Ford Courier Pick-up Automotive Repair Manual

by J H Haynes
Member of the Guild of Motoring Writers
and Peter Ward

Models covered

Ford Courier Pick-up, 109.6 cu in (1796 cc),
120.1 cu in (2000 cc) and 140.3 cu in (2300 cc)

ISBN 0 85696 853 6

(8Y7 - 36008)
(268)

Haynes Publishing Group
Sparkford Nr Yeovil
Somerset BA22 7JJ England

Haynes North America, Inc
861 Lawrence Drive
Newbury Park
California 91320 USA

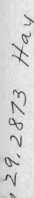

Acknowledgements

Thanks are due to the Ford Marketing Corporation for the supply of technical information and certain illustrations, and to Castrol Limited for information regarding lubrication.

About this manual

Its aim

The aim of this manual is to help you get the best value from your vehicle. It can do so in several ways. It can help you decide what work must be done (even should you choose to get it done by a garage), provide information on routine maintenance and servicing, and give a logical course of action and diagnosis when random faults occur. However, it is hoped that you will make full use of the manual by tackling the work yourself. On simpler jobs it may even be quicker than booking the car into a repair station, and having to go there twice, to leave and collect it. Perhaps most important, a lot of money can be saved by avoiding the costs the repair station must charge to cover its labor and overheads.

The manual has drawings and descriptions to show the function of the various components so that their layout can be understood. Then the tasks are described and photographed in a step-by-step sequence so that even a novice can do the work.

Its arrangement

The manual is divided into thirteen Chapters, each covering a logical sub-division of the vehicle. The Chapters are each divided into consecutively numbered Sections and the Sections into paragraphs (or sub-sections), with decimal numbers following on from the Section they are in, eg 5.1, 5.2, 5.3 etc.

It is freely illustrated, especially in those parts where there is a detailed sequence of operations to be carried out. There are two forms of illustration: figures and photographs. The figures are numbered in sequence with decimal numbers, according to their position in the Chapter: eg Fig. 6.4 is the 4th drawing/illustration in Chapter 6. Photographs are numbered (either individually or in related groups) the same as the Section or sub-section of the text where the operation they show is described.

There is an alphabetical index at the back of the manual as well as a contents list at the front.

References to the 'left' or 'right' of the vehicle are in the sense of a person facing forwards in the driver's seat.

Whilst every care is taken to ensure that the information in this manual is correct no liability can be accepted by the authors or publishers for loss, damage or injury caused by any errors in, or omissions from, the information given.

Introduction to the Ford Courier pick-up

This manual covers the pick-up manufactured by the Toyo Kogyo Company for the Ford Marketing Corporation. There is only one basic body style, although a 4- or 5-speed fully synchromesh transmission or an automatic transmission are available as options, according to the model.

The engine is a single overhead camshaft unit of crossflow design and apart from a chain driven oil pump on the smaller engine, can be regarded as conventional. Drive to the rear wheels is via a diaphragm type clutch and manual or automatic transmission, a propeller shaft, a hypoid removable carrier rear axle and semi-floating driveshafts.

Contents

Page

Acknowledgements   2

About this manual   2

Introduction to the Ford Courier Pick-up   2

Use of English   4

Jacking points and spare wheel location   6

Buying spare parts and vehicle identification numbers   6

Routine maintenance   7

Tools and working facilities   9

Recommended lubricants and fluids   11

Chapter 1   Engine   12   **1**

Chapter 2   Cooling system   43   **2**

Chapter 3   Carburation, fuel, exhaust and emission control systems   48   **3**

Chapter 4   Ignition system   75   **4**

Chapter 5   Clutch   85   **5**

Chapter 6 Part I   Manual gearbox   92   **6A**

Chapter 6 Part II   Automatic transmission   107   **6B**

Chapter 7   Driveshaft   112   **7**

Chapter 8   Rear axle   115   **8**

Chapter 9   Braking system   118   **9**

Chapter 10   Electrical system   134   **10**

Chapter 11   Suspension and steering   173   **11**

Chapter 12   Bodywork and fittings   186   **12**

Chapter 13   Supplement: Revisions and information on later models   205   **13**

Safety first!   268

Conversion factors   269

Index   270

Use of English

As this book has been written in England, it uses the appropriate English component names, phrases, and spelling. Some of these differ from those used in America. Normally, these cause no difficulty, but to make sure, a glossary is printed below. In ordering spare parts remember the parts list may use some of these words:

English	American	English	American
Accelerator	Gas pedal	Locks	Latches
Aerial	Antenna	Methylated spirit	Denatured alcohol
Anti-roll bar	Stabiliser or sway bar	Motorway	Freeway, turnpike etc
Big-end bearing	Rod bearing	Number plate	License plate
Bonnet (engine cover)	Hood	Paraffin	Kerosene
Boot (luggage compartment)	Trunk	Petrol	Gasoline (gas)
Bulkhead	Firewall	Petrol tank	Gas tank
Bush	Bushing	'Pinking'	'Pinging'
Cam follower or tappet	Valve lifter or tappet	Prise (force apart)	Pry
Carburettor	Carburetor	Propeller shaft	Driveshaft
Catch	Latch	Quarterlight	Quarter window
Choke/venturi	Barrel	Retread	Recap
Circlip	Snap-ring	Reverse	Back-up
Clearance	Lash	Rocker cover	Valve cover
Crownwheel	Ring gear (of differential)	Saloon	Sedan
Damper	Shock absorber, shock	Seized	Frozen
Disc (brake)	Rotor/disk	Sidelight	Parking light
Distance piece	Spacer	Silencer	Muffler
Drop arm	Pitman arm	Sill panel (beneath doors)	Rocker panel
Drop head coupe	Convertible	Small end, little end	Piston pin or wrist pin
Dynamo	Generator (DC)	Spanner	Wrench
Earth (electrical)	Ground	Split cotter (for valve spring cap)	Lock (for valve spring retainer)
Engineer's blue	Prussian blue	Split pin	Cotter pin
Estate car	Station wagon	Steering arm	Spindle arm
Exhaust manifold	Header	Sump	Oil pan
Fault finding/diagnosis	Troubleshooting	Swarf	Metal chips or debris
Float chamber	Float bowl	Tab washer	Tang or lock
Free-play	Lash	Tappet	Valve lifter
Freewheel	Coast	Thrust bearing	Throw-out bearing
Gearbox	Transmission	Top gear	High
Gearchange	Shift	Torch	Flashlight
Grub screw	Setscrew, Allen screw	Trackrod (of steering)	Tie-rod (or connecting rod)
Gudgeon pin	Piston pin or wrist pin	Trailing shoe (of brake)	Secondary shoe
Halfshaft	Axleshaft	Transmission	Whole drive line
Handbrake	Parking brake	Tyre	Tire
Hood	Soft top	Van	Panel wagon/van
Hot spot	Heat riser	Vice	Vise
Indicator	Turn signal	Wheel nut	Lug nut
Interior light	Dome lamp	Windscreen	Windshield
Layshaft (of gearbox)	Countershaft	Wing/mudguard	Fender
Leading shoe (of brake)	Primary shoe		

Ford Courier Pick-up — front three-quarter view

Ford Courier Pick-up — rear three-quarter view (step bumper not standard)

Jacking points and spare wheel location

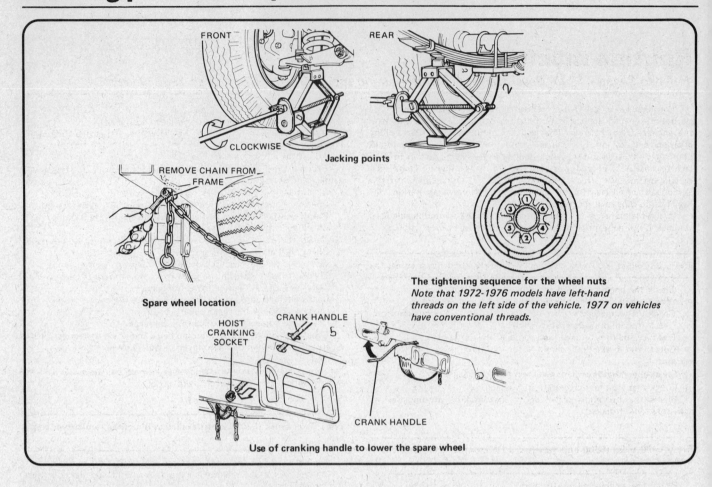

FRONT

REAR

CLOCKWISE

Jacking points

REMOVE CHAIN FROM FRAME

Spare wheel location

The tightening sequence for the wheel nuts
*Note that 1972-1976 models have left-hand
threads on the left side of the vehicle. 1977 on vehicles
have conventional threads.*

HOIST CRANKING SOCKET

CRANK HANDLE

CRANK HANDLE

Use of cranking handle to lower the spare wheel

Buying spare parts and vehicle identification numbers

Buying spare parts

Replacement parts are available from many sources, which generally fall into one of two categories – authorized dealer parts departments and independent retail auto parts stores. Our advice concerning these parts is as follows:

Retail auto parts stores: Good auto parts stores will stock frequently needed components which wear out relatively fast, such as clutch components, exhaust systems, brake parts, tune-up parts, etc. These stores often supply new or reconditioned parts on an exchange basis, which can save a considerable amount of money. Discount auto parts stores are often very good places to buy materials and parts needed for general vehicle maintenance such as oil, grease, filters, spark plugs, belts, touch-up paint, bulbs, etc. They also usually sell tools and general accessories, have convenient hours, charge lower prices and can often be found not far from home.

Authorized dealer parts department: This is the best source for parts which are unique to the vehicle and not generally available elsewhere (such as major engine parts, transmission parts, trim pieces, etc.).

Warranty information: If the vehicle is still covered under warranty, be sure that any replacement parts purchased – regardless of the source – do not invalidate the warranty!

To be sure of obtaining the correct parts, have engine and chassis numbers available and, if possible, take the old parts along for positive identification.

Vehicle identification numbers

Modifications are a continuing and unpublicized process in vehicle manufacturer. Spare parts manuals and lists are compiled on a numerical basis, the individual vehicle numbers being essential to identify correctly, the component required.

The vehicle identification information is stamped on the model plate which is attached to the rear right corner of the engine compartment.

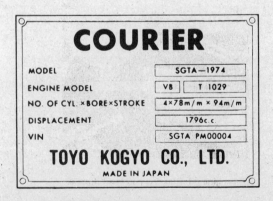

COURIER		
MODEL	SGTA—1974	
ENGINE MODEL	VB	T 1029
NO. OF CYL. ×BORE×STROKE	4×78m/m × 94m/m	
DISPLACEMENT	1796c.c.	
VIN	SGTA PM00004	

TOYO KOGYO CO., LTD.

MADE IN JAPAN

The vehicle model plate (typical)

Routine maintenance

Refer to Chapter 13 for Specifications and information applicable to 1974 through 1982 models.

Maintenance is essential for ensuring safety and desirable for the purpose of getting the best in terms of performance and economy from the vehicle. Over the years the need for periodic lubrication - oiling, greasing and so on - has been drastically reduced if not totally eliminated. This has unfortunately tended to lead some owners to think that because no such action is required the items either no longer exist or will last for ever. This is a serious delusion. It follows therefore that the largest initial element of maintenance is visual examination. This may lead to repairs or renewals.

In the maintenance summary, certain items are not applicable to all vehicles; if not appropriate to your vehicle, these should be ignored.

Every 250 miles (400 km) travelled, or weekly - whichever comes first

---

Check the engine oil level and top-up if necessary.
Check the battery electrolyte level and top-up if necessary.
Check the windshield washer fluid level and top-up if necessary.
Check the tire pressures (when cold).
Examine the tires for wear and damage.
Check the brake and clutch reservoir fluid level and top-up if necessary.
Check the radiator coolant level and top-up if necessary.
Check that the brake operation is satisfactory.
Check the operation of all lights, instruments, warning devices, accessories, controls etc.

Every 4000 miles (6500 km) travelled, or 4 months - whichever occurs first

---

Drain the engine oil when warm, and top-up with the correct quantity and grade of oil.
Check and adjust the valve/rocker clearance (lash).
Inspect the condition of all the drivebelts. Replace or adjust the tension as necessary.
Adjust the idle speed and mixture.
Examine the fuel lines and connections for security of attachment, damage and deterioration.
Clean the air cleaner element and air pump air filter element*
Check the contact breaker points; clean and adjust as necessary.
Check the spark plugs; clean and adjust the gaps as necessary.
Check and adjust the ignition timing.
Check the operation of the accelerator switch; adjust as necessary.
Check the battery specific gravity.
Check and adjust the clutch pedal free-travel.
Check the automatic transmission fluid level; top-up as necessary.
Check and adjust the steering wheel play.
Check and adjust the brake shoe to drum clearances.
Check and adjust the brake pedal travel.
Check and adjust the parking brake operation.
Check the condition of the seat belts and their anchorage points; renew any seat belts which are frayed or otherwise damaged.

In very dusty conditions the air cleaner element and air pump air filter element should be cleaned every 1000 miles

---

Every 8000 miles (13000 km) travelled or 8 months - whichever comes first

---

Replace the engine oil filter when the engine oil is drained.
Tighten the intake manifold, exhaust manifold and cylinder head attachment bolts.

The engine oil filler cap and level dipstick

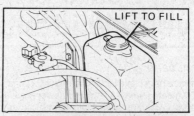

The windshield washer reservoir

The brake and clutch master cylinders

Replace the in-line fuel filter.

Check and adjust the carburetor throttle and choke linkage.

Examine the evaporative emission control system, fuel tank and vapor lines for security of attachment, damage and deterioration.

Check the operation of the throttle solenoid (fuel cut valve).

Examine the distributor cap, rotor and condenser. Clean or replace parts as necessary.

Check the ignition coil and HT leads. Clean or replace parts as necessary.

Check the condition of the ventilating hoses; replace as necessary.

Check the operation of the positive crankcase ventilation valve. Clean or replace as necessary.

Check the condition of the vacuum sensing hoses; replace as necessary.

Check the air pump and relief valve for correct operation; replace as necessary.

Check the air bypass valve for correct operation; replace as necessary.

Check the anti-afterburn valve for correct operation; replace as necessary.

Check the speed switch for correct operation; replace as necessary.

Check the coasting richer valve for correct operation; replace as necessary.

Check the clutch switch for correct operation; adjust or replace as necessary.

Check the condition of the air injection system hoses; replace as necessary.

Check the tightness of the air pump air manifolds.

Check the air pump check valve for correct operation; replace as necessary.

Examine the brake linings, installing new ones as necessary.

Top-up the oil level in the steering gear.

Check the condition of the cooling system hoses; replace as necessary.

Apply a few drops of general purpose lubricating oil to the door, hood, pedal, carburetor controls etc., pivot points. Smear the tailgate hinge pins with a general purpose grease.

Every 12000 miles (20000 km) travelled, or 12 months - whichever comes first

Check and adjust the carburetor float level.
Check the manual transmission oil level; top-up if necessary.
Check the rear axle oil level, top-up if necessary.

Every 20000 miles (32000 km) travelled, or 2 years - whichever comes first

Replace the positive crankcase ventilation valve.
Check the engine cylinder compression pressures.
Replace the evaporative emission canister.
Check the operation of the evaporative emission check valve; replace as necessary.
Replace the air cleaner element and the air pump air filter element*
Replace the piston cups (seals) in the brake and clutch systems.
Lubricate and adjust the front wheel bearings.
Lubricate the front suspension balljoints and upper arm shafts.
Lubricate the steering balljoints and idler arm.
Drain, flush and refill the cooling system, using new antifreeze.
*In very dusty conditions the air cleaner element and the air pump air filter element should be renewed every 12000 miles.

Every 40000 miles (65000 km) travelled, or 4 years - whichever comes first

Replace the flexible hoses in the braking system.

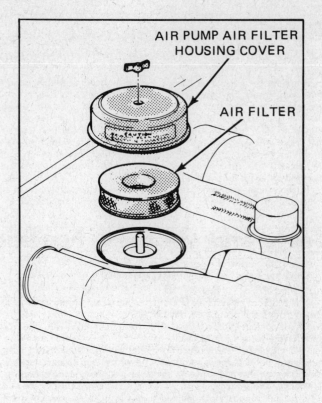

The air pump air filter element

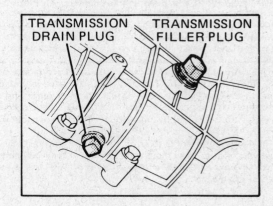

The transmission oil filler and drain plugs

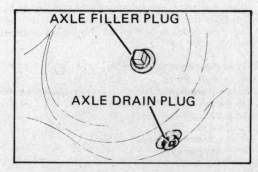

The rear axle oil filler and drain plugs

Tools and Working Facilities

Introduction

A selection of good tools is a fundamental requirement for anyone contemplating the maintenance and repair of a motor vehicle. For the owner who does not possess any, their purchase will prove a considerable expense, offsetting some of the savings made by doing-it-yourself. However, provided that the tools purchased meet the relevant national safety standards and are of good quality, they will last for many years and prove an extremely worthwhile investment.

To help the average owner to decide which tools are needed to carry out the various tasks detailed in this manual, we have compiled three lists of tools under the following headings: *Maintenance and minor repair, Repair and overhaul,* and *Special.* The newcomer to practical mechanics should start off with the *Maintenance and minor repair* tool kit and confine himself to the simpler jobs around the vehicle. Then, as his confidence and experience grow, he can undertake more difficult tasks, buying extra tools as, and when, they are needed. In this way, a *Maintenance and minor repair* tool kit can be built up into a *Repair and overhaul* tool kit over a considerable period of time without any major cash outlays. The experienced do-it-yourselfer will have a tool kit good enough for most repair and overhaul procedures and will add tools from the *Special* category when he feels the expense is justified by the amount of use these tools will be put to.

It is obviously not possible to cover the subject of tools fully here. For those who wish to learn more about tools and their use there is a book entitled *How to Choose and Use Car Tools* available from the publishers of this manual.

Maintenance and minor repair tool kit

The tools given in this list should be considered as a minimum requirement if routine maintenance, servicing and minor repair operations are to be undertaken. We recommend the purchase of combination wrenches (ring one end, open-ended the other); although more expensive than open-ended ones, they do give the advantages of both types of wrench.

Combination wrenches - 10, 11, 13, 14, 17 mm
Adjustable wrench - 9 inch
Engine oil pan/gearbox/rear axle drain plug key (where applicable)
Spark plug wrench (with rubber insert)
Spark plug gap adjustment tool
Set of feeler gauges
Brake adjuster wrench (where applicable)
Brake bleed nipple wrench
Screwdriver - 4 in long x ¼ in dia (flat blade)
Screwdriver - 4 in long x ¼ in dia (cross blade)
Combination pliers - 6 inch
Hacksaw, junior
Tire pump

Tire pressure gauge
Grease gun
Oil can
Fine emery cloth (1 sheet)
Wire brush (small)
Funnel (medium size)

Repair and overhaul tool kit

These tools are virtually essential for anyone undertaking any major repairs to a motor vehicle, and are additional to those given in the *Maintenance and minor repair* list. Included in this list is a comprehensive set of sockets. Although these are expensive they will be found invaluable as they are so versatile - particularly if various drives are included in the set. We recommend the ½ inch square-drive type, as this can be used with most proprietary torque wrenches. If you cannot afford a socket set, even bought piecemeal, then inexpensive tubular box wrenches are a useful alternative.

The tools in this list will occasionally need to be supplemented by tools from the *Special* list.

Sockets (or box wrenches) to cover range in previous list
Reversible ratchet drive (for use with sockets)
Extension piece, 10 inch (for use with sockets)
Universal joint (for use with sockets)
Torque wrench (for use with sockets)
Self-grip wrench - 8 inch
Ball pein hammer
Soft-faced hammer, plastic or rubber
Screwdriver - 6 in long x 5/16 in dia (flat blade)
Screwdriver - 2 in long x 5/16 in square (flat blade)
Screwdriver - 1½ in long x ¼ in dia (cross blade)
Screwdriver - 3 in long x 1/8 in dia (electricians)
Pliers - electricians side cutters
Pliers - needle nosed
Pliers - circlip (internal and external)
Cold chisel - ½ inch
Scriber (this can be made by grinding the end of a broken hacksaw blade)
Scraper (this can be made by flattening and sharpening one end of a piece of copper pipe)
Center punch
Pin punch
Hacksaw
Valve lapping tool
Steel rule/straight edge
Allen keys
Selection of files
Wire brush (large)
Axle stands
Jack (strong scissor or hydraulic type)

Special tools

The tools in this list are those which are not used regularly, are expensive to buy, or which need to be used in accordance with their manufacturers' instructions. Unless relatively difficult mechanical jobs are undertaken frequently, it will not be economic to buy many of these tools. Where this is the case, you could consider clubbing together with friends (or an automobile club) to make a joint purchase, or borrowing the tools against a deposit from a local repair station or tool hire specialist.

The following list contains only those tools and instruments freely available to the public, and not those special tools produced by the vehicle manufacturer specifically for its dealer network. You will find occasional references to these manufacturers' special tools in the text of this manual. Generally, an alternative method of doing the job without the vehicle manufacturer's special tool is given. However, sometimes, there is no alternative to using them. Where this is the case and the relevant tool cannot be bought or borrowed you will have to entrust the work to a franchised dealer.

Valve spring compressor
Piston ring compressor
Balljoint separator
Universal hub/bearing puller
Impact screwdriver
Micrometer and/or vernier gauge
Dial gauge
Stroboscopic timing light
Dwell angle meter/tachometer
Universal electrical multi-meter
Cylinder compression gauge
Lifting tackle
Trolley jack
Light with extension lead

Buying tools

For practically all tools, a tool factor is the best source since he will have a very comprehensive range compared with the average garage or accessory shop. Having said that, accessory shops often offer excellent quality tools at discount prices, so it pays to shop around.

There are plenty of good tools around at reasonable prices, but always aim to purchase items which meet the relevant national safety standards. If in doubt, ask the proprietor or manager of the shop for advice before making a purchase.

Working facilities

Not to be forgotten when discussing tools, is the workshop itself. If anything more than routine maintenance is to be carried out, some form of suitable working area becomes essential.

It is appreciated that many an owner mechanic is forced by circumstances to remove an engine or similar item, without the benefit of a garage or workshop. Having done this, any repairs should always be done under the cover of a roof.

Wherever possible, any dismantling should be done on a clean flat workbench or table at a suitable working height.

Any workbench needs a vise: one with a jaw opening of 4 in (100 mm) is suitable for most jobs. As mentioned previously, some clean dry storage space is also required for tools, as well as the lubricants, cleaning fluids, touch-up paints and so on which soon become necessary.

Another item which may be required, and which has a much more general usage, is an electric drill with a chuck capacity of at least 5/16 in (8 mm). This, together with a good range of twist drills, is virtually essential for fitting accessories such as wing mirrors and back-up lights.

Last, but not least, always keep a supply of old newspapers and clean, lint-free rags available, and try to keep any working area as clean as possible.

Care and maintenance of tools

Having purchased a reasonable tool kit, it is necessary to keep the tools in a clean serviceable condition. After use, always wipe off any dirt, grease and metal particles using a clean, dry cloth, before putting the tools away. Never leave them lying around after they have been used. A simple tool rack on the garage or workshop wall, for items such as screwdrivers and pliers is a good idea. Store all normal spanners and sockets in a metal box. Any measuring instruments, gauges, meters, etc, must be carefully stored where they cannot be damaged or become rusty.

Take a little care when the tools are used. Hammer heads inevitably become marked and screwdrivers lose the keen edge on their blades from time-to-time. A little timely attention with emery cloth or a file will soon restore items like this to a good serviceable finish.

Wrench jaw gap comparison table

Jaw gap (in)	Wrench size
0.250	¼ in AF
0.275	7 mm AF
0.312	5/16 in AF
0.315	8 mm AF
0.340	11/32 in AF; 1/8 in Whitworth
0.354	9 mm AF
0.375	3/8 in AF
0.393	10 mm AF
0.433	11 mm AF
0.437	7/16 in AF
0.445	3/16 in Whitworth; ¼ in BSF
0.472	12 mm AF
0.500	½ in AF
0.512	13 mm AF
0.525	¼ in Whitworth; 5/16 in BSF
0.551	14 mm AF
0.562	9/16 in AF
0.590	15 mm AF
0.600	5/16 in Whitworth; 3/8 in BSF
0.625	5/8 in AF
0.629	16 mm AF
0.669	17 mm AF
0.687	11/16 in AF
0.708	18 mm AF
0.710	3/8 in Whitworth; 7/16 in BSF
0.748	19 mm AF
0.750	¾ in AF
0.812	13/16 in AF
0.820	7/16 in Whitworth; ½ in BSF
0.866	22 mm AF
0.875	7/8 in AF
0.920	½ in Whitworth; 9/16 in BSF
0.937	15/16 in AF
0.944	24 mm AF
1.000	1 in AF
1.010	9/16 in Whitworth; 5/8 in BSF
1.023	26 mm AF
1.062	1.1/16 in AF; 27 mm AF
1.100	5/8 in Whitworth; 11/16 in BSF
1.125	1.1/8 in AF
1.181	30 mm AF
1.200	11/16 in Whitworth; ¾ in BSF
1.250	1¼ in AF
1.259	32 mm AF
1.300	¾ in Whitworth; 7/8 in BSF
1.312	1.5/16 in AF
1.390	13/16 in Whitworth; 15/16 in BSF
1.417	36 mm AF
1.437	1.7/16 in AF
1.480	7/8 in Whitworth; 1 in BSF
1.500	1½ in AF
1.574	40 mm AF; 15/16 in Whitworth
1.614	41 mm AF
1.625	1.5/8 in AF
1.670	1 in Whitworth; 1.1/8 in BSF
1.687	1.11/16 in AF
1.811	46 mm AF
1.812	1.13/16 in AF
1.860	1.1/8 in Whitworth; 1¼ in BSF
1.875	1.7/8 in AF
1.968	50 mm AF
2.000	2 in AF
2.050	1¼ in Whitworth; 1.3/8 in BSF
2.165	55 mm AF
2.362	60 mm AF

Recommended lubricants and fluids

Component	Castrol Product
Engine (1)	Castrol GTX
Gearbox (2)	
Manual	Castrol Hypoy (90 EP)
Automatic	Castrol TQ Dexron ®
Rear axle (differential) (3)	Castrol Hypoy B (90 EP)
Steering gear	Castrol Hypoy (90 EP)
Upper and lower balljoints and upper arm shafts (4)	Castrol MS3 Grease
Front wheel bearings and idler arm (5)	Castrol LM Grease
Brake and clutch fluid (6)	Castrol Girling Universal Brake and Clutch Fluid

Note: The above are general recommendations. Lubrication requirements vary from territory-to-territory and also depend on vehicle usage. Consult the operators handbook supplied with your vehicle.

Chapter 1 Engine

Refer to Chapter 13 for Specifications and information applicable to 1974 through 1982 models

Contents

Big-end and main bearing shells - examination and renovation ... 28	Engine - removal without transmission 6
Camshaft and camshaft bearings - examination and renovation ... 32	Engine - removal with transmission 5
Camshaft and cylinder head installation - engine in the vehicle ... 40	Engine supports (mounts) - removal and installation (engine in the vehicle) 7
Camshaft and cylinder head removal and installation - engine out of the vehicle ... 22	Fault diagnosis - engine 44
Camshaft and cylinder head removal - engine in the vehicle ... 21	General description 1
Clutch pilot bushing, flywheel and crankshaft rear oil seal - removal and installation (engine in the vehicle) 8	Major operations possible with the engine installed 2
Connecting-rod (big-end) bearings - removal and installation (engine in the vehicle) 14	Major operations which require removal of the engine 3
Connecting-rods - examination 31	Methods and equipment for engine removal 4
Crankshaft - examination and renovation 27	Miscellaneous items - inspection and renovation 37
Cylinder block reassembly - engine out of the vehicle ... 39	Oil filter - removal and installation 18
Cylinder block dismantling - engine out of the vehicle ... 25	Oil pan (sump) and oil pump - removal and installation (engine in the vehicle) 12
Cylinder bores - examination and renovation 29	Oil pump - dismantling, inspection and reassembly 17
Cylinder head assembly - dismantling and reassembly ... 24	Pistons and connecting-rods - dismantling and reassembly ... 16
Cylinder head - decarbonisation and inspection 36	Pistons and connecting-rods - removal and installation (engine in the vehicle) 15
Engine ancillary components - removal 20	Pistons and piston rings - examination and renovation ... 30
Engine dismantling - general 19	Rocker arm assembly - dismantling and reassembly 23
Engine examination and renovation - general 26	Rocker arm and shaft assembly - inspection and renovation ... 33
Engine front cover oil seal - renewal (engine in the vehicle) ... 9	Timing chain tensioner - adjustment, removal and installation (engine in the vehicle) 11
Engine front cover, timing chain, oil pump chain and sprockets - removal and installation (engine in the vehicle) 10	Valve guides - examination and renovation 35
Engine - initial start-up after overhaul 43	Valve lash (clearance) - adjustment 41
Engine - installation 42	Valves and valve seats - examination and renovation ... 34
Engine reassembly - general 38	

Specifications

Engine general

Engine type	4-cylinder, 4-stroke, water cooled
Cylinder arrangement	In-line
Valve operation	Overhead camshaft
Firing order	1 - 3 - 4 - 2 (No. 1 nearest radiator)
Bore	3.07 in. (78 mm)
Stroke:	
B1600	3.27 in. (83 mm)
Courier	3.70 in. (44 mm)
Piston displacement:	
B1600	96.8 in^3 (1586 cc)
Courier	109.6 in^3 (1796 cc)
Compression ratio	8.6 : 1
Compression pressure:	
Standard	169 lbf/in^2 (11.9 kgf/cm^2)
Limit	118 lbf/in^2 (8.3 kgf/cm^2)
Oil pressure:	
Hot at 3000 rpm	50 to 64 lbf/in^2 (3.5 to 45 kgf/cm^2)
Idle	4.3 lbf/in^2 (0.3 kgf/cm^2)

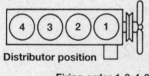

Distributor position

Firing order 1-3-4-2

Cylinder location and distributor rotation

Cylinder head

Material	Aluminium alloy
Maximum permissible distortion	0.006 in. (0.15 mm)
Maximum regrind	0.010 in. (0.25 mm)
Valve lash (clearance), warm engine:	
Intake and exhaust, valve side	0.012 in. (0.30 mm)
Intake and exhaust, cam side	0.009 in (0.23 mm)
Valve seat angle, intake and exhaust	45°
Valve guide:	
Outer diameter	0.5525 to 0.5529 in. (14.03 to 14.04 mm)
Inner diameter	0.3174 to 0.3182 in. (8.06 to 8.08 mm)

Valve stem to guide clearance:
Intake	...	...	...	...	...	...	...	...	0.0007 to 0.0021 in. (0.0178 to 0.053 mm)
Exhaust	...	...	...	...	...	...	...	...	0.0007 to 0.0023 in. (0.0178 to 0.058 mm)
Wear limit	...	...	...	...	...	...	...	...	0.008 in. (0.20 mm)

Intake valve:
Overall length	...	...	...	...	...	...	...	...	4.2717 in. (108.5 mm)
Head diameter	...	...	...	...	...	...	...	...	1.6536 ± 0.0039 in. (42 ± 0.1 mm)
Stem diameter, new	...	...	...	...	...	...	...	...	0.3161 to 0.3167 in. (8.029 to 8.044 mm)
Stem, wear limit	...	...	...	...	...	...	...	...	0.002 in. (0.05 mm)

Valve margin (thickness at edge of valve head):
New	...	...	...	...	...	...	...	...	0.0591 ± 0.0079 in. (1.5 ± 0.2 mm)
Wear limit	...	...	...	...	...	...	...	...	0.0197 in. (0.5 mm)

Exhaust valve:
Overall length	...	...	...	...	...	...	...	...	4.2127 in. (107 mm)
Head diameter	...	...	...	...	...	...	...	...	33 ± 0.1 in. (1.2992 ± 0.0039 mm)
Stem diameter, new	...	...	...	...	...	...	...	...	0.3159 to 0.3167 in. (8.024 to 8.044 mm)
Stem, wear limit	...	...	...	...	...	...	...	...	0.002 in. (0.05 mm)

Valve margin (thickness at edge of valve head):
New	...	...	...	...	...	...	...	...	0.0591 ± 0.0079 in. (1.5 ± 0.2 mm)
Wear limit	...	...	...	...	...	...	...	...	0.0197 in. (0.5 mm)

Valve spring (outer):
Wire diameter	...	...	...	...	...	...	...	...	0.169 in. (4.3 mm)
Outside diameter	...	...	...	...	...	...	...	...	1.295 in. (32.9 mm)

Free length:
New	...	...	...	...	...	...	...	...	1.469 in. (37.3 mm)
Limit	...	...	...	...	...	...	...	...	1.425 in. (36.2 mm)
Fitted length ...	...	...	...	...	...	...	...	...	1.339 in. (34 mm)

Load at fitted length:
New	...	...	...	...	...	...	...	...	31.4 lbf (14.25 kgf)
Limit	...	...	...	...	...	...	...	...	26.7 lbf (12.1 kgf)

Valve spring (inner):
Wire diameter	...	...	...	...	...	...	...	...	0.118 in. (3.0 mm)
Outside diameter	...	...	...	...	...	...	...	...	0.909 in. (23.1 mm)

Free-length:
New	...	...	...	...	...	...	...	...	1.449 in. (36.8 mm)
Wear limit	...	...	...	...	...	...	...	...	1.406 in. (35.7 mm)
Fitted length	...	...	...	...	...	...	...	...	1.26 in. (32.0 mm)

Load at fitted length:
New	...	...	...	...	...	...	...	...	20.9 lbf (9.5 kgf)
Limit	...	...	...	...	...	...	...	...	17.9 lbf (8.1 kgf)

Rocker arm bore	...	...	...	...	...	...	...	...	0.7488 to 0.7501 in. (19.02 to 19.053 mm)

Rocker arm shaft:
Diameter	...	...	...	...	...	...	...	...	0.7469 to 0.7477 in. (18.72 to 18.93 mm)

Length:
Intake	...	...	...	...	...	...	...	...	6.26 in. (159 mm)
Exhaust	...	...	...	...	...	...	...	...	13.229 in. (336 mm)

Rocker arm/shaft clearance:
New	...	...	...	...	...	...	...	...	0.0011 in. (0.028 mm)
Limit	...	...	...	...	...	...	...	...	0.004 in. (0.1 mm)

Camshaft journal diameter:
Front	...	...	...	...	...	...	...	...	1.7701 to 1.7695 in. (44.96 to 44.945 mm)
Center	...	...	...	...	...	...	...	...	1.7691 to 1.7697 in. (44.94 to 44.95 mm)
Rear	...	...	...	...	...	...	...	...	1.7701 to 1.7695 in. (44.96 to 44.945 mm)
Wear limit	...	...	...	...	...	...	...	...	0.002 in. (0.05 mm)

Cam lobe elevation:
Intake	...	...	...	...	...	...	...	...	1.7605 in. (44.715 mm)
Exhaust	...	...	...	...	...	...	...	...	1.7592 in. (44.682 mm)
Wear limit	...	...	...	...	...	...	...	...	0.008 in. (0.20 mm)

Camshaft:
Endplay	...	...	...	...	...	...	...	...	0.001 to 0.007 in. (0.02 to 0.18 mm)
Wear limit	...	...	...	...	...	...	...	...	0.008 in. (0.20 mm)

Camshaft:
Run-out, new	...	...	...	...	...	...	...	...	0.0004 in. (0.01 mm)
Wear limit	...	...	...	...	...	...	...	...	0.0012 in. (0.03 mm)

Camshaft bearing, material	...	...	...	...	...	...	...	...	Babbitt metal

Camshaft bearing, clearance:
Front and rear	...	...	...	...	...	...	...	...	0.0007 to 0.0027 in. (0.019 to 0.069 mm)
Center	...	...	...	...	...	...	...	...	0.0011 to 0.0031 in. (0.029 to 0.079 mm)
Undersize availability	...	...	...	...	...	...	...	...	0.010 in. (0.25 mm)
									0.020 in. (0.50 mm)
									0.030 in. (0.75 mm)

Camshaft drive	...	...	...	...	...	...	...	...	Chain and sprockets
Number of links in chain	...	...	...	...	...	...	...	100

Number of sprocket teeth:
Camshaft	...	...	...	...	...	...	...	...	39
Crankshaft	...	...	...	...	...	...	...	...	19

Valve timing (B1600):
Intake opens	...	...	...	...	...	...	...	13º b.t.d.c.
Intake closes	...	...	...	...	...	...	...	54º a.b.d.c.
Exhaust opens	...	...	...	...	...	...	...	57º b.b.d.c.
Exhaust closes	...	...	...	...	...	...	...	10º a.t.d.c.

Valve timing (Courier, California 1972):
Intake opens	...	...	...	...	...	...	...	26º b.t.d.c.
Intake closes	...	...	...	...	...	...	...	50º a.b.d.c.
Exhaust opens	...	...	...	...	...	...	...	62º b.b.d.c.
Exhaust closes	...	...	...	...	...	...	...	14º a.t.d.c.

Valve timing (Courier, other markets 1972):
Intake opens	...	...	...	...	...	...	...	13º b.t.d.c.
Intake closes	...	...	...	...	...	...	...	57º a.b.d.c.
Exhaust opens	...	...	...	...	...	...	...	62 b.b.d.c.
Exhaust closes	...	...	...	...	...	...	...	8º a.t.d.c.

Valve timing (Courier, 1973):
Intake opens	...	...	...	...	...	...	...	26º b.t.d.c.
Intake closes	...	...	...	...	...	...	...	50º a.b.d.c.
Exhaust opens	...	...	...	...	...	...	...	62º b.b.d.c.
Exhaust closes	...	...	...	...	...	...	...	14º a.t.d.c.

Valve timing (Courier, 1974):
Intake opens	...	...	...	...	...	...	...	13º b.t.d.c.
Intake closes	...	...	...	...	...	...	...	57º a.b.d.c.
Exhaust opens	...	...	...	...	...	...	...	62º b.b.d.c.
Exhaust closes	...	...	...	...	...	...	...	8º a.t.d.c.

Connecting rods, pistons and bearings

Connecting-rods (B1600):
Length, center to center	...	...	...	...	...	...	5.6694 ± 0.002 in. (144 ± 0.05 mm)

Connecting-rods (Courier):
Length, center to center	...	...	...	...	...	...	6.5335 to 6.5375 in. (165.951 to 166.051 mm)
Connecting-rod, permissible distortion	...	...	...	...	...	0.002 in/5 in. (0.02 mm/50 mm)

Side-clearance:
New	...	...	...	...	...	...	...	0.004 to 0.008 in. (0.11 to 0.21 mm)
Limit	...	...	...	...	...	...	...	0.014 in. (0.356 mm)

Small-end bush:
Inner diameter	...	...	...	...	...	...	...	0.8663 to 0.8668 in. (22.003 to 22.014 mm)
Outside diameter	...	...	...	...	...	...	...	0.9857 to 0.9865 in. (25.035 to 25.056 mm)
Connecting-rod, bore	...	...	...	...	...	...	...	0.9838 to 0.9851 in. (24.988 to 25.021 mm)
Piston pin/bush clearance	...	...	...	...	...	...	0.0004 to 0.0012 in. (0.01 to 0.03 mm)
Connecting-rod bearing material	...	...	...	...	...	...	Aluminium alloy
Bearing clearance	...	...	...	...	...	...	0.0011 to 0.003 in. (0.027 to 0.077 mm)
Undersize bearing availability	...	...	...	...	...	...	0.010 in. (0.25 mm)
								0.020 in. (0.50 mm)
								0.030 in. (0.75 mm)

Piston type	...	...	...	...	...	...	...	Conical elliptic, with split skirt
Piston material	...	...	...	...	...	...	...	Aluminium alloy

Piston diameter, measured 0.67 in. (17 mm) below oil ring groove
(B1600):
Piston marked 'A'	...	...	...	...	...	...	...	3.0689 to 3.0691 in. (77.949 to 77.955 mm)
Piston unmarked	...	...	...	...	...	...	...	3.0687 ± 0.002 in. (77.945 ± 0.004 mm)
Piston marked 'C'	...	...	...	...	...	...	...	3.0683 to 3.0685 in. (77.935 to 77.941 mm)
Piston diameter (Courier)	...	...	...	...	...	...	3.0683 to 3.0691 in. (77.935 to 77.955 mm)
Piston pin hole bore diameter	...	...	...	...	...	...	0.8661 to 0.8657 in. (21.998 to 21.988 mm)

Ring groove width:
Top	...	...	...	...	...	...	...	0.0601 to 0.0607 in. (1.526 to 1.542 mm)
Second	...	...	...	...	...	...	...	0.0599 to 0.0604 in. (1.521 to 1.534 mm)
Oil control	...	...	...	...	...	...	...	0.1583 to 0.1588 in. (4.021 to 4.034 mm)
Ring groove depth	...	...	...	...	...	...	...	0.1516 in. (3.85 mm)

Piston/cylinder clearance:
New	...	...	...	...	...	...	...	0.0022 to 0.0028 in. (0.057 to 0.072 mm)
Wear limit	...	...	...	...	...	...	...	0.006 in. (0.15 mm)
Oversize piston availability	...	...	...	...	...	...	0.010 in. (0.25 mm)
								0.020 in. (0.50 mm)
								0.030 in. (0.75 mm)
								0.040 in. (1.00 mm)

Piston rings:
Width:
Top and second	...	...	...	...	...	...	...	0.0579 to 0.0587 in. (1.471 to 1.491 mm)
Oil	...	...	...	...	...	...	...	0.1563 to 0.1571 in. (3.97 to 3.99 mm)

Thickness:
Top and second	...	...	...	...	...	...	...	0.1417 ± 0.0039 in. (3.6 ± 0.1 mm)
Oil	...	...	...	...	...	...	...	0.1181 ± 0.0039 in. (3.0 ± 0.1 mm)

Side clearance:

Top	0.0014 to 0.0025 in. (0.035 to 0.070 mm)
Second	0.0012 to 0.0025 in. (0.030 to 0.064 mm)
Oil	0.0012 to 0.0025 in. (0.030 to 0.064 mm)
End gap	0.008 to 0.016 in. (0.2 to 0.4 mm)
Oversize piston ring availability	0.010 in. (0.25 mm)
	0.020 in. (0.50 mm)
	0.030 in. (0.75 mm)
	0.040 in. (1.00 mm)

Piston pin:

Diameter	0.8655 to 0.8659 in. (21.984 to 21.994 mm)
Length	2.5394 $\pm$ 0.002 in. (64.5 $\pm$ 0.05 mm)
Piston pin/piston clearance	−0.0006 to −0.0002 in. (−0.014 to + 0.005 mm)

Crankshaft, main bearing journal diameter:

New	2.4779 to 2.4875 in. (62.94 to 63.18 mm)
Wear limit	0.002 in. (0.05 mm)

Crankpin, diameter:

New	2.0842 to 2.0848 in. (52.94 to 52.95 mm)
Wear limit	0.002 in. (0.05 mm)

Crankshaft endplay:

New	0.003 to 0.009 in. (0.08 to 0.24 mm)
Wear limit	0.012 in. (0.30 mm)

Crankshaft run-out (measured at flywheel face):

New	0.008 in. (0.02 mm)
Limit	0.0012 in. (0.03 mm)
Oversize thrust bearing availability	0.010 in. (0.25 mm)
	0.020 in. (0.50 mm)
	0.030 in. (0.75 mm)

Main bearing:

Material	Aluminium alloy
Bearing clearance	0.0012 to 0.0024 in. (0.031 to 0.061 mm)
Undersize bearing availability	0.010 in. (0.25 mm)
	0.020 in. (0.50 mm)
	0.030 in. (0.75 mm)

Cylinder block

Material	Special cast iron
Bore (B1600):	
Mark A	3.0714 to 3.0716 in. (78.013 to 78.019 mm)
Unmarked	3.0711 to 3.0714 in. (78.006 to 78.013 mm)
Mark B	3.0709 to 3.0711 in. (78.000 to 78.006 mm)
Bore (Courier)	3.0709 to 3.0716 in. (78.000 to 78.019 mm)
Wear limit of bore	0.006 in. (0.15 mm)
Boring oversizes	0.010 in. (0.25 mm)
	0.020 in. (0.50 mm)
	0.030 in. (0.75 mm)
	0.040 in. (1.00 mm)
Maximum regrind to rectify distortion of the top face	0.010 in. (0.25 mm)

Oil pump

Type	Rotor
Feeding capacity	3.4 US gal/min, 2.9 Imp. gal/min, 13 litres/min. at 2000 engine rpm
Oil pump drive	Chain and sprockets
Number of chain links	46
Number of sprocket teeth	33
Outer rotor/body clearance:	
New	0.006 to 0.010 in. (0.14 to 0.25 mm)
Wear limit	0.012 in. (0.30 mm)
Clearance between rotor lobes:	
New	0.002 to 0.004 in. (0.04 to 0.10 mm)
Wear limit	0.006 in. (0.15 mm)
Rotor endfloat:	
New	0.002 to 0.004 in. (0.04 to 0.10 mm)
Wear limit	0.006 in. (0.15 mm)

Oil filter

Type	Full flow, cartridge
Relief valve opens	11 to 12 lbf/in^2 (0.8 to 1.2kgf/cm^2)

Engine lubrication

Engine oil capacity (approximate)*	8 US pints, 6.5 Imp. pints, 3.8 litres

Add 1 US pint, 0.8 Imp. pint, 0.5 litres with filter change.

Lubricant type (SAE):

Above 32º F (0º C)	.	...	...	...	...	...	...	20W-50	
14º F to 60º F (−10º C to +15º C)	...	...	...	...	...	...	20W-20		
14º F to 104º F (−10º C to +40º C)	...	...	...	...	...	20W-40			
0º F to 85º F (−18º C to +30º C)	...	...	...	...	...	10W-30			
Below 0º F (−18º C)	...	...	...	...	...	...	5W-20		

Torque wrench settings

									lb f ft	kg fm
Main bearing caps	...	...	...	...	...	...	...	...	61 to 65	8.4 to 9.0
Connecting-rod caps	...	...	...	...	...	...	...	...	30 to 33	4.1 to 4.6
Oil pump sprocket	...	...	...	...	...	...	...	...	22 to 25	3.0 to 3.5
Oil pan (sump)	...	...	...	...	...	...	...	...	5 to 7	0.65 to 0.95
Cylinder head:										
Cold engine (initial)	...	...	...	...	...	...	...	...	56 to 60	7.7 to 8.3
Warm engine (final)	...	...	...	...	...	...	...	...	69 to 72	9.5 to 10.0
Camshaft sprocket	...	...	...	...	...	...	...	...	51 to 58	7.0 to 8.0
Distributor drive gear	...	...	...	...	...	...	...	...	51 to 58	7.0 to 8.0
Valve rocker arm cover	...	...	...	...	...	...	...	...	1.1 to 1.4	0.15 to 0.2
Crankshaft pulley	...	...	...	...	...	...	...	...	80 to 94	11.0 to 13.0
Intake manifold	...	...	...	...	...	...	...	...	14 to 19	1.9 to 2.6
Exhaust manifold	...	...	...	...	...	...	...	...	12 to 17	1.6 to 2.3
Spark plugs	...	...	...	...	...	...	...	...	11 to 15	1.5 to 2.1
Oil filter cartridge	...	...	...	...	...	...	...	...	12 to 17	1.6 to 2.3
Oil pressure switch	...	...	...	...	...	...	...	...	9 to 13	1.2 to 1.8
Temperature sender unit	...	...	...	...	...	...	...	...	4 to 7	0.5 to 1.0
Flywheel	...	...	...	...	...	...	...	...	112 to 118	15.5 to 16.3
Miscellaneous:										
6 mm bolt	...	...	...	...	...	...	...	...	5.8	0.8
8 mm bolt	...	...	...	...	...	...	...	...	13.7	1.89
10 mm bolt	...	...	...	...	...	...	...	...	27.5	3.8
12 mm bolt	...	...	...	...	...	...	...	...	47	6.5
14 mm bolt	...	...	...	...	...	...	...	...	65.8	9.1

1 General description

The engine has been designed to provide the vehicle with a lively and economical performance, and in most respects is of conventional overhead camshaft type.

Beginning at the top, the cylinder head is of 'crossflow' design. The intake and exhaust valves are arranged on a near hemispherical combustion chamber. They are operated by rockers in contact with a single chain driven camshaft, mounted centrally on the aluminium alloy cylinder head.

The distributor, which is mounted on the exhaust side of the cylinder head, is driven by a helical gear at the forward end of the camshaft next to the camshaft chain sprocket.

A single compound carburetor is fitted to the intake manifold and the devices which comprise the emission control systems have been added onto the carburation, ignition and exhaust systems on the engine.

The cylinder block is an iron casting, and provides support for the crankshaft at five main bearings. An uncommon feature of this engine is the provision of a chain driven oil pump. The pump is situated at the front of the engine and is driven by a sprocket fitted adjacent to the timing sprocket on the front end of the crankshaft.

The oil pump delivers oil to the main oil gallery from which it passes to the main bearing journals and then to the connecting rod bearing journals through drillings in the crankshaft. Oil spillage from the connecting-rod big-ends, as well as a jet hole drilled through the connecting-rod into the big-ends, provides splash lubrication for the piston and connecting-rod small end. At the top of the engine, galleries drilled in the camshaft supports and rocker shaft provide oil for the rocker journals and tappets.

The impressions gained of this engine are of ruggedness and austerity of design - both essential attributes when there is a requirement for a reliable and economical unit for a lightweight utility vehicle.

2 Major operations possible with the engine installed

1 The following major tasks can be performed with the engine installed. However, the degree of difficulty varies and for anyone who has lifting tackle available it is recommended that items such as the flywheel, pistons, connecting-rods and crankshaft bearings are attended to after removal of the engine from the vehicle.

1 *Removal and installation of the cylinder head.*
2 *Removal and installation of the camshaft and bearings.*
3 *Removal and installation of the engine supports (mounts).*
4 *Removal and installation of the crankshaft rear oil seal.*
5 *Removal and installation of the flywheel.*
6 *Renewal of the clutch pilot bearing.*
7 *Renewal of the engine front cover oil seal.*
8 *Removal and installation of the engine front cover.*
9 *Removal and installation of the timing chain and sprockets.*
10 *Removal and installation of the oil pan (sump).*
11 *Removal and installation of the oil pump.*
12 *Removal and installation of the main bearings.*
13 *Removal and installation of the pistons and connecting-rods.*
14 *Removal and installation of the connecting-rod big-end bearings.*

3 Major operations which require removal of the engine

1 The only item which cannot be removed and installed without the engine being removed, is the crankshaft.

4 Methods and equipment for engine removal

1 The engine can either be removed complete with the transmission, or the two units can be removed separately. If the transmission is to be removed, it is preferable to remove it while still coupled to the engine.
2 Essential equipment includes a suitable jack or support(s) so that the vehicle can be raised whilst working underneath, and a hoist or lifting tackle capable of taking the engine (and transmission, if applicable) weight. (The engine and manual transmission weigh in the order of 300 lb (135 kg); if the engine alone is being lifted allow for approximately three-quarters of this weight; if the lifting tackle demands a reduction of weight, such items as the cylinder head, manifolds and engine ancillaries can be removed before lifting out the engine, provided that a suitable sling can be used for lifting purposes. If an inspection pit is available some problems associated with jacking will be alleviated, but at some time during the engine removal procedure a jack will be required beneath the transmission (a trolley jack is very useful for this application).

5 Engine - removal with transmission

1 Before commencing work it will be necessary to drive the vehicle onto ramps, over an inspection pit or to jack it up for access to the exhaust and transmission.

2 Initially mark the position of the hood (bonnet) hinges, using a pencil or ball-point pen to aid installation. Remove the hood, referring to Chapter 12 if necessary.

3 Detach the battery leads, and stow them to one side where they are out of the way.

4 Drain the cooling system (refer to Chapter 2 if necessary). Remove the coolant hoses between the engine, radiator and heater.

5 Remove the air cleaner (refer to Chapter 3 if necessary).

6 Detach the fan shroud. Remove the radiator followed by the fan shroud (refer to Chapter 2 if necessary).

7 Remove all electrical connections to the engine and transmission, identifying each lead with a tag as it is detached. Note the routing of cables and provisions for clipping and support (photo).

8 The carburetor controls may now be disengaged. Begin by detaching the accelerator linkage and choke control cables. The system varies according to the vehicle and intended market, but typical arrangements are shown in Chapter 3.

9 Disconnect the cable at the air bypass valve.

10 Remove the fuel line(s) from the carburetor and keep a clean dry cloth handy to catch any spillage. Plug the line(s) with a clean metal bar to prevent the ingress of dirt and excessive spillage of fuel.

11 Next undo the four bolts which secure the fan to the pulley boss and remove the fan. It is not essential to remove the fan drive clutch (where applicable).

12 Remove the fanbelt and position the alternator inwards towards the engine.

13 Where applicable, remove the thermactor pump bolts and take off the drivebelt. Disconnect the thermactor hoses at the pump, then remove the bracket and adjusting arm bolts so that the pump can be positioned out of the way.

14 Remove the water hoses from the intake manifold.

15 Where applicable, disconnect the thermactor air filter hose at the air bypass valve.

16 Now go through the following check list of items that should have been removed from the engine at this stage.
    a) Radiator.
    b) Fan and fan shroud.
    c) Coolant hoses between engine/radiator/heater.
    d) Battery cables.
    e) Starter cables.
    f) Engine temperature and oil pressure sender leads.
    g) Distributor, coil and spark plug leads.
    h) Alternator leads.
    j) Thermactor pump (where applicable).
    k) Ground lead between engine and bodyshell.
    l) Carburetor controls, fuel line and air cleaner.

17 From beneath the vehicle drain the engine oil into a container of suitable capacity.

18 Remove the engine lower front stone guard (four nuts and washers).

19 Disconnect the exhaust pipe from the manifold and transmission (refer to Chapter 3 if necessary), and allow it to hang down.

20 The next step is to disconnect the transmission shift linkage on column-shift manual transmission or automatic transmission versions, or the gearshift tower on floor-shift manual transmission versions. On automatic transmissions, disconnect the oil cooler lines. These items are dealt with in Chapter 6.

21 Drain the transmission oil into a container of suitable capacity and disconnect the speedometer drive cable.

22 Index mark the installed position of the propeller shaft, then remove it from the vehicle (refer to Chapter 7 if necessary). Ensure that it is stored in a safe place whilst removed from the vehicle, since damage may result in it becoming unbalanced. Now lower the vehicle to the ground.

23 Before proceeding any further, examine the engine and transmission to ensure that all connections have been detached, stowed and labelled as necessary. It is essential that the space around the transmission and engine is clear of pipes, wires, rods, etc., because any of them could be damaged if knocked when the engine/transmission assembly is being hoisted out of the vehicle.

24 Now bring the hoist over the engine and attach the sling to the lifting eyes on the front of the engine and transmission housing.

25 Support the weight of the transmission with a jack, using a suitable wooden packer between the jack head and the transmission.

26 Take the weight of the engine and transmission on the hoist, then proceed to remove the nuts and bolts from the engine mounts, followed by those from the rear transmission mount. Remove the rear (transmission) crossmember completely (photo). Further information on these items will be found in Section 7.

27 The hoist should now be taking the weight of the engine, which means that the transmission supporting jack can be carefully lowered and the engine and transmission slowly lifted out. Take care not to let the engine sway or damage to accessories, wiring or vehicle paintwork may occur (photo).

28 Now that the engine and transmission assembly is out of the vehicle, the two units may be separated. Undo the nuts and bolts securing the flywheel housing and starter motor to the engine. Remove the starter motor.

29 Gently ease the transmission away from the engine, taking particular care to prevent the weight of the transmission being taken on the input shaft. **Note:** With automatic transmissions use a pry bar between the engine flex-plate and the converter to prevent the converter disengaging from the transmission as it is moved away.

6 Engine - removal without transmission

1 Initially proceed as described in the preceding Section up to and including paragraph 19.

2 Remove the flywheel housing bolts.

3 Remove the lower starter motor nuts and the one lower bolt.

4 Lower the vehicle and remove the upper starter motor bolts, then remove the starter motor.

5 Support the transmission with a jack, using a suitable wooden packer between the jack head and the transmission.

6 Before proceeding any further, examine the engine to ensure that all connections have been detached, stowed and labelled as necessary. It is

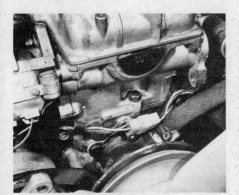

5.7 Disconnect and identify all the electrical leads

5.26 Disconnect the transmission mount

5.27 Lifting out the engine and transmission

essential that the space around the engine is clear of pipes, wires, etc., because any of them could be damaged if knocked when the engine is being hoisted out of the vehicle.

7 Now bring the hoist over the engine and attach the sling to the lifting eye on the front of the engine and around the rear end of the exhaust manifold or rear lifting eye.

8 Take the weight of the engine on the hoist, then proceed to remove the nuts and bolts from the engine mounts. For further information on the mounts refer to Section 7.

9 Carefully draw the engine forwards, away from the transmission,

taking care that the engine weight is not taken by the transmission input shaft (manual transmission), then lift it upwards and away from the vehicle. **Note:** With automatic transmissions, use a pry bar between the engine flex-plate and the converter to prevent the converter disengaging from the transmission as the engine is moved away. Take care not to let the engine sway, or damage to accessories, wiring or vehicle paintwork may occur.

10 Now that the engine is removed, do not attempt to move the vehicle if the transmission is still installed, unless some method can be devised of suspending it from the vehicle frame.

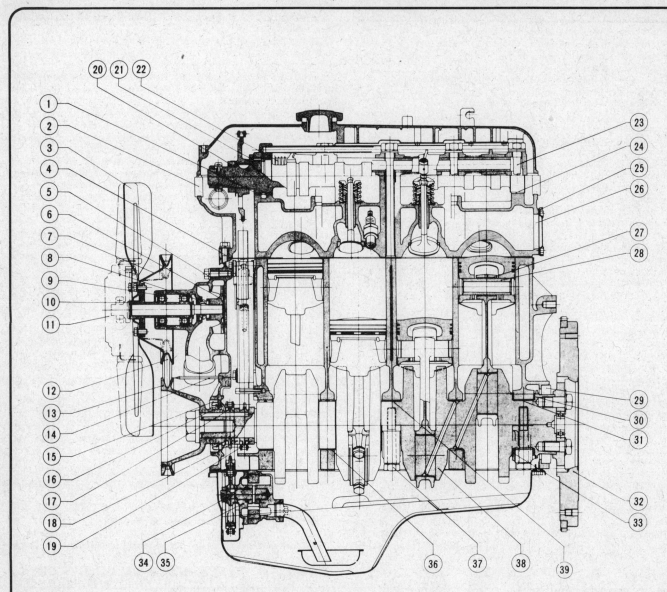

Fig. 1.1 Longitudinal section of the 1600 cc engine

1 Camshaft bearing (front)	11 Fan drive	21 Thrust plate	31 Main bearing (lower)
2 Oil seal	12 V-belt	22 Spring	32 Flywheel
3 Cooling fan	13 Crankshaft pulley	23 Cylinder head bolt	33 Thrust bearing (lower)
4 Cylinder head gasket	14 Timing pointer	24 Camshaft bearing (rear)	34 Oil pump shaft
5 Water pump	15 Oil seal	25 Blind cover	35 Oil pump cover
6 Impeller	16 Thrower	26 Gasket	36 Main bearing
7 Water pump pulley	17 Crankshaft sprocket	27 Small end bush	37 Main bearing cap bolt
8 Water seal	18 Spacer	28 Piston pin	38 Crankshaft
9 Bearing	19 Spacer	29 Oil seal	39 Main bearing
10 Pulley boss	20 Lock nut	30 Thrust bearing (upper)	

7 Engine supports (mounts) - removal and installation (engine in the vehicle)

1 In order to gain access to the underside of the vehicle, it will need to be raised on a hoist or suitable jacks, or alternatively placed over an inspection pit.

Engine front support

2 Remove the engine mount to block lower bolt.
3 Remove the engine lower front stone guard (four nuts and washers)

and unscrew the oil filter (refer to Section 18 if necessary).
4 Position a jack beneath the oil pan (sump), with a wooden block spacer on the jack head, then raise the engine so that a further wooden block can be wedged between the oil pan and the crossmember.
5 Remove the jack. If the vehicle has been raised from the ground it can now be lowered.
6 Remove the bolts and washers from the attachment points and remove the mount. Note that a heat shield is used on the right-hand mount.
7 Installation is the reverse of the removal procedure but do not forget to install the heat shield on the right-hand mount.

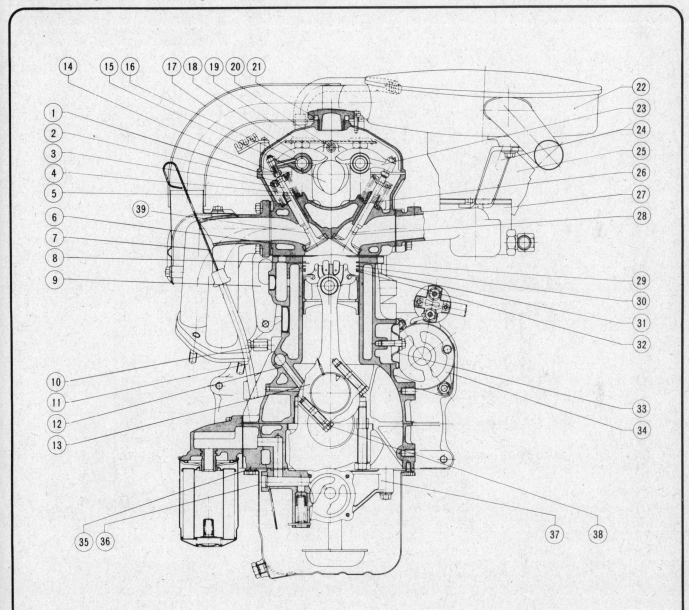

Fig. 1.2 Transverse section of the 1600 cc engine

1 Rocker arm cover gasket	11 Dipstick tube	21 Gasket	31 Piston ring (oil)
2 Exhaust taper sleeve	12 Cylinder block	22 Air cleaner	32 Expander
3 Exhaust valve	13 Connecting rod	23 Inlet taper sleeve	33 Crankcase cover
4 Valve spring (outer)	14 Spring seat (upper)	24 Air cleaner support	34 Starting motor
5 Valve spring (inner)	15 Camshaft	25 Carburettor	35 Gasket
6 Cylinder head	16 Exhaust rocker shaft	26 Intake valve guide	36 Oil pan (sump)
7 Dipstick	17 Hot air duct	27 Intake manifold	37 Oil pump body
8 Piston	18 Rocker arm	28 Intake valve	38 Connecting rod cap bolt
9 Engine hanger	19 Rocker arm cover	29 Piston ring (top)	39 Exhaust valve
10 Water drain cock	20 Oil distribution pipe	30 Piston ring (second)	

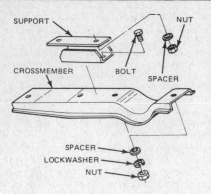

Fig. 1.3 Engine support (mount) - rear (Sec. 7)

7.8 The rear support insulator attaching nuts

7.9 The insulator attachment point on the crossmember

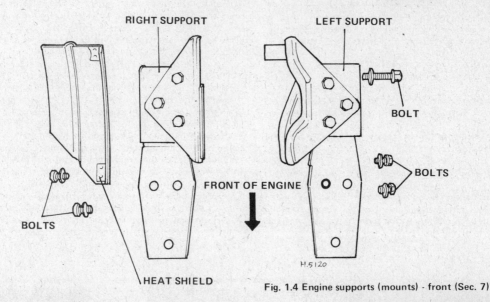

Fig. 1.4 Engine supports (mounts) - front (Sec. 7)

Engine rear support

8   Remove the rear support insulator attaching nuts and washers from the transmission extension housing (photo).

9   Remove the bolts, nuts and washers attaching the insulator to the crossmember (photo).

10 Place a wooden block and a jack under the transmission and raise it just enough to permit removal of the insulator.

11 Installation is the reverse of the removal procedure.

---

8   Clutch pilot bushing, flywheel and crankshaft rear oil seal - removal and installation (engine in the vehicle)

Note: The procedure given in this Section describes oil seal replacement where it is **not** required to replace the rear main bearing. If the rear main bearing requires replacement also, the two jobs must be carried out separately since the engine cannot be conveniently supported if the transmission and oil pan are both removed at the same time.

1   Remove the transmission, as described in Chapter 6.

2   Remove the clutch (refer to Chapter 5 if necessary).

3   If it is required to remove the clutch pilot bushing, it can be done at this stage provided that a suitable extractor is available. If the bearing cannot be extracted do not use too much force, but remove the flywheel first as described in paragraph 4. When installing the replacement bearing it should be carefully driven in using a suitable arbor so that load is applied to the bearing outer race.

4   Remove the flywheel attaching bolts and carefully draw off the flywheel. Great care should be taken if leverage is required, in order to prevent damage to the ring gear and block endface. Remember that the flywheel is fairly heavy and cumbersome, particularly in view of the limited accessibility.

5   If the oil seal requires replacement, use an awl to punch two holes in it on opposite sides of the crankshaft just above the split line of the

Fig. 1.5 Crankshaft rear oil seal removal (Sec. 8)

bearing cap to cylinder block.

6   Install two sheet metal (self-tapping) screws then pry at each screw to extract the seal. Small blocks of wood placed against the cylinder block will provide a fulcrum point for prying. Take great care that the crankshaft seal surface is not scored whilst the seal is being removed.

7   Carefully clean the oil seal recess in the cylinder block and bearing cap. Clean the crankshaft seal surface and inspect it for any scoring, etc.

8   When installing the new seal, lubricate the surfaces of the seal, crankshaft, cylinder block and bearing cap with engine oil. Insert the seal with the lips inwards, carefully pressing it in. If it is stubborn use a small wooden block and light hammer blows; take care to ensure that the seal is not crooked as it is pressed home.

9   The flywheel can now be examined for damage to the ring gear. If there are any broken or chipped teeth, or if other damage exists, the old ring gear can be removed from the flywheel. This can be done by heating the ring gear with a blowlamp as evenly as possible to a

temperature of 250 to 260ºC (480 to 500ºF) and driving it off, or cutting a small groove at the root of two adjacent teeth and then splitting the ring with a cold chisel.

10 To install a new ring gear, it must be heated evenly to a temperature of 250 to 260ºC (480 to 500ºF) in a domestic oven or an oil bath (a naked flame is not very suitable unless the heat can be applied evenly), then carefully driving it on to the cold flywheel. Note that the ring gear tooth chamfer should be towards the engine.

11 When the flywheel has cooled, it can be installed on the engine. Align the 'O' marked hole on the flywheel with the reamer hole on the crankshaft. Coat the bolt threads with a gasket sealer and install the reamer bolt and washer in the 'O' marked hole. Install the remaining bolts and washers and tighten them in a crosswise sequence to the specified torque (photos).

12 Install the clutch (refer to Chapter 5 if necessary).

13 Install the transmission (refer to Chapter 6 if necessary).

9 Engine front cover oil seal - renewal (engine in the vehicle)

1 Remove the engine compartment hood (refer to Chapter 12 if necessary).

2 Drain the cooling system (refer to Chapter 2 if necessary).

3 Remove the radiator (refer to Chapter 2 if necessary).

4 Remove the alternator (and thermactor) drive belt(s).

5 Unscrew the nut and washer from the crankshaft pulley, then use a suitable extractor to pull the pulley off. Take care that the Woodruff key is not lost.

6 Carefully pry out the oil seal. Take care not to damage the sealing face on the front cover, and check that it is clean once the seal is removed.

7 Lubricate the sealing faces with engine oil and carefully press in a new seal (photo).

8 Install the pulley and tighten the bolt to the specified torque.

9 Install the drive belts, radiator, and engine compartment hood in the reverse order to removal. Finally fill the cooling system (refer to Chapter 2 if necessary).

10 Engine front cover, timing chain, oil pump chain and sprockets - removal and installation (engine in the vehicle)

1 Initially proceed as in paragraph 1 thru 5, of the previous Section.

2 Remove the water pump (refer to Chapter 2 if necessary).

3 Remove the single cylinder head to front cover bolt.

4 Raise the vehicle as necessary to remove the engine lower front stone guard (four nuts and washers).

5 Where applicable, disconnect the emission line to the oil pan (sump).

6 Remove the oil pan, as described in Section 12.

7 Lower the vehicle to the ground then remove the alternator bracket to block bolts and position the alternator aside. Where applicable, remove the thermactor pump to block bolts and position the pump aside. Remove the shell tube bolts and tube from the front of the engine.

8 Remove the bolts which retain the engine front cover and take the cover off. This will probably be stuck to the front of the block, but a few taps with a soft faced hammer should free it. Alternatively, provided that care is taken not to damage the sealing faces, a knife blade can be carefully inserted to break the seal.

9 If the timing chain and/or oil pump drive chain are to be removed, remove the cylinder head, as described in Section 21. (The intake and exhaust manifolds need not be removed from the head unless considered necessary.)

10 Remove the oil pump as described in Section 12, then take off the oil pump drive chain.

11 Remove the timing chain tensioner (two bolts).

12 Loosen the screws which retain the timing chain guide strip.

13 Remove the oil slinger from the crankshaft.

14 Remove the oil pump sprocket and chain together. Where applicable, remove the spacer from the crankshaft.

15 Remove the timing chain and crankshaft sprockets, drawing them off with a suitable puller. Take care that the Woodruff key is not lost.

16 When installing, position the crankshaft sprocket to the timing chain, then position them both to the crankshaft. Where applicable,

1

8.11a The O-mark on the flywheel

8.11b The reamer hole on the crankshaft is shown at the top

8.11c The reamer bolt is shown on the right

8.11d The flywheel bolts installed and tightened

9.7 The front cover oil seal installed

install the spacer.

17 Position the oil pump drive chain and sprocket to the crankshaft.

18 Ensure that the sprockets are pushed fully home then install the oil slinger.

19 Install the oil pump, as described in Section 12.

20 Install the cylinder head and camshaft as described in Section 40. Take careful note of the procedure to ensure that the correct valve timing is obtained, then install the rocker arm assembly. See Fig. 1.6 for the chain to sprocket relationship.

21 Where a hydraulic timing chain tensioner is used, compress the snubber spring and wedge a screwdriver in the release mechanism to hold it in place. Install the tensioner and tighten the retaining bolts (screwdriver still in place), then press the top of the chain guide strip towards the chain. Tighten the retaining screws.

22 Where a spring loaded timing chain tensioner is used, depress the slide pin fully and turn it clockwise through 90° to lock the wedge. Install the tensioner and tighten the retaining bolt.

23 Remove the screwdriver from the tensioner (hydraulic type) or turn the slide pin using a screwdriver from the aperture at the side of the camshaft sprocket (spring type), to allow the tensioner to release.

24 Before installing the engine front cover, clean the gasket surface of the cover, cylinder block and water pump.

25 Position the front cover gasket to the block using a non-setting gasket sealant. Install the front cover and tighten the bolts in a crosswise order to the specified torque.

26 Install the thermactor pump and bracket (where applicable).

27 Install the alternator and bracket.

28 Install the water pump (refer to Chapter 2 if necessary).

29 Check that the crankshaft pulley is clean and smear engine oil on the sealing surface. Install the pulley and torque tighten the attaching bolt.

30 The remainder of the installation procedure is the reverse of the removal procedure. On completion, fill the cooling system and adjust the drivebelt tension (refer to Chapter 2 if necessary). Finally, adjust the valve clearances, as described in Section 41.

---

11 Timing chain tensioner - adjustment, removal and installation (engine in the vehicle)

1 Timing chain adjustment is not part of any routine maintenance programme and is normally taken care of automatically. However, after removal and installation of the cylinder head, it is recommended that the adjustment procedure given in this Section is followed (paragraphs 2 thru 9, or 15 thru 22, as appropriate).

Adjustment - hydraulic type

2 Remove the water pump (refer to Chapter 2 if necessary).

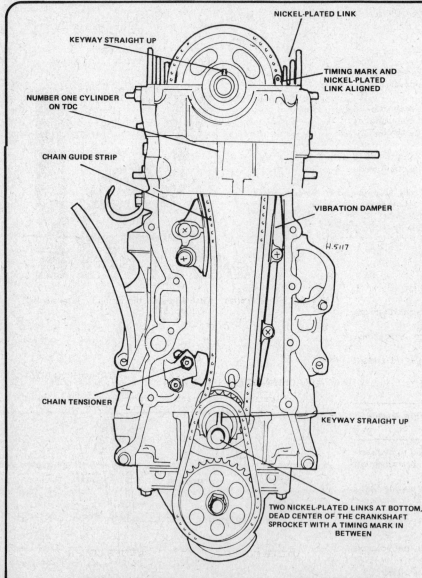

Fig. 1.6 Timing chain installation and alignment (Secs. 10 and 39)

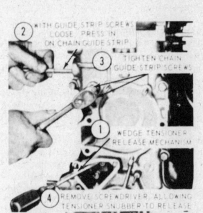

Fig. 1.7 Timing chain tensioner adjustment (Sec. 11)

11.12 Wedging a screwdriver in the hydraulic tensioner

3 Remove the cover from the timing chain tensioner (three nuts and washers). Take care not to damage the sealing faces if the cover is stuck to the engine front cover.
4 Rotate the crankshaft slightly in the direction of normal rotation, then lift the release on the tensioner and compress the snubber spring fully. Wedge a screwdriver in the tensioner to prevent it from releasing.
5 Remove the two blind plugs and aluminium washers from the holes in the cylinder head and timing chain cover. Loosen the chain guide strip attaching screws through the holes in the front cover.
6 Press the top of the guide strip with a lever through the adjusting hole in the cylinder head, then tighten the guide strip attaching screws.
7 Remove the screwdriver from the tensioner to allow the snubber to take-up the spring slack.
8 Install the chain tensioner cover and gasket, using a new gasket and non-setting sealant.
9 Install the water pump (refer to Chapter 2 if necessary).

Removal and installation - hydraulic type
10 To remove the tensioner, initially proceed as in paragraphs 2 and 3.
11 Remove the attaching bolts from the tensioner then withdraw the tensioner through the hole in the front cover.
12 When installing, wedge a screwdriver in the tensioner release mechanism whilst compressing the snubber spring (photo).
13 Without removing the screwdriver, insert the tensioner through the hole in the cover, then install and tighten the retaining bolts.
14 Adjust the tension by following the procedure of paragraphs 5 thru 9, of this Section.

Adjustment - spring type
15 Remove the water pump (refer to Chapter 2 if necessary).
16 Remove the cover from the timing chain tensioner (three nuts and washers). Take care not to damage the sealing faces if the cover is stuck to the engine front cover.
17 Rotate the crankshaft slightly in the direction of normal rotation, then pass a screwdriver down the aperture at the side of the camshaft sprocket. Depress the slide pin fully and turn it clockwise through 90 degrees.
18 Remove the two blind plugs and aluminium washers from the holes in the cylinder head and timing chain cover. Loosen the chain guide strip through the holes in the front cover.
19 Press the top of the guide strip with a lever through the adjusting hole in the cylinder head, then tighten the guide strip attaching screws.
20 Release the tensioner slide pin by turning it counter-clockwise.
21 Install the chain tensioner cover and gasket using a new gasket and non-setting sealant.
22 Install the water pump (refer to Chapter 2 if necessary).

Removal and installation - spring type
23 To remove the tensioner, initially proceed as in paragraph 15 and 16 of this Section.
24 Remove the attaching bolt and withdraw the tensioner through the hole in the front cover.
25 When installing, depress the slide pin fully and turn it clockwise through 90 degrees to lock the wedge.
26 Insert the tensioner through the hole in the front cover then install and tighten the retaining bolt.
27 Adjust the tension, as described in paragraphs 15 thru 22.

12 Oil pan (sump) and oil pump - removal and installation (engine in the vehicle)

1 In order to gain access beneath the vehicle, it will need to be raised on a hoist or suitable jacks, or alternatively placed over an inspection pit.
2 Remove the engine front lower stone guard (four nuts and washers).
3 Drain the crankcase oil into a container of suitable capacity. Remove the oil dipstick.
4 Remove the clutch release cylinder (refer to Chapter 5 if necessary) and let the cylinder hang.
5 Remove the engine rear brace attaching bolts; loosen the bolts on the left-hand side.
6 Where applicable, disconnect the emission line from the oil pan.
7 Remove the oil pan nuts and bolts and lower the oil pan onto the crossmember. If the oil pan is sticking to the block a few careful blows with a soft faced hammer may remove it but take care that the oil pan

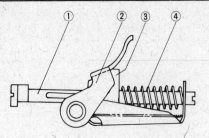
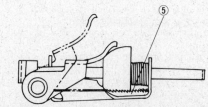

Fig. 1.8 The spring type chain tensioner (Sec. 11)

1 Slide pin	4 Spring
2 Arm	5 Wedge plate
3 Wedge	

Fig. 1.9 Timing chain adjustment with the spring type tensioner (Sec. 11)

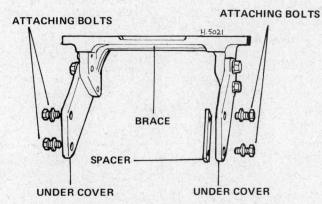

Fig. 1.10 The engine rear brace (Sec. 12)

is not damaged. If this does not move it, a thin bladed knife may be very carefully inserted between the sealing faces, but extreme care must be taken not to damage this sealing face.

8 Remove the oil pump pick-up tube (two nuts and washers) and withdraw the oil pan.

9 To remove the oil pump, first fold back the tab on the lock-washer then unscrew the sprocket nut.

10 Remove the oil pump to block attaching bolts, loosen the sprocket on the pump, then remove the pump (and sprocket, if necessary).

11 When installing the oil pump, position the sprocket to the chain and the pump to the block. Ensure that an 'O' ring is installed in the recess in the body, then install the pump, tightening the bolts to the specified torque.

12 Install the sprocket, tab washer and nut, then check the chain slack as described in Section 39, paragraph 15. Tighten the nut to the specified torque and fold over the locking tab.

13 When installing the oil pan, first ensure that all the gasket surfaces are perfectly clean and undamaged. Clean the pick-up tube and screen and the oil pan.

14 Install a new gasket to the block using a non-setting gasket sealant.

15 Install the oil pump pick-up tube, followed by the oil pan and torque tighten the bolts. The oil pan bolts should be tightened in a crosswise order to prevent any distortion.

16 The remainder of the installation procedure is the reverse of the removal procedure.

17 On completion, top-up the engine with the correct quantity and grade of oil. Start the engine and check for any leakage.

13 Main bearings - removal and installation (engine in the vehicle)

Note: It is of the utmost importance that this operation is carried out in conditions which are as clean as practically possible to prevent ingress of dirt to the bearings.

1 Initially remove the oil pan and oil pump as described in the previous Section.

2 Remove one bearing at a time by removing the retaining bolts and washers from the bearing cap. Take the bearing shell out of the cap.
Note: When removing the rear main bearing cap, install two bolts into the tapped holes so that leverage can be applied directly downwards. Do not rock or twist the bearing cap.

3 Now insert a small bolt into the oil hole in the crankshaft. The bolt head must be larger than the oil hole but must not project a greater distance than the thickness of the bearing shell.

4 Rotate the crankshaft in the normal direction of rotation to force the bearing out of the block.

5 Clean the crankshaft journals and inspect for nicks, burrs and bearing pick-up.

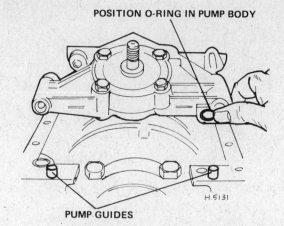

POSITION O-RING IN PUMP BODY

PUMP GUIDES

Fig. 1.11 Installing the oil pump (Sec. 12)

GASKET

Fig. 1.12 Installing the oil pan gasket (Sec. 12)

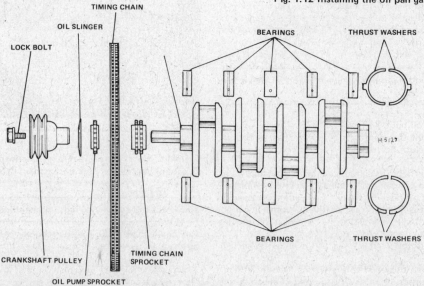

TIMING CHAIN

OIL SLINGER

LOCK BOLT

BEARINGS   THRUST WASHERS

CRANKSHAFT PULLEY

OIL PUMP SPROCKET

TIMING CHAIN SPROCKET

BEARINGS   THRUST WASHERS

Fig. 1.13 The crankshaft and associated parts

Note: The double row timing chain is used on 1800 cc engines and later 1600 cc engines. On early 1600 cc engines a single row chain is used, and a spacer is installed on each side of the timing chain sprocket.

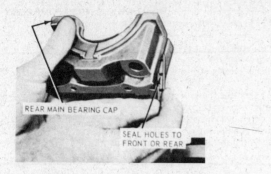

Fig. 1.14 Alternative types of rear main bearing seals (Secs. 13 and 39)

6   When installing an upper bearing shell, place the plain end over the shaft on the locking tang side of the block. Partially install the bearing so that the bolt (see paragraph 3) can be inserted in the crankshaft oil hole; rotate the crankshaft in the opposite direction to normal rotation until the bearing seats. Remove the bolt.

7   The bearing cap and shell can now be installed, after lubricating the bearing surface with engine oil. Tighten the bolts to the specified torque. **Note:** When installing the rear main bearing cap, it is good practice to renew the crankshaft thrust washers and the main bearing cap side seals. Note that the thrust washers are fitted to the block with the oil grooved surface facing the crankshaft thrust side.

8   Install the oil pump and pan as described in the previous Section.

14 Connecting-rod (big-end) bearings - removal and installation (engine in the vehicle)

Note: It is of the utmost importance that this operation is carried out in conditions which are as clean as practically possible to prevent ingress of dirt to the bearings.

1   Initially remove the oil pan and pump as previously described.

2   Remove one bearing at a time by rotating the crankshaft as necessary, to gain access to the cap bolts. Remove the cap bolts, take off the cap, then remove the bearing shell from the cap and connecting-rod.

3   Clean the crankshaft journals, and inspect for nicks, burrs and bearing pick-up. Check that the bearing shell seatings in the cap and connecting-rod are clean.

4   Install the bearing shells in the connecting-rod and bearing cap, with the tangs located in the slots.

5   Lubricate the bearing surfaces with engine oil, install the cap and tighten the bolts to the specified torque.

6   Install the oil pump and pan as described previously.

15 Pistons and connecting-rods - removal and installation (engine in the vehicle)

1   Remove the cylinder head as described in Section 21.

2   Remove the oil pan and oil pump as described in Section 12.

3   Turn the crankshaft until the piston to be removed is at bottom dead centre (bdc). Place a cloth on top of the piston crown to collect any carbon deposits, etc.

4   Carefully scrape off any deposits at the top of the cylinder bore, remove the bearing cap and carefully drive the piston and connecting-rod up out of the bore using a hammer handle. Ensure that the bearing cap and connecting-rod are marked as to their relative cylinder positions. If the piston will eventually be removed from the connecting-rod, this too must be marked.

5   When installing, lubricate the pistons, rings and cylinder bores with engine oil.

6   Ensure that the rings are positioned correctly (see Section 30) and install a piston ring compressor. Press the piston and connecting rod into the correct bore, ensure that the 'F' mark on the piston is towards the front of the engine (see Fig. 1.15). Guide the connecting-rod towards the journal, lubricate the bearing shells with engine oil, then install the bearing cap. Tighten the bolts to the specified torque.

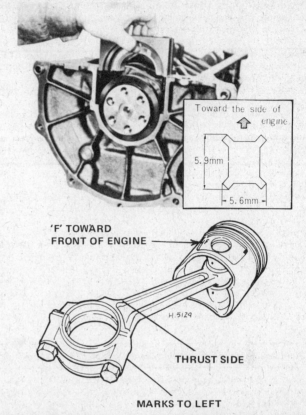

'F' TOWARD
FRONT OF ENGINE

Toward the side of engine

5.9mm

5.6mm

THRUST SIDE

MARKS TO LEFT

Fig. 1.15 Positioning of the piston and connecting rod (Secs. 15 and 16)

16.4 A piston pin retaining clip

7   Install the oil pan and pump, as described in Section 12.

8   Install the cylinder head as described in Section 40.

16 Pistons and connecting-rods - dismantling and reassembly

1   If the engine block is to be rebored, or the pistons are going to be renewed, it will be necessary to remove the pistons from the connecting-rods.

2   Mark the pistons and piston pins to identify them with their respective connecting-rods.

3   Carefully remove the piston rings by opening them out at their ends and sliding them up over the piston crown.

4   Using suitable pliers, remove the piston pin retaining clips. Provided that they are undamaged, they can be saved for re-use (photo).

5 Hold the piston in hot water for about fifteen seconds, then press out the pin. This should not be difficult as the piston will expand, but provided that great care is taken to support the piston, light hammer blows against a suitable drift will do the job.

6 Inspection of the piston, piston rings and cylinder bores, and assembly of the rings to the pistons are dealt with in Sections 29 and 30 later in this Chapter.

7 Check that the piston pin slides through the small end bush, but is not loose.

8 Lubricate the piston pin with engine oil. Install it through the piston and small end bush and install the retaining clips. Note that the 'F' mark on the piston will eventually point towards the front of the engine. See Fig. 1.15 for the correct relationship to the connecting-rod.

17 Oil pump - dismantling, inspection and reassembly

1 If the pick-up tube was not removed prior to removal of the pump (eg: when the engine has been removed from the vehicle), remove its two retaining nuts and washers. Take off the tube and discard the 'O' ring.

2 Remove the pump cover attaching screws. Remove the cover, the inner rotor and shaft assembly then the outer rotor.

3 Remove the split cotter pin from the body, then pull out the cap, spring and plunger.

4 Wash all the parts in gasoline (petrol) or kerosene (paraffin) and dry them with compressed air. Use a small brush to clean out the pump

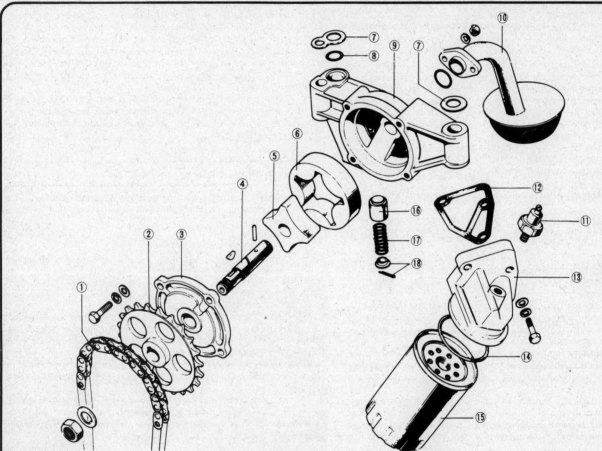

Fig. 1.16 The oil pump and filter (Secs. 17, 18 and 39)

1   Oil pump drive chain
2   Oil pump sprocket
3   Pump cover
4   Shaft
5   Inner rotor
6   Outer rotor
7   Adjusting shims (as required - see Section 39, paragraph 15)
8   'O' ring
9   Pump body
10 Oil strainer
11 Oil pressure switch
12 Gasket
13 Filter cover
14 Oil seal
15 Oil filter cartridge
16 Plunger
17 Control spring
18 Cap and split pin

(a) Outer race to housing clearance

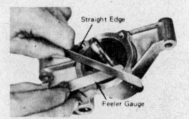

(b) Rotor end play

Fig. 1.17 Oil pump checks (Sec. 17)

housing and the relief valve chamber to ensure that all dirt is removed.

5 Check the pump housing and cover for wear and scoring; check the outer race and rotor for wear. Replace parts which are obviously unserviceable.

6 Measure the outer rotor to housing clearance and compare it with that specified. Replace parts as necessary.

7 With the rotor assembly installed in the housing, place a straight-edge over the assembly and the housing. Measure the clearance (rotor end-play) and compare it with that specified. Replace parts as necessary.

8 Lubricate all the parts of the oil pump with engine oil.

9 Install the relief valve plunger, spring and cap, and secure them with a new split cotter pin.

10 Install the outer rotor, and the inner rotor and shaft assembly. Install and tighten the cover.

11 Position a new 'O' ring on the pick-up tube. Install the tube and secure it with the washers and nuts (except where the engine is installed). Prime the pump with engine oil.

18 Oil filter - removal and installation

1 In order to gain access to the underside of the vehicle, it will need to be raised on a hoist or suitable jacks, or alternatively placed over an inspection pit.

2 Remove the engine front lower stone guard.

3 Place a drip pan beneath the oil filter, then unscrew the filter. If it is stubborn, wrapping a strip of emery cloth around it will provide a better grip.

3 When installing, coat the seal with engine oil and install the filter firmly by hand.

4 Lower the vehicle, run the engine at a fast idle and check for leaks.

5 Top-up the oil level, raise the vehicle and install the stone guard. Lower the vehicle to the ground.

19 Engine dismantling - general

1 It is best to mount the engine on a dismantling stand, but if one is not available stand the engine on a strong bench with wooden blocks so that it is at a comfortable working height. It can be dismantled on the floor but this is not so easy.

2 During the dismantling process, great care should be taken to keep the exposed parts free from dirt. As an aid to achieving this, thoroughly clean down the outside of the engine, removing all traces of oil and congealed dirt.

3 Use kerosene (paraffin) or one of the proprietary cleaning solvents. These solvents will make the job much easier for, after the solvent has been applied and allowed to stand for a time, a vigorous jet of water will wash off the solvent, together with all the grease and dirt. If the

dirt is thick and deeply embedded, work the solvent into it with a wire brush.

4 Finally wipe down the exterior of the engine with a rag and only then, when it is quite clean, should the dismantling process begin. As the engine is stripped, clean each part in a bath of kerosene (paraffin) or gasolene (petrol).

5 Never immerse parts with oilways (for example the crankshaft) in solvents, but to clean wipe down carefully with a petrol dampened cloth. Oilways can be cleaned out with nylon pipe cleaners. If an air line is available, all parts can be blown dry and the oilways blown through as an added precaution.

6 Re-use of the old gaskets is false economy and will lead to oil and water leaks, if nothing worse. Always use new gaskets throughout.

7 Do not throw the old gasket away for it sometimes happens that an immediate replacement cannot be found and the old gasket is then very useful as a template. Hang up old gaskets as they are removed.

8 To strip the engine it is best to work from the top down. The underside of the crankcase, when supported on wooden blocks, acts as a firm base. When the stage is reached where the crankshaft and connecting rods have to be removed, the engine can be upturned and all other work carried out in this position.

9 Whenever possible replace nuts, bolts and washers finger-tight from wherever they were removed. This helps avoid loss and muddle later. If they cannot be replaced, lay them out in such a fashion that it is clear from whence they came.

20 Engine ancillary components - removal

Before basic engine dismantling begins it is necessary to strip it of ancillary components. Typically these will be as follows:

1 Alternator
2 Water pump
3 Oil filter and mounting bracket
4 Distributor
5 Inlet manifold and carburetor
6 Exhaust manifold
7 Engine mount brackets
8 Engine rear brace

1 Remove the alternator together with its mounting bracket (photo).

2 Remove the water pump (refer to Chapter 2 if necessary). **Note:** If a fan clutch is installed and was not removed at the same time as the fan, this should be removed now (photo).

3 Unscrew the oil filter from the mounting bracket, then remove the bracket from the cylinder block. The bracket is retained by three bolts and washers (photos).

4 Remove the distributor from its mounting on the side of the cylinder head (refer to Chapter 4, if necessary).

5 Remove the inlet manifold complete with the carburetor (refer to Chapter 3, if necessary).

1

20.1 Remove the alternator   20.2 Remove the water pump

20.3a Remove the oil filter mounting bracket

20.3b Remove the oil filter mounting bracket

20.7a Removal of the engine mounts

20.7b Removal of the engine mounts

20.7c Removal of the engine mounts

20.8 Removing the rear engine brace

6   Remove the exhaust manifold and heat stove (refer to Chapter 3 if necessary).

7   Remove the engine mounts from the block (for further information on the mounts, see Section 7 (photos)).

8   Remove the engine rear brace from the cylinder block (Fig. 1.10) (photo).

21 Camshaft and cylinder head removal - engine in the vehicle

1   Begin by removing the battery leads and stowing them out of the way to prevent short-circuiting.

2   Drain the cooling system (refer to Chapter 2 if necessary).

3   Remove the top hose from the radiator and thermostat housing on the cylinder head.

4   Remove the air cleaner (refer to Chapter 3 if necessary).

5   Rotate the engine crankshaft so that number 1 piston is at top-dead-centre (tdc) on its firing stroke; this is most easily done by selecting 3rd gear and moving the vehicle a little until the top-dead-centre (tdc) mark on the crankshaft pulley aligns with the timing pointer, whilst at the same time checking that the distributor rotor aligns (approximately) with number 1 spark plug lead in the distributor cap. (See Chapter 4 for further information). For vehicles with automatic transmission, remove the spark plugs and rotate the crankshaft, using the fanbelt, to obtain tdc.

6   Apply the handbrake with 3rd gear still engaged as the installation procedure is simplified a little if this position is not disturbed.

7   Index mark the distributor body and cylinder head, and the rotor and the body, to ensure that correct alignment can be obtained when reassembling. Disconnect the distributor leads, noting their relative positions, then remove the clamp and withdraw the distributor.

8   The next step is to remove the inlet manifold and carburetor from the cylinder head which will require removal of the hoses, carburetor controls, fuel pipes and all pneumatic and electrical connections associated with the emission control equipment. Ensure that all the connections are suitably identified so that they cannot be mixed up when reconnecting. **Note:** Removal of the inlet manifold is described in Chapter 3, but there is no need to remove the assembly completely

from the engine compartment, provided that it can be adequately supported. This will mean that a little work may be saved in not having to remove some of the connections.

9   Remove the exhaust manifold from the cylinder head (refer to Chapter 3 if necessary).

10 Remove the radiator and water pump (refer to Chapter 2 if necessary). Ensure that all the hose connections and electrical leads are suitably identified, then remove them from the cylinder head.

11 Having removed the water pump (which entails removing the crankshaft pulley), remove the cover from the timing chain tensioner. It is retained by three nuts and washers.

12 Slacken each rocker arm cover nut slightly, then remove all the nuts and washers. Lift off the cover; if it is found to be sticking, either tap around the joint with a soft-faced hammer, or insert a knife between the cover and the cylinder head to break the seal. Take great care not to damage the sealing faces.

13 Once the rocker cover has been removed, check the position of the camshaft and sprocket wheel. If the engine number one piston is at tdc on its firing stroke, the two cam lobes operating the number 1 cylinder valves should be both pointing downwards and the rockers should be slack. Examination of the sprocket should show a reference dot being adjacent to a bright link in the timing chain - both mark and link should be in the plane of the cylinder head top surface and axis of the camshaft (photo).

14 It is now necessary to relieve the tension on the timing chain. Ideally this will mean that the crankshaft needs to be rotated slightly in the direction of rotation, but it is important that it is restored to its original position if the timing datum is not to be lost. To relieve the tension, lift the release on the tensioner and compress the snubber spring fully (hydraulic type) or depress the slide pin fully and turn it clockwise through 90 degrees (spring type). For further information refer to Section 11, Figs. 1.7 and 1.9 and photo 11.12.

15 Fold back the locking tab on the nut which secures the distributor drive gear to the front end of the shaft. Use a large wrench to remove the nut, then take off the gear and remove the pin.

16 Fold back the tab on the sprocket retaining nut, then remove the nut, washer and sprocket. Support the sprocket with a piece of wire until the cylinder head has been removed (paragraph 21).

17 It is now time to undo the cylinder head fixing bolts. The same bolts also fix the rocker assembly and camshaft in position on the cylinder head.

18 Once all the bolts have been undone and removed in the reverse order to that shown in Fig. 1.29, carefully lift the rocker arm assembly from the cylinder head. The assembly does not hold together by itself, because there is nothing to restrain the movement of the rocker pedestals along the rocker shafts. Pay particular attention to how this assembly is arranged - it is easier to ensure that it does not accidentally fall apart! Also mark the installed position of the camshaft bearing shells (photo).

19 Having removed the rockers, lift the camshaft out of the bearings in the cylinder head. Extract the camshaft from the sprocket which must remain in the timing chain. Let the sprocket and chain rest on the top chain guides in the engine front cover. Ensure that the chain does not move on the sprockets. Before the bearing shells are removed, mark their installed positions.

20 Undo the single bolt which secures the cylinder head to the top of the engine front cover (photo).

21 Carefully lift the cylinder head off the cylinder block. The weight of the block is not unreasonable but in view of the posture to be adopted to reach the cylinder head, it would be as well to have assistance for this final task.

22 If the cylinder head appears to be stuck to the engine block, **do not** try to prise it off with a screwdriver or cold chisel, but tap the cylinder head firmly with a plastic or wooden-headed hammer. The mild shocks should break any bond between the gasket, the head and engine block.

22 Camshaft and cylinder head - removal and installation - engine out of the vehicle

1 Remove the ancillary components, and proceed as directed in Section 21. **Note:** To obtain more leverage when removing the cylinder head, the manifolds can be removed from the head after removal of the head from the block if wished.

2 Installation is the reverse of this procedure (see Section 40).

23 Rocker arm assembly - dismantling and reassembly

1 The rocker arm assembly will have been removed by necessity before the cylinder head's removal from the engine and the components may now be separated, paying particular attention to their position and orientation.

2 There are no pins or fasteners which hold the rocker assembly together and once free from the cylinder head, it can easily, too easily perhaps, be taken apart.

3 **Note:** For the orientation of the rockers and the small supporters mounted on the shafts between the camshaft bearing caps, see Fig. 1.18.

4 If necessary, unbolt the camshaft thrust bearing plate from the front shaft bearing cap.

5 Recover the oil distribution pipe which passes from front to rear camshaft bearing caps.

6 All components should now be carefully laid out ready for

21.13 Note the position of the bright link with No 1 piston at tdc on its firing stroke

21.18 Lifting off the rocker arm assembly

21.20 The single front cylinder head retaining bolt

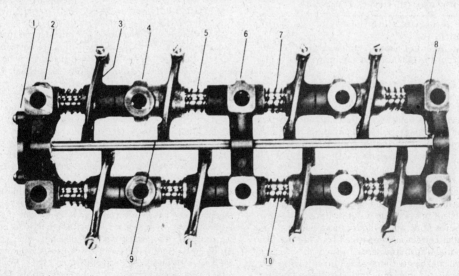
Fig. 1.18 The rocker arm assembly (Sec. 21)

1 Thrust plate	4 Supporter	6 Center bearing cap	9 Oil pipe
2 Front bearing cap	5 Rocker arm shaft	7 Spring	10 Rocker arm shaft
3 Rocker arm (Exhaust)	(Exhaust)	8 Rear bearing cap	(Intake)

inspection (photo).

7   When reassembling the rocker arm assembly, note that a single rocker arm shaft is used on the exhaust side, whereas two short shafts are used on the intake side. These two short shafts are interchangeable but the longer distance between the oil hole and the tip faces towards the center bearing cap (see Fig. 1.20).

8   The center bearing cap is assembled with the oil hole facing towards the intake valve side and the oil distribution pipe is installed with the oil ejection hole facing the camshaft. Note that the 'O' ring on the pipe is pressed into the recess in the center bearing cap after installation, to prevent vibration.

---

24 Cylinder head assembly - dismantling and reassembly

1   Remove the cylinder head to a clean bench and stand it on wooden blocks.

2   The valves can be removed from the cylinder head by the following method. Using a valve spring compressor, compress each set of valve springs in turn, until the valve spring retainer locks (split collets) near the top of the valve stem, can be removed. Release the compressor and then remove the upper spring seat, springs, lower spring seat (if applicable) and finally the valve itself. **Note:** If when the spring compressor is screwed down the spring cap refuses to budge and expose the locks, do not continue to screw the compressor down as there is a likelihood of damaging it. Gently tap the top of the tool directly over the locks with a light hammer; this should free the seat. Hold the compressor to prevent it from kicking aside when the seat is released (photo).

3   It is essential that the valves and their associated components are kept to their respective places in the cylinder head. Therefore, if they are being kept and used again, place them in a piece of card with slots

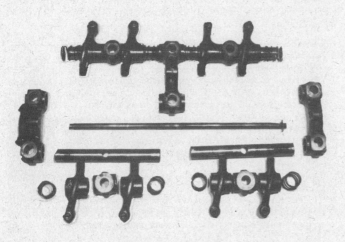

23.6 The component parts of the rocker arm assembly

Fig. 1.19 The cylinder head to front cover bolt (Sec. 23)

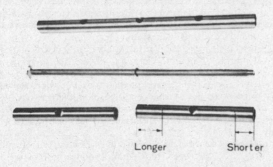

Longer   Shorter

Fig. 1.20 The rocker arm shafts (Sec. 23)

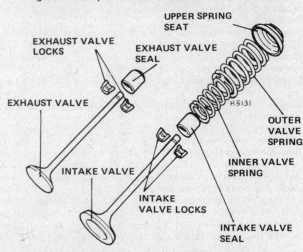

Fig. 1.21 The valves and associated parts (Sec. 24)

24.2a Using a compressor to remove the locks (split collets)

2.42b Removing a valve spring ...

24.2c ...and a valve

cut in it marked 1 to 4 exhaust and 1 to 4 intake. Keep the valve springs, seats and locks in order as well.

4 Finally remove the spark plugs.

5 Having dismantled the cylinder head to this stage, the next step is inspection, as described in Sections 32 thru 36.

6 When reassembling the cylinder head, the procedure is basically the reverse of that used when dismantling. Ensure that the valves are installed in their original positions if they are being re-used; if the valves have been reground the seats these must also be installed in their correct positions. Lubricate each valve stem with a little engine oil as it is being installed to prevent any chance of possible binding in the valve guides.

25 Cylinder block dismantling - engine out of the vehicle

1 With the engine removed from the vehicle, and the cylinder head removed from the block, as described in Section 21, prepare to dismantle the engine as described in the following Sections. Since many of the operations can be carried out with the engine installed, cross-references are made to later Sections for full details of many of the steps, in order to prevent repetition of procedures.

2 On manual transmission models, remove the clutch, as described in Chapter 2.

3 Remove the oil pan (sump) retaining nuts and bolts and remove the oil pan. Take great care that the oil pan is not distorted or the sealing faces damaged, particularly if the oil pan is stubborn to remove. For urther information see Section 12.

4 Remove the oil pump gear attaching nut and the oil pump to block attaching bolts. Loosen the sprocket, remove the pump and take off the sprocket. For further information see Section 12.

5 The next step is to remove the timing chain cover (engine front cover), which is bolted to the cylinder block. For further information see Section 10.

6 With the engine front cover removed, take off the oil pump drive chain, the crankshaft oil slinger, the timing chain tensioner and the timing chain guide. For further information on the timing chain and tensioner see Section 11.

7 Using a suitable extractor, draw off the crankshaft sprocket and timing chain. The Woodruff key can be left in the key-way, provided that it is a tight fit. If it is loose, or if the crankshaft will be machined or renewed, remove the key.

8 Remove the flywheel attaching bolts and carefully ease the flywheel off.

9 Loosen the connecting-rod (big-end) bearing caps on each connecting-rod in turn. Remove one cap, and its associated connecting-rod and piston, one at a time: ensuring that the relative position of the cap, bearing and connecting-rod is not lost. If there are no identification markings (cylinder numbers) on the caps and connecting-rods, mark them now using a center-punch. For further information on removal of the connecting-rods and bearings, refer to Section 14.

10 Loosen the crankshaft main bearing caps then remove them one at a time. If there are no identification markings as to their correct installed positions, mark them now using a center-punch. The crankshaft can now be lifted out, followed by the bearing shells and thrust washers. Ensure that the bearing shells are suitably marked to ensure that they

can be installed in the correct positions (if they are to be used again).

11 If any machining of the block is required, or an exchange block is going to be obtained, remove any remaining items such as dowels, coolant drain plug, oil separator, lifting eyes, etc.

26 Engine examination and renovation - general

1 With the engine stripped and all parts thoroughly cleaned, every component should be examined for wear. The items listed in the Sections following should receive particular attention and where necessary be renewed or renovated.

2 So many measurements of engine components require accuracies down to tenths of a thousandth of an inch. It is advisable therefore to either check your micrometer against a standard gauge occasionally to ensure that the instrument zero is set correctly, or use the micrometer as a comparative instrument. This last method however, necessitates that a comprehensive set of slip and bore gauges is available.

3 Before any inspection of parts is commenced, clean them using gasoline (petrol) or kerosene (paraffin), then blow them dry with compressed air.

27 Crankshaft - examination and renovation

1 Examine the crankpin and main journal surfaces for signs of scoring or scratches and check the ovality and taper of the crankpins and main journals. If the bearing surface dimensions do not fall within the tolerance ranges given in the Specifications at the beginning of this Chapter, the crankpins and/or main journals will have to be reground.

Big-end and crankpin wear is accompanied by distinct metallic knocking, particularly noticeable when the engine is pulling from low revs.

Main bearing and main journal wear is accompanied by severe engine vibration/rumble, getting progressively worse as engine revs increase.

If the crankshaft is reground the workshop should supply the necessary undersize bearing shells.

2 Ensure that the crankshaft oilways are unobstructed.

28 Big-end and main bearing shells - examination and renovation

1 Big-end bearing failure is accompanied by a noisy knocking from the crankcase and a slight drop in oil pressure. Main bearing failure is accompanied by vibration which can be quite severe as the engine speed rises and falls, and a drop in oil pressure.

2 Bearings which have not broken up, but are badly worn will give rise to low oil pressure and some vibration. Inspect the big-ends, main bearings and thrust washers for signs of general wear, scoring, pitting and scratches. The bearings should be matt grey in colour. Renew the bearings if they are not in this condition or if there is any sign of scoring or pitting. **You are strongly advised to renew the bearings - regardless of their condition. Re-installing used bearings is a false economy.**

3 The undersizes available are designed to correspond with crankshaft regrind sizes, ie; 0.020 inch (0.50 mm) bearings are correct for a

Fig. 1.22 Typical bearing conditions (Sec. 28)

crankshaft reground - 0.020 inch (0.50 mm) undersize. The bearings are in fact, slightly more than the stated undersize as running clearances have been allowed for during their manufacture.

4   Very long engine life can be achieved by changing big-end bearings at intervals of 30000 miles (48000 km) and main bearings at intervals of 50000 miles (80000 km) irrespective of bearing wear. Normally, crankshaft wear is infinitesimal and regular changes of bearings will ensure mileages in excess of 100000 miles (160000 km) before crankshaft regrinding becomes necessary. Crankshafts normally have to be reground because of scoring, due to bearing failure.

29 Cylinder bores - examination and renovation

1   The cylinder bores must be examined for taper, ovality, scoring and scratches. Start by carefully examining the top of the cylinder bores. If they are at all worn a very slight ridge will be found on the thrust side. This marks the top of the piston travel. The owner will have a good indication of the bore wear prior to dismantling the engine, or removing the cylinder head. Excessive oil consumption accompanied by blue smoke from the exhaust is a sure sign of worn cylinder bores and piston rings.

2   Measure the bore diameter just under the ridge with a micrometer and compare it with the diameter at the bottom of the bore, which is not subject to wear. If the difference between the two measurements is more than 0.006 inch (0.15 mm) then it will be necessary to fit oversize pistons and rings. If no micrometer is available, remove the rings from a piston and place the piston in each bore in turn about three quarters of an inch below the top of the bore. If an 0.010 inch (0.25 mm) feeler gauge can be slid between the piston and the cylinder wall on the thrust side of the bore then remedial action must be taken. Oversize pistons are available as stated in the Specifications.

3   These are accurately machined to just below the rebore measurements so as to provide correct running clearances in bores bored out to the exact oversize dimensions.

4   If the bores are slightly worn but not so badly worn as to justify reboring them, special oil control rings can be installed to the existing pistons, which will restore compression and stop the engine burning oil. Several different types are available and the manufacturer's instructions concerning their installation must be followed closely.

30 Pistons and piston rings - examination and renovation

1   If the old pistons are to be re-installed, carefully remove the piston rings and thoroughly clean them. Take particular care to clean out the piston ring grooves. At the same time do not scratch the aluminium. If new rings are to be installed to the old pistons, then the top ring should be stepped to clear the ridge left above the previous top ring. If a normal but oversize new ring is installed, it will hit the ridge and break, because the new ring will not have worn in the same way as the old, which will have worn in unison with the ridge.

2   Before installing the rings on the pistons, each should be inserted approximately 3 inches (0.118 mm) down the cylinder bore and the gap measured with a feeler gauge as shown in Fig. 1.24. This should be

as detailed in the Specifications at the beginning of this Chapter. It is essential that the gap is measured at the bottom of the ring travel. If it is measured at the top of a worn bore and gives a perfect fit it could easily seize at the bottom. If the ring gap is too small rub down the ends of the ring with a fine file, until the gap, when fitted, is correct. To keep the rings square in the bore for measurement, line each up in turn with an old ring down about 3 inches (0.118 mm). Remove the piston and measure the piston ring gap.

3   Check the side clearance of the piston rings using a feeler gauge as shown in Fig. 1.25. Compare the clearance with that given in the Specifications, and renew the rings or pistons as appropriate, if they are outside the specified limits.

4   When installing new pistons and rings to a rebored engine the ring gap can be measured at the top of the bore as the bore will now not taper. It is not necessary to measure the side clearance in the piston ring groove with rings installed, as the groove dimensions are accurately machined during manufacture. When installing new oil control rings to old pistons it may be necessary to have the groove widened by machining to accept the new wider rings. In this instance the manufacturer's representative will make this quite clear and will supply the address to which the pistons must be sent for machining (photo).

5   When installing the rings on the pistons, make sure that the ring gaps are properly spaced around the piston circumference. They should be positioned about 120 degrees apart, so that the gap is not located on the thrust side or the piston pin side. Apply a little engine oil to the rings and make sure that they are not binding in the piston grooves.

31 Connecting-rods - examination

1   The connecting-rod is a fairly robust item, but its loading is very harsh and therefore the examination required is directed at finding deep scratches or notches. Generally if the engine is being overhauled, simply because it has worn out, then it is unlikely that the connecting-rods will be anything but completely unserviceable.

2   However, if overhaul was necessitated by a failure of a particular component - piston or valve, then the rod should be wiped clean and its surface thoroughly inspected for damage. If there are sizeable dents or if a crack is found, the rod should be replaced.

32 Camshaft and camshaft bearings - examination and renovation

1   Remove the camshaft bearing shells from the cylinder head and bearing caps, and clean them using gasoline (petrol) or kerosene (paraffin). Inspect each bearing for scoring, chips and wear marks. Unless they are in an 'as new' condition, they should be renewed.

2   Inspect the camshaft lobes for scoring and signs of abnormal wear. Slight dressing of the cam lobes is permissible using an oilstone - provided that the overall cam lobe lift (elevation) is not reduced by more than 0.008 in. (0.20 mm). This can be checked by running the camshaft on lathe centers or V-blocks (or with the camshaft installed on the cylinder head). If the wear pattern is unsatisfactory, the camshaft must be renewed.

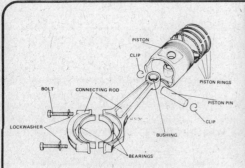

Fig. 1.23 A piston and connecting rod - exploded view (Sec. 30)

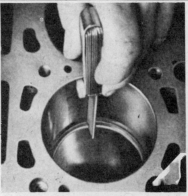

Fig. 1.24 Checking the piston ring gap (Sec. 30)

Fig. 1.25 Checking the piston ring side clearance (Sec. 30)

30.4 Note the piston identification letter (used on some models - see Specifications)

35.2 A valve guide seal

33 Rocker arm and shaft assembly - inspection and renovation

1   Ensure that all the oilways are unobstructed.
2   Inspect the ends of the rockers for wear, indentations and scoring. Light wear is permissible, but if there is evidence of grooving, the rockers must be replaced. Rockers should not be refaced by grinding.

34 Valves and valve seats - examination and renovation

1   Examine the heads of the valves for pitting and burning, especially the heads of the exhaust valves. The valve seatings should be examined at the same time. If the pitting on the valve and seats is very slight the marks can be removed by grinding the seats and valves together with coarse, and then fine, valve grinding paste. Where bad pitting has occurred to the valve seats it will be necessary to recut them to install new valves. If the valve seats are so worn that they cannot be recut, then it will be necessary to install valve seat inserts. These latter two jobs should be entrusted to a vehicle main dealer or automobile engineering works. In practice it is very seldom that the seats are so badly worn that they require renewal. Normally, it is the valve that is too badly worn, and the owner can easily purchase a new set of valves and match them to the seats by valve grinding.
2   Valve grinding is carried out as follows: Place the cylinder head upside down on a bench with a block of wood at each end to give clearance for the valve stems. Alternatively, place the head at 45 degrees to a wall with the combustion chambers away from the wall.
3   Smear a trace of coarse carborundum paste on the seat face and apply a suction grinder tool to the valve heads. With a semi-rotary action, grind the valve head to its seat, lifting the valve occasionally to redistribute the grinding paste. When a dull matt surface finish is produced on both the valve seat and the valve, then wipe off the paste and repeat the process with fine carborundum paste, lifting and turning the valve to redistribute the paste as before. A light spring placed under the valve head will greatly ease this operation. When a smooth unbroken ring of light grey matt finish is produced, on both valve and the valve seat faces, the grinding operation is complete.
4   Scrape away all carbon from the valve head and the valve stem. Carefully clean away every trace of grinding compound, taking great care to leave none in the ports or in the valve guides. Clean the valves and valve seats with a kerosene (paraffin) soaked rag, then with a clean rag. Finally, if an air line is available, blow the valve, valve guides and valve ports clean.

35 Valve guides - examination and renovation

1   If it is found that the valve guides require renewal, where the cylinder head is in an otherwise serviceable condition (or can easily be made serviceable), it is not recommended that any attempt is made to remove them as they are an interference fit. This is a job for a specialist and should either be carried out by a vehicle main dealer or by an automobile engineer with the necessary equipment.
2   If it is found necessary to renew the seals on the ends of the valve guides, these can be pulled off and replacements pressed on. A tool is available from the vehicle manufacturer's for this purpose (photo).

36 Cylinder head - decarbonisation and inspection

1   It is very unlikely that with modern fuels and oils, decarbonisation will be necessary at anything shorter than 60000 mile (100000 km) intervals.
2   This operation can be carried out with the engine either in or out of the vehicle, but the procedure given here is described as though the engine is installed. The spark plugs can remain installed as this helps to prevent carbon deposits from entering the screw threads.
3   With the cylinder head off, carefully remove with a wire brush and blunt scraper all traces of carbon deposits from the combustion spaces and ports. The valve stems and valve guides should be also freed from any carbon deposits. Wash the combustion spaces and ports down with gasoline (petrol) and scrape the cylinder head surface of any foreign matter with the side of a steel rule or a similar article. Take care not to scratch the surface.
4   Clean the pistons and top of the cylinder bores. If the pistons are still in the cylinder bores then it is essential that great care is taken to ensure that no carbon gets into the cylinder bores as this could scratch the cylinder walls or cause damage to the piston and rings. To ensure that this does not happen, first turn the crankshaft so that two of the pistons are on top of the bores. Place a clean lint-free cloth into the other two bores or seal them off with paper and masking tape.
    The water-ways and oilways should also be covered with a small piece of masking tape to prevent particles of carbon entering the cooling system and damaging the water pump, or entering the lubrication system and damaging the oil pump or bearing surfaces.
5   There are two schools of thought as to how much carbon ought to be removed from the piston crown. One is that a ring of carbon should be left around the edge of the piston and on the cylinder bore wall as an aid to keeping oil consumption low. Although this is probably true for older engines with heavily worn bores, on later engines it is best to remove all traces of carbon during decarbonisation.
6   If all traces of carbon are to be removed, press a little grease into the gap between the cylinder walls and the two pistons which are to be worked on. With a blunt scraper carefully scrape away the carbon from the piston crown, taking care not to scratch the aluminium. Also scrape away the carbon from the surrounding lip of the cylinder wall. When all carbon has been removed, scrape away the grease which will now be contaminated with carbon particles, taking care not to press any into the bores. To assist prevention of carbon build up the piston crown can be polished with a metal polish, but take great care that none seeps between the piston and the cylinder wall or the rings may seize in their

grooves. Remove the cloth or masking tape from the other two cylinders and turn the crankshaft so that the two pistons which were at the bottom are now at the top. Place a lint-free cloth into the other two bores or seal them off with paper and masking tape. Do not forget the water-ways and oilways as well. Proceed as previously described.

7   If a ring of carbon is going to be left around the piston then this can be helped by inserting an old piston ring into the top of the bore to rest on the piston and ensure that carbon is not accidentally removed. Check that there are no particles of carbon in the cylinder bores. Decarbonisation is now complete.

8   Using a straight-edge and feeler gauge, check the cylinder head for distortion and corrosion. The maximum permissible distortion and maximum permissible amount to be removed during any regrind, are given in the Specifications. Replace any cylinder head which is outside the acceptable limits.

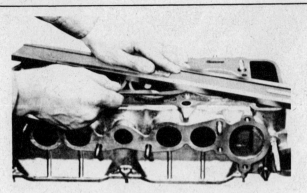

Fig. 1.26 Checking for cylinder head distortion (Sec. 36)

37 Miscellaneous items - inspection and renovation

Timing chain and sprockets
1   Replace a timing chain and sprockets if there is obvious wear or damage, or in the case of a major engine overhaul.

Distributor drive gear
2   Replace a drive gear which is damaged or has wear marks on the teeth.

Manifolds
3   Manifolds are dealt with in Chapter 3, but in the case of engine overhaul they should be examined for cracks, and cleaned of any carbon deposits and traces of gasket material.

Chain tensioner and guide strip
4   Wear on the chain tensioner snubber or guide strip will entail replacement items being fitted as spare parts are not supplied.

Oil pan (sump)
5   The oil pan should be cleaned, and traces of gasket material removed. Check for cracks and damaged sealing faces. If damage cannot be rectified by localized dressing or repair, a replacement item should be obtained.

Crankshaft pulley
6   Clean the oil seal contact surface to remove sludge, corrosion or varnish deposits. Light dressing with crocus cloth is permitted, but do not polish the surface as this can produce an inferior seal and lead to premature seal wear.

Cylinder block core plugs
7   Leaking core plugs can be removed by drilling a hole in the center and then prying them out. Before installing a new core plug, ensure that the bore is clean and dry. Smear a gasket sealing compound around the bore before installing the plug, with the flanged edge inward. Do not strike the crowned portion of the plug as this will damage it, but use a proper installation tool.

Spark plugs
8   Spark plugs should normally be renewed at the time of a major engine overhaul, but provided that their condition is satisfactory, cleaning will suffice. Full details of spark plugs are given in Chapter 4.

38 Engine reassembly - general

1   To ensure maximum life with minimum trouble from a rebuilt engine, not only must every part be correctly assembled, but everything must be spotlessly clean, all the oilways must be clear, locking washers and spring washers must always be fitted where indicated and all bearings and other working surfaces must be thoroughly lubricated during assembly. Before assembly begins, renew any bolts or studs whose threads are in any way damaged; whenever possible use new spring washers and cotter pins.

2   Apart from your normal tools, a supply of lint-free cloths, an oil can filled with engine oil (an empty washing-up fluid plastic bottle thoroughly clean and washed out will invariably do just as well), a supply of new spring washers, a set of new gaskets and a torque wrench should be collected together.

3   The order of assembly for the engine is as follows:
   a) *Install the crankshaft and main bearings.*
   b) *Install the pistons, connecting rods and bearings.*
   c) *Install the oil pump.*
   d) *Install the timing chain and oil pump drive chain.*
   e) *Install the engine front cover and oil pan.*
   f) *Install the cylinder head and valves.*
   g) *Assemble the rocker arm assembly.*
   h) *Install the timing chain tensioner.*
   j) *Install the water pump and crankshaft pulley.*
   k) *Adjust the valve lash (clearances).*
   l) *Install the flywheel and clutch.*
   m) *Install the remaining ancillaries.*

4   Since many of the reassembly operations can be carried out on an already installed engine as described previously in this Chapter, only an outline procedure together with any necessary precautions, is now given to avoid repetition.

39 Cylinder block reassembly - engine out of the vehicle

1   Ensure that the crankcase is thoroughly clean and that all oilways are clear. A thin twist drill is useful for clearing the oilways, or if possible they may be blown out with compressed air. Treat the crankshaft in the same fashion, and then inject engine oil into the oilways.

2   Never re-use old bearing shells; wipe the shell seats in the crankcase clean and then install the upper halves of the main bearing shells into their seats.

3   Install the main bearing shells in the cylinder block and lubricate them with engine oil (photo).

4   Install the crankshaft using the original thrust washers in the cylinder block with the oil grooved surface towards the crankshaft thrust side (photos).

5   Install a new oil seal on the rear end of the crankshaft after applying engine oil to the seal lip (photo).

6   Insert the side seals into the grooves in the rear main bearing cap (see Fig. 1.14).

7   Position the bearing shells and original thrust washers in the caps, lubricate the crankshaft journals, then install and torque tighten the bearing caps. Take great care to ensure that they are installed in their original positions (photos).

8   Using a wooden block and hammer, take-up the crankshaft endplay in one direction, then measure the endplay between the crankshaft thrust face and thrust washer using a feeler gauge. If necessary, remove the crankshaft and install replacement thrust washers to bring the endplay within the specified limits.

9   With the crankshaft installed, position bearing shells in the connecting-rods and bearing caps, lubricate the running surfaces with engine oil, then install them in their correct positions. Ensure that they are in the correct relationship with the cylinder block (front to rear) also. A piston ring compressor will be required to retain the rings while the piston is being installed. The piston can then be positioned into the lubricated bore by pressing down on the crown with a hammer handle or similar, until the connecting-rod mates with the crankshaft journal (crankpin). For further information see Section 15 (photos).

39.3 Install the main bearing shells in the block

39.4a Don't forget the thrust washers ...

39.4b ...before installing the crankshaft

39.5 Install the oil seal at the rear end of the crankshaft

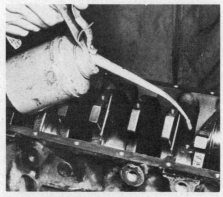
39.7a Lubricate the journals

39.7b Tightening a main bearing cap

1

Fig 1.27 Checking crankshaft end play (sec.39)

39.9a Install the bearing shells ...

39.9b ...push the piston down the bore ...

39.9c ...install the bearing cap...

39.9d ...and tighten it

39.11 Install the oil pump

10 Rotate the crankshaft to ensure that there is no binding or undue friction (high spots).

11 Install an 'O' ring in the outlet hole in the oil pump body. Install the oil pump and torque tighten the attaching bolts. For further information refer to Section 12 (photo).

12 Install the spacer on the crankshaft (where applicable) (photo).

13 Install the timing chain and sprocket on the crankshaft, aligning the crankshaft sprocket and crankshaft keyways with the key in position. Refer to Fig. 1.6 for the position of the bright links (photo).

14 Install the second spacer on the crankshaft (where applicable) (photo).

15 Install the oil pump drive chain and sprockets, aligning the keyways. Check the chain slack before installing the tab washer and nut. If this exceeds 0.157 in. (4 mm), remove the oil pump and install adjusting shims between the oil pump body and the cylinder block (see Figs. 1.16 and 1.28). When the chain slack is satisfactory, install the tab washer and nut on the oil pump drive, then fold over the tab (photos).

16 Install the timing chain guide strip and vibration damper to the front face of the block (photo).

17 Install the crankshaft oil thrower, concave side outwards. Install a new oil seal in the engine front cover and lubricate the lips with engine oil. Do not forget the front cover gasket which can be retained in position, using a non-setting gasket sealant. Install the front cover and torque-tighten the bolts (photos).

18 Cut off any excess gasket material along the mounting surface of the cylinder head and oil pan.

19 Position a new gasket on the oil pan using a non-setting gasket sealant. Install the oil pan, torque-tightening the bolts in a crosswise order.

20 Invert the engine and support the timing chain with a piece of wire, to prevent it from dropping inside the front cover (photo).

21 Install the cylinder head which has already been assembled as described previously, using a new cylinder head gasket.

22 If the camshaft sprocket is not in the timing chain, position it as

39.12 Install the first spacer (where applicable)

39.13 Install the timing chain and sprocket

39.14 Install the second spacer (where applicable)

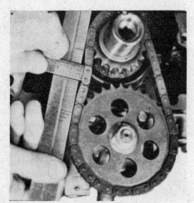

Fig. 1.28 Checking the oil pump chain slack (Sec. 39)

39.15a Install the oil pump sprocket

39.15b Tighten the nut and bend over the washer tab

39.16 Install the guide strip and vibration damper

39.17a Install the crankshaft oil thrower, concave side out

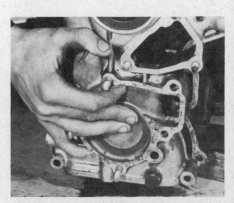

39.17b Install the engine front cover

39.20 Use a piece of wire to support the timing chain

shown in Fig. 1.6, position the camshaft onto the cylinder head and install the sprocket. Ensure that the camshaft journals are lubricated with engine oil. Install the tab washer and torque-tighten the nut, then fold over the tab. For further information, see Section 40.

23 Install the rocker arm assembly and torque-tighten the bolts in the order shown in Fig. 1.29. Refer to Section 40, for further details of this procedure.

24 The timing chain tensioner can now be installed, following the procedure given in Section 11.

25 Install the dowel pin, distributor drive gear, tab washer and nut. Fold over the tab on the washer (photos).

26 Install the distributor, aligning the index marks made when it was removed.

27 Install the water pump (refer to Chapter 2, if necessary).

28 Install the crankshaft pulley, washer and bolt. Tighten the bolt to the specified torque (photo).

29 Adjust the valve lash as described in Section 41. Do not forget the semi-circular oil seals before installing the rocker arm cover.

30 Install the flywheel. Refer to Section 8, for further information (photo).

31 Install the clutch. Refer to Chapter 5, for further information.

32 All that is now required is installation of the ancillaries, which can be done in the reverse order to removal (see Section 20). Note that it is considered preferable to install the oil filter cartridge after installation of the engine, since there is a possibility of damage occurring to it as the engine is lowered into the vehicle engine bay. When installing the intake and exhaust manifolds, ensure that new gaskets are used (photos).

Fig. 1.29 Cylinder head torque tightening sequence (Secs. 21,39, 40 and 41)

39.25a Install the dowel pin and drive gear ...

39.25b ...the tab washer ...

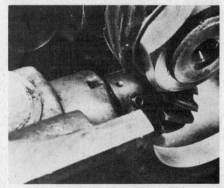

39.25c ... and the nut. Fold over the washer tab

39.28 Install the crankshaft pulley

39.30 Install the flywheel

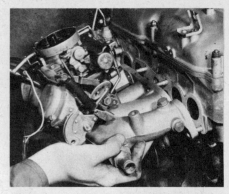

39.32a Install the intake manifold using a new gasket

39.32b Install the exhaust manifold gaskets ...

39.32c ...and the manifold

40.2 Position a new cylinder head gasket

40.3 Install the camshaft bearing shells

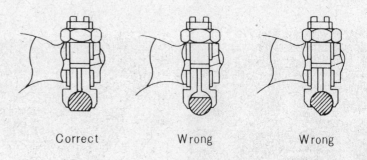

Correct   Wrong   Wrong

Fig. 1.30 The rocker arm adjusting screws (Sec. 40)

40 Camshaft and cylinder head installation - engine in the vehicle

1 Ensure that the cylinder block and cylinder head mating faces are clean.

2 Position a new cylinder head gasket on the block then feed the timing chain and sprocket up through the aperture in the cylinder head as it is positioned on the block. **Note:** If the sprocket has been removed from the chain, ensure that the bright link aligns with the dot on the sprocket (see Fig. 1.6) (photo).

3 Install the cambelt bearing shells into their locations in the cylinder head and lubricate them with engine oil (photo).

4 Position the camshaft and install the sprocket, aligning the keyway. Install the tab washer and nut; torque-tighten the nut and fold over the washer tab.

5 The assembled rocker arm assembly (see Section 23) can now be positioned on the cylinder head. (Don't forget to lubricate the camshaft journals with engine oil). Ensure that the flat surfaces of the balls contact the ends of the valve stems (see Fig. 1.30).

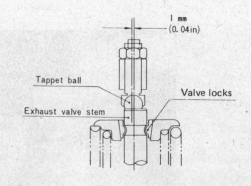

1 mm
(0.04 in)

Tappet ball

Valve locks

Exhaust valve stem

Fig. 1.31 The exhaust rocker arm offset (Sec. 40)

6 Refer to Fig. 1.29 for the bolt tightening sequence and lightly tighten each bolt. Now move each rocker arm supporter on the exhaust side to offset each exhaust rocker arm 0.04 in. (1 mm) from the valve center, then fully tighten the bolts to the specified cold (initial) torque.

7 Install and tighten the single bolt which secures the cylinder head to the engine front cover.

8 Install the dowel pin, distributor drive gear, tab washer and nut. Torque-tighten the nut and fold over the tab on the washer.

9 Adjust the timing chain tensioner, as described in Section 11. Install the tensioner cover using a new gasket.

10 The remainder of the installation procedure is the reverse of the removal procedure, but do not install the rocker arm cover until valve lash adjustment has been carried out, as described in Section 41.

11 On completion, fill the cooling system and run the engine at a fast idle until warm. Switch off and re-torque the cylinder head bolts to the specified final value.

41 Valve lash (clearance) - adjustment

1 If the cylinder head has been dismantled, it will be necessary to adjust the valve lash initially with the engine cold. The figures given in the Specifications are suitable for this purpose, provided that the engine is warmed up properly after installation. Care must be taken during this warming up period to ensure that excessive engine speeds and temperatures are not attained.

2 Having warmed up the engine, shut off the engine and remove the rocker arm cover.

3 Refer to the cylinder head torque-tightening sequence (Fig. 1.29), loosen No. 1 bolt about ¼-turn and retighten to the specified torque. Repeat this procedure for the other bolts in the correct order.

4 Rotate the crankshaft so that No. 1 piston is at top-dead-center (tdc) on the compression stroke. This position can be checked by aligning the tdc mark on the pulley with the timing pointer, when the distributor rotor is pointing to No. 1 spark plug terminal in the distributor cap (or where the valve rockers of No. 1 cylinder can be moved slightly up and down).

5 Using a feeler gauge between the rocker and camshaft, or rocker and valve stem, check for the specified clearance.

6 If adjustment is required, loosen the adjusting screw locknut and turn the adjusting screw until the correct clearance is obtained. Tighten the locknut afterwards and recheck the clearance (photo).

7 Repeat the procedure for the remaining cylinders with the piston at tdc on the compression stroke, in the firing order 1-3-4-2.

8 On completion ensure that the semi-circular grommet is installed as shown in the photograph. Use a new rocker cover gasket, install the rocker cover and tighten the nuts to the specified torque in a crosswise order (photo).

42 Engine - installation

1 Whether the engine is to be installed on its own, or together with the transmission, the procedure is basically the reverse of the removal procedure.

2 Raise the engine (and transmission, where appropriate), using a hoist, and lower it into position in the vehicle engine bay. A jack will be required to support the transmission until the rear support is installed if the transmission is connected to the engine (photo).

3 Install the engine and transmission mounts.

4 Where applicable, install the starter motor and the flywheel housing bolts.

5 Install the exhaust pipe.

6 Install the oil filter (where applicable) and engine lower front stone guard.

7 Connect the electrical, ground, fuel and air lines to the engine.

8 Install the carburetor controls and linkages.

9 Connect the heater and thermactor hoses.

10 Install the thermactor pump (and alternator if not already installed) and drivebelts.

11 Install the fan, radiator and hoses.

12 If applicable, connect the gearshift linkage, speedometer drive cable and propeller shaft.

13 Top-up the engine oil and coolant (and transmission oil, where applicable) (photos).

14 Install the air cleaner.

1

41.6 Adjusting the valve lash (clearance)

41.8 Note the marking on the semi-circular grommet

42.2 Installing the engine and transmission

42.13a Don't forget to top-up the engine ...

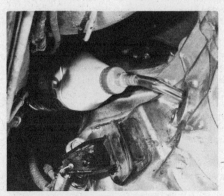

42.13b ...and transmission oil

15 Install the engine compartment hood.
16 Install the battery connections.

43 Engine - initial start-up after overhaul

1   Make sure that the battery is fully charged and that all lubricants, coolant and fuel are replenished.
2   If the fuel system has been dismantled it will require several revolutions of the engine on the starter motor to pump the fuel up to the carburetor.
3   As soon as the engine fires and runs, keep it going at a fast idle only, (no faster) and bring it up to the normal working temperature.
4   As the engine warms up there will be odd smells and some smoke from parts getting hot and burning off oil deposits. The signs to look for are leaks of water or oil which will be obvious if serious. Check also the exhaust pipe and manifold connections, as these do not always 'find' their exact gas tight position until the warmth and vibration have acted on them, and it is almost certain that they will need tightening further. This should be done of course, with the engine stopped.
5   When normal running temperature has been reached adjust the engine idling speed as described in Chapter 3, then set the valve lash as described in Section 41.
6   Stop the engine and wait a few minutes to see if any lubricant or coolant is dripping out when the engine is stationary.
7   Road test the car to check that the timing is correct and that the engine is giving the necessary smoothness and power. Do not race the engine - if new bearings and/or pistons have been fitted it should be treated as a new engine and run in at a reduced speed for the first 300 miles (500 km).

44 Fault diagnosis - engine

Symptom	Reasons	Remedy
Engine fails to turn over when starter control operated		
No current at starter motor	Flat or defective battery	Charge or replace battery. Push start car.
	Loose battery leads	Tighten both terminals and earth ends of ground leads.
	Defective starter solenoid or switch or broken wiring	Run a wire direct from the battery to the starter motor or by-pass the solenoid.
	Engine ground strap disconnected	Check and retighten strap.
Current at starter motor	Jammed starter motor drive pinion	Place car in gear and rock to and fro.
	Defective starter motor	Remove and recondition.
Engine turns over but will not start		
No spark at spark plug	Ignition damp or wet	Wipe dry the distributor cap and ignition leads.
	Ignition leads to spark plugs loose	Check and tighten at both spark plug and distributor cap ends.
	Shorted or disconnected low tension leads	Check the wiring on the coil and to the distributor.
	Dirty, incorrectly set, or pitted contact breaker points	Clean, file smooth, and adjust.
	Faulty condenser	Check contact breaker points for arcing, remove and install new.
	Defective ignition switch	By-pass switch with wire.
	Ignition leads connected wrong way round	Remove and replace leads to spark plugs in correct order.
	Faulty coil	Remove and install new coil.
	Contact breaker point spring earthed or broken	Check spring is not touching metal part of distributor. Check insulator washers are correctly placed. Renew points if the spring is broken.
No fuel at carburetor float chamber or at jets	No fuel in fuel tank	Refill tank!
	Vapour lock in fuel line (in hot conditions or at high altitude)	Blow into fuel tank, allow engine to cool, or apply a cold wet rag to the fuel line.
	Blocked float chamber needle valve	Remove, clean and replace.
	Fuel pump filter blocked	Remove, clean and replace.
	Choked or blocked carburetor jets	Dismantle and clean.
	Faulty fuel pump	Remove, overhaul and replace.
Engine stalls and will not start		
Excess of petrol in cylinder or carburetor flooding	Too much choke allowing too rich a mixture to wet plugs	Remove and dry spark plugs or with wide open throttle, push start the car.
	Float damaged or leaking or needle not seating	Remove, examine, clean and replace float and needle valve as necessary.
	Float lever incorrectly adjusted	Remove and adjust correctly.
No spark at spark plug	Ignition failure - sudden	Check over low and high tension circuits for breaks in wiring.
	Ignition failure - misfiring precludes total stoppage	Check contact breaker points, clean and adjust. Renew condenser if faulty.
	Ignition failure - in severe rain or after traversing water splash	Dry out ignition leads and distributor cap.
No fuel at jets	No fuel in fuel tank	Refill tank!
	Sudden obstruction in carburetor	Check jets, filter, and needle valve in float chamber for blockage.
	Water in fuel system	Drain tank and blow out fuel lines.
Engine misfires or idles unevenly		
Intermittent spark at spark plug	Ignition leads loose	Check and tighten as necessary at spark plug and distributor cap ends.
	Battery leads loose on terminals	Check and tighten terminal leads.
	Battery ground strap loose on body attachment point	Check and tighten ground lead to body attachment point.
Intermittent sparking at spark plug	Engine ground lead loose	Tighten lead.
	Low tension leads to coil loose	Check and tighten leads if found loose.
	Dirty, or incorrectly gapped plugs	Remove, clean and regap.
	Dirty, incorrectly set, or pitted contact breaker points	Clean, file smooth and adjust.
	Tracking across inside of distributor cover	Remove and install new cover.
	Ignition too retarded	Check and adjust ignition timing.
	Faulty coil	Remove and install new coil.

1

Symptom	Reason/s	Remedy
Fuel shortage at engine	Mixture too weak	Check jets, float chamber needle valve, and filter for obstruction. Clean as necessary.
	Carburetor incorrectly adjusted	Remove and overhaul carburetor.
	Air leak in carburetor	Remove and overhaul carburetor.
	Air leak at inlet manifold to cylinder head, or inlet manifold to carburetor	Test by pouring oil along joints. Bubbles indicate leak. Renew manifold gasket as appropriate.
Lack of power and poor compression		
Mechanical wear	Incorrect valve clearances	Adjust rocker arms to take up wear.
	Burnt out exhaust valves	Remove cylinder head and renew defective valves.
	Sticking or leaking valves	Remove cylinder head, clean, check and renew valves as necessary.
	Weak or broken valve springs	Check and renew as necessary.
	Worn valve guides or stems	Renew valve guides and valves
	Worn pistons and piston rings	Dismantle engine, renew pistons and rings.
Fuel/air mixture leaking from cylinder	Burnt out exhaust valves	Remove cylinder head, renew defective valves.
	Sticking or leaking valves	Remove cylinder head, clean, check, and renew valves as necessary.
	Worn valve guides and stems	Remove cylinder head and renew valves and valve guides.
	Weak or broken valve springs	Remove cylinder head, renew defective springs.
	Blown cylinder head gasket (accompanied by increase in noise)	Remove cylinder head and install new gasket.
	Worn pistons and piston rings	Dismantle engine, renew pistons and rings.
	Worn or scored cylinder bores	Dismantle engine, rebore, renew pistons and rings.
Incorrect adjustments	Ignition timing wrongly set. Too advanced or retarded	Check and reset ignition timing.
	Contact breaker points incorrectly gapped	Check and reset contact breaker points.
	Incorrect valve clearances	Check and reset rocker arm to valve stem gap.
	Incorrectly set spark plugs	Remove, clean and regap.
	Carburation too rich or too weak	Tune carburetor for optimum performance.
Carburation and ignition faults	Dirty contact breaker points	Remove, clean and replace.
	Fuel filters blocked causing poor top end performance through fuel starvation	Dismantle, inspect, clean and replace all fuel filters.
	Distributor automatic balance weights or vacuum advance and retard mechanisms not functioning correctly	Overhaul distributor.
	Faulty fuel pump giving top end fuel starvation	Remove, overhaul, or install exchange reconditioned fuel pump.
Excessive oil consumption	Excessively worn valve stems and valve guides	Remove cylinder head and fit new valves and valve guides.
	Worn piston rings	Install oil control rings to existing pistons or purchase new pistons.
	Worn pistons and cylinder bores	Install new pistons and rings, rebore cylinders.
	Excessive piston ring gap allowing blow-up	Install new piston rings and set gap correctly.
	Piston oil return holes choked	Decarbonise engine and pistons.
Oil being lost due to leaks	Leaking oil filter gasket	Inspect and install new gasket if necessary.
	Leaking rocker cover gasket	Inspect and install new gasket as necessary.
	Leaking timing gear cover gasket	Inspect and install new gasket as necessary.
	Leaking oil pan gasket	Inspect and install new gasket as necessary.
	Loose oil pan plug	Tighten and install new gasket if necessary.
Unusual noises from engine		
Excessive clearances due to mechanical wear	Worn valve gear (noisy tapping from rocker box)	Inspect and renew rocker shaft, rocker arms, and ball pins as necessary.
	Worn big-end bearing (regular heavy knocking)	Drop oil pan, if bearings broken up clean out oil pump and oilways, install new bearings. If bearings not broken but worn install bearing shells.
	Worn timing chain and gears (rattling from front of engine)	Remove timing cover, install new timing wheels and timing chain.
	Worn main bearings (rumbling and vibration)	Drop oil pan, remove crankshaft, if bearing worn but not broken up, renew. If broken up strip oil pump and clean out oilways.
	Worn crankshaft (knocking, rumbling and vibration)	Regrind crankshaft, install new main and big-end bearings.

Chapter 2 Cooling system

Contents

Antifreeze and rust inhibitors 6	Fault diagnosis - cooling system 13
Cooling system - draining 3	General description 1
Cooling system - filling 5	Radiator - removal and installation 8
Cooling system - flushing 4	Thermostat - removal, testing and installation 9
Cooling system - routine maintenance 2	Water pump - dismantling, overhaul and reassembly 12
Fan/alternator drivebelt - tension adjustment 7	Water pump - removal and installation 11
Fan drive clutch - testing 10	

Specifications

Type of system ... ... Pressurized and sealed, with centrifugal pump, thermostat, fan and radiator

Radiator
Type ... ... Corrugated fin
Pressure cap setting ... ... 13 lbf/in^2 (0.91 kgf/cm^2)

Thermostat
Type ... ... Wax pellet
Starts to open ... ... 180° F (82.2° C)
Fully open ... ... 203° F (95° C)
Lift height (nominal) ... ... 0.315 in. (8 mm)

Water pump type ... ... Impeller (centrifugal)

Fan/alternator belt tension
New belt ... ... 3/8 to 1/2 in. (9.5 to 12.7 mm)
Used belt ... ... 1/2 to 5/8 in. (12.7 to 15.9 mm)

Coolant capacity (with heater)
Courier ... ... 15 US pints /12.5 Imp. pints/7.1 liters
B1600 ... ... 13.6 US pints/11.3 Imp. pints/6.4 liters

Fan clutch test speeds (Courier - California)

	Fan speed	Pulley speed	Engine speed
Fan clutch starts to slip	1950 rpm	2200 rpm	1700 rpm
Maximum fan slip	3200 rpm	5000 rpm	3840 rpm

1 General description

1 The cooling system comprises a radiator, fan, thermostat, pressure cap and centrifugal water pump. The fan and water pump are driven by a 'V' belt from the crankshaft pulley (this belt also drives the alternator). On Courier models for California, the fan pulley drives the fan thru a slipping clutch in the interests of obtaining less fan noise and a reduction of engine loading.

2 When the engine is cold, coolant circulates in the engine thru the bypass hoses since the thermostat is closed. As the engine warms up, the thermostat starts to open the outlet to the radiator which provides additional cooling for the engine. Coolant now circulates thru the radiator, and into the cylinder and block water jackets and then to the outside surfaces of the combustion chambers which are the hottest parts of the engine. After cooling the combustion chambers, the coolant circulates back thru the block, thru the thermostat and back into the radiator.

3 The coolant is cooled in the radiator by the combined effects of the cooling fan and the forward motion of the vehicle as air passes the cooling fins.

4 An internal combustion engine runs most efficiently when hot and in order to increase the temperature above the boiling point of water, but at the same time control the temperature within suitable limits, a pressurized system is used. This is accomplished by the use of a radiator pressure cap which contains two valves. The main valve will relieve the system pressure when it increases to 13 lbf/in^2 (0.91 kgf/cm^2), which occurs as the temperature rises to the maximum permitted for the vehicle. When the system cools down, the coolant contracts and in order to prevent low pressures which cause the radiator and hoses to collapse, another relief valve comes into operation. This allows air to enter the system and thus balance the pressure.

2 Cooling system - routine maintenance

1 The cooling system requires very little routine maintenance but in view of its important nature, this maintenance must not be neglected.

2 The maintenance intervals are given in the Routine Maintenance Section at the beginning of this manual.

3 Apart from regular checking of the coolant level, and inspection for leaks and deterioration of hose connections, the only other items of major importance are the use of antifreeze solutions or rust inhibitors suitable for aluminium engines, and renewal of the coolant. These items

2

are covered separately in this Chapter.

4 If must be remembered that the cooling system is pressurized. This means that when the engine is hot, the coolant will be at a temperature in excess of 212°F (100°C). Great care must therefore be taken if the radiator pressure cap has to be removed when the engine is hot since steam and boiling water will be ejected. If possible, let the engine cool down before removing the pressure cap. If this is not possible, place a cloth on the cap and turn it slowly counter-clockwise to the first notch. Keep it in this position until all the steam has escaped then turn it further until it can be removed.

3 Cooling system - draining

1 Place the vehicle on level ground. If the coolant is to be re-used, place suitable containers under the drain cocks for its collection.
2 Remove the radiator cap. If the engine is hot see paragraph 4, of the previous Section.
3 Open the radiator and engine block drain cocks and drain off all the coolant. Ensure that the heater water valve is in the hot position to permit the coolant to be drained from the heater matrix.
4 When coolant ceases to flow from the drain cocks, probe them with a piece of stiff wire to ensure that there is no sediment blocking the drain orifices.
5 On completion, refer to Section 4 or 5, as appropriate.

4 Cooling system - flushing

1 With the passage of time deposits can build up in an engine which will lead to engine overheating and possibly serious damage.
2 It is a good policy, whenever the cooling system is drained, to flush the system with cold water from a hosepipe. This can conveniently be done by leaving a hosepipe in the radiator filler orifice for about 15 minutes while water is allowed to run thru. This will usually be sufficient to clear any sediment which may be present.
3 If there appears to be a restriction, first try reverse flushing; this is the application of the hose to the drain orifices and forcing water back thru the radiator tubes and out of the filler.

4 If the radiator flow is restricted by something other than loose sediment, then no amount of flushing will shift it and it is then that a proprietary chemical cleaner, suitable for aluminium engines, is needed. Use this according to the directions and make sure that the residue is fully flushed out afterwards. If leaks develop after using a chemical cleaner, a proprietary radiator sealer may cure them, but the signs are that the radiator has suffered considerable chemical corrosion and that the metal is obviously getting very thin in places.

5 Cooling system - filling

1 When draining (and flushing if applicable) has been accomplished, close the drain cocks and top-up the cooling system with water which contains the correct proportion of antifreeze or inhibitor (see Section 6). Ensure that the heater water valve is open to prevent airlocks from occurring in the heater matrix.
2 When the radiator is full, run the engine for 5 to 10 minutes at a fast idle. As the water circulates, and then as the thermostat opens, the coolant level will be seen to fall. Top-up to the radiator to about halfway up the fill elbow, install the cap, then run the engine for a few more minutes and check carefully for water leaks.
3 Allow the system to cool, then recheck the coolant level. Top-up if necessary until halfway-up the fill elbow then install the cap firmly.

6 Antifreeze and rust inhibitors

1 Tap water alone should not be used in an aluminium engine except in an emergency. If it has to be used, if should be drained off at the earliest opportunity and the correct coolant mixture used instead.
2 Generally speaking, the basis of the coolant mixture can be tap water, except where this has a high alkali content or is exceptionally hard. If these conditions exist, clean rainwater or distilled water should be used.
3 Antifreeze must be of a type suitable for use with aluminium engines (ethylene glycol based antifreeze is suitable) and many proprietary

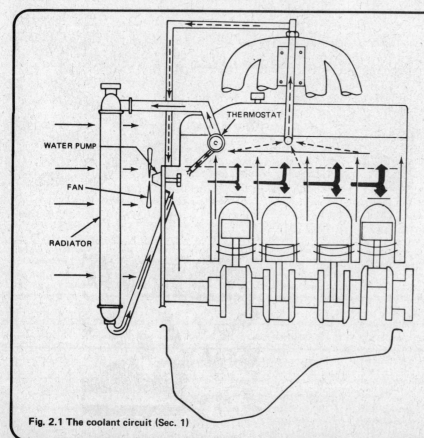

Fig. 2.1 The coolant circuit (Sec. 1)

WATER PUMP

FAN

RADIATOR

THERMOSTAT

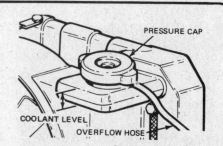

PRESSURE CAP

COOLANT LEVEL

OVERFLOW HOSE

Fig. 2.2 The radiator pressure cap
(Sec. 3)

Fig. 2.3 The engine coolant drain plug
(Sec. 3)

products will be available for use. The fact that all products tend to be expensive should not deter you from using them, since they are a good insurance against freezing and corrosion.

4 The following table gives suitable concentrations of antifreeze. Do not use concentrations in excess of 55% except where protection to below −35°F (−37°C) is required as there is a possibility of overheating in very hot weather.

Coolant freezing water point	Mixture percentage (volume)		Specific gravity of mixture at 68°F (20°C)
	Anti-freeze	Water	
−4°F (−20°C)	35	65	1.051
−49°F (−45°C)	55	45	1.078

5 Antifreeze mixtures are normally suitable for use for a period of two years (even so-called permanent antifreeze) after which they should be discarded and a fresh mixture used.

6 Antifreeze normally contains suitable corrosion inhibitors for protection of the engine. However, if antifreeze is not used for some reason, the vehicle manufacturers market suitable inhibitors which will give satisfactory protection to the engine. Any inhibitors which are used must be mixed in accordance with the instructions on the container.

7 Fan/alternator drivebelt - tension adjustment

1 In order to obtain satisfactory engine cooling and alternator charge rate, allied to a long drivebelt life, the belt must be tensioned correctly.
2 To check the belt tension, apply a pressure of approximately 22 lb f (10 kg f) to the belt midway between the pulleys and check for a deflection as given in the Specifications.
3 If adjustment is required, loosen the alternator mounting bolts and pivot bolt and move the alternator as necessary. Avoid prying against the side of the alternator or irreparable damage may result.
4 Tighten the bolts after adjustment has been made, then recheck the tension. After running the vehicle for about 150 miles (250 km), recheck the belt tension and adjust if necessary.

8 Radiator - removal and installation

1 Drain the cooling system. Refer to Section 3, if necessary.
2 Where applicable, remove the fan shroud retaining screws and move the shroud back over the fan.
3 Remove the cooling fan (and fan clutch, where applicable) from the water pump.
4 Loosen the hose clamps then disconnect the top and bottom radiator hoses (photo).
5 Remove the radiator mounting bolts then carefully lift the radiator out of its supports followed by the shroud, if necessary (photos).
6 If necessary, clean the radiator internally as described in Section 4. If the exterior cooling fins are blocked with dirt, bugs, grease etc, they should be cleared using compressed air on a water jet.
7 When installing, position the radiator against the supports then install and tighten the bolts.
8 Connect the hoses and tighten the clamps.
9 Install the fan (and fan clutch, if applicable) and tighten the bolts.
10 Position and install the fan shroud (where applicable).
11 Fill the cooling system. Refer to Sections 5 and 6, for further information.

9 Thermostat - removal, testing and installation

1 Drain the coolant until it is below the thermostat housing. Disconnect the wire from the temperature sender.
2 Remove the nuts and bolts from the coolant outlet elbow. Where applicable, the vacuum control valve will have to be detached (refer to Chapter 3, Section 21 or 24 for details).
3 Remove the coolant elbow from the thermostat housing studs and the coolant hose.
4 Disconnect the bypass hose from the thermostat housing then remove the thermostat and housing from the engine.

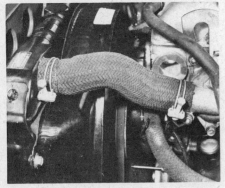
8.4 The top radiator hose

8.5a Lift out the radiator ...

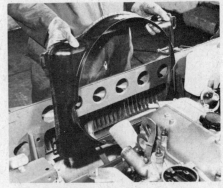
8.5b ...followed by the shroud

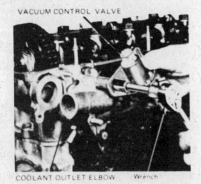
Fig. 2.4 Removing the coolant outlet elbow (Sec. 9)

Fig. 2.5 Removing the thermostat housing (Sec. 9)

Fig. 2.6 Installing the thermostat (Sec. 9)

5   Remove the thermostat from the housing, noting the position of its jiggle pin.

6   Carefully remove all traces of gasket material from the parts using a blunt knife.

7   To test a thermostat for correct operation, suspend it in a container of hot water. Using a thermometer to measure the water temperature, heat the water and note the temperature at which the thermostat begins to open. Also measure the lift and compare the figures obtained with those specified.

Replace the thermostat with a new one if it does not meet the specified lift and operating temperature.

8   Installation of the thermostat is the reverse of the removal procedure, but the following points must be observed:

a) *Ensure that the jiggle pin is in its original position.*

b) *Use new gaskets for the thermostat housing and coolant elbow, and use a non-setting gasket compound on the sealing faces.*

c) *Refer to the procedure given in Section 5, when filling the cooling system.*

10 Fan drive clutch - testing

1   Where a fan drive clutch is used, it can only be checked satisfactorily using a tachometer and stroboscopic lamp. If the clutch does not operate at the specified speeds, is extremely noisy in operation or shown signs of lubricant leakage, a replacement should be installed.

11 Water pump - removal and installation

1   Remove the hood (bonnet). Refer to Chapter 12, if necessary.

2   Drain the cooling system as previously described, then remove the lower hose from the water pump.

3   Disconnect the lower radiator hose and the upper engine hose which leads to the radiator. Remove the radiator.

4   Loosen the alternator and thermactor pump (where applicable) adjusting and mounting bolts, then remove the drivebelts.

5   Remove the fan and pulley and the crankshaft pulley.

6   Remove the water pump securing bolts and remove the pump and gasket from the block.

7   When installing, ensure that the mating faces are clean then install the pump to the block using a new gasket and following the reverse of the removal procedure.

8   Adjust the alternator and thermactor pump drive belts.

9   Fill the cooling system and check for leaks.

12 Water pump - dismantling, overhaul and reassembly

1   If the water pump is leaking, has excessive end play or looseness of the shaft, or is unduly noisy in operation, it should be dismantled for overhaul. However, before commencing, ascertain the availability of spare parts; if these are not available, your only course of action is to obtain an exchange pump. This will obviously be more expensive but will save a certain amount of work.

2   Having removed the water pump from the engine, remove the impeller from the rear of the assembly using a suitable extractor.

3   Using a suitable extractor, remove the pulley boss from the shaft.

4   Remove the spacer and the front dust seal plate assembly.

5   Remove the snap-ring (circlip) from the groove in the water pump housing.

6   Support the pump body then press out the shaft, spacer and bearings assembly (from the rear) thru the front of the body.

7   Remove the seal assembly from the pump body.

8   Using a suitable puller, draw the bearings off of the shaft, then remove the baffle, rear dust seal plate washer and stop-ring.

9   If the bearings run smoothly and do not show signs of corrosion they should (in theory) be suitable for re-use. However, where other parts of the pump are unserviceable, which will only normally occur after a considerable period of time, it is worthwhile fitting new bearings. The seal assembly should be renewed regardless of its condition. The snap-ring and dust seal plates should be renewed if their condition warrants it.

10   Commence reassembly by installing the stop-ring into the groove on the shaft, followed by the rear dust seal plate.

11   Drive the baffle plate onto the shaft taper then install the shaft into

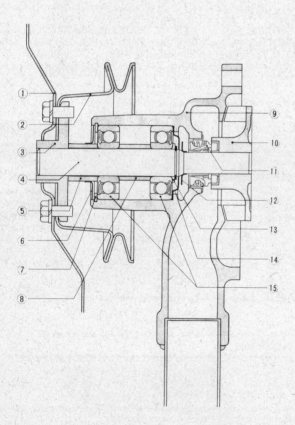

Fig. 2.7 Sectional view of the water pump (Sec. 12)

1	Fan	9	Body
2	Pulley	10	Impeller
3	Pulley boss	11	Seal assembly
4	Shaft	12	Baffle plate
5	Spacer	13	Washer
6	Dust seal plate (front)	14	Dust seal plate (rear)
7	Snap ring	15	Bearing
8	Spacer		

Fig. 2.8 Removing the pulley boss (Sec. 12)

Fig. 2.9 The water pump bearing and shaft assembly (Sec. 12)

the body.

12 Install the washer on the shaft and press in the bearing with the seal side rearwards (towards the impeller).

13 Position the spacer against the installed bearing and fill the cavity with a general purpose grease.

14 Install the remaining bearing with the seal side forwards (towards the fan) then install the snap-ring.

15 Position the spacer and dust seal plate on the bearing.

16 Press the pulley boss onto the shaft until it is flush with the shaft endface.

17 Install the seal assembly into the impeller side of the body.

18 Press the impeller onto the shaft until it is flush with the shaft endface.

Fig. 2.10 Installing the seal assembly (Sec. 12)

2

13 Fault diagnosis - cooling system

Symptom	Reason/s	Remedy
Loss of coolant	Leak in system	Examine all hoses, hose connections, drain taps and the radiator and heater for signs of leakage when the engine is cold, then when hot and under pressure. Tighten clips, renew hoses and repair radiator as necessary.
	Defective radiator pressure cap	Examine cap for defective seal and renew if necessary.
	Overheating causing too rapid evaporation due to excessive pressure in system	Check reasons for overheating.
	Blown cylinder head gasket causing excess pressure in cooling system forcing coolant out	Remove cylinder head for examination.
	Cracked block or head due to freezing	Strip engine and examine. Repair as required.
Overheating	Insufficient coolant in system	Top up.
	Water pump not turning properly due to slack fan belt	Tighten fan belt.
	Kinked or collapsed water hoses causing restriction to circulation of coolant	Renew hose as required.
	Faulty thermostat (not opening properly)	Check and replace as necessary.
	Engine out of tune	Check ignition setting and carburetor adjustments.
	Blocked radiator either internally or externally	Flush out cooling system and clean out cooling fins.
	Cylinder head gaskets blown forcing coolant out of system	Remove head and renew gasket.
	New engine not run-in	Adjust engine speed until run-in.
Engine running too cool	Missing or faulty thermostat	Check and replace as necessary.

Chapter 3 Carburation;
fuel, exhaust and emission control systems

Refer to Chapter 13 for Specifications and information applicable to 1974 through 1982 models.

Contents

Accelerator pump lever - adjustment 12	Exhaust manifold - removal and installation 18
Air cleaner - removal and installation 3	Exhaust system - removal and installation 16
Carburetor (B1600) - dismantling, servicing and reassembly ... 9	Fast idle adjustment 13
Carburetor (Courier) - dismantling, servicing and reassembly ... 10	Fault diagnosis - carburation; fuel, exhaust and emission control
Carburetor - removal and installation 8	systems 25
Carburetor throttle and choke controls 7	Float level (all carburetors) - adjustment 11
Emission control system (B1600) - general description 19	Fuel pump - dismantling, servicing and reassembly 5
Emission control system (B1600) - removal and installation of	Fuel pump - removal, installation and testing 4
component parts 21	Fuel system - routine maintenance 2
Emission control system (B1600) - tests and adjustments ... 20	Fuel tank - removal and installation 6
Emission control system (Courier) - general description ... 22	General description 1
Emission control system (Courier) - removal and installation of	Idle speed and mixture - adjustments 15
component parts 24	Intake manifold - removal and installation 17
Emission control system (Courier) - tests and adjustments ... 23	Secondary throttle valve - adjustment 14

Specifications

B1600

Air cleaner type ... ...   Dry paper element

Carburetor

Type	Two barrel, downdraft type
Throat diameter:	
Primary	1.10 in. (28 mm)
Secondary	1.26 in. (32 mm)
Venturi diameter:	
Primary	0.91 x 0.55 x 0.31 in. (23 x 14 x 8 mm)
Secondary	1.10 x 0.55 x 0.28 in. (28 x 14 x 7 mm)
Main nozzle:	
Primary	0.0827 in. (2.1 mm)
Secondary	0.0984 in. (2.5 mm)
Main jet:	
Primary	No. 106 (General); No. 110 (USA)
Secondary	No. 160
Main air bleed:	
Primary	No. 50
Secondary	No. 70
Slow jet:	
Primary	No. 46 (General); No. 48 (USA)
Secondary	No. 80
Slow air bleed:	
Primary:	
No. 1	0.0551 in. (1.4 mm)
No. 2	No. 160 (General and 1972 USA)
	No. 170 (1973 onwards USA)
Secondary	No. 130 (General and 1972 USA)
	No. 160 (1973 onwards USA)
Slow economiser, primary	0.0630 in. (1.6 mm)
Idle hole	0.0669 in. (1.7 mm)
Power jet	No. 70 (General and 1972 USA); No. 55 (1973 onwards USA)
Pump piston diameter	0.5512 in. (14.0 mm)
Pump nozzle diameter	0.0197 in. (0.5 mm)
Vacuum jet:	
Primary	0.0472 in. (1.2 mm)
Secondary	0.0472 in. (1.2 mm)
Idle speed	600 ± 50 rpm (General); 800 to 850 rpm (USA)
CO concentration at idle	1.5 to 2.5%
Fast idle (primary throttle opening angle)	19.5 ± 1.5°

Secondary throttle starts to open	... ...	When primary valve is 50° open

Fuel pump

Type		12 volt, electro-mechanical
Fuel pressure		2.8 to 3.6 lbf/in^2 (0.2 to 0.25 kgf/cm^2)
Fuel feed capacity		1.76 Imp. pints/min. (1000 cm^3/min — 2 US pints/min.)

Fuel filter type ... ...   Paper element

Fuel octane requirement ... ...   Regular or low lead, 91 octane

Fuel tank capacity ... ...   9.9 Imp. gallons (11.7 US gallons/45 liters)

Courier

Air cleaner type ... ...   Dry paper element

Carburetor ... ...   No details of jet and venturi sizes available

Idle speed ... ...   800 to 850 rpm

CO concentration at idle ... ...   Less than 2%

Fuel pump

		12 volt, electro-mechanical
Fuel pressure		2.8 to 3.6 lbf/in^2 (0.2 to 0.25 kgf/cm^2)
Fuel feed capacity		2 US pints/min. (1000 cm^3/min — 1.76 Imp. pints/min.)

Fuel filter type ... ...   Paper element

Fuel octane requirement ... ...   Regular or low lead, 91 octane

Fuel tank capacity ... ...   9.9 Imp. gallons (11.7 US gallons/45 liters)

Torque wrench settings

	lbf ft	kg fm
Intake manifold stud nuts	14 to 19	1.9 to 2.6
Exhaust manifold stud nuts	12 to 17	1.6 to 2.3
Air injection nozzles	20	2.8
Air manifold nuts	15	2.1
Check valve	20	2.8
Air pump mounting bolts	22	3
Miscellaneous:		
6 mm bolt	6	0.83
8 mm bolt	15	2.1
10 mm bolt	30	4.1
12 mm bolt	50	6.9
14 mm bolt	65	9

1 General description

The fuel system for all models comprises a rear mounted fuel tank, an in-line filter, an electro-mechanical fuel pump, a carburetor and an air cleaner. The air cleaner is installed directly on the carburettor whereas the remaining items are connected via metal and flexible pipes.

The fuel tank is mounted between the chassis frame side rails and has a sender unit for the fuel gauges mounted on top. Fuel is drawn from the tank, through an in-line filter, by an electro-mechanical fuel pump which delivers the fuel to the carburetor float chamber. According to the particular vehicle and its intended market, there may be a condenser tank mounted on top of the fuel tank, an in-line check valve and carbon canister between the pump and the carburetor, and an excess fuel return line from the carburetor to the fuel tank. These items are referred to later in this Chapter as part of the Emission Control System.

For all versions, the carburetor is a two-stage, two-venturi, down-draft type, although there are differences according to the intended market. These differences are primarily associated with the emission control requirements in order to obtain satisfactory combustion allied to clean exhaust gases. The primary carburetor stage incorporates a curb idle system, accelerator pump system, idle transfer system, main metering system and power enrichment system. The secondary stage incorporates an idle transfer system, main metering system and power enrichment system. Choking action is by means of a cable operated manual control; the throttle is controlled by a foot pedal and either a rod or cable linkage. The carburetor incorporates a slow fuel cut

(throttle solenoid) valve. This is used to prevent dieseling (running-on) after the ignition has been switched off, and operates by shutting off the fuel supply in the slow fuel passage.

The air cleaner varies according to the model, but all types incorporate a Summer/Winter control position which permits cool air to be drawn from the engine compartment or warm air from a heat stove attached to the exhaust manifold.

Due to the complexities of the emission control system, and the variations for different markets, models and years of manufacture, these are dealt with separately later in this Chapter.

The exhaust system comprises two main parts, these being the inlet pipe (which incorporates a resonator on some models) and the muffler (silencer) and outlet pipe assembly.

2 Fuel system - routine maintenance

Note: The items listed in this Section are those applicable to a basic fuel system. For all items of routine maintenance associated with emission control, refer to Section 20 or 23. The maintenance intervals for the item in this Section are given in the Routine Maintenance summary at the beginning of the manual.

Air cleaner element - cleaning

1 Unscrew the wing nut from the air cleaner cover, (where appliable also remove the air intake duct clamp at the carburetor opening). Remove the cover and lift out the element. Taking care that no dirt enters the carburetor, dust out the air cleaner case with a lint-free

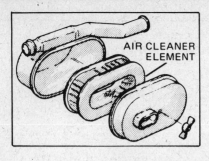

Fig. 3.1 Typical air cleaner elements (Sec. 2)

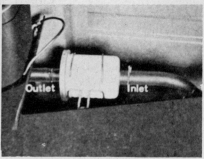

Fig. 3.2 The fuel filter (Sec. 2)

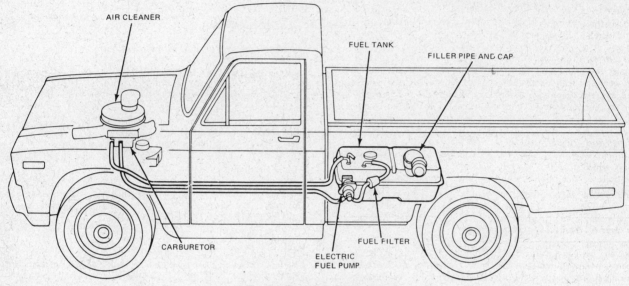

Fig. 3.3 Typical fuel lines (Sec. 2)
(The fuel return line is not installed on all models)

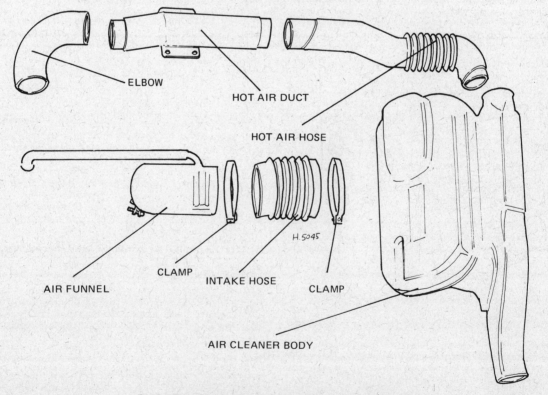

Fig. 3.4 The component parts of the oblong air filter (Sec. 3)

cloth or a dry paintbrush. Tap the element sharply on a hard, clean, surface or use a low pressure air line to remove any traces of dust etc. Do not rub the element as it may absorb some dust which will eventually enter the carburetor. When installing the element ensure that it is seated correctly, where applicable install a new cover gasket, then install the cover and secure it with the wing nut. (Where applicable, also install the air duct clamp).

Idle speed, idle mixture and CO emissions

2   Idle speed and idle mixture adjustments, together with the routine maintenance operations given in Chapter 4, are of a fairly critical nature to maintain the correct exhaust emission standards. For this reason, a separate Section is devoted to them in this Chapter and reference should be made to this when adjustment is required.

Fuel filter

3   Loosen the clips at each end of the fuel filter, remove the existing item and install a replacement.

Carburetor controls and linkages

4   Inspect the choke and throttle pedal linkages for lost motion and general wear and tear, particularly for fraying cables. Where necessary, take up any slackness then apply two or three drops of engine oil or general purpose lubricating oil to all the running surfaces and pivot points.

Fuel lines and connections

5   Examine all the fuel lines and connections for signs of leakage or looseness which may lead to early failure. Tighten connections and/or replace parts as necessary, but only use genuine replacements for your particular vehicle.

3   Air cleaner - removal and installation

1   The air cleaner is either a round flat type, seated above the carburetor, or an oblong type mounted at the side of the carburetor with an air funnel and hose leading to the carburetor. Removal of the filter element is described in Section 2.

2   Regardless of the type of air cleaner it will be necessary to remove the associated hot air intake hose leading from the heat stove where it joins the air cleaner. The air cleaner can then be detached from its mounting stays and lifted off the carburetor, at the same time re-moving any emission control hoses which are applicable.

3   Installation is a reverse of removal procedure.

4   Fuel pump - removal, installation and testing

1   Remove the fuel pump shield from the vehicle frame (photo).
2   Disconnect the fuel line(s) from the pump.
3   Remove the bolts attaching the fuel pump to the mounting bracket then lift away the pump.
4   Installation is a direct reversal of the removal procedure.
5   To test the pump operation (which can only be done satisfactorily with the item installed), first run the engine up to normal operating temperature.
6   Remove the air cleaner as described previously then carefully dis-connect the fuel inlet line or fuel filter at the carburetor, taking care that there is no fuel spillage.

4.1 The fuel pump shield. The fuel filter is to the right

3

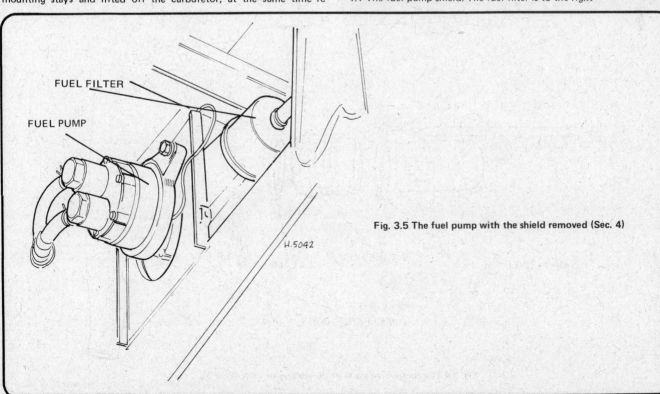

FUEL FILTER

FUEL PUMP

H.5042

Fig. 3.5 The fuel pump with the shield removed (Sec. 4)

7   Connect a pressure gauge, a suitable hose clamp which can act as a restrictor and a flexible hose between the fuel inlet and the carburetor as shown in Fig. 3.6.

8   Position the flexible hose and restrictor so that the fuel can be discharged into a suitable graduated container.

9   Operate the engine at idle speed and vent the system into the container by opening the hose restrictor clip.

10 Close the restrictor, allow the pressure to stabilise and note the reading. Compare it with that given in the Specifications. If the pressure is other than that specified, and the fuel lines and filter are in good condition, the pump should be dismantled for servicing or an exchange unit installed.

11 If the fuel pump meets the pressure requirement, again operate the engine at idle speed.

12 Open the hose restrictor and allow the fuel to flow into the container for a period of 30 seconds. Close the restrictor and check the fuel flow rate. If the flow rate is low, repeat the test using an auxiliary fuel supply and a new filter. If the flow rate is not satisfactory, check for a restriction in the fuel supply line from the tank, and the tank for not venting properly.

5   Fuel pump - dismantling, servicing and reassembly

1   Remove the fuel pump as previously described.

2   Index mark the air chamber (cover), valve chamber and body so that

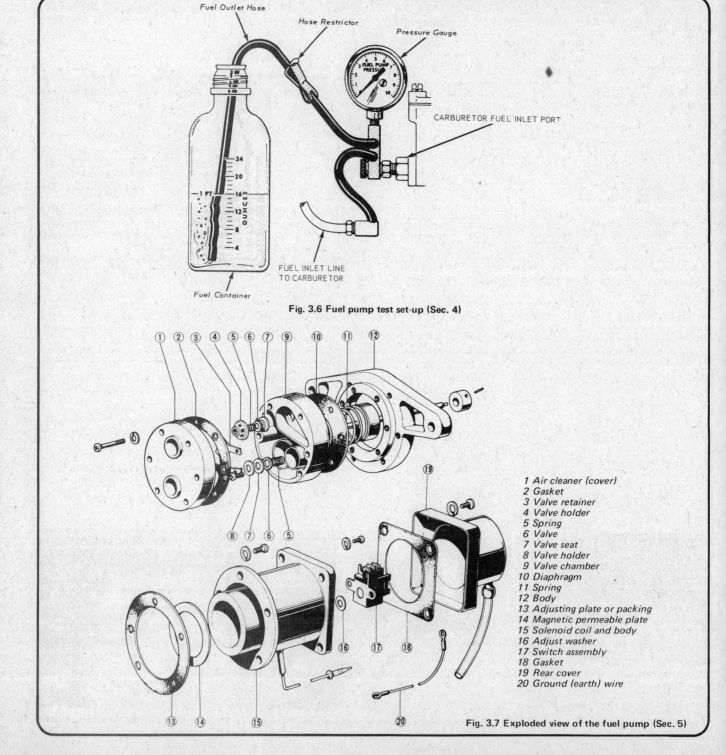

Fig. 3.6 Fuel pump test set-up (Sec. 4)

1 Air cleaner (cover)
2 Gasket
3 Valve retainer
4 Valve holder
5 Spring
6 Valve
7 Valve seat
8 Valve holder
9 Valve chamber
10 Diaphragm
11 Spring
12 Body
13 Adjusting plate or packing
14 Magnetic permeable plate
15 Solenoid coil and body
16 Adjust washer
17 Switch assembly
18 Gasket
19 Rear cover
20 Ground (earth) wire

Fig. 3.7 Exploded view of the fuel pump (Sec. 5)

they can eventually be reassembled in the same positions.

3   Remove the air chamber and valve chamber attaching screws. Remove the air chamber, the gasket and the valve chamber.

4   Remove the valve retainer attaching screws. Remove the retainers and valves from the valve chamber.

5   Remove the screws retaining the rear cover then remove the cover.

6   Disconnect the electrical lead from the switch.

7   Remove the screws which secure the switch assembly to the solenoid, remove the switch assembly.

8   Remove the solenoid from the body by removing the attaching screws.

9   Clean all the mechanical parts in a suitable cleaning solvent or gasoline (petrol). Inspect the air chamber, valve chamber and body for cracks and other damage. Inspect the inlet and outlet valves and obtain replacements if they do not function properly. Examine the diaphragm for damage and deterioration. Inspect the switch assembly contact points for wear, pitting and burning. Light dressing with a suitable contact file or an oil stone is permitted, but if there is severe deterioration new points must be obtained. Before assembling the pump it is recommended that new gaskets are obtained since these are relatively cheap.

10 Assembly of the pump is the reverse of the dismantling procedure. However, the following points need particular attention.

a   Diaphragm shaft stroke

After installation of the body and diaphragm to the solenoid, depress the diaphragm with a finger and check the diaphragm shaft stroke at the end of the shaft. This should be 0.11 to 0.12 in (2.8 to 3.0 mm) and can be adjusted by altering the thickness of the adjusting plate (packing); these are available in thicknesses of 0.004, 0.010 and 0.020 in (0.1, 0.25 and 0.50 mm).

b   Switch make-and-break

After installing the switch assembly to the body, place the stylus of a dial test indicator on the end of the diaphragm shaft and check when the contact points open and close by depressing and releasing the diaphragm. The specified switch position is 0.02 to 0.04 in (0.5 to 1.0 mm) from each end of the stroke. If the points open too early and close too late, decrease the thickness of the adjusting washer. If the points close too early and open too late, increase the thickness of the adjusting washer. Washers are obtainable in thicknesses of 0.010 and 0.024 in (0.25 and 0.6 mm). If the points open too early, bend the upper stopper upwards; if the points open too late bend the upper stopper downwards. If the points close too late, bend the lower stopper upwards; if the points close too early, bend the lower stopper downwards. It may mean that both stoppers will have to be adjusted, but the point gap must finally be 0.039 in (1.0 mm).

6   Fuel tank - removal and installation

1   Chock the front wheels of the vehicle, raise the rear end and remove the tank drain plug. Drain the contents into a suitable container, then firmly install the drain plug.

2   Disconnect the fuel line to the tank. As appropriate, disconnect the line from the condenser tank and the fuel return line.

3   Disconnect the fuel tank sender unit in-line connector.

4   Remove the fuel tank attaching bolts at the mounting bracket and lower the tank to the ground.

5   When installing, raise the tank into position and install the retaining bolts.

6   Connect the fuel sender unit leads and the fuel pipes.

7   Lower the vehicle to the ground and refill the tank.

7   Carburetor throttle and choke controls

1   The throttle and choke controls vary according to the vehicle and the intended market.

2   Figs. 3.10 and 3.11 show typical throttle linkages for left-hand drive vehicles, whereas a typical pedal control for right-hand drive vehicles is shown in the photograph. With the latter type an inner and outer cable is used to operate the throttle butterfly (photos).

3   Regardless of the system, it is important that backlash is eliminated either by adjustment of the long rod or at the outer cable end fitting (photo).

3

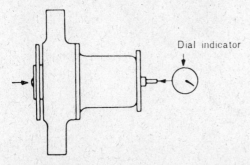

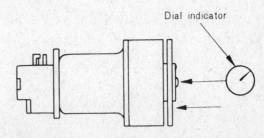

Fig. 3.9 Checking the pump switch make-and-break (Sec. 5)

Fig. 3.8 Checking the pump diaphragm stroke (Sec. 5)

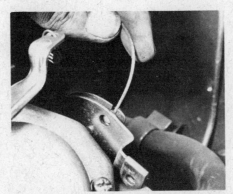

7.2a A typical cable operated throttle pedal

7.2b Removing a typical cable operated throttle control cable

7.3 The adjusting point for the cable operated throttle linkage

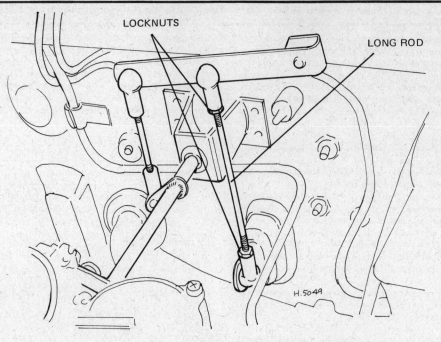

LOCKNUTS

LONG ROD

H.5049

Fig. 3.10 Throttle linkage adjustment - rod operated type (Sec. 7)

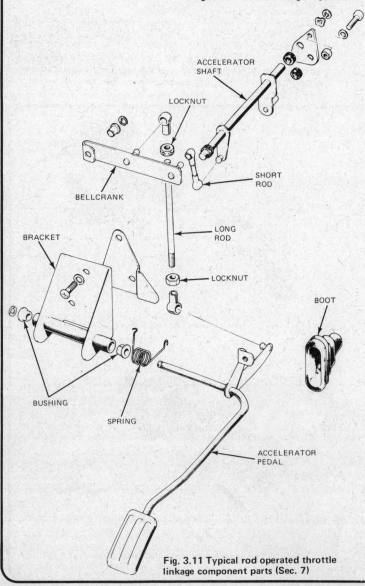

ACCELERATOR
SHAFT

LOCKNUT

BELLCRANK

SHORT
ROD

LONG
ROD

BRACKET

LOCKNUT

BOOT

BUSHING

SPRING

ACCELERATOR
PEDAL

Fig. 3.11 Typical rod operated throttle
linkage component parts (Sec. 7)

7.4 The choke cable adjusting point on the
carburetor bracket

CHOKE CABLE ATTACHING SCREWS

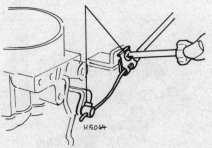

H.5064

Fig. 3.12 Choke cable attaching screws
(Sec. 7)

4 The choke control is dash-mounted and feeds thru the engine compartment firewall by means of an inner and outer cable. This is adjustable for backlash at the choke cable bracket on the carburetor (photo).

5 For the purpose of cable renewal, the locknut on the dash panel can be loosened slightly, then by reaching beneath the panel to the large hexagon nut on the choke control body can be unscrewed. This allows the control to be separated.

8 Carburetor - removal and installation

1 Remove the air cleaner, as described in Section 3.

2 As applicable, remove the bolts attaching the accelerator shaft to the throttle lever or open the throttle butterfly manually and disengage the cable from the cut-out in the cam.

3 Disconnect the fuel line to the carburetor (and return line, if applicable) (photo).

4 Disconnect the vacuum line from the carburetor, where applicable, remove the leads from the coasting richer (deceleration control) valve and the slow fuel cut valve (throttle solenoid).

5 Disconnect the throttle return spring and the choke control cable.

6 Using a suitable cranked spanner remove the carbuetor attaching nuts from the manifold studs. Lift off the carburetor.

7 When installing, position a new gasket on the intake manifold studs, position the carburetor and install the attaching nuts. The remainder of the installation procedure is the reverse of removal. Ensure that any backlash is taken up in the throttle and choke linkage.

8 On completion, start the engine and check for fuel leaks.

9 Carburetor (B1600) - dismantling, servicing and reassembly

1 Disconnect and remove the throttle return spring.

2 Remove the split cotter pin and washer from the end of the pump lever and separate the rod from the lever.

3 Remove the pump lever retaining clip and remove the lever from the air horn and pump piston rod.

4 Disconnect the choke rod from the lever by removing the retaining clip.

5 Remove the air horn attaching screws. Remove the brackets and lift off the air horn.

8.3 The carburetor fuel feed pipe

Fig. 3.13 Removing the split cotter pin and lever retaining clip arrowed (Secs. 9 and 10)

Fig. 3.14 The pump connecting rod removed (Secs. 9 and 10)

Fig. 3.15 Lifting off the air horn (Secs. 9 and 10)

Fig. 3.16 The air horn and associated parts (Secs. 9 and 10)

3

6 Remove the accelerator pump piston assembly from the main body.

7 Remove the slow fuel cut solenoid valve attaching screws; lift away the solenoid valve.

8 Invert the main body. Remove the bolts attaching the main body to the throttle body (one of these is on the underside of the main body). Separate the main body from the throttle body.

9 Remove the sight glass retainer attaching screws. Remove the retainer, sight glass and gasket.

10 Remove the spacer and float from the float pin then remove the needle valve assembly.

11 Remove the fuel inlet fitting, noting the number of copper seat gaskets used.

12 Remove the main air bleeds, the slow air bleeds and the slow jets.

13 Using a suitable screwdriver, remove the power valve.

14 Remove the idle adjusting screw and spring from the main body.

15 Remove the plugs, and the primary and secondary main jets from the main body.

16 Remove the clip from the throttle lever connecting link then disconnect the link from the primary throttle shaft arm.

17 Remove the diaphragm unit cover attaching screws then remove the cover and return spring.

18 Remove the throttle return lever and dust cover from the diaphragm unit body.

19 Remove the clip then disconnect the diaphragm rod and remove the diaphragm and rod assembly.

20 If considered necessary, remove the throttle valve attaching screws and dismantle the throttle valve and shaft.

21 If considered necessary, remove the venturi attaching screws then

Fig. 3.17 Removing the main body (Secs. 9 and 10)

Fig. 3.18 The float and needle valve components parts (Secs. 9 and 10)

1	Float (typical)	5	Needle valve
2	Spacer	6	Copper seat gaskets
3	Valve stem	7	Fuel inlet fitting
4	Spring	8	Filter (strainer)

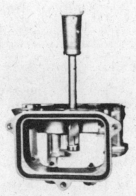

Fig. 3.19 Removing the power valve (Secs. 9 and 10)

Fig. 3.20 Removing the main jets (Secs. 9 and 10)

| 1 | Plug and secondary jet | 3 | Plug |
| 2 | Primary jet | | |

Fig. 3.21 The diaphragm and rod assembly (Secs. 9 and 10)

| 1 | Screws | 3 | Return spring |
| 2 | Diaphragm cover | 4 | Diaphragm and rod assembly |

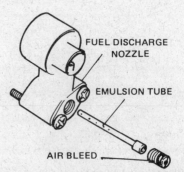

FUEL DISCHARGE NOZZLE

EMULSION TUBE

AIR BLEED

Fig. 3.22 A venturi assembly (fuel discharge nozzle assembly) (Secs. 9 and 10)

remove the venturi by carefully tapping it from the bottom.

22 Remove the air bleeds, jets and check valve (see Fig. 3.23), taking great care that these parts are not damaged or lost.

23 Wash all the parts in clean gasoline (petrol) and dry by shaking and wiping with a lint free cloth or paper tissue. Alternatively, use clean, dry compressed air.

24 Blow through all the jets and passages to ensure that they are un-obstructed. Never probe the jets and passages, or irrepairable damage may result.

25 Inspect the air horn, body and body flange for cracks, nicks and burrs on their respective sealing faces.

26 Inspect the float for leaking, deformation, a damaged tab and worn retaining pin bore.

27 Check the float needle valve for wear and correct seating. Invert the main body, assemble the needle valve and the float, and then suck at the main fuel passage. The seating is unsatisfactory if any leakage is present.

28 Inspect the filter for corrosion and damage.

29 Check the choke valve for excessive play. Ensure that it operates smoothly and closes fully.

30 Check for wear on the sliding portion of the pump piston and for smooth operation. Check the spring for corrosion, wear and damage.

31 Check the idle adjuster screw for damage to its screw thread and seating surface.

32 Check for satisfactory operation of the primary and secondary

Fig. 3.23 The jets and air bleeds (Secs. 9 and 10)

1 Secondary slow air bleed	5 Check valve
2 Secondary slow jet	6 Primary slow air bleed
3 Secondary main air bleed	7 Primary slow jet
4 Primary main air bleed	

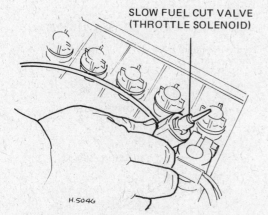

SLOW FUEL CUT VALVE
(THROTTLE SOLENOID)

H.5046

Fig. 3.24 Checking the throttle solenoid (Secs. 9 and 10)

throttle valves, and for wear of the shafts.

33 Check the vacuum control unit diaphragm and spring for damage.

34 Energize the throttle solenoid from a 12v dc source and check that the valve stem is drawn in. De-energize the solenoid and check that the valve stem is extended.

35 Assembly of the carburetor is essentially the reverse of the removal procedure. Always use new gaskets and ensure that the primary and secondary system parts are not mixed up. Ensure that the primary and secondary throttle valves close correctly when in the closed position. When assembling the float, adjust the float level as described in Section 11, followed by the idle and running adjustments given in Sections 12, 13, 14 and 15.

---

10 Carburetor (Courier) - dismantling, servicing and reassembly

1 Remove the cotter key, spring and washer which attach the accelerator pump connecting rod to the pump lever. Disconnect the rod.

2 Remove the pump lever by taking out the retaining screw.

3 Unhook the throttle return spring and remove the choke cable support bracket from the main body.

4 Disconnect the fast idle rod from the fast idle lever by removing the cotter key, spring and washer.

5 Where applicable, remove the coasting richer (deceleration) valve by taking out the three screws. Note the spring and plunger.

6 Disconnect the secondary throttle rod from its shaft by removing the cotter key.

7 Remove the screws and washers attaching the secondary throttle actuator for the body.

8 Carefully pry open the clips retaining the slow fuel cut valve (throttle solenoid) lead. Unscrew the slow fuel cut valve from the main body and remove it.

9 Remove the left rear air horn to body attaching screw. Remove the screw retaining the fuel inlet assembly bolt lock; remove the lock and spacer.

10 Remove the two remaining air horn to body attaching screws then lift off the air horn.

11 Remove the fuel inlet fitting; it is retained by one bolt.

12 Remove the fuel strainer (fitted) then remove the fuel inlet bolt and needle valve assembly.

13 Remove the sight glass cover, gasket, sight glass and second gasket after taking out the three screws.

14 Remove the float level pin collar, then remove the float.

15 Remove the accelerator pump piston cover screws. Remove the cover, piston and gasket.

16 Remove the piston then invert the carburetor and remove the check ball.

17 Remove the screw and washer which retain the pump discharge weight and ball, then invert the carburetor to tip the weight and ball out.

18 Remove the idle jets, main jets and air bleed from the main body.

19 Using a suitable screwdriver, remove the power valve from the main body.

20 Screw the curb idle and idle mixture adjusting screws in, counting the number of turns to make each one *just* bottom on its seat. Remove both screws and their springs.

21 Remove the primary and secondary discharge nozzle retaining screws and washers; remove the nozzles and gaskets.

22 Remove the air bleed screws and emulsion tubes from the discharge nozzles.

23 Remove the lower body from the main body after removing the retaining screws and washer.

24 Remove the retaining nut and washer from the end of the primary throttle shaft, and the throttle operating lever washer. Where applicable remove the servo diaphragm operating lever.

25 Remove the accelerator pump actuating lever, choke actuating lever, throttle return lever and idle adjusting lever.

26 Index mark the primary throttle plate to its bore and to the relative position on the throttle shaft. Remove the throttle plate retaining screws and the plate, then slide the primary throttle shaft out of the lower body. Repeat for the secondary throttle plate.

27 Wash all the parts in clean gasoline (petrol) and dry by shaking and wiping with a lint-free cloth or paper tissue. Alternatively, use clean, dry compressed air.

3

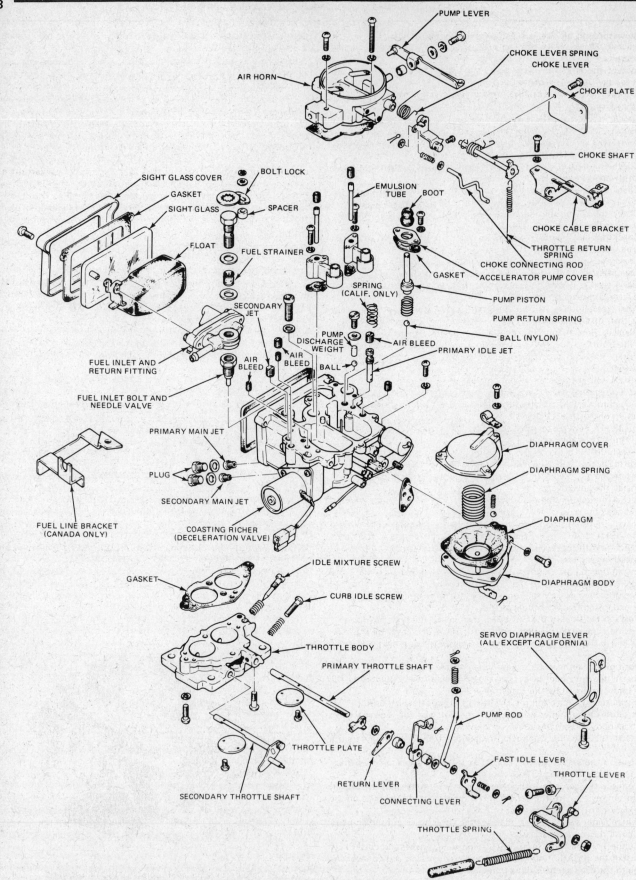

Fig. 3.25 Exploded view of the carburetor used on 1972 Courier models (Sec. 10)

Other carburetors vary in minor detail only. Note that the Coasting Richer valve is used on Couriers with manual transmission.

28 Blow through all the jets and passages to ensure that they are unobstructed. Never probe the jets and passages or irrepairable damage may result.

29 Inspect the air horn, body and body flange for cracks, nicks and burrs on their respective sealing faces.

30 Inspect the float for leaking, deformation, a damaged tab and worn retaining pin bore.

31 Check the float needle valve for wear and correct seating. Invert the main body, assemble the needle valve and the float and then suck at the main fuel passage. The seating is unsatisfactory if any leakage is present.

32 Inspect the fuel strainer for corrosion and damage.

33 Check the choke valve for excessive play. Ensure that it operates smoothly and closes fully.

34 Check for wear on the sliding portion of the pump piston and for smooth operation. Check the spring for corrosion, wear and damage.

35 Check the idle mixture screws and curb idle screw for damage to the screw threads and sealing surfaces.

36 Check for satisfactory operation of the primary and secondary throttle valves and for wear of the shafts.

37 Check the vacuum control unit diaphragm and spring for damage.

38 Energize the slow fuel cut valve from a 12v dc source and check that the valve stem is drawn in. De-energize the solenoid and check that the valve stem is extended.

39 When reassembling, slide the primary throttle shaft into the lower body then install the throttle plate, making sure that the index marks are aligned. Repeat for the secondary throttle shaft and plate. Ensure that the throttle plate operation is smooth and that there is no binding.

40 Install the idle adjusting lever, throttle return lever and choke actuating lever on the primary throttle shaft.

41 Install the accelerator pump actuating lever. Install the washer, throttle operating lever and the retaining washer and nut on the primary throttle shaft; tighten the remaining nut and check for smooth operation of the throttle plate.

42 Position a new gasket and the main body on the lower body and install the screws and washers.

43 Install the curb idle screw and spring, and the idle mixture screw and spring at this original positions as determined in paragraph 20.

44 Install the air bleeds, main jets and idle jets in the main body.

45 Install the power valve.

46 Install the pump discharge check ball and weight or spring, followed by the retaining screw.

47 Install the inlet check ball in the accelerator pump bore, followed by the piston and spring. Ensure that the spring ear seats in the slot at the bottom of the bore. Position the piston, cover and gasket and install the attaching screws.

48 Install the air emulsion tubes in the primary and secondary discharge nozzles, followed by the air bleed screws.

49 Position the primary and secondary discharge nozzles in the main body and install their attaching screws.

50 Position the float in the fuel bowl, then install the float pin collar.

51 Position the rubber gasket, sight glass, gasket and cover on the main body and install the retaining screws. Tighten them evenly and alternately.

52 Position the air horn and a new gasket on the main body.

53 Install the fuel inlet bolt, washer and needle valve assembly in the main body, followed by the fuel strainer.

54 Install the fuel inlet and return fitting and the attaching bolt.

55 Posiiton the fuel inlet bolt lock on the bolt and the lock spacer on the main body. Install the attaching screw.

56 Install the slow fuel cut valve, tightening carefully to compress the gasket.

57 Position the secondary throttle actuator assembly on the main body then install the retaining screws.

58 Connect the secondary throttle rod to its throttle shaft and install the cotter key. Secure the slow fuel cut valve lead into the clips on the secondary throttle actuator.

59 Where applicable, position the coasting richer valve in to main body and install the retaining screws.

60 Connect the fast idle lever, install the spring, washer and cotter key.

61 Install the throttle return spring on the return lever and connect the spring to the choke cable support bracket.

62 Position the choke cable bracket over the choke lever spring tang, and onto the carburetor. Install the washer and attaching screw.

63 Position the accelerator pump lever to the main body and install the attaching screw, spacer and washer.

64 Slide the accelerator pump lever pin into the pump piston rod.

Connect the pump rod and spring to the pump lever and install the cotter key and washer.

11 Float level (all carburetors) - adjustment

1 Under normal running conditions, the fuel level can be checked by reference to the line on the sight glass.

2 If the level is found to be incorrect, dismantle the carburetor as far as necessary, then allow the float to drop under its own weight. Check the clearances between the end of the float and the edge of the bowl, and bend the float tab 'A', if necessary to obtain a dimension of 0.004 to 0.047 in (0.1 to 1.2 mm). Now invert the main body so that the float is uppermost and check the clearance between the end of the float and the edge of the bowl. Bend the float tab 'B' if necessary to obtain a dimension of 0.256 $\pm$ 0.020 in (6.5 $\pm$ 0.5 mm) for USA models or 0.236 $\pm$ 0.020 in (6 $\pm$ 0.5 mm) for other models (Fig. 3.26).

12 Accelerator pump lever - adjustment

1 On some carburetors, at the end of the accelerator pump lever there are two holes for the connecting rod which provide different settings for the amount of fuel injected. (Where there are two holes in the connecting rod, the lower one should be used).

2 With the fuel level at the correct setting, operation of the throttle linkage over its full range of travel will provide an injection of 0.6 cc at the 'A' hole or 0.8 cc at the 'B' hole (see Fig. 3.27). The injection rate

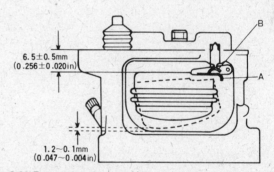

Fig. 3.26 Float level adjustment (Sec. 11) Note: The dimension of 0.256 in. (6.5 mm) is applicable to USA models.

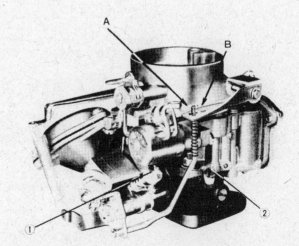

Fig. 3.27 Carburetor adjustment points (B1600 illustrated)
(Secs. 12 and 15)

1 Throttle adjusting screw   2 Idle adjusting screw (mixture)
   (idle speed)
A 0.6 cc injecting setting   B 0.8 cc injection setting

Fig. 3.28 The correct accelerator pump setting where there are holes in the connecting rod (Sec. 12)

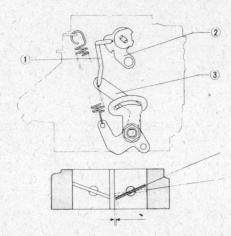

Fig. 3.29 Adjusting the choke connecting rod (Sec. 13)

1 Connecting rod   *3 Connecting lever*
2 Choke lever

Refer to the text for the angle and dimension of butterfly opening

should be adjusted to obtain the most satisfactory performance related to ambient temperature, engine condition and throttle response.

13 Fast idle - adjustment

1 To obtain an increased idle speed when the engine is cold, a fast idle adjustment is provided. When correctly set, this will provide an increase in idle speed of approximately 400 rpm above the normal idle speed.
2 If the carburetor is installed, this can be obtained by using a suitable protractor and pointer on the end of the primary throttle shaft and checking that when the choke is pulled out fully (ie; choke valve closed) the throttle shaft has turned thru the specified angle. Adjustment is made either at the fast idle adjustment screw or by bending the fast idle lever where it contacts the throttle lever tang. If a protractor cannot be used, for most practical purposes it is satisfactory to adjust for a suitable increase of idling speed. However, it must be appreciated that this is a 'hit-or-miss' adjustment, which may contravene local emission control regulations.
3 If the carburetor is removed from the vehicle, eg; after overhaul, the same adjustment procedure as described in the previous paragraph is used but to obtain the correct amount of primary throttle opening, an unmarked No 65 drill shank (0.063 in/1.6 mm) is passed between the throttle wall and the edge of the throttle plate.

14 Secondary throttle valve - adjustment

1 To obtain the specified primary throttle opening at which the secondary throttle just commences to open, adjustment can be made by bending the throttle lever link where it contacts the throttle arm shaft.

15 Idle speed and mixture - adjustments

1 It must be appreciated that in order to obtain satisfactory idle speed, idle mixture and exhaust emissions, careful adjustment of the carburetor is required. In all cases, it is important that before any adjustment is commenced, the distributor contact breaker point gap or dwell angle must be correct, and the timing must have been set for the particular vehicle. These items are dealt with in Chapter 4. Additionally, all items of the emission control system must be in a satisfactory state of tune; these items are dealt with later in this Chapter.
2 Before commencing any adjustment on a vehicle which is already running, ensure that no local regulations are being contravened. Where a carburetor has been dismantled, it is recommended that after setting as described in the following paragraphs, a qualified engineer checks these settings at the earliest possible date. Failure to do this may result in excessive pollutants in the exhaust gases.
3 If possible, obtain an engine speed tachometer and connect it in accordance with the manufacturer's instructions.
4 Set the transmission in neutral then run the engine to attain the normal running temperature. Ensure that the choke is fully open.
5 Set the engine idle speed to that specified, by means of the curb idle screw (throttle adjusting screw).
6 If an exhaust gas analyzer is available, connect it in accordance with the manufacturer's instructions.
7 Adjust the idle (mixture) screw to obtain the specified idle CO content. If no exhaust gas analyzer is available, adjust the idle (mixture) adjusting screw to obtain the fastest steady idle speed. Screwing the screw outwards will tend to give a 'lumpy' running and a sooty exhaust gas which indicates a rich mixture; screwing the screw inwards will cause the engine to increase in speed a little then slow down and will give a 'hollow' exhaust note, indicating a lean (weak) mixture. After obtaining the highest steady speed, re-adjust the throttle adjusting (curb idle) screw to obtain an idle speed of 20 rpm above that specified. Now turn the idle (mixture) adjustment screw in (lean) until the engine speed reduces to that specified.

16 Exhaust system - removal and installation

1 The components of the exhaust system vary slightly according to the particular model and intended market, but the system shown in Fig. 3.30 is typical of what might be installed. The main differences between the various types are the manifold flange, hangers, and the fact that some systems do not incorporate a resonator upstream of the silencer.

Inlet pipe assembly
2 Raise the vehicle on a hoist, or jack it up and use axle stands to provide adequate working room beneath.
3 Remove the three nuts and lockwashers which attach the inlet pipe to the exhaust manifold.
4 Remove the bolt which attaches the inlet pipe to the flywheel housing, and the bolt which attaches it to the bracket on the transmission (photo).
5 As appropriate, remove the two bolts and washers at the muffler (silencer) flange, or the 'U' bolt assembly.
6 Draw the inlet pipe forwards away from the muffler to remove it. Where applicable retrieve the gasket.
7 When installing, initially clean the mating faces of the pipes or flanges, and where applicable position a new flange gasket. Installation is then the reverse of the removal procedure, but do not finally tighten any of the bolts until the installation is complete or difficulties may be encountered. On completion, lower the vehicle to the ground. Muffler

Muffler (silencer) and outlet pipe assembly
8 Raise the vehicle on a hoist, or jack it up and use axle stands to

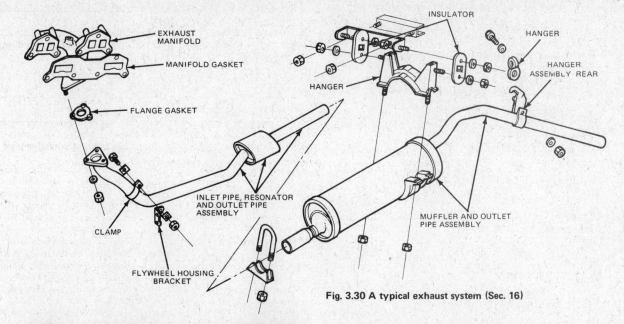

Fig. 3.30 A typical exhaust system (Sec. 16)

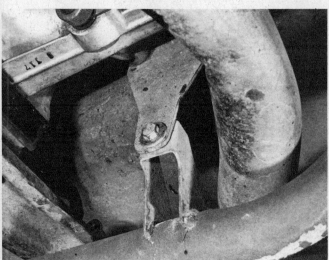

16.4 The exhaust attachment point to the transmission

9 As appropriate, remove the two bolts and washers at the muffler flange, or the 'U' bolt assembly.

10 Remove the insulator/hanger attaching nuts and washers, but take particular note of their relative positions.

11 When installing, initially clean the mating faces of the pipes or flanges and where applicable use a new gasket. Installation is then the reverse of the removal procedure, with new insulators being used where necessary.

17 Intake manifold - removal and installation

1 The procedure given in this Section, describes removal and installation of the manifold complete with carburetor. If considered necessary, the carburetor may first be removed by reference to Section 8 of this Chapter.

2 Drain the cooling system (refer to Chapter 2, if necessary).

3 Remove the air cleaner and accelerator linkage as described previously in this Chapter.

4 Disconnect the choke cable and fuel line to the carburetor.

5 Disconnect the water hoses from the manifold.

6 As appropriate, disconnect the thermactor hoses, crankcase

ventilation hose and distributor vacuum line. Take care to label the hoses if there is any fear of them being inadvertently mixed up when reconnecting.

7 Remove the intake manifold-to-cylinder head nuts and washers, then lift the manifold off the studs on the cylinder block. Remove and discard the gasket.

8 When installing, clean the mating gasket surfaces thoroughly then position a new gasket on the manifold studs. A little non-setting jointing compound is permissible but is not essential.

9 Position the manifold then install and torque tighten the washers and nuts. The remainder of installation is the reverse of the removal procedure, but when filling the cooling system refer to Chapter 2 for details.

18 Exhaust manifold - removal and installation

1 Disconnect the exhaust inlet pipe at the manifold, as described in Section 17.

2 Remove the manifold attaching nuts and washers then lift away the manifold. Remove and discard the gasket(s).

3 When installing, clean the mating gasket surfaces thoroughly then position new gasket(s) on the manifold studs.

3 When installing, clean the mating gasket surfaces thoroughly then position new gasket(s) on the manifold studs.

4 Lightly lubricate the mating flange of the manifold with graphite grease, then position the manifold and install the washers and nuts.

5 Tighten the nuts to the specified torque, then install the exhaust inlet pipe.

19 Emission control system (B1600) - general description

The emission control system is divided into three basic parts as described in the following paragraphs, these being the exhaust emission control system to reduce harmful composites in the exhaust gases; the positive crankcase ventilation system which channels the blow-by gases from the crankcase into the combustion chamber to be burned; and the evaporative emission control system which stores the fuel vapor from the fuel system and leads it to the combustion chamber.

Exhaust emission control system

1 The exhaust emission control system reduces the hydrocarbon, carbon monoxide and oxides of nitrogen content of the exhaust gases. This is effected by the use of a throttle opener system comprising a servo diaphragm and vacuum control valve.

2 During deceleration, an inadequate supply of air/fuel mixture is available for proper combustion which results in a high concentration

of hydrocarbon content in the exhaust. The throttle opener uses the high manifold vacuum which occurs during deceleration to slightly open the primary throttle and thus provide an increase in the fuel/air ratio.

3 The vacuum control valve detects the intake manifold vacuum acting on the servo diaphragm to provide the correct degree of throttle opening, and also controls the vacuum to prevent the throttle being left open too long. The valve comprises a diaphragm, diaphragm return

spring, valve and filter; an altitude corrector with an internal spring provides a change of datum setting for different altitudes.

4 When operating, the high intake manifold vacuum which occurs during deceleration is channelled to the diaphragm chamber. This vacuum overcomes the diaphragm return spring which opens the valve, allowing vacuum to pass to the servo diaphragm chamber. The servo diaphragm moves to partially open the throttle valve but as the vehicle speed decreases, the manifold vacuum decreases so that the primary throttle valve gradually returns towards the normal idling position. The valve of the vacuum control valve is now closed by its spring and as soon as vacuum ceases to act on the servo diaphragm chamber, atmospheric pressure is sensed on the servo diaphragm and returns the throttle fully to the idling position. A small passage through the valve leads air onto the servo diaphragm after the valve is closed.

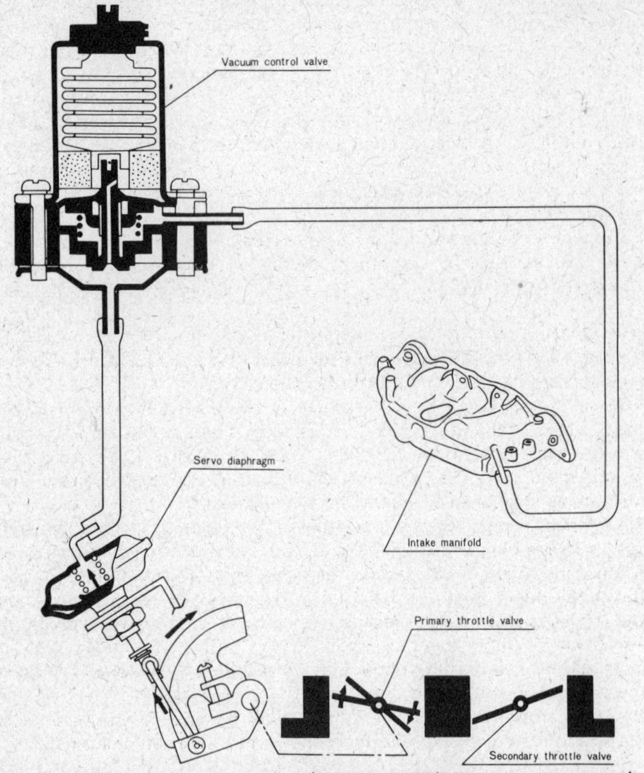

Fig. 3.31 Throttle opener system (B1600, 1972/73 version illustrated) (Sec. 19)

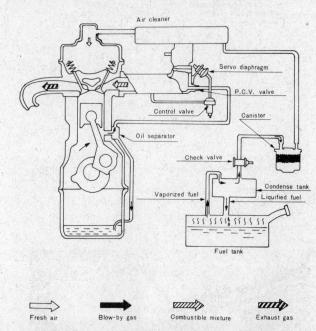

Fig. 3.32 Air pollution control system (B1600, 1972/73) (Sec.19)

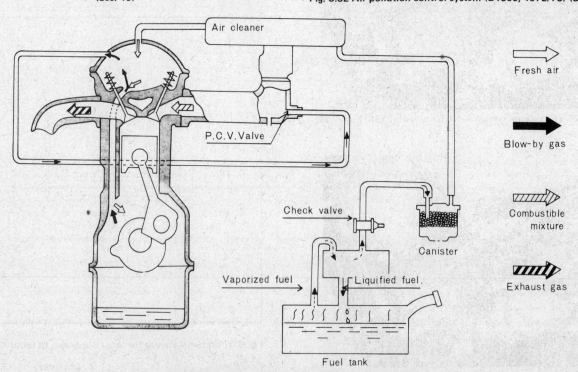

Fig. 3.33 Air pollution control system (B1600, 1974) (Sec. 19)

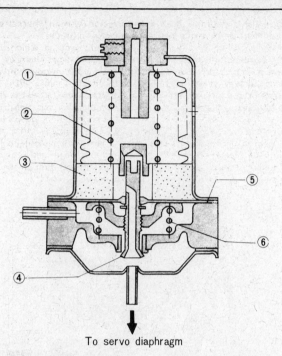

To servo diaphragm

Fig. 3.34 Sectional view of the vacuum control valve (B1600) (Sec. 19)

1 Altitude corrector	4 Valve
2 Spring (internal)	5 Diaphragm
3 Filter	6 Spring

Fig. 3.35 The vacuum control valve (arrowed) (B1600) (Sec. 19)

Fig. 3.36 The servo diaphragm (arrowed) (B1600) (Sec. 19)

5   The servo diaphragm is connected to the primary throttle lever of the carburetor, and responds to the intake manifold vacuum, as controlled by the vacuum control valve, to partly open the throttle.

Positive crankcase ventilation system

6   A positive crankcase ventilation (PCV) system channels the blow-by gases into the intake manifold to be burned during the normal combustion cycle. The system comprises a PCV valve, an oil separator (1972/73 models only), and the associated pipes and hoses.

7   The PCV valve is operated by the pressure difference between the intake manifold and the crankcase. Where there is no pressure difference (engine not rotating) or the manifold pressure is higher than the crankcase pressure (backfire) the valve closes under spring action. If there is a large pressure difference (engine idling or decelerating) the high manifold vacuum opens the valve fully against the spring and a restricted amount of ventilating air is passed to the manifold. When the pressure difference is small (normal operation) the valve is balanced in its approximate mid-position and an unrestricted ventilating airflow is passed.

8   Where an oil separator is used, it is installed on the valve rocker arm cover and is designed to prevent engine lubricant from entering the combustion chamber.

Evaporative emission control system

9   The evaporative emission control system is designed to prevent the emission of fuel vapors into the atmosphere.

10 Fuel vapors rising from the tank are channelled into a condenser tank where ambient temperature changes condense them into fuel which drains back to the fuel tank. When the engine is operating, fuel vapors which have not condensed are routed thru a carbon canister and into the air cleaner to be drawn into the engine.

11 A check valve, located between the condenser tank and canister, allows fuel vapors and ventilation to flow under normal circumstances. If this line becomes clogged or frozen, ventilation does not occur and the engine fuel supply will be cut off. Therefore the valve is opened by the negative fuel tank pressure, allowing a ventilation passage to atmosphere. When the fuel vapor in the tank is expanded due to increased heat, a pressure rise occurs. This opens the valve and releases the pressure to atmosphere.

12 The carbon canister is installed in the engine compartment. Its purpose is to absorb and store fuel vapors until they can be burned.

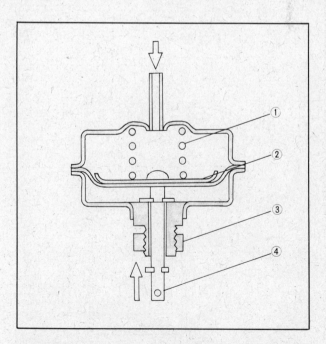

Fig. 3.37 Sectional view of the servo diaphragm (B1600) (Sec. 19)

1 Spring	3 Lock nut
2 Diaphragm	4 Rod

20 Emission control system (B1600) - tests and adjustments

Servo diaphragm

1   Run the engine and check that the idle speed is as specified after it has warmed up.

2   Stop the engine, then disconnect the vacuum sensing tube between the servo diaphragm and the vacuum control valve from the servo diaphragm.

3   Remove the suction hole plug from the intake manifold.

4   Connect the intake manifold and the servo diaphragm using a suitable rubber or plastic tube.

5   Remove the vacuum sensing tube between the carburetor and the

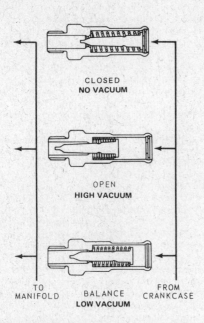

CLOSED
NO VACUUM

OPEN
HIGH VACUUM

TO   BALANCE   FROM
MANIFOLD   LOW VACUUM   CRANKCASE

Fig. 3.38 The operating modes of the positive crankcase ventilation (PCV) valve (B1600 and Courier) (Sec. 19)

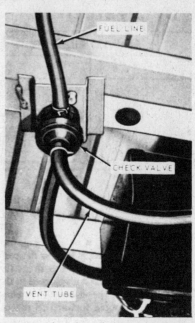

FUEL LINE

CHECK VALVE

VENT TUBE

Fig. 3.39 The check valve (B1600 and Courier) (Secs. 19 and 22)

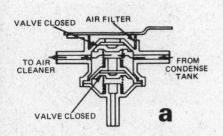

VALVE CLOSED   AIR FILTER

TO AIR   FROM
CLEANER   CONDENSE
                         TANK

VALVE CLOSED   **a**

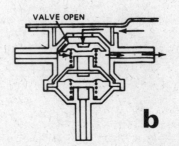

VALVE OPEN

b

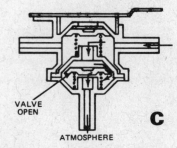

VALVE
OPEN

ATMOSPHERE

c

Fig. 3.40 Operation of the check valve (B1600 and Courier) (Secs. 19 and 22)

a   Normal operation   *b   Open ventilation passage*   *c   Releasing pressure*

Fig. 3.41 The carbon canister (arrowed) (B1600 illustrated) (Secs. 19 and 22)

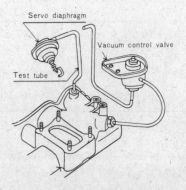

Servo diaphragm

Vacuum control valve

Test tube

Fig. 3.42 Checking the servo diaphragm (B1600) (Sec. 20)

distributor vacuum unit.

6 Run the engine and check that the idle speed is 1300 to 1500 rpm. If outside of this range, adjust using the throttle opener adjusting screw. If the engine idle speed does not rise above that given in the Specifications, or cannot be adjusted to 1300 to 1500 rpm, the servo diaphragm is defective.

7 On completion, connect the system for normal operation.

Vacuum control valve

8 Remove the intake manifold suction hole plug and install a suitable vacuum gauge using pipes and connectors with a minimum inside

Fig. 3.43 The intake manifold suction hole plug (arrowed) (B1600) (Sec. 20)

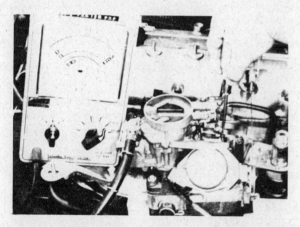

Fig. 3.44 Adjusting the throttle opener (B1600) (Sec. 20)

Fig. 3.46 Adjusting the vacuum control valve (B1600) (Sec. 20)

diameter of 1/8 in (0.125 in/3.0 mm) and a maximum overall length of 6.5 ft (2 metres).

9 Start the engine and run it at approximately 3000 rpm.

10 Suddenly release the accelerator pedal and read the vacuum gauge reading which should momentarily be above 22 in. Hg (560 mm Hg), then fall to 22.05 in. Hg (560 mm Hg) and remain at this value (the operating depression) for a few seconds, then fall gradually to finally indicate the idle speed vacuum. If necessary, adjust the vacuum control valve to obtain satisfactory operation. **Note:** The operating depression of 22.05 in. Hg (560 mm Hg) is set at a barometric pressure of 29.92 in. Hg (760 mm Hg). Where the barometric pressure is not at this value, a correction of 0.4 in. Hg (10 mm Hg) must be allowed for every 0.4 in. Hg (10 mm Hg) variation. For example, where a barometric pressure of 29.52 in. Hg (750 mm Hg) prevails, the operating depression will be 21.65 in Hg (550 mm Hg).

Positive crankcase ventilation (PCV) valve

11 Remove the hose from the PCV valve, then start the engine and run it at 700 to 1000 rpm.

12 Check that suction can be felt at the PCV valve inlet.

Evaporative emission control system hoses

13 Disconnect the check valve to canister hose at the canister.

14 Connect the low pressure side of a water manometer (or 'U' tube) to the hose leading to the check valve, then apply air pressure of 14 in H_2O (356 mm H_2O) to the high pressure side of the manometer. Shut off the pressure source as close to the manometer as possible and check that during a period of five minutes the pressure has not fallen to less than 13.5 in H_2O (343 mm H_2O). If a greater pressure drop has occurred, check for damage and leaks at hose connections, the condense tank, the fuel tank, the fuel line and the fuel filler cap.

Check valve

15 Remove the check valve from the vehicle, as described in Section 21.

16 Connect a 'T' piece to one of the vent line ports.

17 Plug the other vent line port with a finger and check that the valve vents to atmosphere when a pressure and suction of approximately 7 lbf/in^2/0.5 kgf/cm^2) is applied. Replace the valve if the operation is unsatisfactory.

3

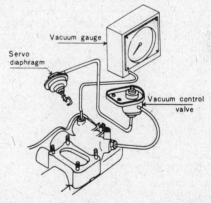

Fig. 3.45 Checking the vacuum control valve (B1600) (Sec. 20)

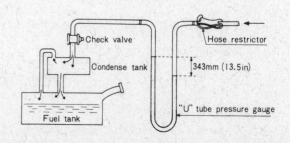

Fig. 3.47 Evaporative emission control system hose check (B1600) (Sec. 20)

21 Emission control sytem (B1600) - removal and installation of component parts

Servo diaphragm

1   Remove the air cleaner then disconnect the vacuum sensing tube from the servo diaphragm.
2   Remove the cotter pin and washer, and take off the link.
3   Slacken the attaching bolts and remove the diaphragm.
4   Installation is the reverse of the removal procedure, following which the diaphragm should be adjusted as described in paragraph 1 thru 7, of the previous Section.

Vacuum control valve

5   Remove the air cleaner and disconnect the vacuum sensing tubes from the vacuum control valve.
6   Remove the vacuum control valve attaching bolts and take off the valve.
7   Installation is the reverse of the removal procedure, following which the valve should be adjusted as described in paragraph 8, thru 10 of the previous Section.

Positive crankcase ventilation (PCV) valve

8   Remove the air cleaner then disconnect the ventilation hose from the ventilation valve.
9   Installation is the reverse of the removal procedure.

Condenser tank

10 Raise the rear end of the vehicle and support it on axle stands. Chock the front wheels for safety.
11 Disconnect the hoses from the condenser tank, then remove the tank mounting bolts and lift off the tank.
12 Installation is the reverse of the removal procedure.

Check valve

13 Raise the rear end of the vehicle and support it on axle stands. Chock the front wheels for safety.
14 Disconnect the check valve hoses, then remove the attaching bolts and take off the valve.
15 Installation is the reverse of the removal procedure.

22 Emission control system (Courier) - general description

1   The emission control system is divided into three basic parts as described in the following paragraphs, these being the exhaust emission control system (thermactor air injection system and deceleration control system) to reduce harmful composites in the exhaust gases; the positive crankcase ventilation system which channels the blowby gases from the crankcase into the combustion chamber to be burned; and the evaporative emission control system which stores the fuel vapor from the fuel system and leads it to the combustion chamber.

Thermactor air injection system (California 1972 and all 1973/74 models)

2   The thermactor system is designed to reduce the hydrocarbon, carbon monoxide and oxides of nitrogen in the exhaust gases. This is accomplished by injecting air under pressure into the exhaust ports near the exhaust valves where the added oxygen (in the air) plus the exhaust heat induces combustion during the piston exhaust stroke.
3   The system comprises the engine-driven air pump, check valve, air injection nozzles, air injection manifold, air bypass valve and interconnecting pipes and hoses.
4   When operating, air is pumped via the check valve to the air manifold and injection nozzles, where it oxidizes the unburned portion of the exhaust gases. A relief valve located in the air pump relieves excess pump pressure, and the check valve prevents backflow of exhaust gases into the air manifold at times when the exhaust gas pressure is higher than the pump pressure (eg; at high engine speeds or in the event of pump drivebelt failure).
5   An air bypass valve is installed between the air pump and check valve and allows the air to be diverted to atmosphere through the air cleaner when the choke control is in operation; this is to prevent overheating of the exhaust system.

Deceleration control system (California 1972 and all 1973/74 models)

6   The deceleration control system is designed to maintain a balanced fuel/air mixture during deceleration. It comprises an anti-afterburn valve to prevent fuel detonation in the exhaust due to an over-rich mixture during the early part of the deceleration mode and a coasting richer valve (manual transmission only) to prevent lean mixtures during the latter part of the deceleration mode.
7   The anti-afterburn valve is operated by intake manifold vacuum. It opens when intake manifold vacuum suddenly increases during decleration and remains open for a period of time in proportion to the amount of pressure change sensed by the valve diaphragm. When opened, the anti-afterburn valve allows additional air from the thermactor pump into the intake manifold, thus weakening the mixture which would otherwise cause detonation in the exhaust afterburning due to its over-richness.
8   As soon as the anti-afterburn valve completes its operation, the coasting rocker valve (where applicable) acts to add additional fuel to the lean mixture created in the intake manifold by the deceleration action, thus ensuring more complete combustion and cleaner exhaust gases. The coasting richer valve is controlled by the speedometer switch, accelerator switch and the clutch switch. In order for the valve to operate, all three switches must be closed at once, and this can only be done when the accelerator pedal is released, the decelerating speed is above 17 to 23 mph, and the clutch pedal is released.

Deceleration control system (1972 except California)

9   The deceleration control system is in three parts: one part controls throttle opening during deceleration; the second part provides a

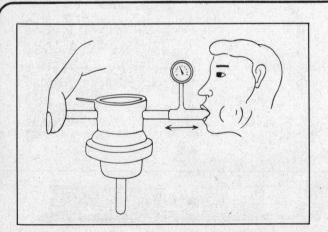

Fig. 3.48 Testing the check valve (B1600 and Courier) (Secs. 20 and 23)

Fig. 3.49 Location of the PCV valve (arrowed) (typical) (Sec. 21)

Fig. 3.50 The deceleration control system (California 1971 and all 1973/74 Couriers) (Sec. 22)

Fig. 3.51 The decleration control system (1972 Courier, except California) (Sec. 22)

retarded spark during deceleration; and the third part provides a retarded spark during idling.

10 A vacuum control valve controls both the spark retard and throttle opening. During deceleration, the vacuum control valve senses the higher intake manifold vacuum and activates both systems. The throttle opening system utilizes a servo diaphragm assembly connected to the primary throttle shaft. A bellows inside this assembly acts as an altitude compensator by changing its datum length in accordance with prevailing atmospheric pressure (or altitude) and thus maintains the correct spring tension on the diaphragm return spring. During deceleration, the vacuum control valve senses the higher intake manifold vacuum and transmits this vacuum to the servo diaphragm. The diaphragm linkage then partly opens the primary throttle plate slightly to supply additional fuel to the lean air/fuel mixture.

11 During deceleration, the vacuum control valve opens to allow vacuum to be applied to the vacuum switch which then closes and activates the distributor retard points. Under all other conditions, the spark is controlled by the normal point set but during deceleration this

point set is bypassed and the retard point set assumes control to give 7 to 10 degrees of spark retard.

12 When idling, the accelerator switch controls the retard points, but at speeds above idling the accelerator switch opens and the normal point set is in use.

Positive crankcase ventilation system

13 A positive crankcase ventilation (PCV) system is used to divert blow-by gases into the intake manifold to be burned by the engine. The system comprises a positive crankcase ventilation valve and hoses (and an oil separator for 1972/73 models) with ventilating air being routed into the rocker cover from the air cleaner and out again into the intake manifold (via the oil separator for 1972/73 models).

14 The PCV valve is operated by the pressure difference between the intake manifold and rocker cover. When there is no pressure difference (engine not rotating), or the intake manifold pressure is higher than the rocker cover pressure (backfire), the valve closes under spring action. If there is a large pressure difference (engine idling or decelerating) the

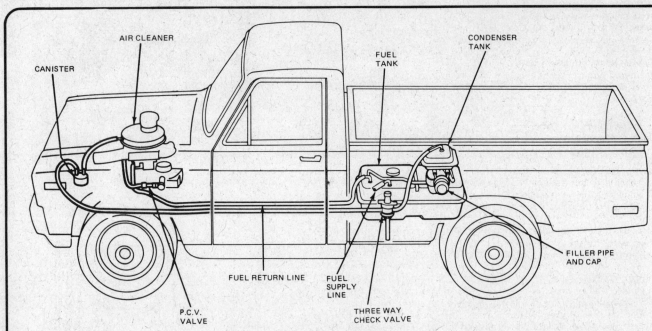

Fig. 3.52 Evaporative emission control system, 1974 Courier (Sec. 22)

Inset A: 1972 differences

Inset B: 1973 differences

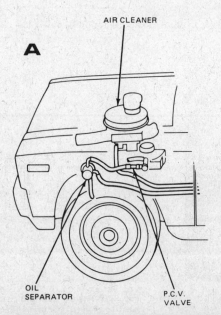

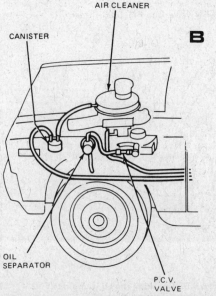

high vacuum in the intake manifold opens the valve against the action of the spring and allows a restricted flow of air through the valve. At small pressure differences (normal operation) the valve is balanced and now the maximum flow of ventilating air occurs.

Evaporative emission control system

15 The evaporative emission control system is designed to prevent the emission of fuel vapors into the atmosphere. The system varies slightly according to the year of manufacture (see Fig. 3.52), but in all cases comprises a fuel tank, condenser tank and check valve.

16 Fuel vapors rising from the tank are channelled into a condenser tank where ambient temperature changes condense them into fuel which drains back to the fuel tank. When the engine is operating, fuel vapors which have not condensed are routed either thru an oil separator and into the PCV valve, or thru a carbon canister and into the air cleaner to be drawn into the engine.

17 A check valve, located between the condenser tank and canister or oil separator, allows fuel vapors and ventilation to flow under normal circumstances. If this line becomes clogged or frozen, ventilation does not occur and the engine fuel supply will be cut off. Therefore the valve is opened by the negative fuel tank pressure, allowing a ventilation passage to atmosphere. When the fuel vapor in the tank is expanded due to intense heat, a pressure rise occurs. This opens the valve and releases the pressure to atmosphere.

18 Where a carbon canister is used, it is installed in the engine compartment. Its purpose is to absorb and store fuel vapors until they can be burned.

---

23 Emission control system (Courier) - tests and adjustments

Air pump drivebelt

1 To check the belt tension, press down midway between the air pump pulley and the water pump pulley. At a downward pressure of 22 lbf ft (10 kgf ft) there should be a belt deflection of ½ to 5/8 in (13 to 16 mm).

2 To adjust the belt, loosen the air pump adjusting bolt and the lower attaching bolt. Pry the pump outward until the correct belt tension is obtained then tighten the bolts to the specified torque.

Air pump

3 Disconnect the air pump outlet hose from the air bypass valve and connect a pressure gauge and 'T' piece as shown in Fig. 3.54.

4 Ensure that the belt tension is correct and run the engine at 1500 rpm with the choke control knob pushed fully in (choke open). Provided that a pump reading of 1 lbf/in^2 (0.07 kgf/cm^2) or more is obtained, the pump is satisfactory.

Air pump relief valve

5 Operate the engine at the specified idle speed and check for airflow at the relief valve (see Fig. 3.55). If airflow is evident, replace the relief

valve.

6 Increase the engine speed to 3000 rpm and check that there is now an airflow. If there is no flow, and the air pump is excessively noisy, or the relief valve is excessively noisy, renew the relief valve and air pump assembly.

Air manifold check valve

7 Remove the check valve from the air manifold and blow through the valve from the intake side, then blow thru from the manifold side. Air should pass from the intake side only; if unsatisfactory, replace the valve.

Fig. 3.53 The air pump adjusting bolt (Courier) (Sec. 23)

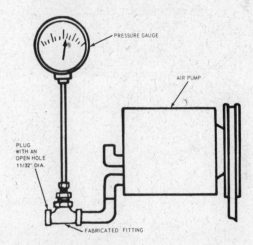

Fig. 3.54 Air pump test set-up (Courier) (Sec. 23)

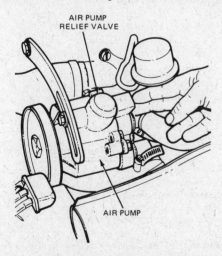

Fig. 3.55 Checking the air pump relief valve (Courier) (Sec. 23)

Fig. 3.56 The location of the air manifold check valve (Courier) (Sec. 23)

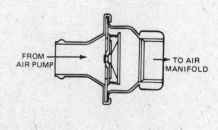

Fig. 3.57 The air manifold check valve (sectioned view) (Courier) (Sec. 23)

3

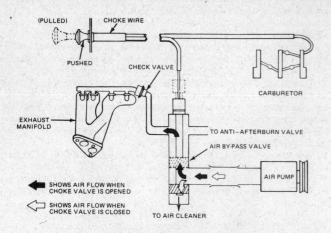

Fig. 3.58 Schematic diagram showing the air by-pass valve operation (Courier) (Sec. 23)

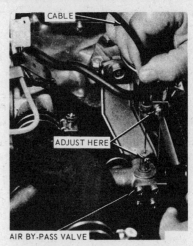

Fig. 3.59 Location of the air by-pass valve (Courier) (Sec. 23)

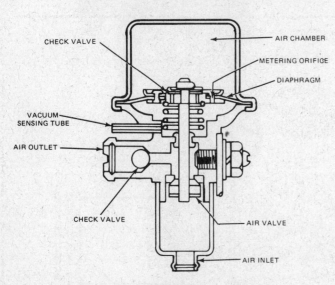

Fig. 3.60 Sectional view of the anti-afterburn valve (Courier) (Sec. 23)

Fig. 3.61 Testing the anti-afterburn valve (Courier) (Sec. 23)

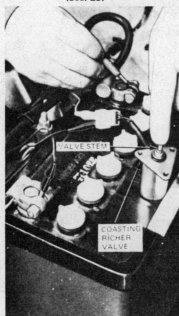

Fig. 3.62 Testing the coasting richer valve (Courier) (Sec. 23)

Air bypass valve

8 Disconnect the air hose at the air manifold check valve then push in the choke control knob fully.

9 Run the engine at approximately 1500 rpm.

10 Check that air flows from the air pump hose, then pull out the choke knob fully and check that the airflow ceases. Replace a valve that is not operating correctly if it cannot be adjusted as described in paragraphs 11 thru 14.

11 To adjust the air bypass valve, push the choke knob fully in and check that the choke plate is fully open.

12 Loosen the cable retaining screw in the valve plunger and the screw in the cable bracket.

13 Ensure that the plunger is fully in, then insert the cable into the plunger and tighten the retaining screw.

14 Push down on the cable to remove any slackness then tighten the bracket screw. Check that when the choke knob is fully out, the valve plunger is pushed to the top of the bracket.

Anti-afterburn valve (California 1972 and all 1973/74 models)

15 Remove the anti-afterburn valve outlet hose.

16 Start the engine, raise the engine rpm then allow the throttle to snap shut. Check that air flows from the anti-afterburn valve for approximately three seconds. Replace a valve where this is not satisfactory.

Coasting richer valve (California 1972 and all 1973/74 models, manual transmission only)

17 Remove the valve from the carburetor and connect the valve leads to a 12 volt dc source of supply. Check that the valve stem is drawn in, then moves out again when the voltage is disconnected. Replace a valve where this does not occur.

18 Install the coasting richer valve, then rig a 12 volt test-lamp and jumper leads to the solenoid supply connections.

19 Raise the rear of the vehicle and place it on axle stands. Chock the front roadwheels for safety.

20 Run the engine in top gear to a speed above 30 mph then release the accelerator pedal. The test-lamp should remain on until the speed falls below 17 to 23 mph.

21 If the tests so far are satisfactory, no further tests are required. If satisfactory operation is now obtained, check the clutch switch, as described in the following paragraph.

22 Using a suitable continuity tester (eg; an ohmmeter or a test-lamp and battery), check that when the clutch pedal is depressed the switch is open and when the pedal is released the switch is closed. If this test is satisfactory, check the accelerator switch as described in the following paragraph.

23 Using a suitable continuity tester, check that when the accelerator pedal is depressed the switch is open and when the pedal is released the switch is closed. If this test is satisfactory, check the speed switch as described in the following paragraph.

24 Remove the instrument cluster (refer to Chapter 10, for details) and attach a 12 volt test-lamp to the speedometer switch relay. Now repeat the test given at paragraphs 19 and 20. If this test is unsatisfactory, check that the relay will energize from a 12 volt dc supply, but for

safety's sake, first disconnect the relay leads.

Servo diaphragm (1972 except California)

25 Start the engine and ensure that the idle speed is as specified.

26 Stop the engine. Disconnect the vacuum line between the vacuum control valve and the servo diaphragm at the diaphragm.

27 Disconnect the vacuum line between the intake manifold and the vacuum control valve at the intake manifold.

28 Disconnect the vacuum line between the carburetor and the distributor vacuum diaphragm.

29 Connect a vacuum line directly from the intake manifold to the servo diaphragm, as shown in Fig. 3.63.

30 Run the engine and check that the idle speed is 1300 to 1500 rpm using an external tachometer. Provided that the speed is between 750 and 1700 rpm adjust it using the servo diaphragm adjusting screw. Replace the servo diaphragm if the specified reading cannot be obtained.

Vacuum control valve (1972 except California)

31 Disconnect the vacuum line between the vacuum control valve and the intake manifold at the intake manifold.

32 Attach a vacuum gauge to the vacuum line using a 'T' piece (see Fig. 3.65.

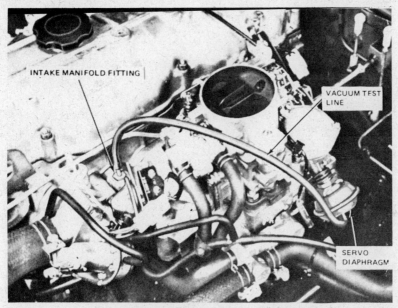

Fig. 3.63 Testing the servo diaphragm (Courier) (Sec. 23)

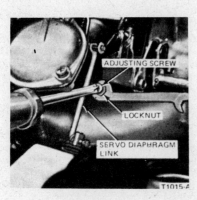

Fig. 3.64 Adjusting the servo diaphragm (Courier) (Sec. 23)

Fig. 3.65 Testing the vacuum control valve (Courier) (Sec. 23)

33 Start the engine, run at approximately 3000 rpm, then release the accelerator. A vacuum reading in excess of 21.3 in Hg should be obtained, and should then fall back to 21.3 in Hg for 1 to 2 seconds. The reading should then fall to 16 to 18 in Hg for ambient conditions at sea level. See Fig. 3.67 for compensation figures for other altitudes. If the vacuum reading is not as specified, adjustment can be made by turning the adjusting screw at the top of the valve. Renew the valve if the correct adjustment cannot be obtained.

Vacuum switch (1972 except California)

34 Disconnect the vacuum line between the vacuum switch and the vacuum control valve then use a 'T' piece to connect a vacuum gauge as shown in Fig. 3.68.
35 Connect one end of the hose to a vacuum source and increase the vacuum reading to above 8 in Hg.
36 Release the vacuum slowly and check that the switch is heard to click at approximately 6 in Hg. If no click is heard, or it occurs above 6½ to 7 in Hg, replace the switch.

Accelerator switch (1972 except California)

37 Check the accelerator switch as described in paragraph 23. If adjustment is required, ensure that the throttle plates are fully closed, then loosen the switch adjusting screw locknut and back the screw out, until it no longer contacts the switch.
38 Turn the screw in, until the switch clicks, then turn in a further 1½ turns. Tighten the locknut and recheck the operation.

Distributor contact breaker retard points (1972 except California)

39 Refer to Chapter 4, Section 8.

Positive crankcase ventilation (PCV) valve

40 Remove the hose from the PCV valve then start the engine and run it at 700 to 1000 rpm.
41 Check that suction can be felt at the PCV valve inlet.

Evaporative emission control system check valve

42 Remove the check valve from the vehicle, as described in Section 24.
43 Connnect a 'T' piece to one of the vent line ports.
44 Plug the other vent line port with a finger and check that the valve vents to atmosphere when a pressure and suction of approximately 7 lbf/in^2 (0.5 kgf/cm^2) is applied. Replace the valve if the operation is unsatisfactory.

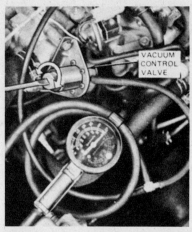

Fig. 3.66 Adjusting the vacuum control valve (Courier) (Sec. 23)

Altitude (Feet)	Vacuum Reading (In. Hg.)
+ 10,000	13.80
+ 9,000	14.55
+ 8,000	15.30
+ 7,000	16.05
+ 6,000	16.80
+ 5,000	17.55
+ 4,000	18.30
+ 3,000	19.05
+ 2,000	19.80
+ 1,000	20.55
Sea Level	21.30
− 1,000	22.05

Fig. 3.67 Altitude correction chart for the vacuum control valve (Courier) (Sec. 23)

Fig. 3.68 Testing the vacuum switch (Sec. 24)

24 Emission control system (Courier) - removal and installation of component parts

Air pump

1 Remove the battery, alternator and alternator V-belt. Refer to Chapter 10, if necessary.
2 Disconnect the air pump inlet and outlet hoses.
3 Remove the air pump adjustment bolt and the drivebelt.
4 Remove the air pump mounting bolt and lift away the pump.
5 Installation is the reverse of the removal procedure. Adjust the alternator drivebelt, as described in Chapter 2, and the air pump drivebelt, as described in paragraph 2 of the previous Section.

Air manifold check valve

6 Disconnect the air hose and unscrew the check valve from the manifold.
7 Installation is the reverse of the removal procedure.

Air manifold

8 Remove the air manifold check valve.
9 Apply penetrating oil to the nozzle unions. Unscrew the unions and remove the air manifold.
10 Installation is the reverse of the removal procedure.

Air injection nozzles

11 Disconnect the hose from the air manifold check valve.
12 Remove the manifold assembly complete with check valve (refer to paragraph 9).
13 Remove the exhaust manifold heat stove.
14 Apply penetrating oil to the nozzle screw threads then remove them from the exhaust ports.
15 Installation is the reverse of the removal procedure.

Air bypass valve

16 Loosen the cable attaching screws at the valve plunger and cable bracket.
17 Pull the cable out of the valve then remove the bypass valve from the bracket (4 screws).
18 When installing, position the valve to the mounting bracket and install the screws.
19 Push the choke knob fully in and insert the end of the cable into the valve plunger. Tighten the retaining screw.
20 Pull down on the cable to remove any slackness then tighten the bracket screw.

Anti-afterburn valve (California 1972 and all 1973/74 models)

21 Remove the two hoses and the vacuum line from the valve.
22 Remove the attaching bolt and remove the valve.
23 Installation is the reverse of the removal procedure.

Coasting richer valve (California 1972 and all 1973/74 models, manual transmission only)

24 Disconnect the electrical lead then remove the valve from the carburetor (3 screws).
25 Installation is the reverse of the removal procedure.

Clutch switch (California 1972 and all 1973/74 models, manual transmission only)

26 Disconnect the electrical lead from the switch then remove the adjusting nut on the rear of the switch mounting bracket.
27 Installation is the reverse of the removal procedure, but adjust the switch to operate when the clutch pedal is depressed.

Accelerator switch (manual transmission only, all models)

28 Disconnect the electrical lead from the switch.
29 Remove the switch from the throttle return spring bracket (3 screws) and remove the switch.
30 Installation is the reverse of the removal procedure, but adjust the switch, as described in paragraphs 37 and 38, of the previous Section.

Speed switch (California 1972 and all 1973/74 models, manual transmission only)

31 The speed switch is integral with the speedometer head and cannot be renewed on its own. Refer to Chapter 10, for removal of the speedometer.

Vacuum control valve (1972 except California)

32 Make a note of the hose connections to the vacuum control valve, then remove them.
33 Remove the bolts from the mounting bracket then remove the valve.
34 Installation is the reverse of the removal procedure, following which the valve should be adjusted, as described in paragraphs 31 thru 33, of the previous Section.

Servo diaphragm (1972 except California)

35 Disconnect the link from the diaphragm after removing the cotter key, spring and washer.
36 Loosen the diaphragm attaching nut then slide the diaphragm from the bracket.
37 Installation is the reverse of the removal procedure, following which the diaphragm should be adjusted, as described in paragraph 25 thru 30, of the previous Section.

Vacuum switch (1972 except California)

38 Remove the electrical lead and vacuum line from the vacuum switch.
39 Remove the single attaching bolt and remove the switch.
40 Installation is the reverse of the removal procedure.

Positive crankcase ventilation (PCV) valve

41 Remove the air cleaner (1973/74 models only).

3

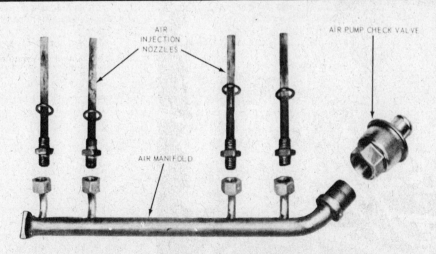

Fig. 3.69 The air manifold, check valve and air injection nozzles (Courier) (Sec. 24)

42 Disconnect the hose from the PCV valve then unscrew the valve from the intake manifold fitting.
43 Installation is the reverse of the removal procedure

Oil separator (1972/73 models only)

44 If necessary, raise the vehicle.
45 Remove the bolt attaching the oil separator to the engine block and disconnect the hoses.
46 Installation is the reverse of the removal procedure.

Condenser tank

47 Raise the rear of the vehicle and place it on axle stands. Chock the front wheels for safety.
48 Disconnect the hoses from the condenser tank, then remove the condenser tank attaching bolts and lift the tank off.

Check valve

49 Disconnect the hoses, then remove the check valve attaching screws and remove the valve.
50 Installation is the reverse of the removal procedure.

---

25 Fault diagnosis - carburation; fuel, exhaust and emission control systems

Unsatisfactory engine performance and excessive fuel consumption are not necessarily the fault of the fuel system or carburetor. In fact they more commonly occur as a result of faults in the emission control system or ignition system. Because of the complexities and interdependence of the components in the emission control system, it is difficult to give a satisfactory diagnostic procedure; however, the checks and adjustments given in this Section are fairly straightforward and should always be carried out when problems occur. Fault finding and servicing of the ignition system should always be carried out before attending to problems which are leading to excessive fuel consumption, erratic or unsatisfactory performance, etc.

The table below assumes that the associated systems are correct.

Symptom	Reason/s	Remedy
Smell of fuel when engine is stopped	Leaking fuel lines or unions	Repair or renew as necessary.
	Leaking fuel tank	Fill fuel tank to capacity and examine carefully at seams, unions and filler pipe connections. Repair as necessary.
Smell of fuel when engine is idling	Leaking fuel line unions between pump and carburetor	Check line and unions and tighten or repair.
	Overflow of fuel from float bowl due to wrong level setting or ineffective needle valve or punctured float	Check fuel level setting and condition of float and needle valve, and renew if necessary.
Excessive fuel consumption for reasons not covered by leaks or float bowl faults	Worn jets	Renew jets.
	Sticking choke mechanism	Check correct movement and operation of choke plate.
	Accelerator pump incorrectly set	Check and adjust as necessary.
Difficult starting, uneven running, lack of power, cutting out	One or more jets blocked or restricted	Dismantle and clean carburetor.
	Float bowl fuel level too low or needle sticking	Dismantle and check fuel level and needle.
	Fuel pump not delivering sufficient fuel	Check pump delivery and clean or repair as required.
	Intake manifold gaskets leaking, or manifold fractured	Check tightness of mounting nuts and inspect manifold.
	Check valve sticking	Check and replace as necessary.
	PCV valve stuck open	Check and clean as necessary.
Engine will not idle	PCV valve sticking	Check and clean as necessary.
	Slow fuel cut solenoid sticking closed	Check and replace as necessary.
	Incorrect idle settings.	Check and adjust as necessary.
Dieseling (running-on)	Slow fuel cut solenoid sticking open	Check and replace as necessary.
Engine will not run	Fuel pump inoperative	Check and repair as necessary.

Chapter 4 Ignition system

Refer to Chapter 13 for Specifications and information applicable to 1974 through 1982 models.

Contents

Condenser - testing, removal and installation	4
Distributor contact points - removal, installation and adjustment ...	3
Distributor - dismantling, servicing and reassembly	6
Distributor - removal and installation	5
Dwell angle - checking and setting	7
Fault diagnosis - ignition system	10
General description	1
Ignition timing	8
Routine maintenance	2
Spark plugs and HT leads	9

Specifications

B1600

Spark plugs

Spark plug type:	
Standard	NGK BP—6ES, NGK BPR—6ES or Denso W-20EP
Cold type	NGK BP—7ES or NGK BPR—7ES
Spark plug thread	14 mm
Spark plug electrode gap	0.031 in. (0.8 mm)
Engine firing order	1, 3, 4, 2 (No. 1 nearest radiator)

Distributor

Type	Single point, with vacuum and centrifugal advance and retard; gear driven from camshaft
Direction of rotation	Clockwise
Point gap	0.020 in. (0.5 mm)
Contact point pressure	1.1 to 1.4 lb (500 to 650 gram)
Dwell angle	49 to 55º
Centrifugal advance:	
Starts	0 at 550 rpm
Maximum	11º at 2000 rpm
Vacuum advance, General and 1972 Federal:	
Starts	0º at 6.3 in. Hg (160 mm Hg)
Maximum	8.5º at 10.24 in. Hg (260 mm Hg)
Vacuum advance, 1972 California and 1973 USA:	
Starts	0º at 12.6 in. Hg (320 mm Hg)
Maximum	7.5º at 21.65 in. Hg (550 mm Hg)
Condenser capacity	0.20 to 0.24 mfd

Ignition timing

General	8º BTDC
USA	5º BTDC
Timing mark location	Crankshaft pulley
Engine idle speed:	
General	600 ± 50 rpm
USA	800 to 850 rpm

Courier

Spark plugs

Spark plug type	Autolite AG32A or AGR 32
Spark plug thread	14 mm
Spark plug electrode gap	0.029 to 0.033 in. (0.74 to 0.84 mm)
Engine firing order	1, 3, 4, 2 (No. 1 nearest radiator)

Distributor

Type	Single or dual point, with vacuum and centrifugal advance and retard; gear driven from camshaft
Direction of rotation	Clockwise
Point gap	0.018 to 0.022 in. (0.46 to 0.56 mm)
Dwell angle	49º to 55º

4

Vacuum advance:
  Manual transmission   ...   .   7.5º at 19.7 in. Hg (500 mm Hg)
  Automatic transmission ...   .   7.5º at 17.8 in. Hg (432 mm Hg)

Ignition timing
Initial advance ...   .   5º BTDC (1972 models); 3º BTDC (1973, 1974 models)
Engine idle speed   ...   .   700 to 750 rpm

Torque wrench settings

	lbf ft	kg fm
Spark plug	11 to 15	1.5 to 2.1

1 General description

1 In order that the internal combustion engine with spark ignition can operate properly, it is essential that the spark be delivered at the spark plug electrodes at the precise moment it is required. This moment varies - in relation to the position of the pistons and crankshaft - depending on the speed and loading of the engine. This control of the spark timing is automatic. When it is realised that at 50 mph approximately 100 sparks per second are being produced then the importance of the need for precise setting is realised. The majority of minor faults and cases of poor performance and economy can be traced to the ignition system.

2 The principles are as follows: Battery voltage is fed through a circuit which passes through a coil developing high voltage. Without going into electrical principles it is sufficient to say that when the circuit is 'made', voltage is fed to a capacitor (condenser). When the circuit is broken the condenser discharges its voltage into the low voltage line, and a high voltage is boosted from the core of the coil and along the HT lead. This voltage is delivered to the center contact of the distributor cap and from there, via the rotor arm, to each of the other four contacts in turn. Each of these is linked by a 'high tension' lead to each spark plug.

3 Obviously the timing of the break in the circuit decides the moment at which the spark is made. The contact points (or breaker points) are in effect a switch. Not only do they open and close four times for every 2 revolutions of the crankshaft - delivering a spark to the four plugs in turn - they also open earlier or later in relation to the position of the crankshaft/pistons. Ignition advance and retard are the terms used to express this condition and it is measured in degrees - being degrees of angle of any crank on the shaft. Zero degrees is top dead center, being the highest point of the arc made by a crank. Timing setting is therefore normally expressed as so many degrees btdc (before top dead center).

4 In order to vary the ignition timing for optimum efficiency at all times, the contact opening cam is able to revolve a certain amount round the center spindle. This is controlled by spring-loaded weights which move out under centrifugal force as the engine speed increases, and by vacuum from the engine intake manifold, according to the prevailing running conditions (ie: the engine 'loading'). At conditions of wide throttle opening there is a low intake manifold depression which gives little or no vacuum advance. At moderate throttle openings, where the vehicle is cruising, there is a comparatively high intake manifold depression which gives full vacuum advance.

5 The dual point distributors used on some early models are similar to the single point type, the extra points being used to give additional timing control (spark retardation) in conjunction with the vacuum switch and accelerate switch of the emission control system.

6 An additional feature of the ignition system is the ballast resistor which is connected in series with the ignition coil. Under normal running conditions, approximately half of the battery voltage is dropped across the ballast resistor and half across the ignition coil, the latter item being a 5 to 6 volt type. Therefore, the correct HT output voltage is obtained when 12 volts is applied to the circuit. Under engine starting conditions, the battery voltage may drop to around 9 volts which would give a poor spark if a 12 volt coil was used. However, when the starter solenoid is energized, this bypasses the ballast resistor and the battery voltage is applied direct to the coil to provide an additional HT voltage since the coil is receiving a higher than normal input voltage (photo).

2 Routine maintenance

1 The ignition system is one of the most important and most neglected systems in any vehicle, and attention to routine maintenance cannot be over-emphasized. The maintenance intervals are given in the Routine Maintenance Section at the beginning of this Manual.

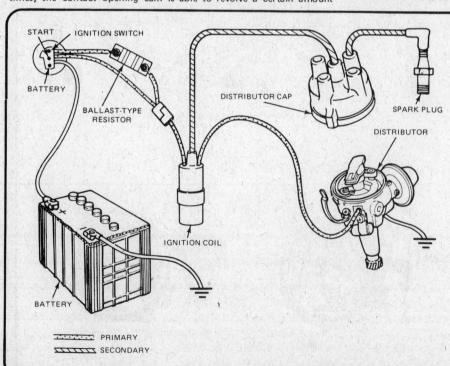

Fig. 4.1 The ignition system circuit (Sec. 1)

Spark plugs

2   Remove the plugs and thoroughly clean away all traces of carbon. Examine the porcelain insulation round the central electrode inside the plug, and if damaged discard the plug. Reset the gap between the electrodes. Do not use a set of plugs for more than 12 000 miles; it is false economy. For further information on spark plugs, see Section 9.

Distributor contact points

3   Remove the distributor cap and rotor, and carefully pry open the contact points with a small screwdriver. Provided that the points are clean (and this is not very likely since there is normally a build-up on one contact and a cavity in the other), all that needs to be done is to check and reset the gap, as described in Section 3. If the points require attention, refer to Section 3, and remove them; then rub the faces smooth using an oilstone. It is important to remove all the build-up on the one contact, and as much as is practically possible of the cavity on the other contact. Also remember that the faces must be square to each other when re-installed or correct setting of the gap will not be possible; a slightly domed profile can assist for this purpose. After cleaning, install the contacts and set the gap, as described in Section 3. The ultimate life of contact breaker points cannot be predicted, but with correct attention at the appropriate maintenance intervals, they should be capable of lasting for at lease 12000 miles (20000 km).

Distributor cap, rotor and HT leads

4   Remove the distributor cap and HT leads from the ignition coil and spark plugs. Wipe the end of the coil, the HT leads and spark plug caps and the internal and external surfaces of the distributor cap with a lint-free cloth moistened with gasoline (petrol) or a cleaning solvent. Ensure that all traces of dirt and oil are removed, then carefully inspect for cracked insulation on the leads, spark plug caps, distributor cap and ignition coil end. At the same time, check that the carbon brush in the center of the distributor cap is intact and returns under the action of its spring when pressed in. Carefully scrape any deposits from the distributor cap electrodes and from the rotor; if any serious erosion has occurred, replacement parts should be fitted.

Lubrication

5   Apply two drops of engine oil to the screw head in the center of the distributor cam, and through the aperture in the baseplate to lubricate the advance mechanism. Apply a trace of the same oil to the breaker point pivot(s), and a trace of petroleum jelly to the cam profile.

Ignition timing

6   After completing the aforementioned, check and adjust the dwell angle and ignition timing, as described in Sections 7 and 8.

---

3   Distributor contact points - removal, installation and adjustment

1   Spring back the distributor cap retaining clips, remove the cap and pull off the rotor.
2   Remove the screws retaining the distributor point set(s) and, where applicable, loosen the nut so that the flying lead can be detached. Take care that no screws, nuts or washers are dropped inside the distributor.
3   Lift out the contact set(s). If they are to be cleaned, refer to Section 2; alternatively obtain a new set of the correct type from your vehicle main dealer.
4   Installation is the reverse of the removal procedure, but before finally tightening down the points it is necessary to set the contact point gap as described in the following paragraph. For most practical purposes this is all that is required, although it is advantageous to obtain a final setting by the dwell angle method, as described in Section 7.

1.6 The ballast resistor

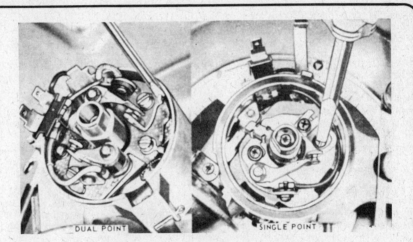

Fig. 4.2 Contact breaker point adjustment - typical (Sec. 3)

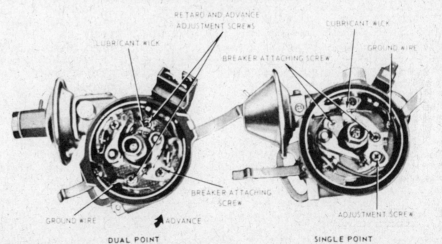

Fig. 4.3 Contact breaker point installation
(Sec. 3)

5   Check that the contact breaker points are correctly aligned. A small amount of misalignment can be corrected for by bending the stationary breaker point bracket but if seriously misaligned, it may mean that points have been refaced incorrectly. Rotate the engine at the crankshaft pulley until the contact rubbing block is on the peak of the cam. Insert a feeler gauge of the specified size between the contact faces and adjust the position of the fixed contact until the feeler gauge is a firm sliding fit. Tighten the fixed contact plate screw and ensure that the other screw(s) is/are tight, then recheck that the gap has not altered. Install the rotor and distributor cap on completion.

4 Condenser - testing, removal and installation

1   A faulty condenser will cause rapid burning of the contact breaker points at the best, and at the worst total failure of the ignition system.
2   Without special test equipment a faulty condenser cannot be readily diagnosed, but where there is an indication of a malfunction, it is best to renew it in view of its very moderate cost.
3   Depending upon the distributor, the condenser is either connected to a screw on the outside of the distributor body or is fed through a grommet into the distributor and connects to a terminal. The condenser body is retained on the exterior of the distributor by a single screw and washer. When reconnecting the lead ensure that all washers are installed in their original positions and that all the screws are tight.

5 Distributor - removal and installation

1   Remove the distributor cap and disconnect the vacuum line from the diaphragm unit.
2   Index mark the distributor body and cylinder block, and the distributor body and rotor, to provide alignment marks for eventual installation so that the timing will not be altered.
3   Disconnect the low tension wire(s) from the distributor body.
4   Remove the distributor attaching nut and associated washers.
5   Lift the distributor out of the cylinder head. Do not rotate the crankshaft after the distributor has been removed or it will be necessary to re-time the engine when it is installed.
6   Installation is a straightforward reversal of the removal procedure but since even the smallest deviation from the original installed position may marginally affect ignition timing, it is recommended that this is checked, as described in Section 8. If the crankshaft was rotated after the distributor was removed, turn the crankshaft until the TDC mark on the pulley is in line with the pointer when No. 1 piston is at top-dead-center on its firing stroke (No. 4 piston will also be at top-dead-center at the same time, but it will be at the end of its exhaust stroke. In this condition the No. 4 cylinder valves are 'rocking', but the No. 1 cylinder valves are both closed. This can be readily detected by placing a finger over No. 1 cylinder spark plug hole, where the compression pressure will be felt). Having determined top-dead-center, slide the distributor into the cylinder head and at the same time align the distributor rotor with the No. 1 cylinder segment of the distributor cap. Provided that the plug leads are already fitted, the angular position of the cap will be pre-determined by the lengths of the leads. On completion, check the ignition timing, as described in Section 8.

6 Distributor - dismantling, servicing and reassembly

1   Remove the distributor as previously described. If the distributor cap has not been removed, remove it now.
2   Remove the terminal cover retainer and cover (where applicable).
3   Remove the rotor and disconnect the condenser lead attaching nuts.
4   Remove the screws which retain the condenser(s); remove the condenser(s).
5   Disconnect the breaker point lead(s) from their terminal(s).
6   Where applicable, lift the primary terminal block from the housing.
7   Remove the 'C' clip which secures the vacuum diaphragm link to the breaker plate.
8   Remove the breaker point securing screw(s) and lift the point(s) and lubricant wick retainer from the breaker plate.
9   Remove the screw from the center of the cam spindle, then lift the cam off.
10 Remove the two screws which retain the vacuum unit (and the reinforcement plate if applicable).

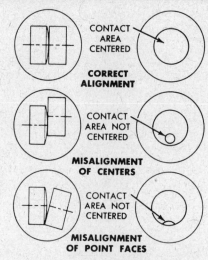

Fig. 4.4 Checking the contact breaker point alignment (Sec. 3)

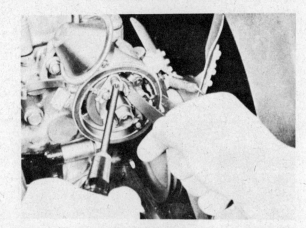

Fig. 4.5 Measuring the contact breaker point gap (Sec. 3)

11 Where applicable, remove the two breaker plate sub-plate attaching screws and anchor plates.
12 Where applicable, remove the two bale clamp (cap retaining clip) attaching screws; remove the bale clamps, ground terminal and insulator.
13 Rotate the breaker plate counter-clockwise, using a small screwdriver until the terminal block recess in the sub-plate is below the vacuum diaphragm link (dual point distributors only) (Fig. 4.8).
14 Disconnect the link from the breaker plate then remove the diaphragm unit.
15 Lift off the breaker plate (and sub-plate if applicable).
16 Lift the cam (and spring on dual point distributors) off the centrifugal weights, and remove it from the housing.
17 Unhook the weight spring from each post. On dual point distributors, remove the 'C' clip from each centrifugal weight. Remove the weights.
18 Check the distributor parts for damage and wear. Refer to Section 2, paragraph 5, for checks and cleaning details of the cap and rotor. Unless the points are known to be in good condition it is advisable to install new ones. Check the weights for excessive looseness on their pivots; it is advisable to fit new springs in view of their modest cost. Suck (by mouth) on the vacuum diaphragm unit and check that the link is drawn in. When the vacuum is held by placing the tongue or a finger over the tube, the link should remain in; if it fails to do so, the vacuum unit must be renewed. Ensure that the driven gear is securely pinned to the cam spindle, and that the gear is undamaged.
19 Apply a trace of molybdenum-disulphide grease to the cam pivots.
20 Position each centrifugal weight on its pivot pin and connect the springs to their posts. On dual point distributors, install new 'C' springs.
21 Apply a trace of molybdenum-disulphide grease to the cam spindle.

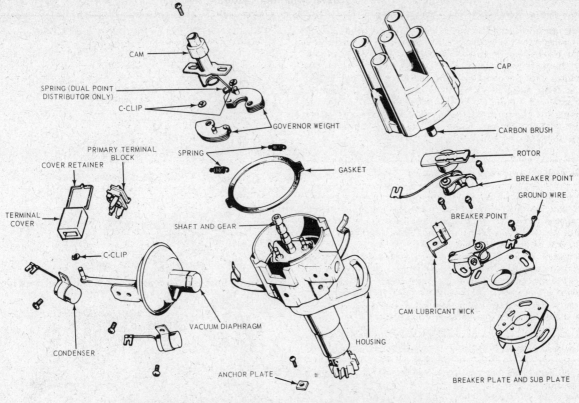

Fig. 4.6 Exploded view of the dual point distributor - typical (Sec. 6)

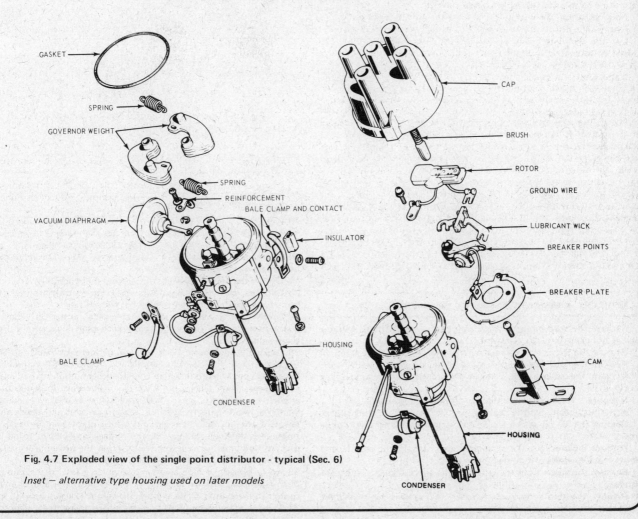

Fig. 4.7 Exploded view of the single point distributor - typical (Sec. 6)

Inset — alternative type housing used on later models

4

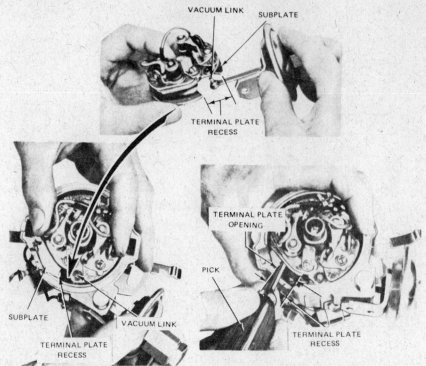

Fig. 4.8 Removing and installing the vacuum diaphragm unit on dual point distributors (Sec. 6)

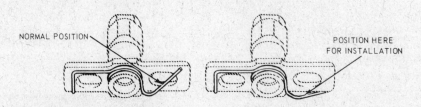

Fig. 4.9 The installation position for the cam return spring on dual point distributors (Sec. 6)

22 On dual point distributors, position the cam return spring as shown in Fig. 4.9. This is to prevent interference with the centrifugal weight drive pin.

23 Place the cam in position on the shaft, ensuring that each pin is entered in the slot. Secure the cam to the shaft with the screw. On dual point distributors, press down on the end of the spring to release it to the normal position.

24 On single point distributors, position the breaker plate in the housing and install the insulator, ground terminal and bale clamps. Ensure that the breaker plate ground wire is placed between the housing and plate, and is secured by the bale clamp attaching screw. Position the vacuum diaphragm and install the reinforcing plate and attaching screws. Secure the link using a new 'C' clip.

25 On dual point distributors, place the vacuum diaphragm unit in the housing, then position the breaker plate and sub-plate. Ensure that the terminal block recess in the sub-plate is opposite the vacuum link. While the sub-plate is held in this position, rotate the breaker plate as required to insert the diaphragm link in the breaker plate. Secure it with a new 'C' clip then secure the diaphragm unit with its two screws.

26 On dual point distributors, rotate the sub-plate with a small screwdriver in a clockwise direction until the terminal block recess in the sub-plate aligns with the terminal block opening in the housing. Position the two sub-plate anchor plates and secure them in place with the two screws and the breaker point ground wire.

27 Install the breaker point(s), the cam lubricant wick and the retainer(s).

28 Secure the condenser(s) to the housing.

29 Where applicable, insert the breaker point terminal block in the housing. Connect the condenser lead(s) and breaker point(s) to the terminals.

30 Install the distributor, check and adjust the points, and set the timing. If a dwell angle meter is available, check the dwell angle before setting the timing.

7 Dwell angle - checking and setting

1 For most practical purposes, the breaker points can be set by adjusting the gap, as described in Section 3. However, a more accurate method of setting the points is obtained by the dwell angle method which requires the use of a proprietary dwell angle meter. This type of meter is supplied complete with operating and connecting instructions.

2 To check the dwell angle, first disconnect the distributor vacuum line.

3 Connect the dwell angle meter and set it up in accordance with the manufacturer's instructions for 4-cylinder engines.

4 Start the engine and run it at idle speed.

5 Check the dwell angle and compare it with that specified. If it is satisfactory, all that needs to be done is to disconnect the meter and its connections.

6 If adjustment is required, you will need to increase the breaker point gap if the angle was too large, or decrease the gap, if the angle was too small. This can be done by re-adjustment, as described in Section 3. However, it is possible to do it whilst the engine is being cranked by an assistant while you carry out the adjustment. First remove the coil HT lead from the distributor and ground it, then remove the distributor cap and rotor. Loosen the breaker point attaching screws then, whilst the engine is being cranked, alter the contact position until the correct dwell angle is obtained. Stop the engine cranking, tighten the attaching screw(s) then recheck the angle. On completion, remove the meter, remake the HT connection, then install the rotor and distributor cap.

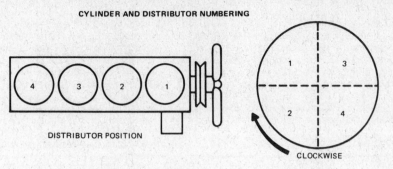

CYLINDER AND DISTRIBUTOR NUMBERING

DISTRIBUTOR POSITION

CLOCKWISE

FIRING - 1-3-4-2

Fig. 4.10 The distributor lead and cylinder numbering (Sec. 8)

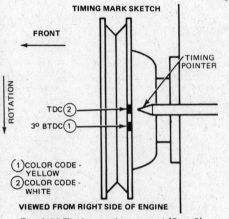

Fig. 4.11 Timing marks - general (Sec. 8)
See Specifications for actual advance on any model

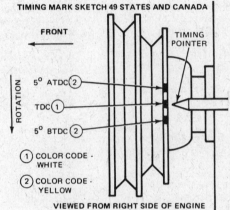

Fig. 4.12 Timing marks for 49 states and Canada models for 1972 (Sec. 8)

8.3 The timing pointer and typical pulley markings

8 Ignition timing

1 In order to obtain a spark at the correct time, it is very important that the distributor is correctly positioned relative to the angular position of the crankshaft. This position varies according to the model and market, but reference to Fig. 4.11 and 4.12 will show the various marks which can be expected to be found on the crankshaft pulley for timing purposes.

2 The simplest way to check and adjust the timing requires no special equipment, although the use of a 12 volt bulb of fairly low wattage, together with two flying leads, can be very helpful.

3 The instant of time at which the distributor contact breaker points open is the time at which the spark is delivered. Therefore, if the appropriate timing mark is aligned with the timing pointer, the breaker points should just be opening. To be able to judge this more accurately, connect the bulb flying leads across the breaker points and switch on the ignition. Rotate the crankshaft at the pulley about 20° counterclockwise from top-dead-center (TDC) at which time the bulb should be extinguished. Now rotate the crankshaft clockwise until the bulb illuminates (ie: the breaker points are just opening) and check the position of the pulley with respect to the pointer. If the marks are correctly aligned, all is well and good. If the marks are not aligned, it will mean slackening the distributor clamp bolt, turning the distributor slightly, tightening the clamp bolt and rechecking. If the timing is too far advanced (ie: the timing mark is too far from the pointer when the points open) you will need to rotate the distributor clockwise; if it is too far retarded (ie: the timing mark is too near the pointer or has gone past it), you will need to rotate the distributor counter-clockwise (photo).

4 The aforementioned procedure is not that recommended by the vehicle manufacturer, although for most practical purposes it can be regarded as perfectly satisfactory. Where there are stringent emission control regulations in force it may be a legal requirement to carry out a dynamic timing check. This will require the use of a stroboscopic timing light, which can be purchased as a proprietary item from any

Fig. 4.13 Using a stroboscopic timing light (Sec. 8)

automobile accessory dealer.

5 For a dynamic timing check, first check that the timing marks on the pulley are clean, then disconnect and plug the vacuum line which goes to the distributor. Connect the timing light to No. 1 spark plug wire and if possible connect an engine speed tachometer to the engine. Start the engine and run it at the specified idle speed, checking for the correct ignition timing as the timing light is shone on to the timing mark on the pulley. If adjustment is required, refer to the procedure given in paragraph 3. Having set the timing at idle speed, increase the speed to 2000 rpm approximately, and note the timing which should now have advanced. Make a note of the engine speed, as it is increased, at which the timing just begins to advance then repeat this check with the vacuum line unplugged and connected to the distributor. A greater amount of advance should be obtained at this second reading, which indicates that the vacuum diaphragm unit is functioning.

6 For dual point distributors, a check of the retard function is also required. To do this, reset the engine to idle speed and check that the timing is now 5° after-top-dead-center (ATDC).

7 Any adjustments to the distributor to obtain the correct dynamic timing will need to be made on a distributor test stand by an automobile engineer specializing in this sort of job. However, before arranging for this, it is best to consider whether the distributor requires major servicing which is most likely after a high mileage has been covered.

8 On completion of any or all of the aforementioned checks and adjustments, ensure that all test gear is disconnected.

9 Spark plugs and HT leads

1 The correct functioning of the spark plugs is vital for the proper running and efficient operation of the engine.

2 At the intervals specified, the plugs should be removed, examined, cleaned, and if worn excessively, renewed. The condition of the spark plug can also tell much about the general condition of the engine.

3 If the insulator nose of the spark plug is clean and white, with no deposits, this is indicative of a weak mixture, or too hot a plug (a hot plug transfers heat away from the electrode slowly - a cold plug transfers heat away quickly).

4 If the insulator nose is covered with hard black looking deposits, then this is indicative that the mixture is too rich. Should the plug be black and oily then it is likely that the engine is fairly worn, as well as the mixture being too rich.

5 If the insulator nose is covered with light tan to greyish brown deposits, then the mixture is correct, and it is likely that the engine is in good condition.

6 If there are any traces of long brown tapering stains on the outside of the white portion of the plug, then the plug will have to be renewed, as this shows that there is a faulty joint between the plug body and the insulator, and compression is being allowed to leak away.

7 Plugs should be cleaned by a sand blasting machine, which will free them from carbon more than by cleaning by hand. The machine will also test the condition of the plugs under compression. Any plug that fails to spark at the recommended pressure should be renewed.

8 The spark plug gap is of considerable importance, as, if it is too large or too small the size of the spark and its efficiency will be seriously impaired. The spark plug gap is given in the Specifications Section.

9 To set it, measure the gap with a feeler gauge, and then bend open, or closed, the outer plug electrode until the correct gap is achieved. The centre electrode should never be bent as this may crack the insulation and cause plug failure, if nothing worse.

10 When installing the plugs, remember to connect the leads from the distributor cap in the correct firing order which is 1, 3, 4, 2, No. 1 cylinder being the one nearest the radiator.

11 The plug leads require no maintenance other than being kept clean and wiped over regularly. The leads used are of the carbon cored type which are used to suppress high frequency radio interference from the ignition system, Although, these leads can give trouble-free performance for many years, they can sometimes cause starting problems after a considerable period of usage. A procedure is given for checking them in Section 11, paragraph 6, but if they are found to be faulty, consideration should be given to replacing them with the copper cored conductor type and using suppressor-type plug caps. Your automobile electrical specialist will be able to help with the supply of approved types.

10 Fault diagnosis - ignition system

There are two general symptoms of ignition faults. Either the engine will not fire, or the engine is difficult to start and misfires. If it is a regular misfire, ie: the engine is only running on two or three cylinders, the fault is almost sure to be in the high tension circuit. If the misfiring is intermittent, the fault could be in either the high or low tension circuits. If the engine stops suddenly, or will not start at all, it is likely that the fault is in the low tension circuit. Loss of power and over-heating, apart from faulty carburetor settings, are normally due to faults in the distributor, or incorrect ignition timing.

Engine fails to start

1 If the engine fails to start and it was running normally when it was last used, first check that there is fuel in the tank. If the engine turns over normally on the starter motor and the battery is evidently well charged, then the fault may be in either the high or low tension circuits. First check the HT circuit. **Note:** If the battery is known to be fully charged, the ignition light comes on, and the starter motor fails to turn the engine, **check the tightness of the leads on the battery terminals** and also the secureness of the ground lead **connection to the body**. It is quite common for the leads to have worked loose, even if they look and feel secure. If one of the battery terminal posts gets very hot when trying to operate the starter motor this is a sure indication of a faulty connection to that terminal. For further information on the battery, refer to Chapter 10.

2 One of the commonest reasons for bad starting is wet or damp spark plug and distributor leads. Remove the distributor cap. If the condensation is visible internally, dry the cap with a rag and also wipe over the leads.

3 If the engine still fails to start, check that voltage is reaching the plugs by disconnecting each plug lead in turn at the spark plug end and holding the end of the cable about 3/16 inch (5 mm) away from the cylinder block. Arrange for an assistant to spin the engine from the ignition switch.

4 Sparking between the end of the cable and the block should be fairly strong with a regular blue spark (hold the lead with a gloved hand or in a dry cloth to prevent electric shocks). If voltage is reaching the spark plugs, remove them and clean and reset them to the specified gaps. The engine should now start.

5 If no voltage is reaching the plugs, disconnect the coil HT lead from the distributor and hold this about 3/16 in. (5 mm) away from the block. Spin the engine as before; a rapid succession of blue sparks between the end of the lead and the block indicates that the coil is in order, and that either the distributor cap is cracked, the carbon brush is stuck or worn, the rotor arm is faulty, the contact points are burnt, pitted or dirty, or the HT leads are at fault.

6 To check the HT leads, an ohmmeter will be required. If a reading in excess of 1000 ohms/inch (394 ohms/cm) is obtained, replacement leads should be obtained.

7 If there are no sparks from the end of the lead from the coil, check the connections of the lead to the coil and distributor, and the lead resistance as described in the previous paragraph. If these are in order, either the ignition coil or low tension circuit is faulty.

8 To check the battery-to-coil voltage, connect a voltmeter between the battery negative terminal and the coil positive terminal. Jumper the coil (distributor) terminal to ground and check the indicated voltage, when the ignition is switched on. This should be 4.5 to 6.9 volts.

9 Now check the voltage drop across the ballast-resistor by connecting the voltmeter between the battery positive terminal and the coil '+' (ignition switch/ballast-resistor) terminal. Leave the jumper lead still connected and switch on the ignition. The voltage should be 4.5 to 6.6 volts.

10 If no voltage is obtained at paragraph 8, the ballast-resistor or its wiring are open-circuit. If no voltage is obtained at paragraph 9, the coil or its wiring are open-circuit. If battery voltage is obtained at paragraph 8, the coil or its wiring are open-circuit. If battery voltage is obtained at paragraph 9, the ballast-resistor or its associated wiring are open-circuit. **Note:** The tests at paragraphs 8 and 9, do not conclusively isolate a fault to the coil or ballast-resistor, since if a failure occurs they will not necessarily fail open-circuit but may just alter their resistance. Before condemning either, it is advisable to check the resistance of each which should be in the order of 1.3 to 1.7 ohms.

11 To check the ignition starting circuit, connect a voltmeter, as described in paragraph 9 with the jumper lead still connected. Crank the engine from the starter and check that the voltage indicated is less than 1 volt. If greater than 1 volt, clean and tighten the connections in the circuit.

12 To check the coil-to-ground voltage, rotate the crankshaft at the pulley until the breaker points are closed. Connect a voltmeter between the battery negative terminal and the coil - (distributor) terminal. Switch on the ignition and check for a voltage of less than 0.25 volts. If the voltage is high, check between the coil and the distributor primary wire; between the distributor primary wire and the moving breaker point; between the moving breaker point and the breaker plate; between the breaker plate and the distributor housing; between the distributor housing and the engine ground. Isolate the source of high voltage and clean/tighten the appropriate connection.

Common spark plug conditions

NORMAL

Symptoms: Brown to grayish-tan color and slight electrode wear. Correct heat range for engine and operating conditions.

Recommendation: When new spark plugs are installed, replace with plugs of the same heat range.

WORN

Symptoms: Rounded electrodes with a small amount of deposits on the firing end. Normal color. Causes hard starting in damp or cold weather and poor fuel economy.

Recommendation: Plugs have been left in the engine too long. Replace with new plugs of the same heat range. Follow the recommended maintenance schedule.

CARBON DEPOSITS

Symptoms: Dry sooty deposits indicate a rich mixture or weak ignition. Causes misfiring, hard starting and hesitation.

Recommendation: Make sure the plug has the correct heat range. Check for a clogged air filter or problem in the fuel system or engine management system. Also check for ignition system problems.

ASH DEPOSITS

Symptoms: Light brown deposits encrusted on the side or center electrodes or both. Derived from oil and/or fuel additives. Excessive amounts may mask the spark, causing misfiring and hesitation during acceleration.

Recommendation: If excessive deposits accumulate over a short time or low mileage, install new valve guide seals to prevent seepage of oil into the combustion chambers. Also try changing gasoline brands.

OIL DEPOSITS

Symptoms: Oily coating caused by poor oil control. Oil is leaking past worn valve guides or piston rings into the combustion chamber. Causes hard starting, misfiring and hesitation.

Recommendation: Correct the mechanical condition with necessary repairs and install new plugs.

GAP BRIDGING

Symptoms: Combustion deposits lodge between the electrodes. Heavy deposits accumulate and bridge the electrode gap. The plug ceases to fire, resulting in a dead cylinder.

Recommendation: Locate the faulty plug and remove the deposits from between the electrodes.

TOO HOT

Symptoms: Blistered, white insulator, eroded electrode and absence of deposits. Results in shortened plug life.

Recommendation: Check for the correct plug heat range, over-advanced ignition timing, lean fuel mixture, intake manifold vacuum leaks, sticking valves and insufficient engine cooling.

PREIGNITION

Symptoms: Melted electrodes. Insulators are white, but may be dirty due to misfiring or flying debris in the combustion chamber. Can lead to engine damage.

Recommendation: Check for the correct plug heat range, over-advanced ignition timing, lean fuel mixture, insufficient engine cooling and lack of lubrication.

HIGH SPEED GLAZING

Symptoms: Insulator has yellowish, glazed appearance. Indicates that combustion chamber temperatures have risen suddenly during hard acceleration. Normal deposits melt to form a conductive coating. Causes misfiring at high speeds.

Recommendation: Install new plugs. Consider using a colder plug if driving habits warrant.

DETONATION

Symptoms: Insulators may be cracked or chipped. Improper gap setting techniques can also result in a fractured insulator tip. Can lead to piston damage.

Recommendation: Make sure the fuel anti-knock values meet engine requirements. Use care when setting the gaps on new plugs. Avoid lugging the engine.

MECHANICAL DAMAGE

Symptoms: May be caused by a foreign object in the combustion chamber or the piston striking an incorrect reach (too long) plug. Causes a dead cylinder and could result in piston damage.

Recommendation: Repair the mechanical damage. Remove the foreign object from the engine and/or install the correct reach plug.

13 In the event of all the aforementioned tests being satisfactory, the fault almost certainly lies in the condenser. This is dealt with in Section 4.

Engine misfires

1 If the engine misfires regularly, run it at a fast idling speed, and short out each of the spark plugs in turn by placing an insulated screwdriver across the plug terminal to the cylinder block.

2 No difference in engine running will be noticed when the plug in the defective cylinder is short circuited. Short circuiting the working plugs will accentuate the misfire.

3 Remove the plug lead from the end of the defective plug and hold it about 3/16 in. (5 mm) away from the block. Restart the engine. If sparking is fairly strong and regular, the fault must lie in the spark plug.

4 The plug may be loose, the insulation may be cracked or the electrodes may have burnt away giving too wide a gap for the spark to jump across. Worse still, the earth electrode may have broken off. Either renew the plug, or clean it, reset the gap and then test it.

5 If there is no spark at the end of the plug lead, or if it is weak and intermittent, check the ignition lead from the distributor to the plug. If the insulation is cracked or damaged, renew the lead. Check the connections at the distributor cap.

6 If there is still no spark, examine the distributor cap carefully for signs of tracking. This can be recognised by a very thin black line running between two or more segments, or between a segment and some other part of the distributor. These lines are paths which now conduct electricity across the cap thus letting it run to ground. The only answer is to fit a new distributor cap.

7 Apart from the ignition timing being incorrect, other causes of misfiring have already been dealt with under the section dealing with failure of the engine to start.

8 If the ignition timing is too far retarded, it should be noted that the engine will tend to overheat, and there will be quite a noticeable drop in power. This is very often accompanied by 'dieseling' (afterburning or running-on after switching off the ignition) and/or backfiring in the exhaust. If the engine is overheating and power is down and the ignition timing is correct, then the carburetor should be checked, as it is likely that this is where the fault lies. See Chapter 3, for details.

Chapter 5 Clutch

Refer to Chapter 13 for Specifications and information applicable to 1974 through 1982 models.

Contents

Clutch linkage - adjustment 5	Clutch release lever and bearing - removal and installation 4
Clutch master cylinder - dismantling and reassembly 7	Clutch - removal and installation 3
Clutch master cylinder - removal and installation 6	Fault diagnosis - clutch 10
Clutch release cylinder - dismantling and reassembly 9	General description 1
Clutch release cylinder - removal and installation 8	Hydraulic clutch system - bleeding 2

Specifications

Type	Single dry plate, diaphragm spring, hydraulically operated
Pressure plate	
Inner diameter	4.96 in. (126 mm)
Outer diameter	7.99 in. (203 mm)
Clutch disc	
Inner diameter	5.12 in. (130 mm)
Outer diameter	7.87 in. (200 mm)
Plate thickness	0.138 in. (3.5 mm)
Lateral runout (maximum):	
New disc	0.028 in. (0.7 mm)
Limit	0.039 in. (1 mm)
Release fork free-play	0.12 ro 0.13 in. (3 to 3.5 mm)
Clutch pedal free-play	0.8 to 1.2 in. (20 to 30 mm)
Master cylinder bore	0.75 in. (19.05 mm)
Clearance, piston to master cylinder bore	
New	0.0016 to 0.0049 in. (0.04 to 0.125 mm)
Wear limit	0.006 in. (0.15 mm)
Release cylinder bore	0.6875 in. (17.46 mm)
Clearance, piston to release cylinder bore	
New	0.0013 to 0.004 in. (0.032 to 0.102 mm)
Wear limit	0.006 in. (0.15 mm)
Clutch fluid specification	SAE J1703, ESA-MC625-A, or MVSS 116, DOT-3 or DOT-4

Torque wrench settings	lbf ft	kg fm
Clutch cover to flywheel	13 to 20	1.8 to 2.7
Clutch housing to engine	24 to 41	3.3 to 5.7
Release lever return spring bracket	5 to 7.5	0.7 to 1.0
Release cylinder nut	11.5 to 17	1.6 to 2.35
Release lever pivot pin	23 to 34	3.2 to 4.7

1 General description

1 The clutch fitted to all vehicles is a single dry disc (plate) type. The assembly comprises the disc assembly, clutch cover and pressure plate assembly, and the release mechanism.

2 The clutch housing also acts as the transmission input shaft bearing retainer; it contains the input shaft bearing oil seal and a selective fit thrust washer for controlling input shaft endplay.

3 A hydraulic operating mechanism is used. This comprises a dash-mounted master cylinder and a clutch release (slave) cylinder mounted on the flywheel housing. Clutch engagement is controlled by a one-way valve mounted on the master cylinder, this controls the flow of return fluid when the clutch pedal pressure is released.

2 Hydraulic clutch system - bleeding

1 In the event of failure of any of the seals in the hydraulic system, or where part of the system has been disconnected, air will enter and need to be bled off as with the braking system.

2 To prepare for the operation, a clean jar, a short length of flexible

tubing, a new supply of the recommended fluid and the services of an assistant will be required. Ensure that the master cylinder reservoir is topped-up to the full mark, and put about 1 in. (2.5 cm) of fluid in the jar (photo).

3   Remove the cap from the release cylinder bleed valve and install the flexible tube to the valve. Put the other end of the tube into the fluid in the jar.

4   With the assistant inside the vehicle, slacken the bleed valve then get the assistant to depress the clutch pedal fully and hold it down. Tighten the bleed valve.

5   The pedal can now be released, the bleed valve loosened again and the procedure repeated until no more air is expelled for each depression of the pedal. During the operation it is essential that the reservoir level is repeatedly topped-up to prevent air from entering, and that the end of the tube is kept submerged in the fluid.

6   Remove the tube on completion and install the bleed valve cap. Discard all the old fluid; it is false economy to try to use it again since it will probably be contaminated with moisture and dirt.

7   Finally check the operation of the clutch during a test drive. If necessary, adjust the linkage as described in Section 5.

3   Clutch - removal and installation

1   In order to remove the clutch, it will be necessary to first remove the transmission, as described in Chapter 6.

2   It will probably be helpful to lock the flywheel whilst the clutch cover bolts are removed. This can usually be done by installing one of the clutch housing bolts and fabricating a small bracket or clip to engage the starter ring teeth and wrap round the bolt.

3   Remove the two pilot bolts and four standard bolts securing the clutch cover to the flywheel. Remove the clutch cover and disc. Mark the relative position of the clutch cover (if it is to be used again), the flywheel and the pilot bolts, to ensure that they are eventually installed correctly. (Note that two opposite holes in the cover are reamed to take the pilot bolts).

4   Inspect the diaphragm spring and clutch cover for wear and damage. Inspect the surface of the pressure plate for warping, burning, scores and ridges. Although it may be possible for a suitably equipped repair shop to regrind the pressure plate surface, this is not really recommended. Great care has to be taken to maintain squareness and flatness, and no more than a few thousandths of an inch can be removed. Generally speaking, if the surface is scored the whole assembly should be renewed. Any grease marks on the pressure plate or the flywheel can be removed, using a lint-free cloth or tissues dampened with a suitable grease solvent. On no account must the pressure plate and cover assembly be immersed. If scoring of the flywheel face is evident, this must be removed by skimming and is a job for an engineering workshop. Where a flywheel face is unmarked but polished, rubbing with very fine emery cloth using circular movements is beneficial. If the flywheel is to be machined, it must first be removed, as described in Chapter 1. If the clutch disc is worn below the permissible limit, is warped, or is contaminated with oil, it must be renewed; similarly if there are loose facings, loose rivets, broken springs or distortion exists a new disc must be obtained. Where there is evidence of oil or grease contamination, this must be rectified before reassembly with new parts begins. Ensure that the clutch disc slides freely on the transmission input shaft and that the pilot bearing in the flywheel is not loose or rough-running (bearing replacement is dealt with in Chapter 1).

5   Position the clutch disc to the flywheel taking care not to touch the friction faces with the hands and ensuring that the shorter splined boss

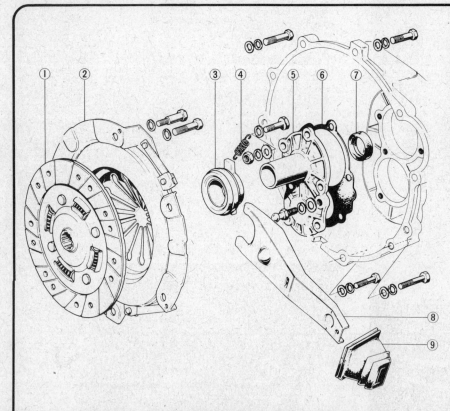

2.2 Clutch (right) and brake (left) master cylinder reservoirs (typical)

Fig. 5.1 The component parts of the clutch (typical) (Sec. 1)

1 Clutch disc	3 Release bearing	7 Oil seal
2 Clutch cover and	4 Spring	8 Release lever
pressure plate	5 Front cover	9 Dust cover
assembly	6 Gasket	

Note: In some cases the spring (4) is not used. The alternative type is shown in photo 4.3 and Fig. 5.4.

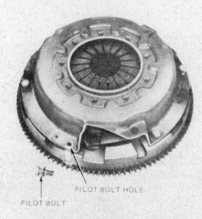

PILOT BOLT HOLE

PILOT BOLT

Fig. 5.2 Marking the clutch pilot bolt holes (Sec. 3)

is towards the flywheel.

6   Position the clutch cover to the flywheel and loosely install the two pilot bolts. The disc must now be centralized on the flywheel and this is most conveniently done by using the transmission input shaft (if the transmission is dismantled) as an alignment tool. Alternatively, a suitable round wooden or steel shaft can be utilized (photo).

Fig. 5.3 Checking the clutch disc for warping (Sec. 3)

7   When the disc has been centralized, install the four remaining bolts and tighten all the bolts to the specified torque. This tightening must be done evenly and in a crosswise order to prevent distortion of the cover.
8   Lightly lubricate the face of the release bearing, the release lever contact area of the release bearing hub and the input shaft bearing retainer, using a general purpose grease.
9   Check that the release bearing and lever move freely, then install the transmission, as described in Chapter 6.

4   Clutch release lever and bearing - removal and installation

1   Remove the transmission, as described in Chapter 6.
2   The clutch release lever is retained on the ball pivot by a spring clip; the lever is removed by simply pulling it off (photos).
3   With the lever removed, the release bearing can be removed from the retaining clip on lever fork-end. If necessary, remove the boot from the aperture in the bellhousing wall (photo).
4   Wipe all the oil and grease from the release bearing but under no circumstances use any cleaning solvents. Light scoring of the release bearing can be dressed out using fine emery cloth, but where scoring is heavy or where there is evidence of any other damage the bearing must be renewed. Where bearing damage has occurred, inspect the input shaft bearing retainer for evidence of scoring. Hold the release bearing inner race and rotate the outer race while applying pressure to it; if there is

3.6 Centralizing the clutch using the transmission input shaft

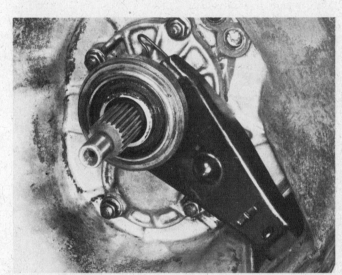

4.2a The clutch release lever

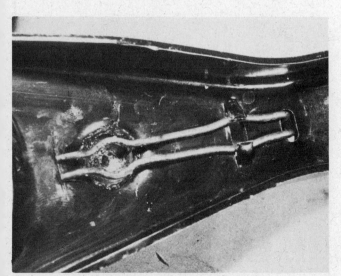

4.2b The clutch release lever spring retaining clip

4.3 The release bearing retaining clip (later type)

5

roughness or noise, a replacement bearing must be used. Where bearing failure has occurred, this may have resulted from incorrect linkage adjustment, or from a damaged or misaligned release lever. Therefore, these points must be checked.

5   When reassembling the clutch, apply a thin film of general purpose grease to the input shaft bearing retainer portion of the clutch housing, to the release lever pivot bolt and to the fork ends of the release lever where they run in the bearing hub.

6   Install the release bearing on the lever, then snap the lever onto the pivot bolt. Also install the release lever boot.

7   Apply a thin film of general purpose grease to the face of the release bearing and check that the bearing hub slides freely on the input shaft bearing retainer.

8   On completion, install the transmission as described in Chapter 6.

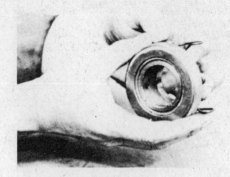

Fig. 5.4 Checking the release bearing for wear (Sec. 4)

5   Clutch linkage - adjustment

1   In order to ensure smooth clutch operation and the maximum

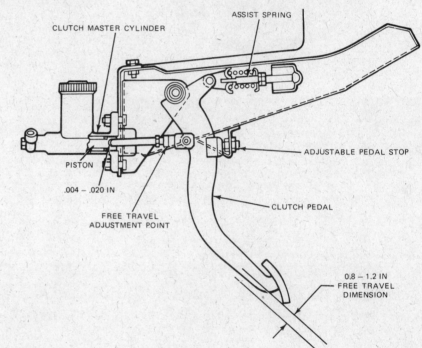

Fig. 5.5 Clutch pedal adjustment (Sec. 5)

CLUTCH MASTER CYLINDER

ASSIST SPRING

ADJUSTABLE PEDAL STOP

PISTON

.004 – .020 IN

FREE TRAVEL ADJUSTMENT POINT

CLUTCH PEDAL

0.8 – 1.2 IN FREE TRAVEL DIMENSION

useful life of the clutch components, it is essential that the linkage is correctly adjusted. Adjustment is taken up at two points, these being the pedal and the release lever.

Pedal adjustment
2   The clutch pedal free-travel is set by loosening the locknut on the pushrod and rotating the rod as necessary, to obtain the specified dimension at the pedal pad. After adjustment has been set, ensure that the locknut is tight.

Release lever adjustment
3   Apply the parking brake and raise the vehicle to obtain access to the clutch release cylinder.

4   Disconnect the release lever return spring at the lever end (photo).

5   Pull back the rubber boot, then loosen the locknut and rotate the adjusting nut to obtain the specified clearance between the bullet-nosed end of the adjusting nut and the release lever.

6   On completion, tighten the locknut and ensure that the boot is moved back to cover the locknut.

6   Clutch master cylinder - removal and installation

1   Disconnect the hydraulic line at the outlet fitting on the master cylinder one-way valve.

2   Remove the nuts and washers from the two master cylinder

5.4 The release lever return spring

mounting bolts and pull the cylinder away from the firewall.

3   When installing, insert the pedal pushrod into the master cylinder piston as the cylinder is positioned onto the firewall.

4   Install and tighten the securing nuts and bolts.

5   Connect the hydraulic line to the outlet fitting on the one-way valve.

6   Bleed the hydraulic system, as described in Section 2, then adjust the linkage, if necessary, as described in Section 5.

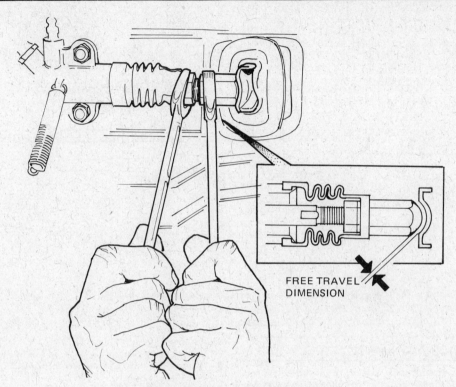

Fig. 5.6 Clutch release lever adjustment (Sec. 5)

FREE TRAVEL DIMENSION

5

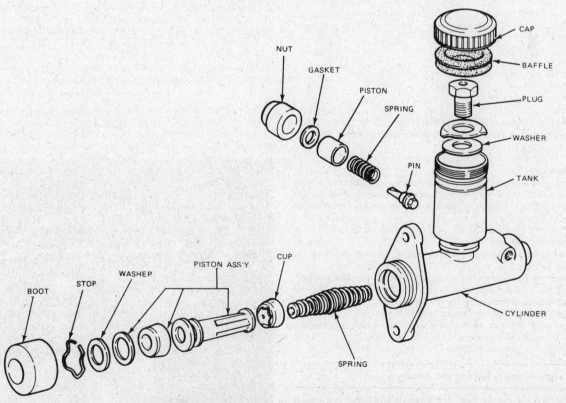

Fig. 5.7 Exploded view of the clutch master cylinder (Sec. 7)

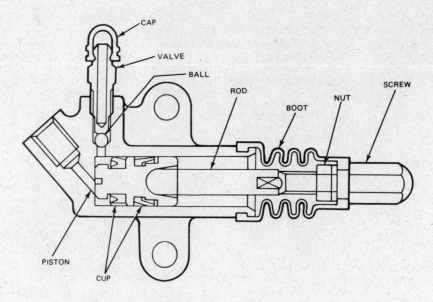

Fig. 5.8 Sectional view of the clutch release cylinder (Sec. 9)

7 Clutch master cylinder - dismantling and reassembly

1 The clutch master cylinder does not normally require attention, and when dismantled it is recommended that all the rubber parts are renewed. It is therefore a good policy to obtain a repair kit which will contain the necessary parts, prior to starting the job.

2 Having removed the master cylinder from the vehicle, clean the outside using a lint-free cloth and drain off the brake fluid. Do not attempt to clean the master cylinder or any of its component parts with gasoline (petrol), kerosene (paraffin) or cleaning solvents. It is generally adequate to use new brake fluid for cleaning purposes but isopropyl alcohol or methylated spirits are also suitable.

3 Remove the dust boot from the pushrod end of the cylinder.

4 Carefully remove the stop-ring using a small screwdriver and take out the stop washer beneath it.

5 Remove the piston, piston cup and the return spring from the cylinder bore.

6 Carefully remove and dismantle the component parts of the one-way valve.

7 Clean all the component parts (see paragraph 2) but discard the rubber cups. Examine the bore for wear, scoring and roughness; check the clearance of the piston in the bore and reject any parts which are unsatisfactory. Ensure that the cylinder compensating port is not blocked and check the parts of the one-way valve for freedom of operation.

8 When reassembling, dip the internal parts of the master cylinder in clean, new, brake fluid.

9 Insert the return spring into the cylinder bore.

10 Install the primary cup with its flat side towards the piston.

11 Fit the secondary cup onto the piston then insert the cup and piston into the cylinder bore.

12 Install the stop washer followed by the stop-ring.

13 Assemble and install the one-way valve to the master cylinder.

14 Fill the reservoir with clean, new, brake fluid and operate the piston with a screwdriver until fluid is ejected from the outlet.

15 Install the dust boot and wipe off any spilled fluid from the outside of the cylinder.

8 Clutch release cylinder - removal and installation

1 Disconnect the hydraulic line from the release cylinder and plug the end to prevent fluid spillage.

2 Unhook the return spring from the release lever.

3 Remove the nuts and washers securing the release cylinder to the clutch housing; remove the cylinder.

4 When installing, position the release cylinder to the clutch housing studs. Install and tighten the nuts and washers.

5 Connect the hydraulic line to the release cylinder.

6 Top-up the master cylinder fluid level. Bleed the system as described in Section 2 and, if necessary, adjust the release lever as described in Section 5. Do not forget to install the release lever return spring.

9 Clutch release cylinder - dismantling and reassembly

1 The clutch release cylinder does not normally require attention, and when dismantled it is recommended that all the rubber parts are renewed. It is therefore a good policy to obtain a repair kit which will contain all the necessary parts prior to starting the job.

2 Having removed the release cylinder from the vehicle, clean the outside using a lint-free cloth. Do not attempt to clean the release cylinder or any of its component parts with gasoline (petrol), kerosene (paraffin) or cleaning solvents. It is generally adequate to use new brake fluid for cleaning purposes but isopropyl alcohol or methylated spirits are also suitable.

3 Remove the dust boot from the cylinder and take out the release rod.

4 Remove the piston by tapping the release rod end of the cylinder sharply on a hard wooden surface. Alternatively, clean compressed air applied at the inlet connection can be used.

5 Unscrew the bleed valve and take out the ball.

6 Clean all the component parts (see paragraph 2) but discard the rubber cups. Examine the bore for wear, scoring and roughness; check the clearance of the piston in the bore and reject any parts which are unsatisfactory. Check that the bleed valve and inlet bores are clear, and that the bleed valve ball is in good condition.

7 When reassembling, dip the internal parts of the release cylinder in clean, new, brake fluid.

8 Assemble the cups to the piston as shown in Fig. 5.8; install the piston, smaller diameter first.

9 Install the release rod and the boot.

10 Install the bleed valve ball followed by the valve and cap.

10 Fault diagnosis - clutch

Symptom	Reason/s	Remedy
Judder when taking up drive	Loose engine/transmission mountings or over flexible mountings	Check and tighten all mounting bolts and replace any 'soft' or broken mountings.
	Badly worn friction surfaces or friction plate contaminated with oil deposits	Remove and replace clutch parts as required. Rectify any oil leakage points which may have caused contamination.
	Worn splines in the friction plate hub or on the transmission input shaft, or damaged plate	Renew friction plate and/or input shaft.
	Badly worn flywheel	Renew bearing.
	Worn or loose input shaft	Examine and rectify.
Clutch drag (or failure to disengage) so that gears cannot be meshed	Clutch clearance too great	Adjust linkage.
	Clutch friction disc sticking because of rust on splines (usually apparent after standing idle for some length of time)	As a temporary remedy engage top gear, apply parking brake, depress clutch and start engine. (If very badly stuck, engine will not turn). When running, rev up engine and slip clutch until disengagement is normally possible. Renew friction plate at earliest opportunity.
	Damaged or misaligned pressure plate assembly	Replace pressure plate assembly.
Clutch slip - (increase in engine speed; does not result in increase in car speed - especially on hills)	Clutch clearance too small resulting in partially disengaged clutch at all times	Adjust linkage.
	Clutch friction surfaces worn out (beyond further adjustment). Clutch surfaces oil soaked	Replace friction plate and remedy source of oil leakage.

5

Chapter 6 Part I: Manual gearbox

Refer to Chapter 13 for Specifications and information applicable to 1974 through 1982 models.

Contents

Clutch housing - dismantling and reassembly 10
Countershaft (layshaft) - dismantling and reassembly 6
Extension housing - dismantling and reassembly 8
Extension housing rear bushing - removal and installation ... 14
Extension housing rear seal - removal and installation ... 13
Fault diagnosis - manual gearbox 15
General description 1
Input shaft - dismantling and reassembly 4

Output shaft - dismantling and reassembly 5
Shift rails - dismantling and reassembly 7
Shift tower and lever - dismantling and reassembly 9
Transmission - cleaning and inspection 11
Transmission - dismantling 3
Transmission - reassembly 12
Transmission - removal and installation 2

Specifications

Transmission type	4-forward and 1-reverse gear, with synchromesh on all forward gears

Gear ratios

1st	4.024 : 1
2nd	2.399 : 1
3rd	1.507 : 1
4th	1.000 : 1
Reverse	4.024 : 1

Lubricant capacity (approximately) ... ... 3.0 US pints (2.5 Imp. pints/1.43 liters)

Lubricant type ... ... SAE 90EP

Input shaft endplay (transmission partly assembled - clutch housing in place)* ... ... 0 to 0.004 in (0 to 0.1 mm)

Output shaft assembly (measured between reverse gear and thrust washer)* ... ... 0 to 0.004 in (0 to 0.1 mm)

Third gear synchronizer insert (key) to synchronizer ring slot* ... ... 0.030 to 0.080 in (0.76 to 2.03 mm)

Four gear shift rail travel* ... ... 0 to 0.028 in (0 to 0.71 mm)

*The above tolerances are controlled by the use of selective thrust washers and snap-rings (circlips)

Synchronizer ring to conical face of gear ... ... 0.032 to 0.060 in (0.8 to 1.5 mm)

Output shaft run-out ... ... 0.0012 in (0.03 mm)

Output shaft to gear bushing ... ... 0.001 to 0.003 in (0.025 to 0.076 mm)

Reverse idler shaft to gear bushing ... ... 0.0009 to 0.0023 in (0.023 to 0.058 mm)

Torque wrench settings	lb f ft	kg f m
Clutch release lever return spring bracket bolt	5 to 7½	0.7 to 1.0
Exhaust pipe bracket to case bolt	11½ to 17	1.6 to 2.35
Shift fork lock bolt	5½ to 9	0.76 to 1.24
Shift lever retainer to shift tower bolt	5 to 7½	0.7 to 1.0
Shift tower to extension housing bolt	11½ to 17	1.6 to 2.35
Speedometer drive attaching bolt	5 to 7½	0.7 to 1.0
Shift control lever end to shaft bolt	20 to 25	2.77 to 3.45
Transmission mount to crossmember bolt and nut	23 to 34	3.2 to 4.7
Shift rail detent spring cap	28½ to 40	3.9 to 5.5
Friction piece spring cap	28½ to 40	3.9 to 5.5
Selector lock spindle detent spring cap	28½ to 40	3.9 to 5.5
Clutch release lever cylinder attaching nut	11½ to 17	1.6 to 2.35
Case assembly stud nut	23 to 34	3.2 to 4.7

Torque wrench settings (continued)	lb f ft	kg fm
Case assembly bolt nut	11½ to 17	1.6 to 2.35
Extension housing to case stud nut	23 to 24	3.2 to 4.7
Clutch housing to case stud nut	40½ to 59½	5.6 to 8.2
Transmission mount to case nut	11½ to 17	1.6 to 2.35
Crossmember to frame nut	23 to 34	3.2 to 4.7
Exhaust bracket to engine nut	8½ to 13	1.2 to 1.8
Pivot, clutch release lever pin	23 to 34	3.2 to 4.7
Interlock pin bore plug	7 to 10½	0.97 to 1.5
Drain plug	15 to 23½	2.1 to 3.2
Filler plug	25 to 36½	3.45 to 5
Reverse idler shaft setscrew	6½ to 10½	0.9 to 1.5
Back-up lamp switch	18 to 25½	2.5 to 3.5

1   General description

1   The Ford Courier is supplied with a 4-speed manual transmission as standard equipment. This transmission has synchromesh on all forward gears, with a selective sliding mesh type reverse gear. The transmission shift lever is centrally located on the cab floor.
2   All forward gears are helically cut which ensures quiet running; the reverse gear and reverse idler gear are spur (straight) cut.
3   The transmission case is of an aluminium alloy construction. It is manufactured in two longitudinal halves, with detachable extension and clutch housings.
4   The floor shift control lever and mechanism are built into the extension housing.

2   Transmission - removal and installation

1   Disconnect the battery ground lead and position the gearshift lever in neutral.
2   Lift up the rubber boot covering the shift lever floor opening and remove the four capscrews, lockwashers and flat washers retaining the gearshift tower.
3   Remove the shift lever, tower and gasket (complete with the two boots), as an assembly from the transmission extension.

4   Cover the opening in the extension with a lint-free cloth or similar to prevent dirt entering.
5   Raise the vehicle or place it over an inspection pit.
6   Disconnect and remove the propeller shaft (refer to Chapter 7 if necessary). Plug the transmission to prevent leakage (or alternatively drain the transmission if no suitable plug can be found).
7   Remove the exhaust pipe to transmission attaching bolts.
8   Remove the nut and bolt attaching the exhaust pipe hanger to the clutch housing.
9   Disconnect and remove the exhaust inlet pipe (refer to Chapter 3, if necessary).
10 Unhook the clutch release lever return spring then remove the release cylinder and secure it to one side.
11 Remove the speedometer cable from the extension (photo).
12 Disconnect the back-up switch wires and starter motor connections. If there is any possibility of them being mixed up, suitably label them.
13 Place a jack, with a wooden block on the jack head, beneath the oil pan.
14 Remove the starter motor from the engine.
15 Remove the bolts, lockwashers and flat washers securing the engine rear plate to the transmission. Position a jack beneath the transmission with a wooden block on the jack head.
16 Remove the nuts and bolts which secure the transmission mound to the crossmember (see Chapter 1, Section 7).
17 Remove the crossmember from the chassis frame side rails (2 nuts

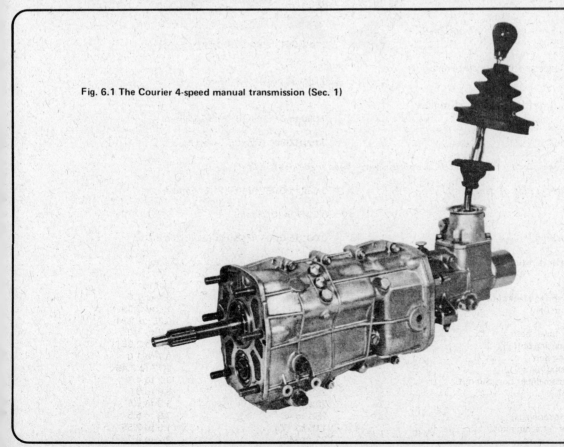

Fig. 6.1 The Courier 4-speed manual transmission (Sec. 1)

6A

2.11 Remove the speedometer drive cable

and washers).

18 Lower the engine support jack, then ease the transmission rearwards off the locating dowels until the input shaft clears the clutch disc. Do not allow the transmission weight to be taken on the input shaft or permanent damage to the shaft may occur.

19 Remove the transmission away from the vehicle to a suitable workbench or storage area.

20 When installing, first ensure that the mating surfaces and locating dowels are free from dirt, paint, machining, burrs etc., which would prevent easy assembly.

21 Mount the transmission on a suitable jack or supports beneath the vehicle.

22 Start the input shaft into the clutch disc, aligning the splines, and move the transmission forward to locate it on the engine rear plate dowels.

23 Install the bolts, flat washers and lockwashers and tighten them to the specified torque.

24 Remove the transmission jack then install the starter motor.

25 Raise the engine and install the rear crossmember. Tighten the nuts to the specified torque.

26 Install the bolts, nuts and washers attaching the transmission mount to the rear crossmember. Tighten the nuts to the specified torque and remove the engine jack.

27 Install the propeller shaft (refer to Chapter 7, if necessary).

28 Install the exhaust inlet pipe.

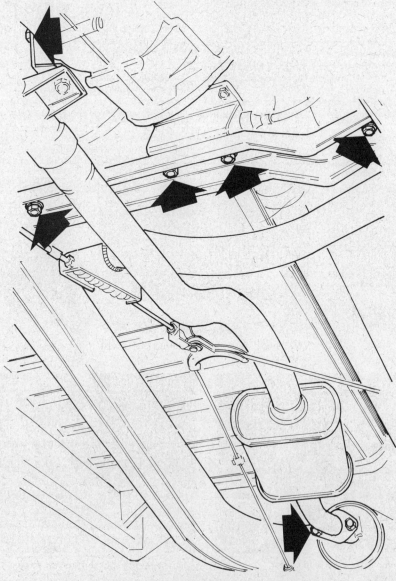

Fig. 6.2 Disconnection points for the transmission (Sec. 2)

29 Connect the back-up lamp switch and starter motor wires.

30 Install the clutch release cylinder, adjust the clutch and install the retracting spring. These operations are described in Chapter 5.

31 Install the speedometer cable then top-up the transmission oil. Lower the vehicle to the ground.

32 Position the shift tower and gasket to the extension housing, ensuring that the shift lever seats in the shift control rod. Install and tighten the capscrews to the specified torque.

33 Install the rubber boot over the floor opening.

34 Reconnect the battery ground lead.

3 Transmission - dismantling

1 Having removed the transmission from the vehicle, remove the clutch release bearing return spring then slide the bearing off the input shaft bearing retainer in the clutch housing.

2 Remove the release lever and boot from the clutch housing.

3 Remove the bolts, washers and lockwashers attaching the clutch housing to the transmission case.

4 Remove the clutch housing, gasket and input shaft bearing thrust washer (photo).

5 Place the transmission on its left-hand side.

6 Remove the nuts, washers and lockwashers which retain the extension housing.

7 With neutral gear position still selected, press the lever to the left or downwards as far as it will go and slide the extension housing away from the transmission case.

8 Remove the nuts, bolts, washers and lockwashers which connect the two halves of the case, then lift the right half off the left half (photos).

9 Lift out the countershaft (layshaft) and gear assembly (photo).

10 Remove the input and output shaft as an assembly, rolling it out from the shift forks (photo).

11 Separate the input shaft from the output shaft, but do not lose the bearing (photo).

12 If necessary, the reverse idler gear can be removed by pushing the center (3rd/4th speed) shift rail forwards as far as it will go. This will provide clearance for the reverse shift fork to be rotated as the idler

3.4 Removal of the clutch housing

3.8a Separating the two halves of the transmission

3.8b Separating the two halves of the transmission

3.9 Lift out the countershaft

3.10 Remove the input and output shafts as an assembly

3.11 Separate the input shaft from the output shaft

6A

3.12 Remove the reverse idler gear

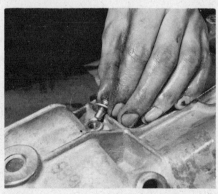
3.13 The reverse idler shift rod set screw

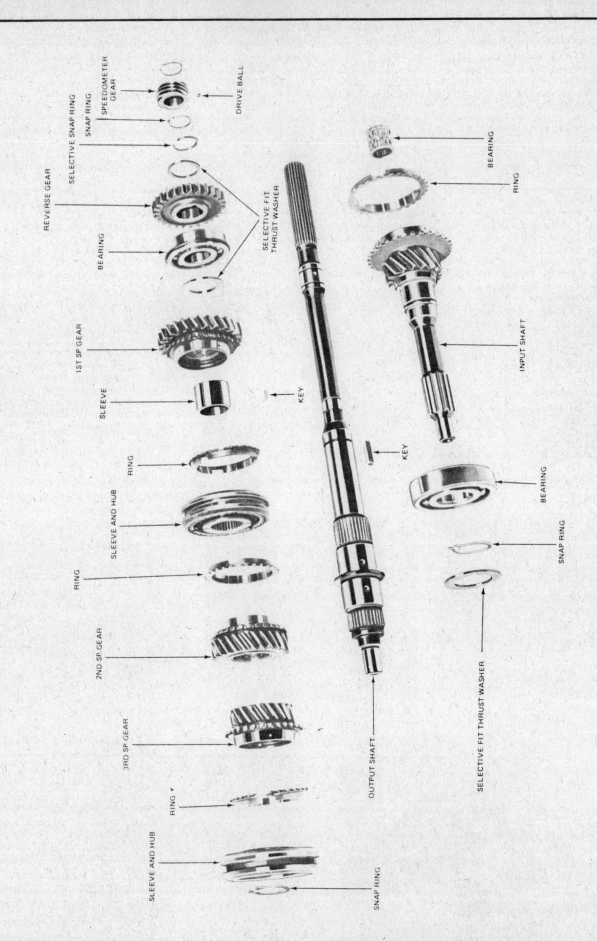

SPEEDOMETER GEAR

SNAP RING

SELECTIVE SNAP RING

REVERSE GEAR

BEARING

DRIVE BALL

SELECTIVE FIT THRUST WASHER

1ST SP GEAR

SLEEVE

KEY

BEARING

RING

INPUT SHAFT

RING

SLEEVE AND HUB

RING

KEY

BEARING

2ND SP. GEAR

SNAP RING

3RD SP GEAR

SELECTIVE FIT THRUST WASHER

RING

OUTPUT SHAFT

SLEEVE AND HUB

SNAP RING

Fig. 6.3 The component parts of the input and output shafts (Secs. 4 and 5)

gear is withdrawn. Remove the idler gear (photo).

13 If necessary, remove the setscrew on the outside of the case to permit the idler shift rod to be pushed out of the case (photo).

14 The transmission is now dismantled into its major sub-assemblies which can now be further dismantled, as described in the following Sections. At all times take care to protect any sub-assemblies which are not to be dismantled, or have been dismantled and reassembled, from dirt and contamination.

4 Input shaft - dismantling and reassembly

1 Remove the needle roller bearing from inside the counterbore of the input shaft.

2 Remove the thrust washer and snap-ring (circlip) from the groove adjacent to the bearing.

3 Support the bearing on a suitable plate, input end uppermost, and press down on the shaft to push it out of the bearing. Take care that loads are not applied to the bearing outer race (as might happen if the bearing was pulled off the shaft using an extractor).

4 Refer to Section 11, which gives information on inspection of the transmission parts.

5 When assembling the shaft, press or drive the bearing into position, applying load to the inner race only, then install the snap-ring in the input shaft groove.

6 Install the needle roller bearing into the input shaft counterbore.

5 Output shaft - dismantling and reassembly

1 Remove the snap-ring (circlip) at the forward end of the shaft (photo).

2 Slide off the 3rd/4th speed synchronizer, synchronizer ring and 3rd gear. (The part number on the synchronizer hub should face rearwards; mark it for identification purposes if no part number is present (photo).

3 Remove the speedometer gear snap-ring, then slide off the speedometer gear and ball. Remove the second snap-ring (photos).

4 Remove the selective snap-ring and thrust washer which retain the reverse gear, bearing, 1st gear, sleeve, 1st/2nd synchronizer hub and 2nd gear on the shaft. Slide the parts off the shaft, noting that the oil groove of the hub faces forwards (photos).

5 Refer to Section 11, which gives information on inspection of the transmission parts.

6 When assembling the shaft, assemble the 3rd gear and synchronizer ring on the front end, along with the 3rd/4th speed synchronizer. Ensure that the appropriate marking is rearwards (see paragraph 2).

7 Install the snap-ring to retain these parts.

8 Slide the 2nd gear and synchronizer ring onto the rear of the shaft.

9 Install the 1st/2nd speed synchronizer and ring onto the shaft, oil groove facing forwards.

10 Install the 1st speed synchronizer ring, 1st gear and sleeve, thrust washer, bearing and reverse gear onto the shaft.

11 Install the original selective fit thrust washer and snap-ring onto the shaft and check the clearance between the rear face of the reverse gear and the thrust washer (photo).

12 Use a thrust washer/snap-ring combination to obtain the specified clearance.

13 Install the speedometer gear snap-ring, speedometer ball and gear, and the outer snap-ring.

Fig. 6.4 Removing the input shaft bearing (Secs 4 and 6)

Fig. 6.5 Installing the input shaft bearing (Sec. 4)

6A

5.1 Remove the snap ring at the forward end of the shaft

5.2 Slide off the 3rd/4th speed synchronizer, synchronizer ring and 3rd gear

5.3a Remove the speedometer gear snap ring

5.3b Slide off the gear and ball

5.4a Remove the snap ring ...

5.4b ... thrust washer ...

5.4c ... reverse gear ...

5.4d ... bearing ...

5.4e ... and associated parts

5.11 Checking the clearance after assembling the shaft

6.1 Remove the countershaft snap ring ...

6.2 ... and remove the reverse gear and roller bearing

6 Countershaft (layshaft) - dismantling and reassembly

1   Remove the snap-ring on the rear end of the shaft (photo).
2   Slide off the reverse gear and roller bearing (photo).
3   If it is necessary to remove the sleeve a knife edge should be inserted between the sleeve and the gear face so that it can be carefully pryed away. Take care not to damage the gear. Once it has moved about 1/16 inch (1.5 mm) the method adopted for the input shaft bearing can be used (see Fig. 6.4).
4   To remove the bearing at the front end of the shaft, remove the snap-ring then press the bearing off the shaft, as described in Section 4 for the input shaft (see Fig. 6.4).
5   Refer to Section 11, which gives information on inspection of the transmission parts.
6   When assembling the countershaft, first install the sleeve (if removed during dismantling).
7   Assemble the roller bearing and reverse gear to the shaft, then install the snap-ring.
8   Press or drive the ball bearing onto the front of the shaft, applying load to the inner race only, then install the snap-ring.

7 Shift rails - dismantling and reassembly

Note: When removing detent caps, springs, shims, balls and associated parts, ensure that they are suitably identified so that they can eventually be re-installed in their original positions.
1   Remove the spring caps, one at a time, and shake out the spring, ball and shim (adjusting plate), (if applicable) (photo).
2   Remove the interlock bore plug and shake out the interlock pins.
3   Remove the shift fork attaching screws then take the shift forks out of the case (photo).
4   Refer to Section 11, which gives information on inspection of the transmission parts.
5   Position the shift fork in the case, then slide in the 1st/2nd speed shift rail.
6   The next step is fairly tricky in that the interlock pins and remaining shift rails have to be inserted. This is best achieved by applying a small amount of grease to one of the pins so that it can be 'stuck' to a small rod or screwdriver shaft, and inserted through the bore in the case until it bottoms against the 1st/2nd speed shift rail (photo).

COUNTERSHAFT GEAR

REVERSE GEAR

SLEEVE

SNAP RING

BEARING

BEARING

Fig. 6.6 The component parts of the countershaft (Sec. 6)

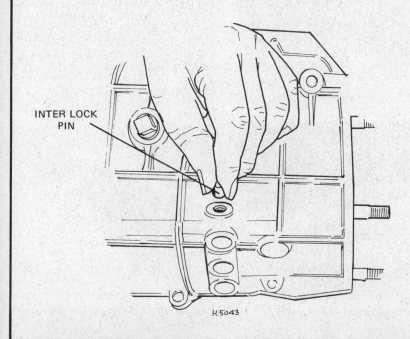

INTER LOCK PIN

H.5043

Fig. 6.7 An interlock pin, showing its location (Sec. 7)

7.1 Remove the spring caps

7.3 Slide out the shift forks after removing the attaching screws

7.6 Installing a interlock pin

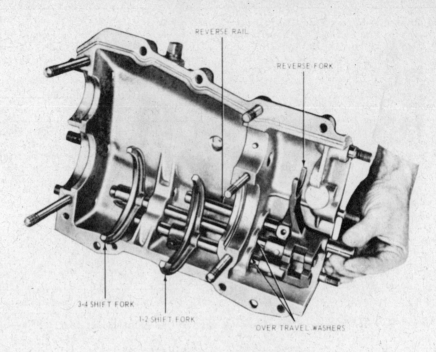

Fig. 6.8 Installing the reverse shift rail (Sec. 7)

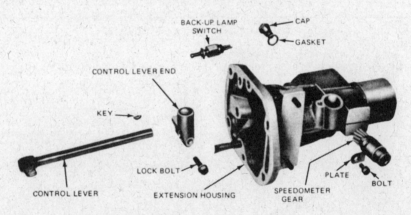

Fig. 6.9 Component parts of the extension housing (Sec. 8)

7.11 Install the spring caps

8.1 Remove the speedometer drive gear

7 Now position the 3rd/4th fork in the case and slide the shift rail (and over-travel washer, if required - see Section 12), into the case and fork. Slightly rotating movement of the shift rail may be necessary during this step.

8 Insert the second interlock pin, following the same method as was used for the first (paragraph 6). The reverse shift rail and fork can now be installed, followed by the final interlock pin.

9 Install and torque tighten the interlock bore plug.

10 Align the shift forks on the rails then install and torque tighten the attaching lock bolts.

11 Position the case open side downwards and install each detent assembly into its correct bore. Tighten the caps to the specified torque (photo).

12 Lubricate the shift forks and rails using SAE 90 EP transmission oil.

8 Extension housing - dismantling and reassembly

1 Place the assembly onto its right-hand side and remove the speedometer gear, back-up light switch, and the spring loaded friction piece (photo).

2 Place the housing in an upright position, then remove the lockbolt holding the cupped control lever end fitting to the lever.

3 Remove the lever end from the rod and slide the rod out of the housing. The key can now be removed.

4 Refer to Section 11, which gives information on inspection of the transmission parts.

5 When reassembling, position the key and slide the control lever rod into the housing.

6 Install the lever end and lockbolt. Tighten the bolt to the specified

torque.

7 Install the friction piece, speedometer gear and back-up light switch. Lubricate the speedometer gear housing seal with SAE 90 EP transmission oil before installation. Tighten the parts to the specified torque.

9 Shift tower and lever - dismantling and reassembly

1 Remove the three bolts, washers and lockwashers attaching the shift lever to the tower. Remove the lever and associated parts.

2 Remove the detent spring cap, spring and ball from the tower so that the selector lock lever and spring can be removed.

3 If the shift lever was excessively loose in its socket, select a thicker shim when reassembling, and use a new wave-washer.

4 Position the selector lock spindle and spring in the shift tower. While applying upward pressure on the spindle to locate the spindle positioning notch, install the detent ball, spring and cap.

5 Check that the ball is in the notch in the spindle then tighten the spring cap to the specified torque.

6 Assemble the lever to the tower.

10 Clutch housing - dismantling and reassembly

1 If the clutch housing is to be replaced by a new one, remove the appropriate parts (refer to Chapter 5).

2 If the housing is not being replaced by a new one, remove the input shaft bearing seal (Fig. 6.11).

3 As applicable, install the items to the clutch housing.

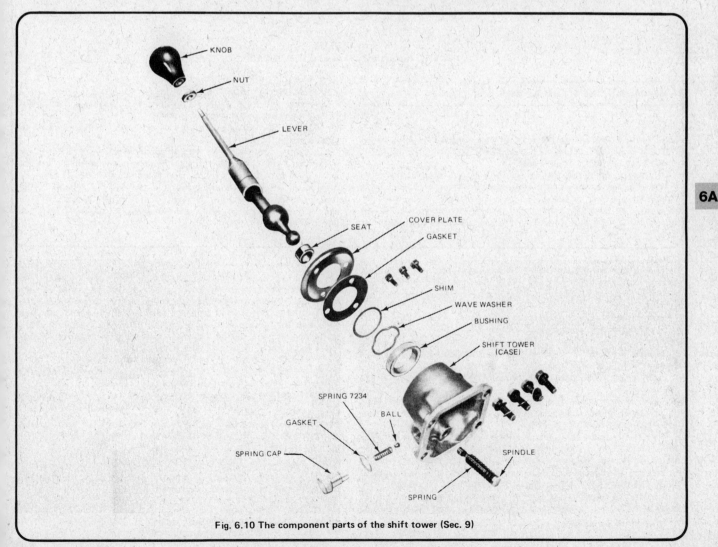

Fig. 6.10 The component parts of the shift tower (Sec. 9)

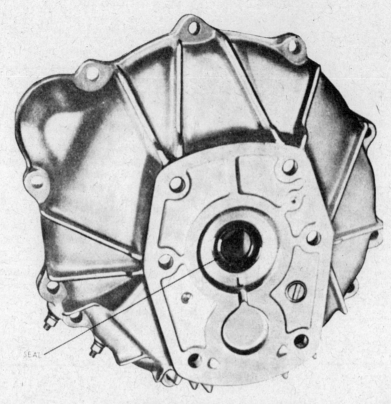

SEAL

Fig. 6.11 The input shaft bearing seal (Sec. 10)

11 Transmission - cleaning and inspection

Cleaning
1 All parts, except seals and ball bearing assemblies, should be soaked in gasoline (petrol) or kerosene (paraffin), brushed or scraped as necessary, and dried with compressed air.
2 Ball bearing assemblies may be carefully dipped into clean gasoline or kerosene, and spun with the fingers. Whilst being prevented from turning, they should be dried with compressed air. After inspection, (paragraphs 14 thru 16), they should be lubricated with SAE 90 EP transmission oil and stored carefully in clean conditions until ready for use.

Inspection - general
3 Inspect the transmission case and extension housing for cracks, worn or damaged bearings and bores, and damaged threads and machined surfaces. Small nicks and burrs can be locally dressed out using a fine file.
4 Ensure that the transmission cover vent hole is unobstructed.
5 Examine the shift levers, forks, shift rails, lever and shafts for wear and damage.
6 Replace roller bearings which are chipped, corroded or rough-running.
7 Examine the countershaft (layshaft) for damage and wear; replace it if this is evident.
8 Examine the reverse idler and sliding gears for damage and wear. Replace them if this is evident. Replace the idler gear shaft if worn, damaged or bent.
9 Replace the input shaft and gear if damaged or worn. If the roller bearing surface in the counterbore is damaged or worn, or the core surface is damaged, replace the gear and gear rollers.
10 Examine all the gears for wear and damage, renewing as necessary.
11 Replace the output shaft if bent, or if the splines are damaged.
12 Inspect the bushing and seal in the rear extension housing. If damaged or worn, replacements must be fitted **after** the extension housing has been installed on the transmission (see Sections 13 and 14).
13 Replace the seal in the transmission input shaft bearing retainer.

Ball bearing assemblies - inspection
14 Examine the inner and outer raceways for pitting and corrosion, replacing any bearings where this is found.
15 Examine the ball cage and races for signs of cracking, replacing any bearings where this is found.
16 Lubricate the raceways with a small quantity of SAE 90 EP transmission oil, then rotate the outer race slowly until the balls are lubricated. Spin the bearings by hand in various attitudes, checking for roughness. If any is found after the bearings have been cleaned (paragraph 2), they should be renewed. If they are satisfactory they should be stored carefully whilst awaiting assembly into the transmission.

Synchronizer mechanism
17 Inspect the synchronizer ring for chipped and worn teeth, renewing parts as necessary.
18 Fit the synchronizer ring to the gear cone and measure the clearance between the side faces of the synchronizer ring and the gear as shown in Fig. 6.12. If outside the specified limits, the parts must be replaced.
19 To check the contact between the cone surface and the inner surface of the synchronizer ring, apply a little Prussian (engineer's) blue to the cone surface and fit it to the ring. If the contact pattern is poor, it can be corrected by lapping with a fine lapping paste.
20 Check that the clutch sleeve slides freely on the clutch hub.
21 Check the synchronizer insert (key), the insert groove in the clutch hub and the inner surface of the clutch sleeve for wear.
22 Check that the synchronizer insert springs are undamaged.

Output shaft runout
23 Mount the output shaft on 'V' blocks and check for runout using a dial test indicator. If the runout exceeds the specified limit, the shaft must be renewed.

Output shaft bushings
24 Check the fit of the output shaft and gear bushings. If outside the specified limit, the gear must be renewed.

Reverse idler gear bushings
25 Check the fit of the reverse idler bushing, gear and shaft. If outside the specified limit, the gear must be renewed.

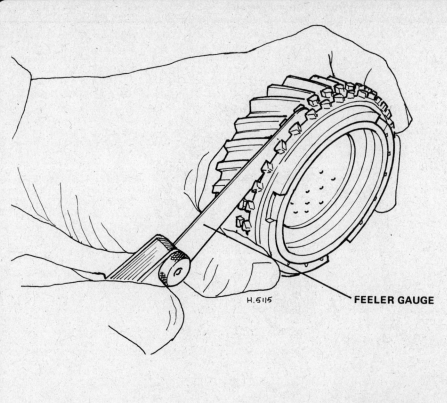

H.5115

FEELER GAUGE

Fig. 6.12 Checking clearance on a synchronizerring (Sec. 11)

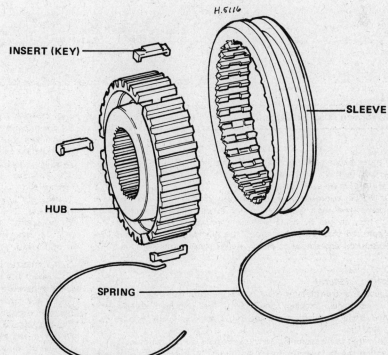

H.5116

INSERT (KEY)

SLEEVE

HUB

SPRING

Fig. 6.13 A typical synchronizer assembly (Sec. 11)

6A

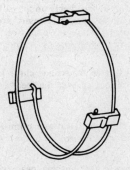

Fig. 6.14 The method of installing the synchronizer insert springs (Sec. 11)

12 Transmission - reassembly

1 Position the reverse idler gear in the case, then install the idler shaft and setscrew. Tighten the screw to the specified torque.

2 Lubricate the input shaft roller bearing with transmission oil and install it in the input shaft counterbore.

3 Set the shift forks in neutral, then assemble the input shaft to the output shaft and install the assembly into the case.

4 Install the countershaft (layshaft) into the case, ensuring that the dowel hole in the roller bearing aligns with the dowel in the case. Check that the main gear train rotates freely (photo).

5 Position the original input shaft thrust washer in the clutch housing. Assemble the clutch housing and a new gasket to the left half of the case and tighten the retaining nuts to the specified torque.

6 Use a feeler gauge to check the endplay between the rear face of the input shaft bearing and the transmission case by moving the input shaft forwards as far as possible. Adjust the endplay to meet the specified limits by selecting a suitable thrust washer.

7 Shift the transmission into 3rd gear then use a feeler gauge to check the clearance between the synchronizer insert and the exposed edge of the synchronizer ring. If the measured clearance is outside the specified limits, the output shaft must be dismantled and another key-slotted thrust washer (between the output shaft bearing and the 1st speed gear) must be selected. Reassemble the output shaft and adjust the overall endplay at the reverse gear, as described in Section 5. Recheck the input shaft endplay on completion (paragraph 6).

8 Shift the transmission into 4th gear and measure the clearance between the shift gate end of the shift rail and the transmission case boss. If the clearance is greater than that specified, it will be necessary to install selective fit thrust washers (over-travel washers) on the 3rd/4th shift rail between the shift gate fitting and the transmission case boss (see Fig. 6.8). Refer to Section 7 for further information on the shift rails.

9 Remove the clutch housing and lubricate all the moving parts with transmission oil, including the input shaft and output shaft seals in the clutch and extension housings.

10 Apply a thin coat of a non-setting gasket sealant to the two halves of the transmission case. Shift the gears into neutral and assemble the two halves of the case. Tighten the bolts and nuts to the specified torque. **Note:** Ensure that a flat washer is placed next to the transmission case so that lockwashers are prevented from damaging the casing material as the nuts are tightened (photo).

11 Position a new gasket on the transmission case and install the extension. Tighten the nuts to the specified torque.

12 Position the clutch housing and gasket on the case. Install the retaining nuts and tighten them to the specified torque (photo).

12.4 The dowel hole in the roller bearing

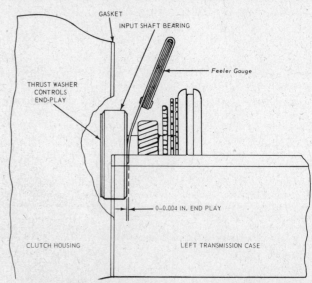

Fig. 6.15 Checking endplay on the input shaft (Sec. 12)

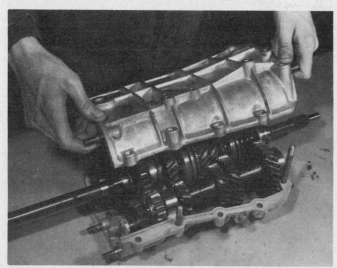

12.10 Assembling the transmission case

12.12 Installing the clutch housing

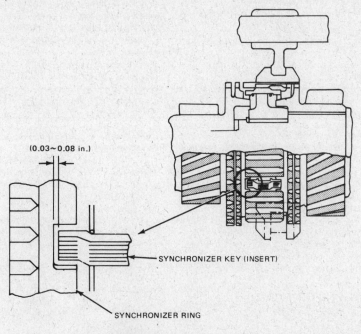

(0.03~0.08 in.)

SYNCHRONIZER KEY (INSERT)

SYNCHRONIZER RING

Feeler Gauge

Fig. 6.16 Checking the insert clearance of a synchronizer ring (Sec. 12)

13 Install the clutch release lever, bearing and associated parts, as described in Chapter 5.

13 Extension housing rear seal - removal and installation

1 Remove the propeller shaft as described in Chapter 7, then carefully pry out the seal. Take care that the sealing face inside the bushing is not marked during this operation.
2 When installing a new seal, lubricate it with SAE 90 EP transmission oil, then install it carefully and squarely into the bushing.
3 Finally install the propeller shaft.

Fig. 6.17 The rear seal and bushing (Secs. 13 and 14)

6A

14 Extension housing rear bushing - removal and installation

1 Initially remove the seal, as described in the previous Section.
2 Using a suitable extractor, draw out the bushing from the extension housing.
3 When installing, lubricate a new bushing with engine oil and carefully press it into the housing. Take great care that the bushing enters squarely and is not damaged in the process.
4 Install the seal, as described in the previous Section.

15 Fault diagnosis - manual gearbox

Symptom	Reason/s	Remedy
Weak or ineffective synchromesh		
General wear	Synchronising cones worn, split or damaged	Dismantle and overhaul transmission. Install new gear wheels and synchronizing cones.
	Synchromesh teeth worn or damaged	Dismantle and overhaul transmission. Install new synchromesh unit.
Jumps out of gear		
General wear or damage	Shift rails worn or damaged	Dismantle and install new shift rails.
	Detent spring, broken	Install new springs.
Excessive noise		
Lack of maintenance	Incorrect grade of oil in transmission or oil level too low	Drain, refill, or top up transmission with correct grade of oil.
	Bush or needle roller bearings worn or damaged	Dismantle and overhaul transmission. Renew bearings.
	Gear teeth excessively worn or damaged	Dismantle and overhaul transmission. Renew gears.
Excessive difficulty in engaging gear		
Clutch not fully disengaging	Clutch pedal adjustment incorrect	Adjust clutch pedal correctly.
Shift rail interlock ineffective	Shift rails or interlock pins damaged or worn	Dismantle and install new shift rails and interlock pins.
General wear	Worn shift linkage	Dismantle extension housing and shift tower for examination. Replace parts as necessary.

Chapter 6 Part II: Automatic transmission

Contents

Automatic transmission - checking the fluid level 18
Automatic transmission - general description 16
Automatic transmission - removal and installation 17
Brake band - adjustment 19
Inhibitor switch - removal, installation and adjustment 23
Kick-down switch - removal, installation and adjustment 22
Selector lever - removal, installation and linkage adjustment ... 21
Vacuum diaphragm - removal and installation 20

Specifications

Transmission type ... ...   Jatco, model 3N71B

Gear ratios

1st	2.458 : 1
2nd	1.458 : 1
3rd	1.000 : 1
Reverse	2.181 : 1

Fluid capacity (total) ... ...   13,2 US pints (10.8 Imp. pints/6.2 liters)

Fluid type
Ford recommendation   ESW M2C33-F (Type F)

Stall speed ... ...   1750 to 2000 rpm

Shift speeds
Throttle condition (Manifold vacuum)

Range	Shift speed (mph)
Kick-down (0 to 1.97 in Hg/ 50 mm Hg)	
D₁ - D₂	28 to 41
D₂ - D₃	51 to 68
D₃ - D₂	44 to 57
D₂ - D₁	19 to 29
Half throttle (7.87 in Hg/ 200 mm Hg) ... ... D₁ - D₂	7 to 17
D₂ - D₃	14 to 36
Minimum throttle (Over 17.7 in Hg/450 mm Hg) ... ... 1₂ - 1₁	22 to 30

Brake band adjustment ... ...   Tighten screw to 9 to 11 lb f ft (1.24 to 1.52 kg f m), then back off 2 turns

Torque wrench settings

	lb f ft	kg f m
Driveplate to crankshaft	100 to 115	13.8 to 15.9
Driveplate to torque converter	29 to 36	4 to 5
Converter housing to engine	29 to 36	4 to 5
Oil pan	3.6 to 5.1	0.5 to 0.7
Inhibitor switch to transmission case	3.6 to 5.1	0.5 to 0.7
Manual shaft locknut	21.7 to 28.9	3 to 4
Oil cooler pipe set bolt to transmission	17.4 to 26	2.4 to 3.6
Actuator for parking rod to extension housing	5.8 to 8	0.8 to 1.1

6B

16 Automatic transmission - general description

1   The automatic transmission is conventional in that it has a torque converter and three gears. The gears are epicyclic, and are engaged by hydraulically actuated clutches and brake bands.

2   The transmission is the model 3N71B made by the Japanese Automatic Transmission Company. A floor-mounted shift lever is used to give the selected speed range, this being 'P', 'N', 'R', 'D', '2' and '1' as described below.

3   When 'P' (Park) is selected, the drive to the rear wheels is locked. This range should never be selected while the vehicle is in motion, but should be used when parking. This position can also be used for starting the engine.

4   When 'N' (Neutral) is selected, there is no drive to the rear wheels. This position can be used for engine starting, and should always be used when the engine is idling for any period of time.

5   'R' (Reverse) corresponds to a normal reverse gear on manual transmissions. Before selecting 'R', ensure that the vehicle is stationary.

6   The 'D' (Drive) selection is the normal driving position where gear changing is automatic.

7   '2' (second gear manual) should be used for slippery surfaces, traffic braking and steep descents. The transmission remains in second gear; it should not be selected at road speeds above 60 mph.

8   '1' (low gear manual). This is for sustained pulling power or braking on hilly roads. To avoid skidding, this range should not be selected

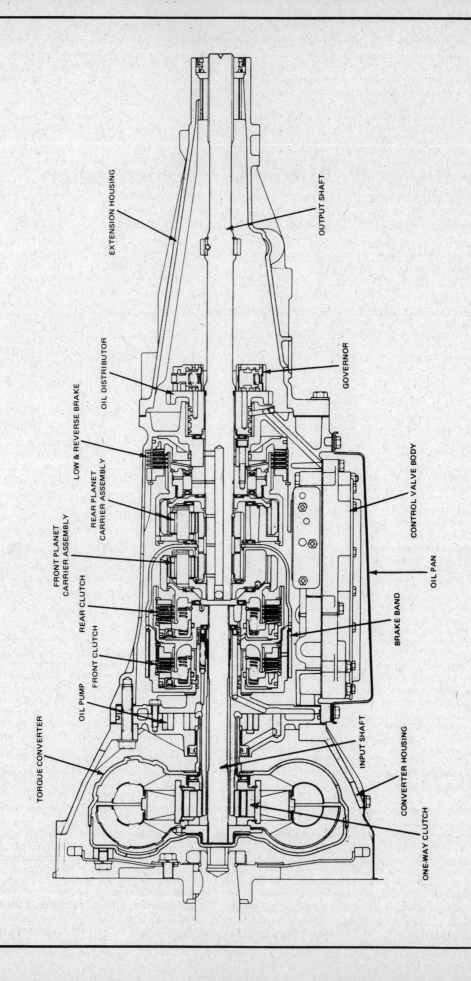

EXTENSION HOUSING

OUTPUT SHAFT

OIL DISTRIBUTOR

GOVERNOR

LOW & REVERSE BRAKE

REAR PLANET CARRIER ASSEMBLY

FRONT PLANET CARRIER ASSEMBLY

CONTROL VALVE BODY

REAR CLUTCH

FRONT CLUTCH

OIL PAN

OIL PUMP

BRAKE BAND

TORQUE CONVERTER

INPUT SHAFT

CONVERTER HOUSING

ONE-WAY CLUTCH

Fig. 6.18 Sectional view of the automatic transmission (Sec. 16)

above 20 mph on slippery surfaces.

9 When in first gear, but with 'D' selected, the car will free-wheel if the engine is on overrun, as the drive goes through the one way clutch. If in '1' then the low and reverse brake is selected, and there is engine braking.

10 There is no oil pump on the output shaft, so tow starting is not possible with the automatic transmission. If the car needs a tow in the event of a breakdown, the propeller shaft should be removed.

11 In view of the complex nature of the automatic transmission, it is not recommended that any attempt is made to carry out any repair operations other than those given in this Chapter. In the event of a transmission fault occurring, the transmission may be removed (see Section 17) and should then be forwarded to a vehicle main dealer or automatic transmission specialist for repair.

12 Normal maintenance of automatic transmission does not require periodic transmission fluid changes.

17 Automatic transmission - removal and installation

1 Disconnect the battery ground lead.

2 Raise the vehicle on a hoist or suitable axle stands, or alternatively place it over an inspection pit, for access beneath.

3 Place a large drain pan beneath the transmission. Starting at the rear of the transmission oil pan, and working towards the front, loosen the attaching bolts and allow the fluid to drain.

4 Remove the oil pan bolts except for two at the front and allow the fluid to drain further. Now install two bolts at the rear to hold the oil pan in place.

5 Remove the bolt which secures the exhaust pipe bracket to the right-hand side of the converter housing.

6 Remove the exhaust pipe flange bolts at the rear of the resonator, then disconnect the pipe.

7 Remove the propeller shaft (refer to Chapter 7 for further information).

8 Disconnect the speedometer drive cable from the extension housing.

9 Disconnect the shift rod from the manual control lever at the transmission.

10 Remove the hose connection from the vacuum diaphragm. Disconnect the wires from the downshift solenoid and inhibitor switch; remove the wires from the clip.

11 Disconnect the transmission oil cooler lines.

12 Remove the access cover from the converter housing lower end.

13 Index mark the driveplate and torque converter relationship, then remove the four bolts attaching the converter to the drive plate.

14 Remove the transmission rear support to crossmember nuts and bolts.

15 Support the transmission with a suitable jack then remove the crossmember to frame attaching bolts and remove the crossmember.

16 Carefully lower the transmission, whilst at the same time supporting it.

17 Remove the starter motor, then the converter housing to engine attaching bolts. Remove the transmission dipstick/filler tube.

18 Using a pry bar, exert pressure between the driveplate (flexplate) and the converter to prevent the converter from disengaging from the transmission.

19 Lower the transmission and move it rearwards as an assembly, from beneath the vehicle.

20 When installing, ensure that the converter is properly installed and raise the transmission on a suitable jack beneath the vehicle.

21 Raise the transmission into position and install the converter housing to engine attaching bolts. Tighten the bolts to the specified torque.

22 Lower the transmission and install the starter motor.

23 Install the dipstick/filler tube and 'O' ring on the transmission case and secure it to the cylinder block with the bolt.

24 Raise the transmission. Install the crossmember to the frame and the rear support to the crossmember.

25 Align the index marks on the torque converter and driveplate. Install and tighten the bolts to the specified torque.

26 Install the converter housing access cover and remove the jack.

27 Connect the oil cooler lines, electrical leads and the vacuum diaphragm hose.

28 Connect the shift rod to the transmission manual lever.

29 Connect the speedometer drive cable.

30 Install the driveshaft (refer to Chapter 7, if necessary).

31 Position the resonator outlet pipe flange to the muffler using a new gasket, and secure with the attaching bolts.

32 Position the exhaust pipe bracket to the converter housing and install the attaching bolt.

33 If the oil pan has not been installed properly, remove it completely, install a new gasket using a non-setting sealant, position the oil pan and install the attaching bolts. Tighten the bolts in a crosswise order to the specified torque.

34 Lower the vehicle and connect the battery. Fill the transmission with the specified fluid, run the engine and check for fluid leaks.

18 Automatic transmission - checking the fluid level

1 The automatic transmission fluid level should be checked at intervals of 4000 miles (6500 km) using the procedure given in the following paragraphs.

2 Park the vehicle on level ground and apply the parking brake.

3 Run the engine at idle speed. (If the engine is cold, run at a fast idle for about five minutes then slow down to normal idle speed).

4 With engine idling, select each position in turn then leave it at 'N' or 'P'.

5 With the engine still idling, pull out the dipstick, wipe it clean with a lint-free cloth, push it back fully into the tube then pull it out again.

6 Observe the level on the dipstick. After idling for about two minutes the level should be read on the cold side of the dipstick; after idling for about five minutes the level should be read on the hot side of the dipstick. The fluid level should be between the 'L' and 'F' marks. **Note:** A cold fluid temperature is approximately 104°F (40°C) and a hot fluid temperature is approximately 176°F (80°C).

7 When any topping-up is done, fluid should be poured into the filler tube to bring it up to the correct level. Under no circumstances must the transmission be overfilled, or foaming of the oil will occur once it gets hot and expands; this will cause loss of fluid from the vent which may lead to a transmission malfunction.

19 Brake band - adjustment

1 Although not part of the routine maintenance procedure, brake band adjustment may become necessary. Typical faults which can be attributed to an incorrectly adjusted brake band are:

   a) *Poor acceleration, with a low maximum speed.*
   b) *The vehicle is braked when 'R' is selected.*
   c) *No 'D₁'–'D₂' change, or excessive shock when changing.*
   d) *Unsatisfactory change to 'N' from 'D₃'.*
   e) *Transmission overheating and/or fluid discharge.*

2 To adjust the brake band, drain the transmission fluid, as described in Section 17.

3 Remove the oil pan completely, thoroughly clean it and discard the

Fig. 6.19 The dipstick (filler tube) (Sec. 18)

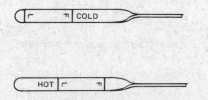

Fig. 6.20 The dipstick level markings (Sec. 18)

COLD

HOT

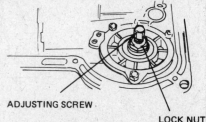

Fig. 6.21 The brake band adjusting point (Sec. 19)

ADJUSTING SCREW

LOCK NUT

6B

gasket.

4 Loosen the locknut on the brake band adjusting screw then tighten the screw to a torque of 9 to 11 lb f ft (1.24 to 1.52 kg f m). Back off the screw two full turns then hold the screw while the locknut is tightened to a torque of 22 to 29 lb f ft (3 to 4 kg f m).

5 Place a new gasket on the oil pan using a non-setting gasket sealant. Install the oil pan, torque-tightening the bolts in a crosswise order.

6 Lower the vehicle to the ground and fill the transmission with the recommended fluid.

20 Vacuum diaphragm - removal and installation

1 Disconnect the vacuum diaphragm hose.

2 Unscrew the diaphragm unit by hand. Remove the 'O' ring and diaphragm rod from the case.

3 When installing, first position the diaphragm rod in the transmission case.

4 Install a new 'O' ring on the vacuum unit. Screw in the vacuum unit firmly by hand and connect the hose.

21 Selector lever - removal, installation and linkage adjustments

1 Raise the vehicle then remove the nut and lockwasher securing the selector lever to the lower selector lever operating arm.

2 Lower the vehicle and lift out the selector lever assembly from the floorpan housing.

3 Unscrew the selector lever handle. Remove the detent rod, plunger and spring.

4 When installing, place the detent spring, plunger and rod in the selector lever then follow the reverse of the removal procedure to complete the installation.

5 To adjust the linkage, select 'N' then disconnect the clevis from the lower end of the selector lever operating arm.

6 Move the transmission manual lever to the third detent from the rear of the transmission.

7 Loosen the clevis retaining nuts and adjust the clevis so that it freely enters the hole in the lever. Tighten the retaining nuts.

8 Connect the clevis to the lever and secure it with the spring washer, flat washer and the retainer.

9 Lower the vehicle and test the transmission operation during a test drive.

22 Kick-down switch - removal, installation and adjustment

1 Disconnect the wire from the kick-down switch.

2 Remove the switch retaining nut and remove the switch from the bracket.

3 When installation the switch, follow the reverse procedure to removal. Adjust the switch to engage when the accelerator pedal is between 7/8 and 15/16 of full pedal travel.

4 On completion, test drive the vehicle to ensure that the switch is functioning correctly.

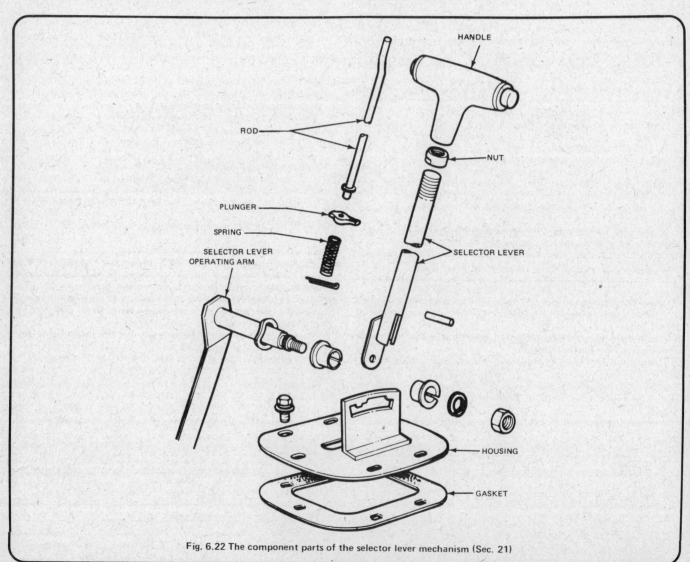

Fig. 6.22 The component parts of the selector lever mechanism (Sec. 21)

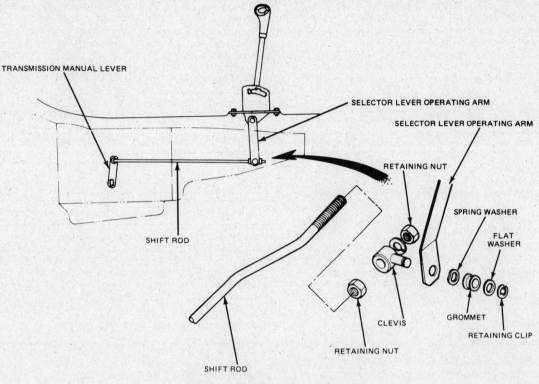

Fig. 6.23 The manual linkage (Sec. 21)

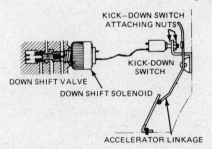

Fig. 6.24 Adjusting the kickdown switch (Sec. 22)

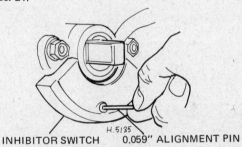

Fig. 6.25 Adjusting the inhibitor switch (Sec. 23)

6B

23 Inhibitor switch - removal, installation and adjustment

1   Place the transmission lever in the 'N' position then raise the vehicle.
2   Remove the transmission manual lever retaining nut; remove the lever.
3   Disconnect the multiple connector then remove the two switch retaining bolts. Lift away the switch.
4   Loosely install a replacement switch and remove the screw from the alignment pin hole at the bottom of the switch.
5   Rotate the switch and insert an alignment pin of 0.059 in/1.5 mm (the unmarked shank of a No. 59 drill should be suitable) through the alignment hole and into the hole of the internal rotor.
6   Tighten the switch attaching bolts and remove the alignment pin.
7   Install the alignment pin screw in the switch body and install the multiple wire connector.
8   Position the transmission manual lever on the manual lever shaft; secure with the flat washer and nut.
9   Check that the engine will only start when 'N' or 'P' is selected.

Chapter 7 Driveshaft

Refer to Chapter 13 for Specifications and information applicable to 1974 through 1982 models.

Contents

Driveshaft - balance and run-out checks 5	Introduction 1
Driveshaft - dismantling and reassembly 4	Universal joints - inspection 3
Driveshaft - removal and installation 2	

Specifications

Maximum permissible run-out	0.016 in (0.4 mm)
Maximum permissible run-out at 4000 rpm	
Front	0.28 oz in (20 gr cm)
Center	0.17 oz in (12.5 gr cm)
Rear	0.28 oz in (20 gr cm)
Universal joint spider diameter	
New	0.6559 ± 0.004 in (16.66 ± 0.011 mm)
Wear limit	0.6515 in (16.549 mm)
Selective snap-ring availability	0.057 in (1.45 mm)
	0.058 in (1.48 mm)
	0.059 in (1.51 mm)
	0.061 in (1.54 mm)
	0.062 in (1.57 mm)
	0.063 in (1.60 mm)
	0.064 in (1.63 mm)

Torque wrench settings	lb f ft	kg f m
Yoke to rear axle companion flange	40 to 47	5.5 to 6.5
Yoke to front propeller shaft	116 to 130	16 to 18
Center bearing support	14 to 21	2 to 2.9

1 General description

1 Drive from the transmission to the rear axle is via a two-piece drive-shaft (propeller shaft) which comprises the front coupling shaft, rear driveshaft, a center support bearing, universal joints and yokes.

2 The rear end of the shaft is attached to the companion flange thru the universal joint, and the front end is attached to the transmission by means of the splined sliding yoke. This permits fore-and-aft movement of the driveshaft as the rear axle moves up and down. The center of the driveshaft is supported by the bearing attached to the underbody.

3 The universal joints are retained in the yokes by snap-rings (circlips) and on some models grease caps are also fitted. The snap-rings are available in different sizes to ensure that the joint spider can be centered correctly in the interests of reducing vibration.

2 Driveshaft - removal and installation

1 Mark the relative position of the driveshaft rear yoke and the differential companion flange to ensure that they can be refitted in the same relative position.

2 Remove the four bolts which secure the rear yoke to the companion flange (photo).

3 Remove the nuts and washers securing the center support bearing to the underbody. Remove the centre support bearing (photo).

4 Carefully withdraw the driveshaft from the transmission, taking care not to damage the rear oil seal. Suitably plug the end of the transmission to prevent loss of the lubricant (photo).

5 Installation is the reverse of the removal procedure but ensure that transmission end of the driveshaft is well lubricated with transmission oil and that care is taken not to damage the oil seal as the shaft is inserted. Also ensure that the alignment marks on the rear yoke are correctly mated with those on the companion flange. Top-up the transmission if any lubricant has been lost.

3 Universal joints - inspection

1 Wear in the needle roller bearings is characterised by vibration in the transmission, 'clonks' on taking up the drive, and in extreme cases of lack of lubrication, metallic squeaking and ultimately grating and shrieking sounds as the bearings break up. If a bearing breaks up at high speed it could be lethal, so they should be changed in good time.

2 It is easy to check whether the needle roller bearings are worn with the driveshaft in position, by trying to turn the shaft with one hand, the other hand holding the companion flange when the rear universal is being checked, and the front half coupling when the front universal is being checked. Any movement between the shaft and the front and the rear half couplings is indicative of considerable wear. If worn, the old bearings and spiders will have to be discarded and a repair kit, comprising new universal joint spiders, bearings, seals and snap-rings purchased. Check also by trying to lift the shaft and noticing any movement in the joints.

3 Examine the driveshaft spline for wear. If worn it will be necessary to purchase a new front half coupling, or if the yokes are badly worn, an exchange shaft. It is not possible to fit oversize bearings and journals to the trunnion bearing holes.

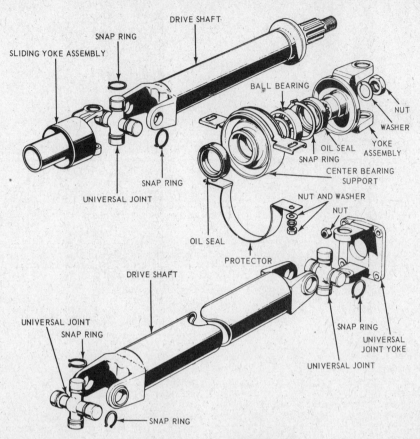

Fig. 7.1 The component parts of the driveshaft (Sec. 1)

2.2 Remove the four bolts at the rear axle companion flange

2.3 Remove the center support bearing

2.4 Withdraw the driveshaft from the transmission

7

4 Driveshaft - dismantling and reassembly

1 Clean away all traces of dirt from around the universal joint. If the joints are of the type where a steel plug is pressed in on top of the snap-rings, these will need to be removed using a small chisel or steel-shaft screwdriver which can be driven thru them to prise them out.

2 Remove the snap-rings using suitable pliers or a small screwdriver. It does not matter if the snap-rings are distorted because new ones must be used on reassembly. If they are difficult to remove a hammer blow on the end of the joint spider may relieve the pressure on them.

3 To remove the bearing cups select two sockets, one large enough to fit completely over the bearing cup and the other to fit on the end of the cup. By compressing in the jaws of a vise or by hammering on the smaller socket (provided that some degree of caution is exercised) the spider and cups can be driven out of one side of the yoke. Penetrating oil will usually assist if the job proves really stubborn. Having removed one cup, the opposite one can be removed by reversing the direction of

applied pressure. The remaining ones are then treated similarly.

4 Having dismantled the joint, carefully clean the parts and inspect them for wear and other damage. If a joint spider is worn below the permissible limit, it must be renewed regardless of the condition of the bearing condition. The oil seals and center driveshaft bearing need not be removed unless damage or wear is evident. If they are to be renewed, remove the nut and washer and draw the front shaft out of the center yoke. The snap-ring can then be removed, and the center bearings support and oil seals can be pulled off. When installing a new bearing, it should be liberally lubricated with a general purpose grease. Apply grease to the shaft splines, install new oil seals with the lips towards the bearing, install the snap-ring and the nut and washer. Tighten the nut to the specified torque.

5 When reassembling the universal joints, ensure that all the parts are free from dirt, then lightly grease the holes in the yokes. Ensure that the bearing cups are approximately 1/3 full of general purpose grease.

6 Insert the spider into the yoke and carefully press in two opposing cups and seals. The vise and sockets can be used for this job as they

Fig. 7.2 The component parts of the universal joint (Sec. 4)

1 Bearing	*4 Yoke*
2 Spider	*5 Driveshaft*
3 Seal	*6 Snap ring (circlip)*

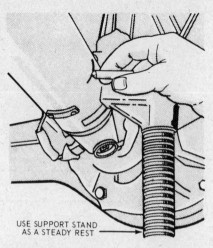

Fig. 7.3 Marking the driveshaft heavy side with chalk (Sec. 5)

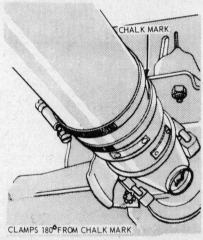

Fig. 7.4 Installed hose clamps, 180° from the chalk mark (Sec. 5)

were when dismantling. Snap-rings are available in selective sizes so that the universal joint can be positioned centrally and then all end-play can be taken up. Ensure that the opposing snap-rings are of equal size to obtain optimum balance.

7   Repeat paragraph 6 for the remaining pair of bearings on the joint.

8   Where applicable, apply a little grease to the end of the bearing cups and install the steel plugs. Apply soft hammer blows to the center of the plugs, if necessary, to enable them to spread and so obtain a tight fit.

5   Driveshaft - balance and run-out checks

1   The driveshaft is balanced during manufacture and will not normally require any further balancing provided that the correct snap-rings have been used on the universal joints, and that accident damage has not occurred.

2   If vibration of the driveshaft is experienced, it is permissible to rotate the two halves relative to each other, or the rear shaft relative to the companion flange, thru 180° (ie; half a revolution) only. If this does not improve the situation, the following balancing procedure may be adopted.

3   Raise the rear of the vehicle so that the wheels can rotate and there is access to the driveshaft. Ensure that the vehicle is really well supported and that there is no possibility of the supports collapsing. If the vehicle front wheels are still on the ground, they must be chocked very securely.

4   Start the engine and engage top gear. Raise the engine speed until 40 to 50 mph is indicated on the speedometer, maintain this speed then carefully bring a piece of chalk into contact with the rotating propeller shaft at its rear end. The points of contact of the chalk indicate the heavy side of the shaft. **Note:** Take great care if balancing weights or clips are fitted to prevent injury to the hands. Also ensure that shirt or jacket cuffs are securely fastened otherwise they could become entangled.

5   Install two screw-type hose clamps to the shaft so that the screws are opposite the chalk marks. Tighten the clamps securely.

6   Run the vehicle on the road, up to 65 to 70 mph (speedometer

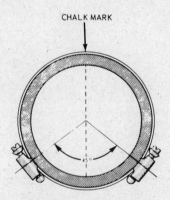

Fig. 7.5 Move the clamps away from each other to obtain optimum balance (Sec. 5)

reading) and check for vibration. If inbalance exists rotate the clamp screws approximately 45 degrees (1/8 revolution) away from each other and recheck. Continue to rotate the clamps at smaller intervals if vibration persists, then finally road test the vehicle. If vibration cannot be eliminated by this method, serious shaft damage is indicated, and an examination should be made by a vehicle main dealer.

Chapter 8 Rear axle

Contents

Axle housing - removal and installation 5	Fault diagnosis - rear axle 6
Axle-shaft assembly - removal and installation (including	General description 1
wheel bearing adjustment) 2	Rear wheel bearing and seals - removal and installation 3
Differential carrier assembly - removal and installation 4	

Specifications

Type ... ... Semi-floating, hypoid

Ratio
Courier:
   Manual ... ... 4.11 : 1
   Automatic ... ... 4.62 : 1
B1600:
   UK ... ... 4.375 : 1
   Other markets ... ... 4.875 : 1

Ring gear to pinion backlash ... ... 0.0075 to 0.0083 in (0.19 to 0.21 mm)

Maximum run-out of ring gear ... ... 0.003 in (0.076 mm)

Axle-shaft endplay
First installed ... ... 0.026 to 0.033 in (0.66 to 0.84 mm)
Second installed ... ... 0.002 to 0.006in (0.05 to 0.15 mm)

Differential bearing preload ... ... 0.0045 in (0.11 mm)

Lubricant type
Above 0°F (−18°C) ... ... SAE 90
Below 0°F (−18°C) ... ... SAE 80

Lubricant capacity
Courier ... ... 3.0 US pints/2.5 Imp. pints/1.4 liters
B1600 ... ... 2.8 US pints/2.2 Imp. pints/1.3 liters

Torque wrench settings

	lb f ft	kg f m
Carrier to housing stud nuts	12 to 16	1.7 to 2.2
Rear axle-shaft bearing housing bolts	12 to 16	1.7 to 2.2
Ring gear to case bolts	40 to 45	5.5 to 6.2
Rear axle-shaft bearing locknut	130 to 190	18 to 26

8

1 General description

1 The rear axle is a conventional semi-floating type and is held in place by semi-elliptic rear springs and telescopic shock absorbers. The differential carrier is removable from the axle casing which permits all the setting up to be done on the bench during any major servicing.

2 The final drive crownwheel and pinion are of the hypoid type, with the pinion center-line below the crownwheel center-line. The pinion runs in two opposed taper roller bearings and can be adjusted for depth-of-mesh with the crownwheel by the use of shims. Pinion bearing preload is adjusted by means of a collapsible spacer on the pinion shaft.

3 The crownwheel is bolted to a differential case and is carried in two opposed taper roller bearings. Adjustment of the side gears is by the use of shims.

4 Adjusters are provided to permit drive pinion to ring gear adjustment.

5 The axle-shafts are of the semi-floating type and are retained at the outer ends by ball bearings and housings which bolt to the axle housing.

6 It is considered beyond the scope of a manual of this type to delve into the complexities of setting up the differential since a number of special tools are required. Also, the procedure is rather complicated, and for those people without a good knowledge of this type of gear train there is a possibility of incorrect meshing and preload which will give rise to noise and backlash which will lead to early failure. In this Section you will find details of the removal procedures for the axle-shafts and differential carrier. In the event of any failure of the differential assembly, it is recommended that a complete exchange assembly is purchased or the existing faulty assembly is repaired by a vehicle main dealer.

2 Axle-shaft assembly - removal and installation (including wheel bearing adjustment)

1 Chock the front wheels then raise the rear of the vehicle.
2 Remove the rear roadwheel, brake drum, brake shoe assembly, parking brake cable retainer and hydraulic lines to the wheel cylinders. For further information on these procedures, refer to Chapter 9.
3 Remove the nuts holding the backing plate and bearing housing to the axle housing.
4 Withdraw the axle-shaft assembly from the housing. If necessary, remove the oil seal from the housing.
5 Where applicable, install a new oil seal carefully into the axle housing. Ensure that the seal lips are inwards and apply a little axle lubricant to the sealing faces.
6 Install the axle-shaft then use two bolts and nuts to temporarily secure the bearing housing and backing plate to the axle housing.
7 Using a dial gauge mounted on the backing plate, check the endplay. If only one axle-shaft has been removed the endplay of the shaft should be set to that specified for the second installed shaft. If both shafts have been removed the endplay for the first installed should be set as specified, after which the endplay for the second installed shaft should be set. Endplay is set by the selective use of shims between the bearing housing and axle housing flanges.
8 Install the remaining bearing housing and backing plate bolts and tighten them to the specified torque.
9 The remainder of the installation procedure is the reverse of removal. Don't forget to bleed the brake system on completion. (Chapter 9).

3 Rear wheel bearing and seals - removal and installation

1 Remove the axle-shaft and axle housing oil seal as described in the previous Section.
2 Fold down the tabs of the lockwasher then remove the locknut

Fig. 8.1 The axle-shaft removed from the vehicle (Sec. 2)

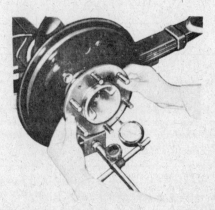

Fig. 8.2 Checking the axle-shaft (wheel bearing) endplay (Sec. 2)

using a suitable spanner.
3 Using a suitable extractor, draw the bearing and housing assembly off the shaft. If necessary, remove the backing plate.
4 Remove the bearing, bearing cup and oil seal from the bearing housing.
5 Install a new outer oil seal in the bearing retainer.
6 Install a new bearing cup in the bearing housing with the taper inwards. This will need to be pressed in or carefully driven in using a hammer and a suitable diameter tube. If driven in, ensure that the bearing cup does not become cocked or it will probably seize.
7 Position the brake backing plate on the axle-shaft (when applicable), followed by the bearing housing assembly. Note: On some models a gasket and baffle are placed outboard of the bearing housing; install these if they are applicable to your vehicle.
8 Smear the bearing cup with a lithium based general purpose grease and pack the inside of the bearing cap about half full. Work the same type of grease into the rollers, ensuring that every part is lubricated.
9 Position the tapered bearing on the shaft so that the taper faces the same way as the bearing cup taper. Press or carefully drive the bearing onto the shaft then install the lockwasher and locknut.
10 Using a suitable spanner, torque tighten the locknut to the specified torque. Fold up the washer tabs afterwards.
11 Install the axle-shaft as described in the previous Section, taking special note of the wheel bearing endplay adjustment procedure. Don't forget to bleed the brake system on completion (Chapter 9).

4 Differential carrier assembly - removal and installation

1 Remove the axle-shafts as previously described in Section 2. Additionally remove the axle drain plug and drain the oil into a container of appropriate capacity. Clean the drain plug (it is magnetic and will probably be very dirty) and install it once the oil is drained.
2 Mark the relative installed position of the driveshaft (propeller shaft) and the differential companion flange. Disconnect the shaft, as described in Chapter 7.
3 Remove the nuts which retain the differential carrier to the axle housing. Remove the carrier.
4 When installing, clean the sealing surfaces of the housing and carrier, then apply a non-setting gasket sealant to these surfaces.
5 Position the carrier to the case then install and tighten the nuts to the specified torque.
6 Install the driveshaft, referring to Chapter 7 for torque figures and other information.
7 Install the axle-shafts as previously described then top-up the axle with lubricant of the specified grade. Don't forget to bleed the brake system on completion (Chapter 9).

5 Axle housing - removal and installation

1 Remove the differential carrier, as previously described.
2 Position axle stands under the rear frame members whilst supporting the axle weight with a suitable jack or jacks.
3 Disconnect the hydraulic brake line from the axle housing.
4 Disconnect each rear shock absorber from the axle. Refer to Chapter 11 if necessary.

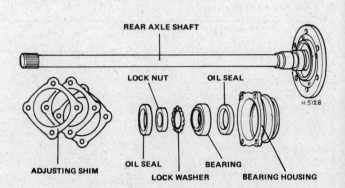

Fig. 8.3 The component parts of the axle-shaft (Sec. 2)

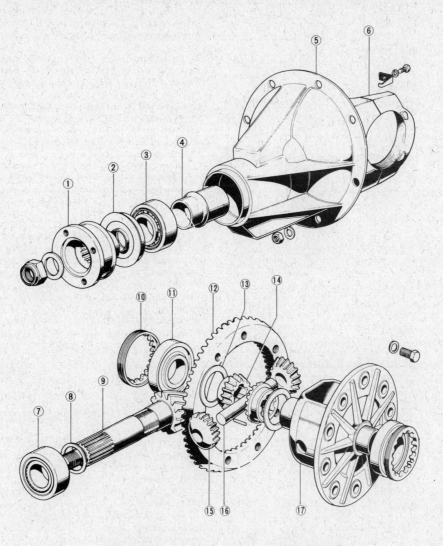

Fig. 8.4 The component parts of the differential (Sec. 4)

1	Companion flange	6	Bearing cap	10	Adjusting screw	14	Side gear
2	Oil seal	7	Rear bearing	11	Differential bearing	15	Pinion gear
3	Front bearing	8	Spacer	12	Ring gear	16	Pinion shaft
4	Collapsible spacer	9	Drive pinion	13	Thrust washer	17	Differential case
5	Carrier						

5   Lower the axle slightly to relax the spring tension then remove the spring clip (U bolt) nuts, spring clips and spring seat caps.
6   Remove the axle housing from the vehicle.

7   Installation is the reverse of the removal procedure. Torque-tighten the spring clips to the specified value (see Chapter 11), and on completion bleed the braking system of air (see Chapter 9).

6   Fault diagnosis - rear axle

Symptom	Reason
Vibration	Worn axle shaft bearing Loose bolts (driveshaft to companion flange). Tires require balancing. Driveshaft out of balance.
Noise on turns	Worn differential gear.
Noise on drive or coasting*	Worn or incorrectly adjusted ring and pinion gear.
'Clunk' on acceleration or deceleration	Worn differential gear cross shaft. Worn driveshaft universal joints. Loose bolts (driveshaft to companion flange).

It must be appreciated that tire noise, wear in the rear suspension bushes and worn or loose shock absorber mountings can all mislead the mechanic into thinking that components of the rear axle are the source of trouble.

8

Chapter 9 Braking system

Refer to Chapter 13 for Specifications and information applicable to 1974 through 1982 models.

Contents

Brake adjustment 2	Parking brake - cable renewal and adjustment 14
Brake lines and hoses - inspection, removal and installation ... 9	Parking brake warning light switch - removal and installation ... 15
Brake master cylinder (single or tandem) - removal and installation 10	Pressure differential valve - removal, installation and centralizing ... 13
Brake pedal adjustment 3	Rear brake shoes - inspection, removal and installation 7
Fault diagnosis - braking system 16	Rear brake wheel cylinder - removal, servicing and installation ... 8
Front brake shoes - inspection, removal and installation ... 5	Single brake master cylinder - dismantling, servicing and
Front brake wheel cylinders - removal, servicing and installation ... 6	reassembly 12
General description 1	Tandem brake master cylinder - dismantling, servicing and
Hydraulic brake system - bleeding 4	reassembly 11

Specifications

Type
Front	Twin leading shoes
Rear	Twin leading shoes with double-acting pistons

Parking brake
Parking brake	Mechanical, hand operated thru cable and linkage to rear wheels

Brake pedal free-travel
Brake pedal free-travel	5/8 to 1.0 in (15 to 20 mm)

Master cylinder
Type	Tandem or single
Clearance between piston and bore:	
New	0.0008 to 0.004 in (0.020 to 0.105 mm)
Wear limit	0.006 in (0.15 mm)

Front brake
Drum diameter:	
New	10.2364 in (260 mm)
Wear limit	10.2758 in (261 mm)
Minimum permissible lining thickness	1/32 in (0.8 mm)
Wheel cylinder bore	1.0 in (25.4 mm)
Clearance between piston and bore:	
New	0.0016 to 0.0049 in (0.04 to 0.125 mm)
Wear limit	0.006 in (0.15 mm)

Rear brake
Drum diameter:	
New	10.2364 in (260 mm)
Wear limit	10.2758 in (261 mm)
Minimum permissible lining thickness	1/32 in (0.8 mm)
Wheel cylinder bore	13/16 in (20.64 mm)
Clearance between piston and bore:	
New	0.0016 to 0.0049 in (0.04 to 0.125 mm)
Wear limit	0.006 in (0.15 mm)

Parking brake handle travel
Parking brake handle travel	5 to 10 notches

Brake fluid specification
Brake fluid specification	SAE J1703, ESA-M6C25-A or MVSS 116, DOT-3 or DOT-4

Brake bleeder adapter
Brake bleeder adapter	Rotunda FRE 1436-27

Torque wrench settings
	lb f ft	kg f m
Master cylinder pushrod locknut	8.5 to 13	1.2 to 1.8
Master cylinder securing nuts	11.4 to 17	1.6 to 2.35
Master cylinder fittings	43 to 51	6 to 7

1 General description

1 Most models are equipped with a tandem master cylinder and reservoirs, pressure differential valve and warning light switch assemblies, single piston hydraulic front wheel cylinders and double piston hydraulic rear wheel cylinders (photos).

2 All brake lines are connected from the master cylinder to the front and rear brakes via the pressure differential valve (where applicable) and rigid and flexible pipes.

3 The dual master cylinder comprises a hydraulic cylinder with two fluid reservoirs, two hydraulic pistons and residual check valves.

4 The pressure differential valve incorporates a warning light which is operated by a piston in the valve assembly. If there is a leak in either the front or rear braking system, or unequal fluid pressure, the piston in the valve assembly will move off-center. When this occurs, the warning light switch is actuated and closes the circuit to the warning light.

5 Vehicles which have a single master cylinder have a simplified system where the pressure in the master cylinder is fed equally to all four wheels from a common cylinder bore. This does not incorporate any loss-of-pressure warning light.

6 Brake adjustment is by means of screw type adjusters incorporated in the wheel cylinder pistons. These adjusters are reached through adjusting slots in the brake backplates; one adjuster is provided for each wheel cylinder.

7 Parking brake operation is from a dash mounted handle via cables and links to the rear wheels only. The handle is pulled out to operate the brakes and is rotated slightly anti-clockwise to release. Adjustment is normally made automatically by adjustment of the rear brakes, but a separate adjustment can be made to compensate for cable stretch.

2 Brake adjustment

1 In order to maintain maximum braking efficiency the front and rear drum brakes should be adjusted at the intervals given in the Routine Maintenance Section at the beginning of this manual. Before commencing adjustment, ensure that the drums are at normal ambient temperature, since brakes which are adjusted to hot drums will tend to bind as the drums cool down.

Front brakes

2 Release the parking brake and chock the rear wheels to prevent movement of the vehicle.

3 Raise the front end of the vehicle and remove the adjusting slot covers in the brake backing plate.

4 Insert a screwdriver through one slot to engage with the star-wheel of the wheel cylinder. Rotate the star-wheel towards the inside of the drum until the wheel is locked, then back off six to eight notches to give clearance of the shoe from the drum.

5 Repeat this procedure for the other adjuster on that wheel then install the adjusting slot covers.

6 Repeat the procedure for the other front wheel then lower the vehicle to the ground.

Rear brakes

7 With the parking brake still released, chock the front wheels then raise the rear end of the vehicle.

8 Remove the adjusting slot covers in the brake backing plate then rotate the wheel to ensure that there is no drag from the parking brake.

1.1a General view of a front brake assembly

1.1b General view of a rear brake assembly

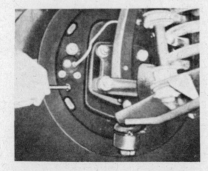

Fig. 9.1 Adjusting the front brakes (Sec. 2)

Fig. 9.2 Adjusting the rear brakes (Sec. 2)

9

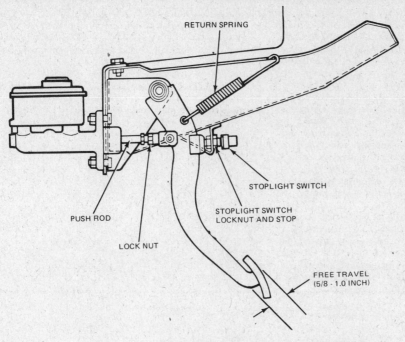

RETURN SPRING

STOPLIGHT SWITCH

STOPLIGHT SWITCH
LOCKNUT AND STOP

PUSH ROD

LOCK NUT

FREE TRAVEL
(5/8 - 1.0 INCH)

Fig. 9.3 Brake pedal free travel adjustment (Sec. 3)

If there is any drag, disconnect the equalizer clevis pin whilst the brakes are adjusted.

9 Using a screwdriver or cranked brake adjusting tool, turn the lower wheel cylinder adjusting wheel to lock the shoe against the drum (see Fig. 9.2).

10 Back off the adjusting screw six to eight notches so that the drum rotates without drag.

11 Repeat this procedure for the upper wheel cylinder and then for the opposite rear wheel.

12 On completition, install the adjusting slot covers and, if applicable, the parking brake equalizer clevis pin.

13 Lower the vehicle to the ground and test drive the car to check for satisfactory brake operation.

3 Brake pedal adjustment

1 At the intervals given in the Routine Maintenance Section, the brake pedal travel should be checked and adjusted using the following procedure.

2 Check the pedal travel at the pedal pad for the specified free-travel.

3 If adjustment is required, loosen the locknut on the master cylinder pushrod at the clevis which attaches the pushrod to the pedal assembly.

4 Rotate the pushrod in, or out, to obtain the specified free-travel then tighten the locknut to the specified torque.

4 Hydraulic brake system - bleeding

1 The system should need bleeding only when some part of it has been dismantled which would allow air into the fluid circuit, or if the reservoir level has been allowed to drop so far that air has entered the master cylinder.

2 Ensure that a supply of clean non-aerated fluid of the correct specification is to hand in order to replenish the reservoir during the bleeding process. It is essential to have someone available to help, as one person has to pump the brake pedal while the other attends to each wheel. The reservoir level has also to be continuously watched and replenished. Fluid bled out should not be re-used. A clean glass jar and a 9 to 12 inch (270 to 300 mm) length of rubber or plastic tube that will fit tightly over the bleed nipple are also required.

3 On vehicles with tandem master cylinders it is necessary to bleed the front and rear sections separately, and on completion it may be necessary to centralize the pressure differential valve. Regardless of the system type, bleeding must commence at the longest run from the

Fig. 9.4 A front brake bleed nipple (Sec. 4)

master cylinder ,(of either half of the system for tandem master cylinders) and when bleeding the rear wheel cylinders the lower one is to be done first.

4 Make sure the bleed nipple is clean and put a small quantity of fluid in the bottom of the jar. Fit the tube onto the nipple and place the other end in the jar under the surface of the liquid. Keep it under the surface throughout the bleeding operation.

5 Loosen the bleed nipple, push the pedal down slowly thru its full travel then close the nipple and release the pedal. Repeat this operation until air ceases to flow from the bleed tube then finally tighten the nipple whilst the pedal is held depressed.

6 Remember to check the reservoir level then repeat this procedure for the next appropriate wheel cylinder. On completion, ensure that the fluid is between the 'Max' and 'Min' levels on the reservoir wall (after centralizing the pressure differential valve) on tandem systems or not less than 1/3 of the way down the cylinder or single systems.

5 Front brakes shoes - inspection, removal and installation

1 Apply the parking brake and raise the front end of the vehicle. Remove the roadwheel.

2 Remove the brake drum attaching screws and install them in the tapped holes in the drum. Rotate the screws inwards evenly to draw off

the drum (photo).

3 Brush all the dust from the backing plate and interior of the drum. Check for any signs of brake fluid leakage at the wheel cylinders and signs of lubricant loss from the hub; refer to Section 6, of this Chapter, and Chapter 11 for corrective action for the wheel cylinders and hub, respectively.

4 Inspect the linings for excessive wear or shoe damage, and contamination from brake fluid or hub grease. Brake linings which are worn down to within 1/32 in. (0.8 mm) of the shoes (or to within this distance of the rivet heads if rivetted linings are used), should be renewed. Shoes which are impregnated with oil or grease should be renewed as it is not very satisfactory to use proprietary solvents which tend to clean the surface but then allow the deposits which have soaked into the linings to come to the surface and form a glazed film.

5 At this stage, also inspect the condition of the drum. If the drum diameter exceeds that specified, or is heavily scored, a replacement item must be installed.

6 To remove the brake shoes, remove the pull-off (retracting) springs.

7 Remove the shoe retaining spring guide pins and the retaining springs by holding the guide pin against the backing plate, and compressing and turning the retaining spring thru 90° to release it. The shoes can now be removed, but to prevent the pistons from coming out of the wheel cylinders inadvertently, rubber bands can be used to hold them in place (photos).

8 Any grease or dirt remaining on the backing plate can now be carefully removed using gasoline (petrol) or proprietary solvents very carefully. Dry carefully afterwards with a lint-free cloth or paper tissues.

9 Unscrew the brake adjusters from the wheel cylinders and apply a little high melting point grease sparingly to the screw threads and to those of the star wheels; then replace them, screwing them fully in. Apply a trace of the same grease to the shoe contact points on the backing plate (photo).

10 Position each new brake shoe to the brake backing plate so that the slot in the shoe web is towards the adjusting screw.

11 Install the shoe retaining spring guide pins, positioning the retaining spring over the guide pin whilst the latter is held in place. Depress the spring and turn it thru 90° to lock it.

12 Install the brake retracting springs, being careful not to bend the hooked ends or stretch them unduly. Note: If the brake shoes have been overheated - caused by maladjustment, abuse or extremely severe operating conditions - it is a good policy to fit new ones at this point.

13 Install the brake drum and its attaching screws.

14 Install the roadwheel and adjust the brake, then repeat the operation for the other side of the vehicle.

15 Road test the car to check for satisfactory operation.

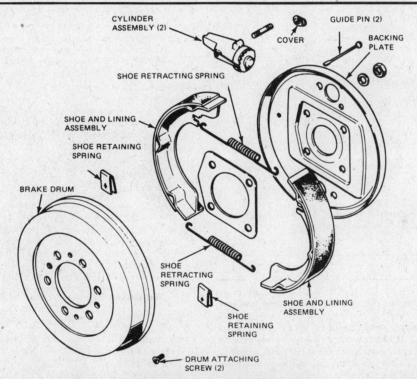

Fig. 9.5 The component parts of the front brake (Sec. 5)

5.2 Removal of the brake drum using screws. The drum retaining screws can be used for this purpose

Fig. 9.6 Removing the front brake drum (Sec. 5)

Fig. 9.7 Removing a front brake shoe retaining spring (Sec. 5)

9

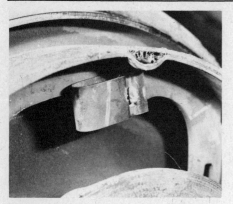

5.7a A retaining spring and guide pin installed

5.7b The retaining spring and guide pin assembly

5.9 The brake adjuster star wheel and spring

16 New brakes normally take a short period of time to 'bed in' properly, and after a few hundred miles of running, the drums should be removed, dusted out, refitted and the brakes adjusted for optimum performance.

6 Front brake wheel cylinder - removal, servicing and installation

1 Remove the brake shoes, as described in the previous Section.
2 Disconnect the hydraulic brake line at the rear of the wheel cylinder(s).
3 Remove the nuts and/or bolts and washers attaching the wheel cylinder(s) to the backing plate; remove the wheel cylinders.
4 Remove the piston and adjusting screw (complete with boot). Separate the adjusting screw and boot from the adjuster.
5 Remove the piston cup, expander and spring from the cylinder. If this proves to be stubborn, the cylinder can be tapped sharply onto a hardwood surface, or placed end down and compressed air applied to the inlet port.
6 Wash all the parts in clean methylated spirits, isopropyl alcohol or brake fluid. Under no circumstances should gasoline (petrol), kerosene (paraffin) or proprietary solvents be used. It is false economy to hope to use the cups again (unless they are known to have been in use for a very short period only), and they are best discarded. Examine the cylinder bore, piston and adjuster for wear, scoring or corrosion. Renew parts as necessary.
7 Apply clean brake fluid to the cylinder bore and internal parts and a trace of high melting point grease to the screw threads of the adjuster and star-wheel.

Fig. 9.8 The slots (arrowed) in the front brake shoes (Sec. 5)

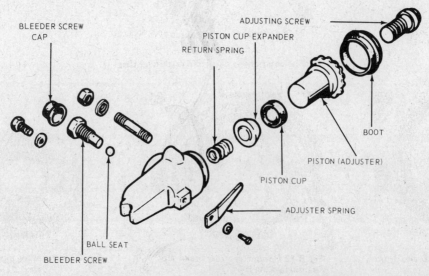

Fig. 9.9. The component parts of a front wheel cylinder (Sec. 6)

8 Position the piston return spring, piston cup expander and piston cup into the cylinder (flat side of piston cup outwards).

9 Assemble the piston boot to the piston/adjuster so that the smaller boot lip is in the piston/adjuster groove.

10 Insert the piston/adjuster into the cylinder and install the larger boot lip onto the groove at the end of the cylinder.

11 Install the adjuster screw then position the wheel cylinder to the backing plate and install the nuts and/or bolts and washers.

12 Ensure that the fitting on the brake line is clean and install it to the cylinder.

13 Install the brake shoes as described in the previous Section.

7 Rear brake shoes - inspection, removal and installation

1 Chock the front wheels and raise the rear end of the vehicle. Release the parking brake and remove the roadwheel.

2 Remove the brake drum attaching screws and install them in the tapped holes in the drum. Rotate the screws inwards evenly to draw off the drum.

3 Brush all the dust from the backing plate and interior of the drum. Check for any signs of brake fluid leakage at the wheel cylinders, and signs of lubricant loss from the hub; refer to Section 8, of this Chapter, and Chapter 8 for corrective action for the wheel cylinders and hub, respectively.

4 Inspect the linings for excessive wear or shoe damage and contamination from brake fluid or hub grease. Brake linings which are worn down to within 1/32 in (0.8 mm) of the shoes (or to within this distance of the rivet heads if rivetted linings are used) should be renewed. Shoes which are impregnated with oil or grease should be renewed as it is not very satisfactory to use proprietary solvents which tend to clean the surface but then allow the deposits which have soaked into the linings to come to the surface and form a glazed film.

5 At this stage, also inspect the condition of the drum. If the drum diameter exceeds that specified, or is heavily scored, a replacement item must be installed.

6 To remove the brake shoes, remove the pull-off (retracting) springs.

7 Remove the shoe retaining spring guide pins and the retaining springs by holding the guide pin against the backing plate, and compressing and turning the retaining spring thru 90° to release it.

8 Remove the parking brake link then withdraw the shoes so that the parking brake cable can be unhooked from the parking brake lever. Remove the shoes completely. To prevent the pistons from coming out of the wheel cylinders inadvertently, rubber bands can be used to hold them in place.

9 Any grease or dirt remaining on the backing plate can now be carefully removed using gasoline (petrol) or proprietary solvents **very** carefully. Dry carefully afterwards with a lint-free cloth or paper tissues.

10 Unscrew the brake adjusters from the wheel cylinders and apply a little high melting point grease sparingly to the screw threads and to those of the star-wheels; then replace them, screwing them fully in. Apply a trace of the same grease to the shoe contact points on the backing plate and the pivot points of the handbrake linkage.

11 When installing, position the parking brake lever on the rear shoe and install its retaining clip.

12 Hold the rear brake shoe near the backing plate and install the eye of the parking brake cable on the parking brake operating lever.

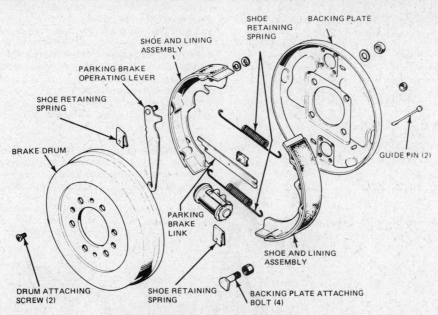

Fig. 9.10. The component parts of a rear brake (Sec. 7))

Fig. 9.11. Removing a rear brake drum (Sec. 7)

Fig. 9.12 Removing a rear brake shoe retaining spring (Sec. 7)

Fig. 9.13 Installing a parking brake cable (Sec. 7)

13 Position both brake shoes to the backing plate, install the parking brake link between the two shoes then engage the shoes with the slots in the wheel cylinder pistons and adjusting screws.

14 Install the shoe retaining spring guide pins, positioning the retaining spring over the guide pin whilst the latter is held in place. Depress the spring and turn it thru 90° to lock it.

15 Install the brake retracting springs, being careful not to bend the hooked ends or stretch them unduly. **Note:** If the brake shoes have been overheated caused by maladjustment, abuse or extremely severe operation conditions, it is a good policy to fit new ones at this point.

16 Install the brake drum and its attaching screws.

17 Install the roadwheel and adjust the brake, then repeat the operation for the other side of the vehicle.

18 Road test the car to check for satisfactory operation.

19 New brakes normally take a short period of time to 'bed in' properly, and after a few hundred miles of running, the drums should be removed, dusted out, refitted and the brakes adjusted for optimum service.

8 Rear brake wheel cylinder - removal, servicing and installation

1 Remove the brake shoes, as described in the previous Section.

2 Disconnect the hydraulic brake line at the rear of the wheel cylinder(s).

3 Remove the nuts and washers which attach the wheel cylinders to the brake backing plate; remove the wheel cylinders.

4 Remove the piston and adjusting screw (complete with boot). Separate the adjusting screw and boot from the adjuster.

5 Remove the other piston and boot and separate the piston from the boot.

6 Press in on either piston cup and force the piston cups, cup expanders and return spring out of the cylinder.

7 Wash all the parts in clean methylated spirits, isopropyl alcohol or brake fluid. Under no circumstances should gasoline (petrol), kerosene (paraffin) or proprietary solvents be used. It is false economy to hope to use the cups again (unless they are known to have been in use for a very short period only) and they are best discarded. Examine the cylinder bores, piston and adjuster for wear, scoring or corrosion. Renew parts as necessary.

8 Apply clean brake fluid to the cylinder bore and internal parts and a trace of high melting point grease to the screw threads of the adjuster and star-wheel.

9 Position the piston return spring in one piston cup expander then place the other expander and a new piston cup on the return spring.

10 Install the return spring, piston cup expanders and piston cups into the cylinder, flat sides of the piston cups outwards.

11 Assemble the piston boot to the piston/adjuster (small lip to the piston/adjuster) then insert them into the cylinder assembly. Install the larger lip of the boot into the groove at the end of the cylinder.

12 Install the adjuster screw into the adjuster then position the wheel cylinder to the backing plate and install the nuts and washers.

13 Ensure that the fitting on the brake line is clean and install it to the cylinder.

14 Install the brake shoes, as described in the previous Section.

9 Brake lines and hoses - inspection, removal and installation

1 At the intervals given in the Routine Maintenance Section, the brake system flexible hoses should be renewed. However, during any servicing of the brake system it is good practice to inspect for deterioration and leakage which at the very least might cause some embarrassment and possibly even disaster, should there be a failure.

2 Failure of the rigid lines is extremely unlikely unless the vehicle has suffered some accident damage. Indeed, these lines can reasonably be expected to last the life of the vehicle, but should there be need for renewal, only the approved parts for your particular vehicle are recommended. This is due to the bending, cutting to length and fitting of the appropriate adapters and unions.

3 When renewing any type of brake line or hose, to prevent excessive fluid spillage, first remove the reservoir cap, place a thin polythene film over the opening and refit the cap firmly. Don't forget that this must be removed when the job is completed and that it is essential to bleed the system of air on completion (see Section 4).

4 To renew flexible brake hoses, follow the procedure given in paragraphs 5 thru 10 below.

5 Disconnect the brake line from the brake hose at the frame support bracket.

6 Remove the hoseshoe type retaining clip from the hose and frame bracket. Disengage the hose from the frame bracket then unscrew the entire hose assembly from the junction block on the brake backing plate or rear axle housing.

7 When installing, fit a new copper washer over the hose-to-junction block fitting, then thread the hose into the junction block and tighten it.

8 Engage the hose upper end to the frame bracket and install the horseshoe type retaining clip. Take care not to twist the hose.

9 Connect the brake line to the hose then tighten the tube fitting nut.

10 On completion bleed the system of air.

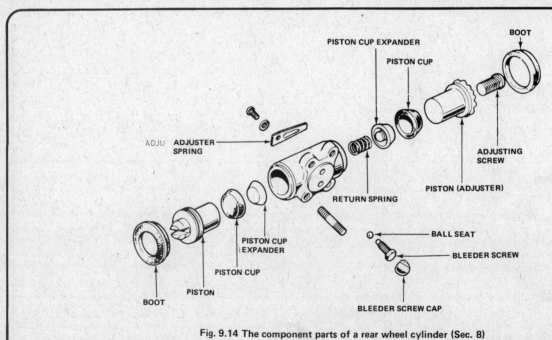

Fig. 9.14 The component parts of a rear wheel cylinder (Sec. 8)

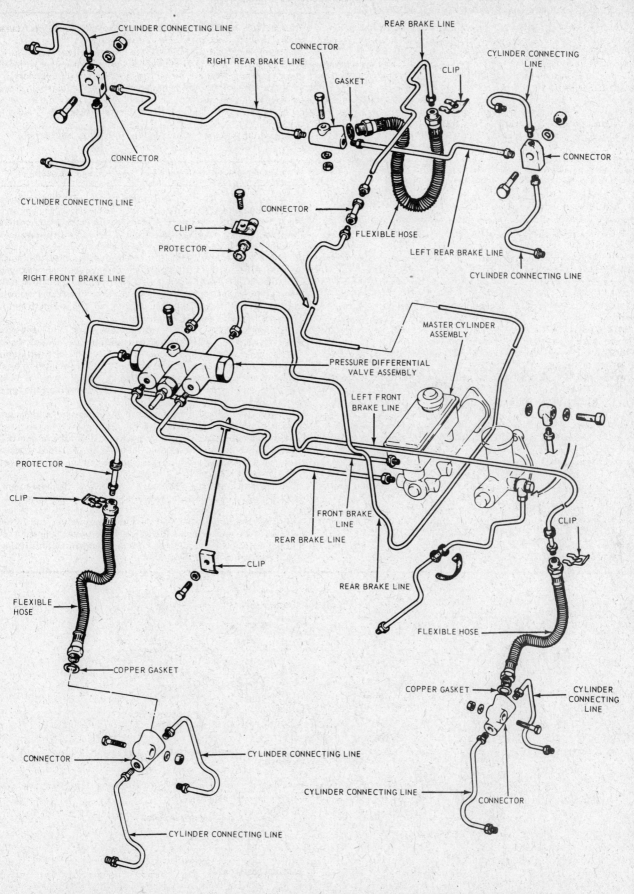

Fig. 9.15 Hydraulic brake lines and hoses - typical for right-hand drive vehicles with tandem master cylinders (Sec. 9)

9

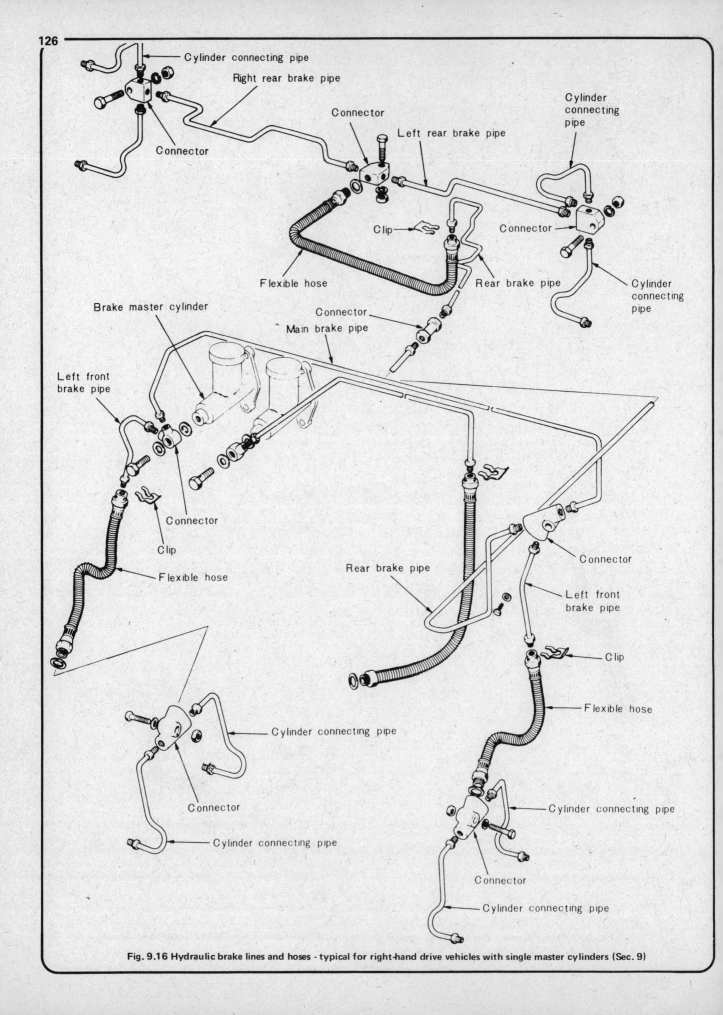

Fig. 9.16 Hydraulic brake lines and hoses - typical for right-hand drive vehicles with single master cylinders (Sec. 9)

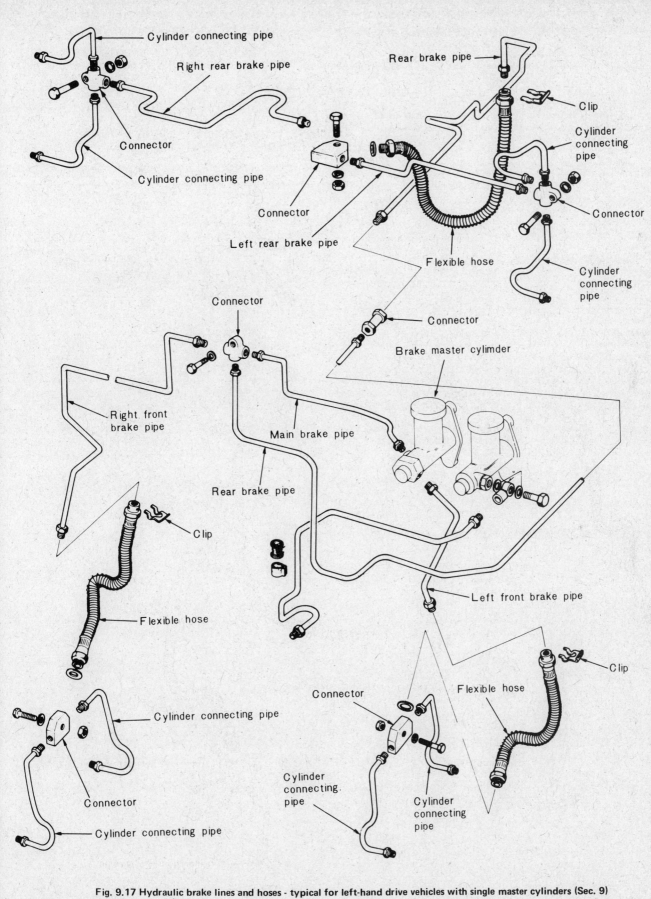

Fig. 9.17 Hydraulic brake lines and hoses - typical for left-hand drive vehicles with single master cylinders (Sec. 9)

9

10 Brake master cylinder (single or tandem) - removal and installation

1   Remove the reservoir cap then place a thin polythene film over the cylinder and replace the cap. This is to prevent excessive fluid loss (which will damage the vehicle paintwork very readily) while the cylinder is being removed.

2   Disconnect the brake lines from the master cylinder's outlet ports and plug them with plastic caps or masking tape to prevent fluid spillage.

3   Remove the two nuts and lockwashers securing the master cylinder to the dashpanel, then lift the cylinder and boot assembly outwards and upwards from the brake pedal pushrod.

4   When installing, position the master cylinder and boot assembly to the dashpanel while carefully guiding the brake pedal pushrod into contact with the master cylinder piston. Install the two nuts and lockwashers and tighten them to the specified torque.

5   Unplug the brake lines and reconnect them to the master cylinder.

6   Remove the polythene film (if still fitted) from the reservoir cap, then top-up and bleed the system, as described in Section 4.

7   On completion, check the brake pedal free-travel and adjust as necessary.

11 Tandem brake master cylinder - dismantling, servicing and reassembly

Note: During any servicing operation on the brake master cylinder, great care must be taken to ensure that there is no contamination from dirt, oil or grease. As far as is practically possible, hands should be clean. Do not use gasoline (petrol), kerosene (paraffin) or proprietary solvents to clean parts, but use only methylated spirits, isopropyl alcohol or clean brake fluid.

1   Drain off the fluid from the reservoir. Separate the reservoir from the cylinder body by removing the two attaching screws then lift the reservoir up and out of the two grommets.

2   Remove the two grommets and the rubber boot at the brake pushrod end.

3   Using a small screwdriver, remove the piston stop ring (retainer).

4   Remove the piston stop washer, primary piston and its return spring.

5   Loosen, but do not remove, the secondary piston stop screw.

6   Make-up a small guide pin, as shown in Fig. 9.20. Push in the secondary piston with a screwdriver, remove the stop screw and 'O' ring and insert the guide pin in its place. Remove the screwdriver and extract the secondary piston and its return spring.

7   Remove the outlet port fittings, gaskets, check valves and check valve springs.

8   Remove the cups (seals) from the primary and secondary pistons. It is false economy to hope to use these cups again (unless they are known to have been in use for a very short period only) and they are best

Fig. 9.18 The attachment points of the single master cylinder (Sec. 10)

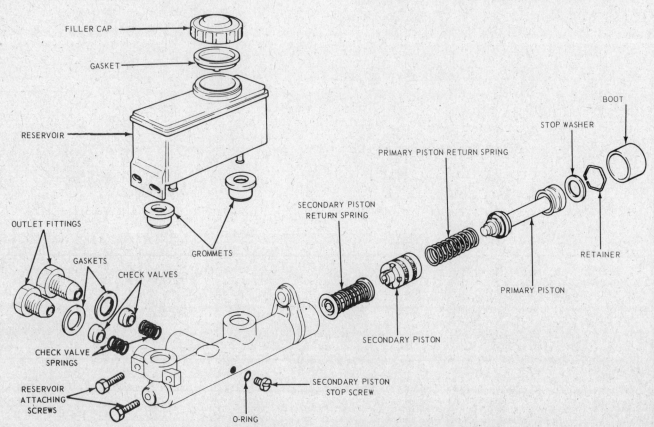

Fig. 9.19 The component parts of the tandem master cylinder (Sec. 11)

WITH GUIDE PIN

Secondary cup
Secondary piston
Cylinder
Guide pin

WITHOUT GUIDE PIN

(0.335")
8.5mm
(0.193")
4.9mm
Guide pin
Chamfer

Fig. 9.2 Use of the guide pin on the tandem master cylinder (Sec. 11)

discarded.

9 Clean all the parts carefully (refer to the 'Note' at the beginning of the Section) and dry them with compressed air, paper tissues or a clean lint-free cloth. Examine the cylinder bores and pistons for wear, scoring and signs of corrosion, replacing as necessary. Ensure that the compensating ports in the cylinder are not blocked.

10 When reassembling, dip all parts in clean brake fluid except the cylinder body and reservoir.

11 Insert the check valve springs and the valves into the cylinder ports and install the gaskets and fittings. Tighten to the specified torque.

12 Fit the cups to the secondary piston so that the flat sides of the cup are towards the piston (see Fig. 9.21).

13 Insert the secondary piston return spring, then fit the guide pin into the stop screw hole and press in the secondary piston as far as it will go.

14 Remove the guide pin and install the stop screw with a new 'O' ring.

15 Fit the primary cup to the primary piston so that the flat side is towards the piston. Fit the secondary cup to the primary piston with the open side facing the secondary piston.

16 Insert the return spring and the primary piston into the cylinder bore; install the piston stop, stop washer and the piston stop ring.

17 Install the two new grommets to the cylinder body and install the reservoir.

18 Install the two reservoir attaching screws.

12 Single brake master cylinder - dismantling, servicing and reassembly

Note: During any servicing operation on the brake master cylinder, great care must be taken to ensure that there is no contamination from dirt, oil or grease. As far as is practically possible, hands should be clean. Do not use gasoline (petrol), kerosene (paraffin) or proprietary solvents to clean parts, but use only methylated spirits, isopropyl alcohol or clean brake fluid.

1 Drain off the fluid from the reservoir.

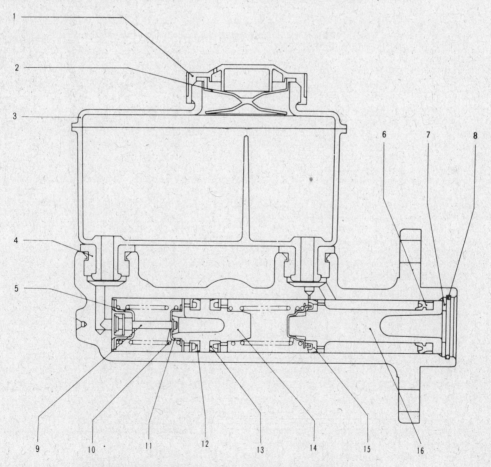

Fig. 9.21 Sectional view of the tandem master cylinder (Sec. 11)

1 Reservoir cap	5 Stopper valve	9 Valve	13 Secondary cup
2 Baffle	6 Secondary cup	10 Spring	14 Secondary piston
3 Reservoir	7 Washer	11 Spring seat	15 Primary cup
4 Bush	8 Stop ring (retainer)	12 Primary cup	16 Primary piston

9

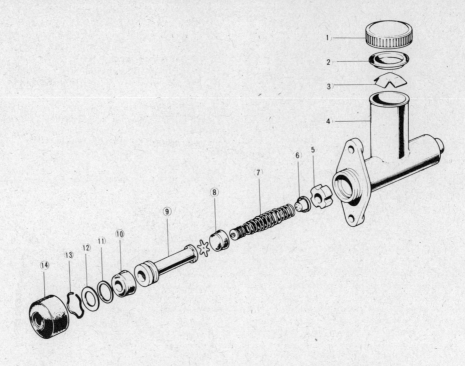

Fig. 9.22 The component parts of the single master cylinder (Sec. 12)

1 Reservoir cap	4 Cylinder and	7 Return spring	11 Clip
2 Baffle	reservoir	8 Primary cup	12 Washer
3 Baffle plate	5 Valve seat	9 Piston	13 Stop ring
	6 Check valve	10 Secondary cup	14 Dust boot

2 Remove the dust boot from the cylinder.
3 Remove the stop ring using a screwdriver and take out the piston stop washer.
4 Remove the piston and secondary cup assembly, the primary cup, return spring, check valve and valve seat.
5 On all left-hand drive vehicles the reservoir can be removed from the cylinder after removing the single bolt and washer.
6 Where applicable, remove the end fitting from the cylinder.
7 Remove the secondary cup from the piston, then discard this and the secondary cup. It is false economy to hope to use these again unless they are known to have been in use for a very short period only.
8 Clean all the parts carefully (refer to the 'Note' at the beginning of this Section) and dry them with compressed air, paper tissues or a clean lint-free cloth. Examine the cylinder bore and piston for wear, scoring and signs of corrosion, replacing as necessary.
9 When installing, where applicable fit the reservoir and the cylinder end fitting.
10 Dip all the moving parts in clean brake fluid then install the valve seat, check valve and return spring into the cylinder.
11 Install the primary cup with the flat side towards the piston then install the secondary cup to the piston to face in the same direction.
12 Install the piston, clip (where applicable), washer and stop ring.
13 Fill the reservoir with fluid and operate the piston with a screwdriver until fluid is ejected.
14 Finally install the dust boot.

13 Pressure differential valve - removal, installation and centralizing

1 Disconnect the warning light switch electrical connector.
2 Remove the master cylinder reservoir cap, place a piece of thin polythene film over the opening then replace the cap firmly. This is to prevent excessive fluid spillage.
3 Remove the brake inlet and outlet lines and plug them with plastic caps or masking tape.
4 Remove the single retaining bolt, then remove the valve and switch assembly.
5 When installing, position the valve and switch assembly on the top cowl panel and install the retaining bolt.

6 Connect the brake lines to the valve assembly.
7 Connect the warning light switch connector.
8 Depress the brake pedal several times then bleed the hydraulic system, as described in Section 4.

Centralizing the pressure differential valve

9 After any repair or bleeding to tandem master cylinder systems the differential valve may move off-center as witnessed by the warning lamp being illuminated. This is itself does not constitute a hazard but will obviously not give a true warning of any further failure. To centralize the valve, follow the procedure given in paragraphs 10 thru 12.
10 Turn on the ignition and check that the reservoir fluid level is correct. Top-up if necessary.
11 Depress the brake pedal and check that the light extinguishes. If it remains illuminated, very carefully bleed a little fluid from the half of the system which did not have a fault or which was not bled last, and as soon as the light extinguishes close the bleed nipple. Failure of light to extinguish will mean that fluid has to be bled from the other half of the system.
12 If this fails to extinguish the light, and it has been ascertained that there is no leakage at the wheel cylinders or from any of the hydraulic lines and unions, a faulty pressure differential valve is indicated and a replacement item must be fitted.

14 Parking brake - cable renewal and adjustment

Front cable

1 Raise one side of the vehicle to provide access beneath. Chock the wheels which are still on the ground and release the parking brake.
2 Slacken the jam nut at the fork joint and remove the adjusting nut. Separate the front cable from the fork joint and remove the jam nut.
3 Remove the cable return spring then pull the protective boot away from the lower end of the front cable housing.
4 Pull the housing forward out of the slotted frame bracket and slide the cable shaft sideways thru the slot until the cable and housing are free.

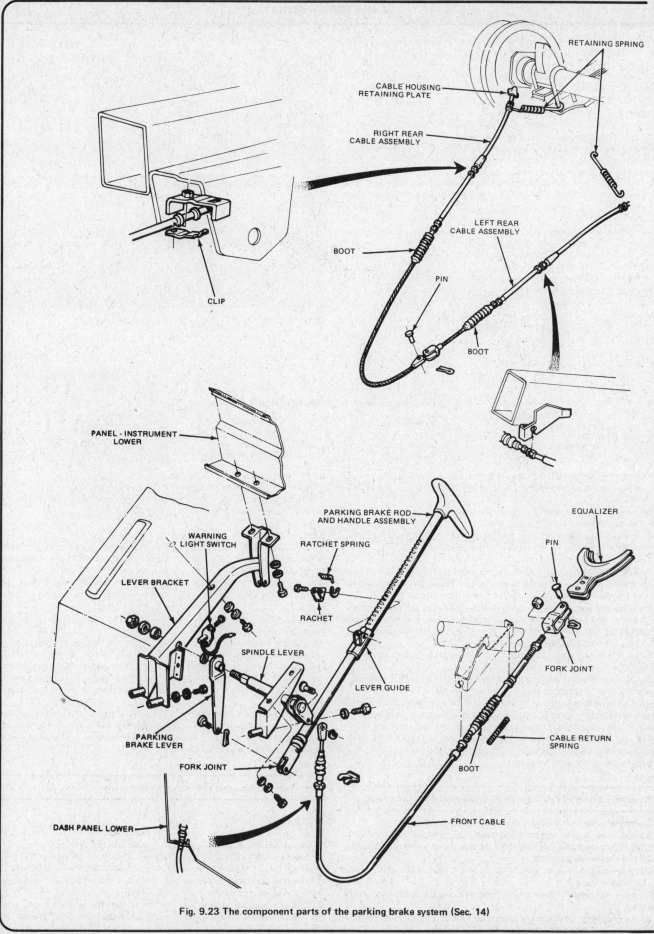

Fig. 9.23 The component parts of the parking brake system (Sec. 14)

RETAINING SPRING

CABLE HOUSING
RETAINING PLATE

RIGHT REAR
CABLE ASSEMBLY

BOOT

LEFT REAR
CABLE ASSEMBLY

PIN

BOOT

CLIP

PANEL - INSTRUMENT
LOWER

PARKING BRAKE ROD
AND HANDLE ASSEMBLY

EQUALIZER

WARNING
LIGHT SWITCH

RATCHET SPRING

PIN

LEVER BRACKET

RACHET

SPINDLE LEVER

FORK JOINT

LEVER GUIDE

PARKING
BRAKE LEVER

FORK JOINT

CABLE RETURN
SPRING

BOOT

DASH PANEL LOWER

FRONT CABLE

9

5 If necessary, remove the two cable housing retainer nuts and bolts then remove the right-hand defroster nozzle tube from the heater plenum chamber and the defroster nozzle inlet.

6 Disengage the upper cable connector from the brake lever by removing the clevis pin.

7 Remove the upper cable housing retaining nut and pull the cable and housing out of the slotted dash panel bracket.

8 Push the upper cable and housing assembly and the grommet, thru the dashpanel into the engine compartment to permit its removal.

9 When installing, route the upper cable assembly thru the opening in the dashpanel and connect it to the parking brake lever.

10 Install the upper cable retaining nut, and if applicable, position the defroster nozzle tube on the inlet to the heater plenum chamber.

11 Route the lower cable and housing assembly rearward and thru the slotted frame bracket. Where applicable, install the two cable housing retaining nuts and bolts.

12 Install the cable boot at the lower end, followed by the cable return spring.

13 Install the jam nut on the cable shaft, feed the shaft thru the fork joint and install the cable adjusting nut.

14 If the rear cable is not in need of renewal, adjust the cable, as described in paragraphs 30 thru 33.

Rear cable

15 Remove the equalizer clevis pin and separate the two parts of the cable at the clevis joint (photo).

14.15 The clevis joint

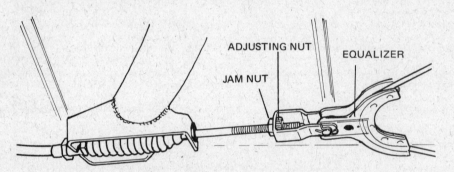

Fig. 9.24 The adjustment point for the parking brake (Sec. 14)

Fig. 9.25 The parking brake warning light switch (Sec. 15)

16 Remove the rear brake shoes, as described in Section 7.

17 Rotate the hooked end of brake shoe parking brake levers out of the cable connector.

18 Remove the cable housing retainer from the brake backing plate then pull the return spring to release the retainer plate from the end of the cable housing.

19 Pull back the boot from the forward end of the housing.

20 Loosen the cable housing to frame bracket lock nut, and remove the forward end of the housing from the frame bracket.

21 Remove the cable housing retaining clip bolts and disengage the cable housing to frame tension springs. Pull the cable housing and cable out of the brake backing plate.

22 When installing, insert the cable and housing into the brake backing plate and install the cable housing retainer plate.

23 Assemble the rear brake shoes, as described in Section 7.

24 Position the forward end of the cable assembly in the cable to housing frame bracket. Tighten the cable housing locknut then install the cable boots.

25 Install the rear cable housing retaining clips and the rear boots.

26 Route the left cable thru the equalizer and connect the two parts of the cable using the clevis.

27 Install the equalizer and clevis pin.

28 Adjust the rear wheel brakes, as described in Section 2.

29 Adjust the parking brakes, as described in paragraphs 30 thru 33.

Parking brake adjustment

30 It will not normally be necessary to adjust the parking brake cable since this is automatically catered for when adjusting the rear wheel brakes. However, after a high mileage when there has possibly been some cable stretch, or in the event of renewal of either of the cables, the following procedure should be carried out.

31 Initially ensure that the rear wheel brakes are correctly adjusted, as described in Section 2.

32 Adjust the length of the front cable at the adjusting nut so that the rear brakes are locked when the parking brake handle is pulled out 5 to 10 notches.

33 After adjustment ensure that the jam nut is tightened then apply the brake several times, checking that the wheels rotate freely when the brake is released. Re-adjust if necessary.

---

15 Parking brake warning light switch - removal and installation

1 Apply the parking brake to provide clearance between the switch assembly and the switch stop tab on the parking brake lever shaft.

2 Disconnect the switch connector then remove the two screws securing the switch mounting bracket.

3 Installation is the reverse of the removal procedure.

16 Fault diagnosis - braking system

Before diagnosing faults in the braking system check that any irregularities are not caused by:
*   1   Uneven and incorrect tire pressures*
*   2   Incorrect 'mix' of radial and crossply tires*
*   3   Wear in the steering mechanism*
*   4   Defects in the suspension and shock absorbers*
*   5   Misalignment of the body frame*

Symptom	Reason/s	Remedy
Pedal travels a long way before the brakes operate	Brake shoes set too far from the drums	Adjust the brake shoes to the drums.
Stopping ability poor, even though pedal pressure is firm	Linings and/or drums badly worn or scored	Dismantle, inspect and renew as required.
	One or more wheel hydraulic cylinders seized resulting in some brake shoes not pressing against the drums	Dismantle and inspect wheel cylinders. Renew as necessary.
	Brake linings contaminated with oil	Renew linings and repair source of oil contamination.
	Wrong type of linings fitted	Verify type of material which is correct for the car and fit it.
	Brake shoes wrongly assembled	Check for correct assembly.
Car veers to one side when the brakes are applied	Brake linings on one side are contaminated with oil/grease/hydraulic fluid	Renew linings and stop leak.
	Hydraulic wheel cylinder on one side partially or fully seized	Inspect wheel cylinders for correct operation and renew as necessary.
	A mixture of lining materials fitted between sides	Standardize on types of linings fitted.
	Unequal wear between sides caused by partially seized wheel cylinders	Check wheel cylinders and renew linings and drums as required.
Pedal feels 'spongy' when the brakes are applied	Air is present in the hydraulic system	Bleed the hydraulic system and check for any signs of leakage.
Pedal feels 'springy' when the brakes are applied	Brake linings not bedded into the drums (after fitting new ones)	Allow time for new linings to bed in after which it will certainly be necessary to adjust the shoes to the drums as pedal travel will have increased.
	Master cylinder or brake backplate mounting bolts loose	Retighten mounting bolts.
Brakes overheating	Brakes used too severely	Drive less hard.
	Brakes binding	Check rear drum adjuster. Check master cylinder free play.
Pedal travels right down with little or no resistance and brakes are virtually non-operative	Leak in hydraulic system resulting in lack of pressure for operating wheel cylinders	Examine the whole of the hydraulic system and locate and repair source of leaks. Test after repairing each and every leak source.
	If no signs of leakage are apparent, the master cylinder internal seals are failing to sustain pressure	Overhaul master cylinder. If indications are that cups have failed for reasons other than wear, all the wheel cylinder cups should be checked also and the system completely replenished with the correct fluid.
Pedal creeps down when held on	Hydraulic leak	If no visible leak, master cylinder cups are being by-passed and need renewal.
Brake juddering	Drum out of true	Measure and renew if necessary.
	Backplate loose	Tighten.
	Lining dust or road dirt inside rear drums	Clean out drums.

9

Chapter 10 Electrical system

Refer to Chapter 13 for Specifications and information applicable to 1974 through 1982 models.

Contents

Alternator - dismantling, testing, servicing and reassembly ...	9
Alternator - general information and precautions ...	6
Alternator - removal and installation ...	8
Alternator - testing in the vehicle ...	7
Back-up (reverse) light ...	19
Battery - charging ...	5
Battery - electrolyte replenishment ...	4
Battery - maintenance ...	3
Battery - removal and installation ...	2
Dome (interior) light ...	23
Fault diagnosis - electrical system ...	46
Flasher units ...	34
Front parking and turn signal lamps ...	20
Fuses and fuse panel ...	35
General description ...	1
Headlight aim - adjustment ...	17
Headlights - removal and installation ...	16
Horn ...	39
Ignition switch - removal, testing and installation ...	24
Instrument panel - dismantling (general) ...	28
Instrument panel lamps - removal and installation ...	32
Instruments - testing (twin dial instrument panel) ...	30
License plate lamp ...	22
Oblong dial instrument panel - removal and installation ...	27
Radio - removal and installation ...	36
Radios and tape players (after market type) - installation (general) ...	37
Radios and tape players - suppression of interference (general) ...	38
Sender units - removal and installation ...	29
Side marker lamps ...	18
Speedometer drive cable - removal and installation ...	31
Starter motor - dismantling, testing, servicing and reassembly ...	15
Starter motor - general description ...	12
Starter motor - removal and installation ...	14
Starter motor - testing in the vehicle ...	13
Steering column mounted combination switch - removal and installation ...	25
Switches (dash panel mounted) - removal and installation ...	33
Tail and rear turn signal lamp ...	21
Twin dial instrument panel - removal and installation ...	26
Voltage regulator - checks and adjustments in the vehicle ...	11
Voltage regulator - removal and installation ...	10
Windshield washer system - removal and installation ...	43
Windshield wiper arms and blades ...	40
Windshield wiper motor and linkage - removal and installation ...	41
Windshield wiper motor - dismantling and reassembly ...	42
Windshield wiper motor - testing ...	44
Windshield wiper relay - testing ...	45

Specifications

System type ... ... 12 volt, negative ground (earth)

Battery capacity ... ... 60 or 70 amp hour, at 20 hour rate

Generator

Type	Alternator
Direction of rotation	Clockwise
No load test	14 volts, 0 amps at 1050 rpm or less
Load test	14 volts, 32 amps at 2500 rpm or less
Brush length:	
New	0.55 in. (14 mm)
Limit	0.24 in. (6 mm)
Brush spring tension	0.7 to 0.9 lb (310 to 410 gram)
Pulley ratio	1 : 22

Regulator

Constant voltage relay:	
Air gap	0.028 to 0.043 in. (0.7 to 1.1 mm)
Point gap	0.012 to 0.016 in. (0.3 to 0.4 mm)
Back gap	0.028 to 0.043 in. (0.7 to 1.1 mm)
Regulated no-load voltage at 4000 alternator rpm	14.5 $\pm$ 0.5 volts
Pilot relay:	
Air gap	0.035 to 0.047 in. (0.9 to 1.2 mm)
Point gap	0.028 to 0.043 in. (0.7 to 1.1 mm)
Back gap	0.028 to 0.043 in. (0.7 to 1.1 mm)
Pilot lamp illuminates	3.0 volts
Pilot lamp extinguishes	3.7 to 5.7 volts

Starter motor

Capacity	1 kw
Brush spring tension	29 to 38 oz (0.8 to 1.1 kg)
Free running test	11.5 volts, 60 amps or less at 5000 rpm or more
Solenoid operating voltage (minimum)	8 volts

Lighting system - bulb wattage

Headlight ...	50W/40W or 50W/37.5W, 37.5W or 40W/45W, 45W
Turn signal, tail and stop lamp	23W/8W or 21W/5W
License plate	7.5W or 8W
Interior light	5W
Side marker	8W
Back-up light	12W or 15W or 10W
Instrument cluster, warning lights, etc.	3W

Note: The wattages given vary according to the vehicle and market. In cases of difficulty, the advice of your local vehicle main dealer should be sought.

1 General description

1 The electrical system is a 12 volt, negative earth type comprising an alternator and its associated regulator, the battery, the starting motor, the ancillaries such as lighting equipment, windshield wipers etc, and the associated wiring and protective circuits.

2 The battery provides starting power and a reserve of energy should the loading of the system exceed the alternator output.

3 When installing electrical accessories to your vehicle it is important to ensure that they are suitable for negative earth vehicles (most vehicles are negative ground, but accessories are still available for positive ground systems). Equipment which incorporates semi-conductor devices may well be permanently damaged if they are not suited to your particular system.

4 If the battery is to be boost-charged from an external charging source, it is important to disconnect the battery positive cable in order to protect the semi-conductor devices in the alternator and possibly any electrical accessories which may have been installed. Similarly, when any electric (arc) welding or power tools are used the same precaution should be taken.

5 Alternative type instrument panels are used, according to the particular vehicle and market; these are shown in Section 26 or 27. A 7-volt instrument stabilizer is used to control the supply to the fuel and temperature gauges. This stabilizer (the IVR) is incorporated in the fuel gauge.

2 Battery - removal and installation

1 The battery is in a special carrier fitted on the right-hand wing valance of the engine compartment. It should be removed once every three months for cleaning. Disconnect the leads from the battery terminals by slackening the clamp retaining nuts and bolts, or by unscrewing the retaining screws if terminal caps are fitted instead of clamps (photos).

2 Unscrew the clamp bar retaining nuts, then remove the clamp.

Carefully lift the battery from its carrier. Hold the battery vertical to ensure that none of the electrolyte is spilled.

3 Installation is a direct reversal of this procedure. **Note:** Install the negative lead before the positive lead and smear the terminals with petroleum jelly to prevent corrosion. NEVER use an ordinary grease as applied to other parts of the car.

3 Battery - maintenance

1 Normal weekly battery maintenance consists of checking the electrolyte level of cell to ensure that the separators are covered by ¼ inch of electrolyte. If the level has fallen, top up the battery using distilled or de-ionized water. Do not overfill. If the battery is overfilled or any electrolyte spilled, immediately wipe away the excess, as electrolyte attacks and corrodes any metal it comes into contact with very rapidly. In an emergency, where the electrolyte level is too low, it is permissible to use boiled drinking water which has been allowed to cool but this is not recommended as a regular practice.

2 If the battery terminals are showing signs of corrosion, brush or scrape off the worst taking care not to get the deposits on the vehicle paintwork or your hands. Prepare a solution of household ammonia, washing soda or bicarbonate of soda and water. Brush this onto all the corroded parts, taking care that none enters the battery. This will neutralize the corrosion and when all the fizzing and bubbling has stopped the parts can be wiped clean with a dry, lint-free cloth. Don't forget to smear the terminals and clamps with petroleum jelly afterwards to prevent further corrosion.

3 Inspect the battery clamp and mounting tray and treat these in the same way. Where the paintwork has been damaged, after neutralizing, the area can be painted with a zinc based primer and the appropriate finishing color, or an underbody paint can be used.

4 At the same time inspect the battery case for cracks. If a crack is found, clean and plug it with one of the proprietary compounds marketed for this purpose. If leakage through the crack has been excessive then it will be necessary to refill the appropriate cell with fresh electrolyte as described later. Cracks are frequently caused at the

2.1a The battery carrier

2.1b The battery ground (earth) terminal)

10

top of the battery case by pouring in distilled water in the middle of winter *after* instead of *before* a run. This gives the water no chance to mix with the electrolyte and so the former freezes and splits the battery case.

5 If topping-up becomes excessive and the case has been inspected for cracks that could cause leakage, but none are found, the battery is being overcharged and the voltage regulator will have to be checked and reset.

6 With the battery on the bench, measure the specific gravity with a hydrometer to determine the state of charge and condition of the electrolyte. There should be very little variation between the different cells and, if a variation in excess of 0.025 is present, it will be due to either:

a) *Loss of electrolyte from the battery at some time caused by spillage or a leak, resulting in a drop in the specific gravity of the electrolyte when the deficiency was replaced with distilled water instead of fresh electrolyte.*

b) *An internal short circuit caused by buckling of the plates or similar malady pointing to the likelihood of total battery failure in the near future.*

7 The specific gravity of the electrolyte for fully charged conditions at the electrolyte temperature indicated, is listed in Table A. The specific gravity of a fully discharged battery at different temperatures of the electrolyte is given in Table B.

Table A

Specific gravity - battery fully charged

1.268 at 100°F or 38°C electrolyte temperature
1.272 at 90°F or 32°C electrolyte temperature
1.276 at 80°F or 27°C electrolyte temperature
1.280 at 70°F or 21°C electrolyte temperature
1.284 at 60°F or 16°C electrolyte temperature
1.288 at 50°F or 10°C electrolyte temperature
1.292 at 40°F or 4°C electrolyte temperature
1.296 at 30°F or -1.5°C electrolyte temperature

Table B

Specific gravity - battery fully discharged

1.098 at 100°F or 38°C electrolyte temperature
1.102 at 90°F or 32°C electrolyte temperature
1.106 at 80°F or 27°C electrolyte temperature
1.110 at 70°F or 21°C electrolyte temperature
1.114 at 60°F or 16°C electrolyte temperature
1.118 at 50°F or 10°C electrolyte temperature
1.122 at 40°F or 4°C electrolyte temperature
1.126 at 30°F or -1.5°C electrolyte temperature

4 Battery - electrolyte replenishment

1 If the battery is in a fully charged state and one of the cells maintains a specific gravity reading which is 0.025 or lower than the others, and a check of each cell has been made with a voltage meter to check for short circuits (a four to seven second test should give a steady reading of between 1.2 and 1.8 volts), then it is likely that electrolyte has been lost from the cell with the low reading at some time.

2 Top up the cell with a solution of 1 part sulphuric acid to 2.5 parts of distilled or de-ionized water. If the cell is already fully topped up draw some electrolyte out of it with a pipette.

3 When mixing the sulphuric acid and water **never add water to sulphuric acid** — always pour the acid slowly onto the water in a glass container. **If water is added to sulphuric acid it will explode.**

4 Continue to top up the cell with the freshly made electrolyte and to recharge the battery and check the hydrometer readings.

5 Battery - charging

Note: If the battery is to remain in the vehicle when being charged always disconnect the battery positive lead.

1 In winter time when a heavy demand is placed on the battery, such as when starting from cold, and much electrical equipment is

continually in use, it is a good idea to occasionally have the battery fully charged from an external source at a rate of approximately 4 amps.

2 Continue to charge the battery at this rate until no further rise in specific gravity is noted over a four hour period.

3 Alternatively, a trickle charger, charging at the rate of 1.5 amps can be safely used overnight.

4 Special rapid 'boost' charges which are claimed to restore the power of the battery in 1 to 2 hours are most dangerous unless they are thermostatically controlled as they can cause serious damage to the battery plates through overheating.

5 While charging the battery note that the temperature of the electrolyte should never exceed 100°F (37.8°C).

6 Alternator - general information and precautions

1 The alternator charging system comprises the alternator, the regulator, an ammeter on some models, the battery, a 40-amp fuse and the associated wiring.

2 The alternator is driven by a 'V' belt from the engine. Current is supplied from the alternator/regulator system to the rotating field of the alternator to two slip rings, via two brushes.

3 Power is generated in the form of alternating current which is then rectified by six diodes for battery charging. The alternator regulator automatically adjusts the field current to maintain the prescribed output voltage.

4 When the ignition is switched on, current passes to the alternator field and as the engine is started the alternator field rotates causing the alternator to generate a voltage. Where applicable current flow will be shown on the ammeter.

5 A 40-amp fuse is located under the hood on the right fender splash shield to give protection in the event of the wiring becoming grounded (earthed).

6 It must be appreciated that the semi-conductors in the alternator can easily be permanently damaged by inadvertently reversing the battery terminals or disconnecting one battery lead while the engine is running.

7 Alternator - testing in the vehicle

1 In order to test the alternator properly, special test equipment will be needed and it is considered outside the scope of a manual of this type. A simple check-out is given in the following paragraphs, but where this fails to isolate a fault it is essential that a vehicle main dealer is contacted or the job is entrusted to an automobile electrical specialist.

2 Disconnect the wire from the alternator 'B' terminal and connect an ammeter into the lead. The ammeter positive lead connects to the 'B' terminal and the negative lead connects to the lead which was disconnected.

3 Remove the electrical connector from the regulator then remake each connection using suitable short flying leads.

4 Run the engine at approximately 2000 rpm and note the ammeter reading.

5 Disconnect the wire at the regulator 'F' terminal and short circuit this wire to the regulator 'A' terminal.

6 If there is a large increase in the charging current, the alternator is satisfactory and the regulator is at fault. If there is no change in current, the alternator is at fault.

8 Alternator - removal and installation

1 Remove the battery, as described in Section 2.

2 Remove the single wire from the alternator 'B' terminal and remove the multiple connector (photo).

3 Remove the alternator adjusting arm bolt and the distributor cap and rotor.

4 Remove the alternator pivot bolt and lift away the alternator.

5 Installation is the reverse of the removal procedure but on completion, adjust the drivebelt tension, as described in Chapter 2.

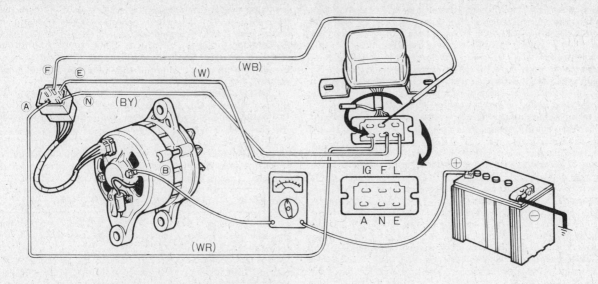

Fig. 10.1 Alternator testing set-up (Sec. 7)

8.2 The alternator, showing the electrical connections

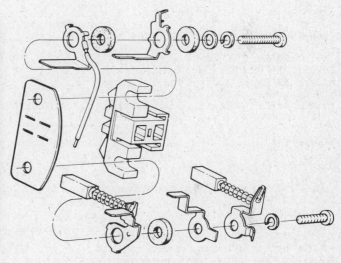

Fig. 10.2 The brush box assembly (Sec. 9)

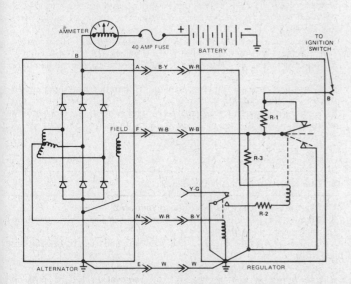

Fig. 10.3 The alternator charging circuit (Sec. 9)

9 Alternator - dismantling, testing, servicing and reassembly

Note: Before attempting to dismantle and repair the alternator, it must be appreciated that more harm than good can be done by anyone not familiar with repair techniques on semi-conductor devices. Also, before dismantling, ensure that there are spare parts available since it is unlikely that any individual components will be capable of being repaired. If parts are not available, or you feel that you do not have the knowledge and experience to do the job yourself, either purchase an exchange unit or entrust the job to a specialist in this type of work.

1 Remove the condenser (capacitor) from the rear of the alternator.
2 Insert a drift through the pulley fan fins then remove the nut, washers, pulley, fan, washer and spacer from the shaft.
3 Remove the three alternator through bolts and remove the front housing and rotor.
4 Remove the rotor from the front housing.
5 Remove the nut, washers and insulator from the 'B' terminal.
6 Remove the three screws attaching the rectifier plates to the housing.
7 Unscrew the brush holder attaching screws but do not pull them out.
8 Carefully remove the stator, rectifiers and brush holder from the rear housing.
9 Using a soldering iron of less than 100 watts, unsolder the stator

leads from the rectifier and brush holder assembly. If necessary, unsolder the brush holder assembly wire from the positive rectifier heat sink.

10 Unsolder the rectifier assemblies using the minimum possible amount of heat.

11 If bearings are to be replaced, the rear one can be drawn off the rotor shaft. To remove the front one, remove the three attaching screws from the bearing retainer and press out the bearing.

12 Carefully clean the parts with a clean paintbrush, paper tissues or a lint-free cloth. Do not immerse them in proprietary solvents. Check the brushes and tension springs in accordance with the Specifications, renewing as necessary.

13 Using a suitable ohmmeter, check for continuity between the stator coil leads, or each pair of leads, as appropriate. If an open circuit exists, the stator must be renewed. (Fig. 10.5).

14 Using a suitable ohmmeter, connect between the stator core and each winding lead. If a short circuit is indicated, the stator must be renewed. (Fig. 10.4).

15 Using a suitable ohmmeter, check for a resistance of .5 to 6 ohms between the slip-rings. If this is not obtained, the rotor should be renewed. (Fig. 10.6).

16 Using a suitable ohmmeter, connect between the rotor core and one slip-ring. Renew the rotor if a short circuit is indicated. (Fig. 10.7).

17 Using a suitable ohmmeter, check between each diode terminal and the heat sink (Fig. 10.8). An indication should be obtained when the leads are connected one way, but an open circuit should be indicated when the ohmmeter leads are reversed. If there is no indication, or a high indication, regardless of the polarity of the ohmmeter leads, the

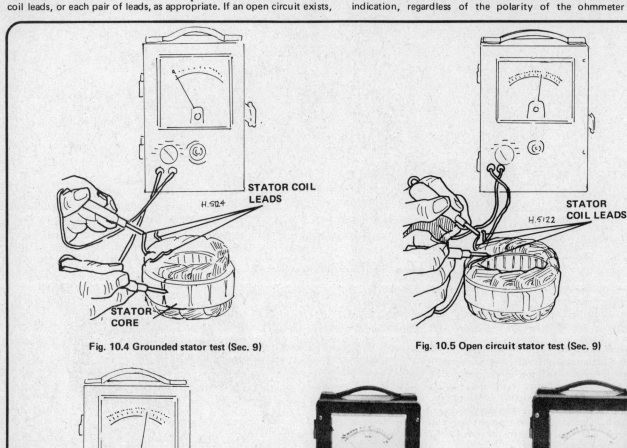

Fig. 10.4 Grounded stator test (Sec. 9)

Fig. 10.5 Open circuit stator test (Sec. 9)

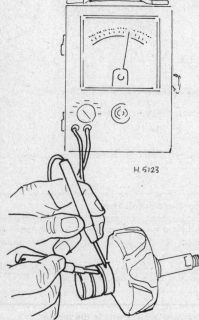

Fig. 10.7 Grounded rotor test (Sec. 9)

Fig. 10.6 Open rotor test (Sec. 9)

Fig. 10.8 Diode test (Sec. 9)

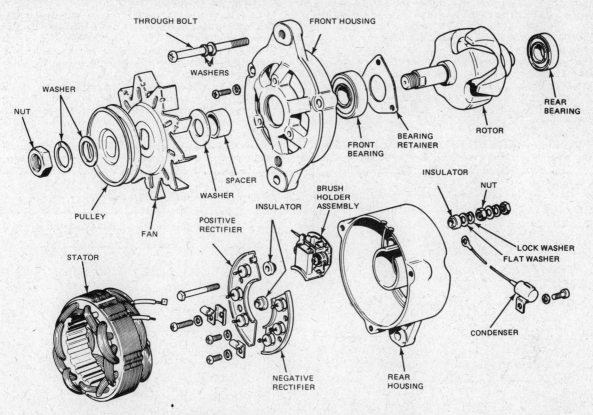

Fig. 10.9 Exploded view of the alternator (Sec. 9)

appropriate diodes and heat sink should be renewed as an assembly.

18 To commence assembly of the alternator, install new bearings if they were removed. When installing the rotor shaft bearing, press on the inner race only; when installing the bearing to the front housing, press on the outer race only.

19 Assemble the stator, rectifiers and brush holder assembly, then using the minimum amount of heat possible, solder the wires.

20 Place the rear housing on the bench, open side up, then carefully lower the stator, rectifiers and brush holder assembly into the rear housing. Securely tighten the brush holder retaining screws.

21 Hold the rear housing and stator assembly with the rear of the housing upwards. Insert the insulator between the positive rectifier heat sink and the rear housing, allowing the shoulder of the insulator to drop into the large hole of the heat sink.

22 Install the longest crosshead screw and washer through the wire clamp, flat insulator, heat sink and round insulator. Start the screw in the threaded hole in the rear housing but do not tighten it.

23 Insert another insulator between the positive rectifier heat sink and the rear housing so that the insulator shoulder fits into the 'B' terminal hole. Tighten the screw to hold the insulator in position against the rear housing.

24 Install the square headed battery terminal screw through the heat sink, insulator and rear housing. Install an insulator, shoulder towards the housing, washer and nut on the 'B' terminal screw. Ensure that the insulator shoulder recesses into the hole in the rear housing.

25 Install the two screws that attach the negative rectifier heat sink to the rear housing, noting that the wire clamp is retained by the screw furthest from the brush holder.

26 Ensure that the insulator shoulders are recessed in the holes, then tighten the rectifier attaching screws and the 'B' terminal nut.

27 Push the brushes into the holder and install a thin wire (eg: a paper clip) into the small hole below the terminal connector at the rear of the alternator, and through the holes in the brushes to hold them in the retracted position.

28 Position the rotor to the front housing and install the spacer, washer, fan, pulley, washers and nut; tighten the nut securely.

29 Assemble the two parts ensuring that the notches are aligned, then install and tighten the three through-bolts.

30 Install the condenser with the lead connected to the 'B' terminal.

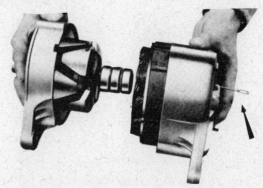

Fig. 10.10 Installing the alternator rotor (Sec. 9)

The arrow indicates the brush retracting wire

31 Remove the brush retracting wire then check that the pulley rotates freely.

10 Voltage regulator - removal and installation

1   Disconnect the wires from the regulator at the multi-way connector.
2   Remove the two regulator securing screws and lift off the regulator (photo).
3   Installation is the reverse of the removal procedure, but ensure that the charging system operation is checked on completion.

11 Voltage regulator - checks and adjustments in the vehicle

1   Ensure that the vehicle battery is in good condition and fully charged.
2   Connect a voltmeter between the 'A' and 'E' terminals of the

10.2 The voltage regulator

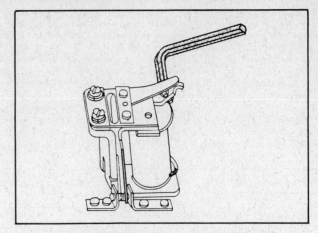

Fig. 10.13 Adjusting the regulator (Sec. 11)

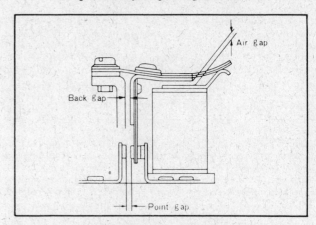

Fig. 10.14 The regulator gaps (Sec. 11)

regulator. Refer to Fig. 10.11.
3   Run the engine at 4000 rpm (alternator speed 1800 rpm) and check for a voltage of 14 to 15 volts.
4   If adjustment is required, first check the air gap, point gap and back gap (see Specifications) and adjust if necessary. Now bend the upper plate down (to decrease the voltage setting) or up (to increase the voltage setting), as necessary.
5   Refer to Fig. 10.12 and make up a test circuit as shown using a suitable wire wound resistor and a 12 volt lamp of less than 10 watts rating. Decrease the voltage from minimum and check that the lamp is initially illuminated but extinguishes between 3.7 and 5.7 volts. Reduce the voltage and check that the lamp is illuminated at 3.5 volts or less.
6   If adjustment is required, adjust as described at paragraph 4, to obtain the voltage at which the lamp is illuminated, then check the range at which it is extinguished.

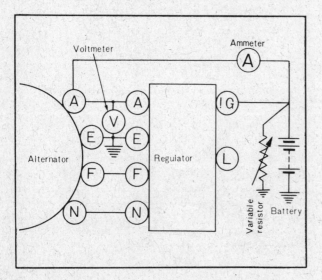

Fig. 10.11 Constant voltage relay checks (Sec. 11)

12 Starter motor - general description

1   The starter motor is a four-brush, four-pole, four-field wound type.
2   The main frame encloses a wound armature running in two bushings; this rotates between four pole shoes around which are four field coils.
3   The field coils are series-parallel connected, and are retained by the pole shoes which are attached to the starter frame.
4   A rubber grommet which prevents foreign matter entering the starter also isolates the field coil strap from the starter frame.
5   The solenoid assembly is mounted on the starter drive end housing and lies parallel to the motor body. The plunger and shift fork are enclosed in the drive end housing where they are protected from mud, dirt, grease, etc.
6   The solenoid incorporates a pull-in winding and a hold-in winding which together provide sufficient magnetic pull to draw the plunger into the solenoid to engage the starter drive gear with the engine flywheel ring gear.

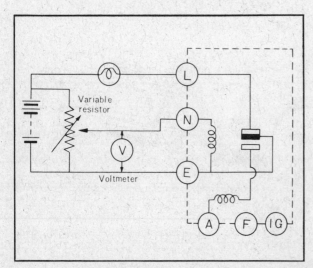

Fig. 10.12 Pilot lamp relay checks (Sec. 11)

7   In the engine starting sequence the solenoid is energized from the ignition switch which moves the starter drive gear into mesh with the flywheel ring gear. At the same moment, the solenoid main contacts close and the motor is energised and starts to rotate.

8   As soon as the engine fires and the ignition key returns to the normal running position, the solenoid is de-energized. This cuts the supply to the motor and the solenoid return spring causes the shift fork to disengage the drive from the flywheel ring gear.

9   To prevent excessive motor speed as the engine fires, an overrunning clutch is incorporated in the drive gear assembly. The drive gear can therefore run at a faster speed than the armature during this brief period of time and disengages itself from the flywheel ring gear.

13 Starter motor - testing in the vehicle

1   In the event of the starter motor failing to operate, a simple check can be made with the use of a voltmeter.

2   Connect the positive lead of a 0 to 20V dc voltmeter to the starter solenoid '50' or 'S' terminal, and the other lead to the battery ground (earth) lead.

3   Crank the starter motor and check the voltage reading. If this is 8 volts or above, remove the starter and check the solenoid as described at paragraphs 16 thru 18 of Section 15. If the voltage is less than 8 volts the trouble is likely to be a discharged battery, high battery terminal resistance (eg: corrosion) or faulty wiring.

14 Starter motor - removal and installation

1   Disconnect the battery ground cable.

2   Remove the carburetor air cleaner and air intake tube for access.

3   Disconnect the battery cable from the starter solenoid 'B' terminal and the ignition switch wire from the '50' or 'S' terminal (photo).

4   Raise the left-hand side of the vehicle if necessary, then working from below remove the two starter attaching nuts, washers and bolts.

5   Tilt the drive end of the starter downwards then remove it from below, working it out through the emission system hoses as necessary.

6   Installation is a direct reversal of the removal procedure.

15 Starter motor - dismantling, testing, servicing and reassembly

1   Disconnect the solenoid field strap then remove the two solenoid retaining screws.

2   Disengage the solenoid plunger hook from the shift fork, then remove the solenoid.

3   Remove the shift fork retaining bolt.

4   Remove the two through bolts. Separate the drive end housing from the starter frame while disengaging the shift fork from the drive assembly.

5   Remove the bearing cover (two screws) at the brush holder end.

6   Remove the 'C' washer, washer and spring from the end of the armature shaft and pull the brush end cover from the starter frame. The armature can now be withdrawn.

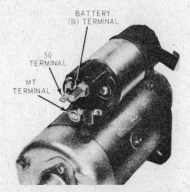

Fig. 10.15 The starter motor solenoid terminals (Sec. 13)

See text for alternative terminology

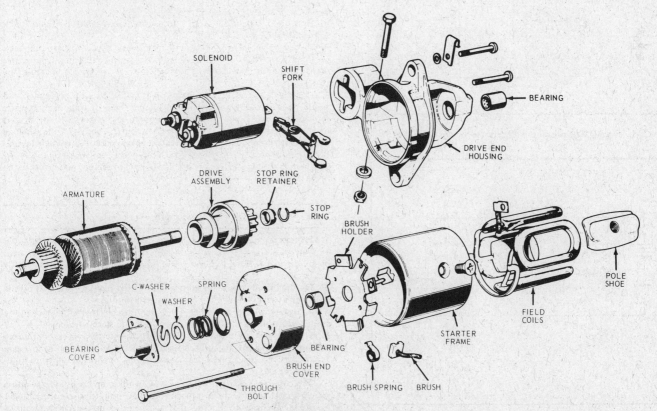

Fig. 10.16 Exploded view of the starter motor (Sec. 15)

14.3 Remove the starter motor and solenoid leads

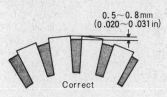

0.5~0.8 mm
(0.020~0.031 in)

Correct

Incorrect

Fig. 10.17 Under-cutting dimensions for the commutator (Sec. 15)

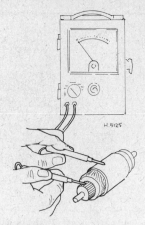

Fig. 10.18 Armature segment to core checks (Sec. 15)

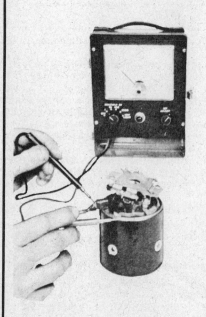

Fig. 10.19 Checking the field coils (Sec. 15)

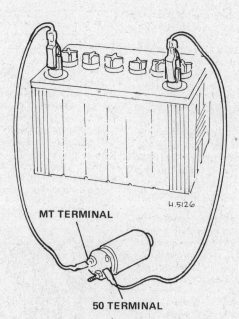

MT TERMINAL

50 TERMINAL

Fig. 10.20 The solenoid pull-in coil test set-up (Sec. 15)

TO SOLENOID

SCREW INSTALLED FOR ELECTRICAL CONNECTION TO BODY

MT TERMINAL

50 TERMINAL

Fig. 10.21 The solenoid hold coil test set-up (Sec. 15)

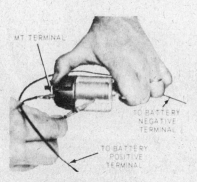

MT TERMINAL

TO BATTERY NEGATIVE TERMINAL

TO BATTERY POSITIVE TERMINAL

Fig. 10.22 The solenoid plunger return test set-up (Sec. 15)

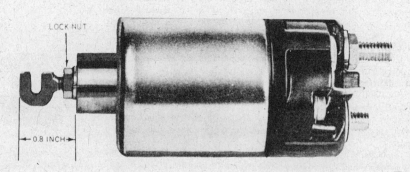

LOCK NUT

0.8 INCH

Fig. 10.23 The solenoid plunger adjustment (Sec. 15)

Fig. 10.24 The starter drive end clearance (Sec. 15)

7 Slide the drive stop ring retainer towards the armature and remove the stop ring. Now remove the retainer and drive assembly from the armature shaft.

8 Remove the brushes from the holder and separate the holder from the starter frame.

9 If it is necessary to remove the field coil (see paragraph 15), remove the pole shoe retaining screws and remove the pole shoes and field coil.

10 If the bearings are worn they can be pressed out.

11 Carefully clean the parts with a clean paintbrush, paper tissues or a lint-free cloth. Do not immerse them in proprietary solvents. Check the brush spring tension in accordance with the Specifications. Obtain new brushes, since it is false economy not to renew them if the starter is being stripped for major servicing.

12 If the commutator is dirty, discolored or worn, it may be cleaned using a strip of fine emery paper. Where scoring or arcing has occurred it may be possible for it to be machined but in serious cases it will be necessary to obtain a replacement armature. After any repair operation to the commutator, undercut the mica segments as shown in Fig. 10.17.

13 Using a suitable ohmmeter, check between the armature core and each segment of the commutator in turn. An infinite reading should be obtained in each case; if this is not obtained the armature must be renewed (see Fig. 10.18).

14 Using a suitable ohmmeter, test the commutator between all adjacent segments, checking for a similar resistance indication in each case. Provided that this test is satisfactory, and there was no indication of arcing at the commutator, the armature can be assumed to be satisfactory. If the test proves satisfactory and there was evidence of arcing at the commutator, it is advisable to have the armature checked by a specialist as there may be an intermittent fault.

15 Using a suitable ohmmeter test the field winding for a short circuit to the frame. If a reading other than infinity is obtained, a new winding will be required.

16 To test the solenoid pull-in coil, apply 12 volts dc between the 'MT' and '50' or 'M' and 'S' terminals. The plunger should be drawn into the solenoid.

17 To test the solenoid holding coil, refer to Fig. 10.21 and connect a 12 volt positive lead to the 'MT' or 'M' terminal and solenoid body. Connect a 12 volt negative lead to the '50' or 'S' terminal then disconnect the lead from the 'MT' terminal. Check that the plunger remains in the retracted position.

18 To check the plunger return, hold the solenoid plunger in, apply 12 volts dc between the 'MT' or 'M' terminal and the solenoid body. Release the plunger and check that it does **not** hold in.

19 To commence assembly, install new bearings if applicable. If the field coils were removed, these too should now be installed; ensure that the retaining screws are fully tightened.

20 Position the drive assembly on the armature shaft followed by the stop ring retainer and the stop ring. Slide the retainer over the stop ring to secure it.

21 Position the armature in the starter frame; position the brush holder to the armature and starter frame then install the brushes.

22 Position the drive end housing to the armature shaft and engage the shift fork with the drive assembly as the drive end housing is moved towards the starter frame.

23 Position the brush end cover to the starter frame, ensuring that the ear tabs of the brush holder align with the through-bolt holes. Install

the through-bolts.

24 Install the rubber washer, spring, washer and 'C' washer on the armature shaft and position the bearing cover to the brush end cover. Install the two screws.

25 Align the shift fork with the pivot bolt hole. Install the pivot bolt, lockwasher and nut.

26 If the solenoid has an adjustable plunger, check the dimension as shown in Fig. 10.23. If necessary loosen the locknut and adjust the plunger length to suit.

27 Position the solenoid to the drive end housing, making sure that the plunger hook engages with the shift fork. Install the solenoid retaining screws and washers.

28 Apply 8 volts dc to the solenoid '50' and 'MT' or 'S' and 'M' terminals and check the clearance between the starter drive and the drive stop ring retainer. For adjustable type plungers, this should be 0.08 to 0.160 in. (2.0 to 4.0 mm) and if not obtained the plunger will need to be adjusted, as described in paragraph 26; to increase the clearance lengthen the plunger and vice versa. For non-adjustable type plungers, the dimension should be 0.02 to 0.08 in. (0.5 to 2.0 mm) and adjustment is by inserting packing washers between the solenoid body and the motor drive end housing.

29 Install the field strap to the solenoid 'MT' or 'M' terminal and tighten the nut.

16 Headlights - removal and installation

1 The headlights vary, depending on the vehicle and the country in which it is used.

2 According to the model, it may be necessary to remove the grille (Chapter 12) or headlight surround (this is retained by four screws).

3 Loosen the headlight unit rim retaining screws, rotate the rim clockwise and remove it whilst supporting the headlight unit (photos).

4 Remove the plug connector from the rear of the headlight unit (photo).

5 Installation is a direct reversal of the removal procedure but take care to locate the tabs on the glass with the positioning slots of the headlight housing. On completion, it is advisable to arrange for the headlight beam to be checked, so it may be preferable to leave the headlight surround or grille (if applicable) off the vehicle until this has been done.

HOUSING   BULB   RING

10

Fig. 10.25 A typical single headlight unit (Sec. 16)

Fig. 10.26 Removing the headlight frame on a typical twin headlight unit (Sec. 16)

Fig. 10.27 The beam aiming screws on a twin headlight unit (Sec. 16)

16.3a Removal of the headlight unit

16.3b Removal of the headlight unit

16.4 The headlight unit plug connector

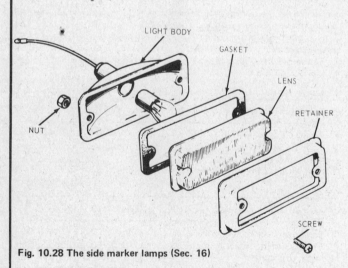

LIGHT BODY
GASKET
LENS
RETAINER
NUT
SCREW

Fig. 10.28 The side marker lamps (Sec. 16)

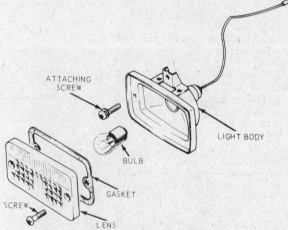

ATTACHING SCREW
BULB
LIGHT BODY
GASKET
SCREW
LENS

Fig. 10.29 The back-up (reverse) light (Sec. 16)

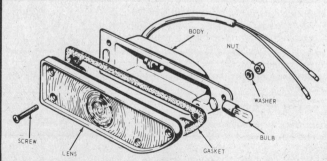

BODY
NUT
WASHER
BULB
SCREW
LENS
GASKET

Fig. 10.30 A typical front parking light (Sec. 16)

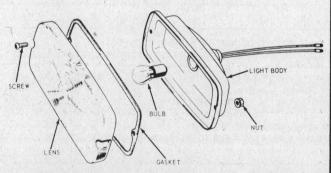

SCREW
LIGHT BODY
BULB
NUT
LENS
GASKET

Fig. 10.31 A typical tail light (Sec. 16)

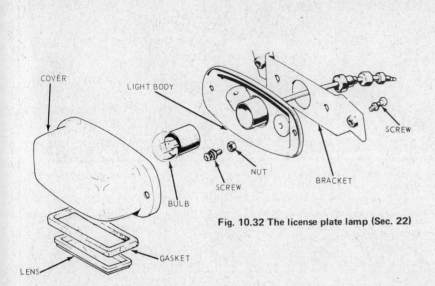

Fig. 10.32 The license plate lamp (Sec. 22)

COVER
LIGHT BODY
SCREW
NUT
SCREW
BRACKET
BULB
LENS
GASKET

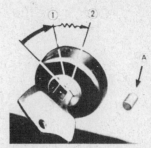

Fig. 10.33 The ignition switch

1 Ignition on   *2 Engine start*

A. This button is provided on some vehicles to switch on the parking lights when the vehicle is parked. When the ignition switch is switched on, the button retracts and the parking lights are extinguished.

17 Headlight aim - adjustment

1 Headlight aim adjusting screws are provided on each light unit but it is not advisable to adjust the aim haphazardly since not only may it be illegal, but it is not very easy to do it accurately.
2 A vertical and horizontal aim screw is fitted to each light unit, and these are the larger crosshead screws alongside two of the headlight unit securing screws.

18 Side marker lamps

1 To gain access to the bulb, either remove the two lens securing screws, or remove the screws and nuts attaching the assembly to the vehicle, then take off the retainer and lens.
2 The bulb is removed by pressing in and turning it counter-clockwise.
3 To remove the light body, either remove the two securing screws and nuts, then lift off the body and gasket, or if these screws and nuts have been removed, to gain access to the bulb, push the light unit out and remove the gasket. Separate the feed wire at the bullet connector.
4 Installation is a reverse of the removal procedure, but ensure that the gasket is fitted tidily.

19 Back-up (reverse) light

1 To gain access to the bulb, remove the two lens securing screws, then take off the lens and gasket. Now press in the bulb and rotate it counter-clockwise to remove it.
2 If the complete light unit is to be removed, disconnect the bullet connector and remove the single securing screw from beneath the vehicle.
3 Installation is the reverse of the removal procedure.

20 Front parking and turn signal lamps

1 Remove the four lens retaining screws and pull off the lens and gasket to gain access to the bulb(s). To remove the bulb(s), press in and turn counter-clockwise.
2 To remove the lamp body disconnect the leads at the bullet connectors, then remove the two lamp body mounting nuts and washers. Withdraw the lamp body.
3 Installation is the reverse of the removal procedure.

21 Tail and rear turn signal lamps

1 If two-piece lens assemblies are in use, it is necessary to remove the larger lens (3 screws) before the smaller lens (1 screw) can be removed. For single piece lenses, remove the two lens retaining screws. The bulbs can now be removed by pressing in and turning counter-clockwise.
2 If the light unit is to be removed, disconnect the wires at the bullet connectors and unhook them from the clip.
3 Remove the two nuts retaining the light unit and withdraw it.
4 Installation is the reverse of the removal procedure.

22 License plate lamp

1 To gain access to the bulb, disconnect the wire at the bullet connector then, working from behind the support bracket, remove the two light unit retaining screws.
2 Remove the light unit, take out the two cover attaching screws and remove the cover.
3 To remove the bulb, press in and turn counter-clockwise.
4 Installation is the reverse of the removal procedure.

23 Dome (interior) light

1 Press on the ends of the lens to remove it, then pull out the bulb.
2 To remove the base, unsolder the wire then remove the two attaching screws.
3 Installation is the reverse of the removal procedure.

24 Ignition switch - removal, testing and installation

1 Disconnect the battery ground (earth) cable.
2 Reach beneath the instrument panel and pull off the ignition switch electrical connector.
3 Hold the switch from behind the panel, then remove the switch retaining nut by turning it counter-clockwise.
4 Push the switch through to the rear of the instrument panel.
5 Installation is the reverse of the removal procedure.

25 Steering column mounted combination switch - removal and installation

1 The combination switch operates the direction (turn signal) indicators on all models. On many models it also operates the windscreen wipers and washers, and incorporates the headlight switch knob.
2 If the combination switch develops a fault, it will have to be replaced as an assembly by reference to the following paragraphs.
3 Disconnect the battery ground cable and remove the steering wheel, as described in Chapter 11.

10

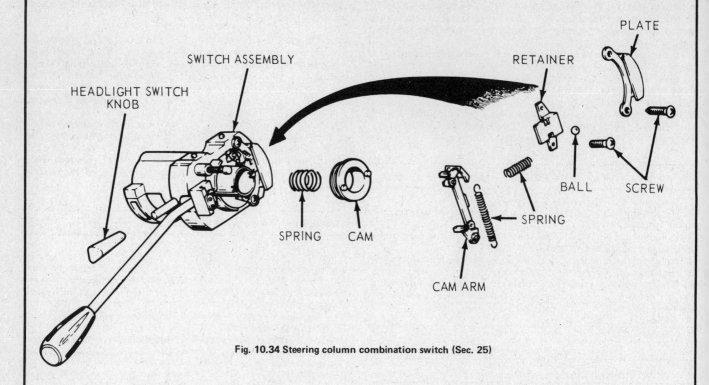

HEADLIGHT SWITCH KNOB

SWITCH ASSEMBLY

RETAINER

PLATE

SPRING

CAM

CAM ARM

SPRING

BALL

SCREW

Fig. 10.34 Steering column combination switch (Sec. 25)

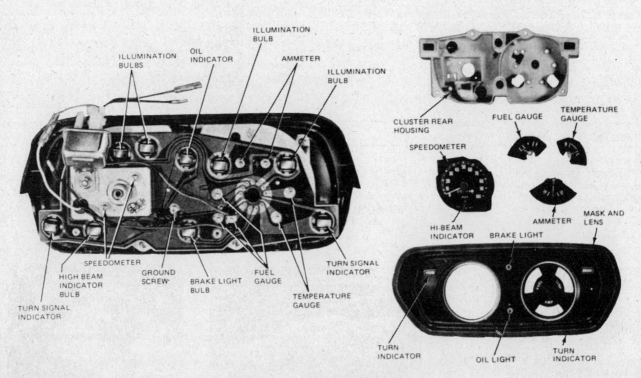

ILLUMINATION BULBS

OIL INDICATOR

ILLUMINATION BULB

AMMETER

ILLUMINATION BULB

SPEEDOMETER

HIGH BEAM INDICATOR BULB

TURN SIGNAL INDICATOR

GROUND SCREW

BRAKE LIGHT BULB

FUEL GAUGE

TEMPERATURE GAUGE

TURN SIGNAL INDICATOR

CLUSTER REAR HOUSING

FUEL GAUGE

TEMPERATURE GAUGE

SPEEDOMETER

HI-BEAM INDICATOR

BRAKE LIGHT

AMMETER

MASK AND LENS

TURN INDICATOR

OIL LIGHT

TURN INDICATOR

Fig. 10.35 The twin dial instrument cluster (Sec. 26)

4 Remove the plastic lights and hazard indicator, where applicable.
5 Remove the steering column shroud retaining screws and remove the shroud. On column change models remove the stop ring for the upper support shaft.
6 Disconnect the multiple connectors at the combination switch or at the base of the column, as applicable.
7 Where applicable, pull off the headlight switch knob.
8 Where applicable, remove the snap-ring (circlip) and pull off the turn indicator cancelling cam.
9 Either remove the switch clamp bolt, or remove the single retaining bolt near the bottom of the switch, and pull the switch off the column.
10 Installation is the reverse of the removal procedure.

26 Twin dial instrument panel - removal and installation

1 Disconnect the battery ground cable.
2 Remove the four crosshead screws which secure the cluster assembly to the instrument panel.
3 Pull the cluster away from the instrument panel so that the speedometer cable can be unscrewed.
4 Pull the multiple connector out of the printed circuit panel.
5 Note the lead colors to the ammeter then disconnect them.
6 Remove the single crosshead screw which secures the ground lead to the rear of the cluster. On vehicles equipped with a thermactor, remove the two connections from the speedometer sensor switch.
7 Withdraw the instrument panel.
8 Installation is the reverse of the removal procedure.

27 Oblong dial instrument panel - removal and installation

1 Disconnect the battery ground cable.
2 Reach up behind the instrument panel and remove the two bolts, spring washers and flat washers, and two nuts, spring washers and flat washers retaining the panel. These are not very accessible and tubular socket wrenches will probably be required together with a torch, in order to do the job properly.
3 Draw the instrument panel forward a little and unscrew the speedometer cable ferrule (photo).
4 Carefully identify all the wires, then disconnect them from their terminals and withdraw the panel (photo).
5 Installation is the reverse of the removal procedure.

28 Instrument panel - dismantling (general)

Printed circuit
1 For instrument panels with a printed circuit, this can be removed after taking out the bulb and socket assemblies and removing the four screws attaching the mask and lens to the rear housing. Remove the fuel gauge, temperature gauge and ammeter retaining screws (see next

paragraph), and lift off the printed circuit. Installation is the reverse of the removal procedure.

Speedometer, fuel gauge, temperature gauge and ammeter
2 *Twin dial instrument panel:* Remove the four screws which retain the mask and lens assembly, lift off the assembly and remove the nuts or screws retaining the instrument(s) to be removed. Installation is the reverse of the removal procedure, but it is advisable to put a trace of petroleum jelly (vaseline) on all the points of electrical contact with the printed circuit, to improve electrical continuity.
3 *Oblong dial instrument panel:* Remove the five crosshead screws retaining the escutcheon strip at the top rear of the panel, and the four crosshead screws retaining the instrument cluster to the panel. Carefully identify the wiring to the instrument(s) to be removed, then remove the retaining nuts or screws. Installation is the reverse of the removal procedure.

29 Sender units - removal and installation

Temperature sender
1 The temperature sender unit is located adjacent to the engine front lifting bracket. It can be removed by pulling off the electrical lead and unscrewing it from the block. Installation is the reverse of the removal procedure.

Oil pressure switch
2 The oil pressure switch is mounted in the oil filter bracket on the right-hand side of the engine. It can be removed by pulling off the

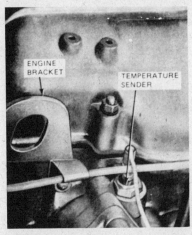

Fig. 10.36 The engine temperature sender unit (Sec. 29)

27.3 Disconnecting the speedometer drive

27.4 The rear of the oblong instrument panel

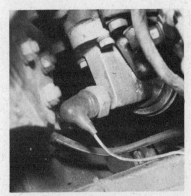

Fig. 10.37 The engine oil pressure switch (Sec. 29)

electrical lead and unscrewing it from the bracket. Installation is the reverse of the removal procedure

Fuel gauge sender unit

3 Remove the fuel tank, as described in Chapter 3, then remove the six sender unit retaining screws. Installation is the reverse of the removal procedure.

---

30 Instruments - testing (twin dial instrument panel)

Fuel and temperature gauges

1 Withdraw the instrument panel far enough to gain access to the rear of the units.
2 Remove the ground lead from the panel 'J' terminal (ground).

3 Connect the 'J' terminal to a good vehicle ground point, then connect a 12 volt bulb between the following points:
   a) *Between the 'F' and 'J', 'I' and 'J', and 'E' and 'J' terminals; the bulb should glow.*
   b) *Between the 'G' and 'J', and 'D' and 'J' terminals; the bulb should flash.*

Oil pressure switch

4 If the oil pressure switch does not illuminate with the ignition on and the engine stopped, short the oil pressure switch lead to ground. The indicator should illuminate now with the ignition on.

Temperature gauge and fuel gauge sender units

5 With the ignition switched on, short the sender unit terminal to ground. The sender unit is inoperative if the gauge unit registers full.

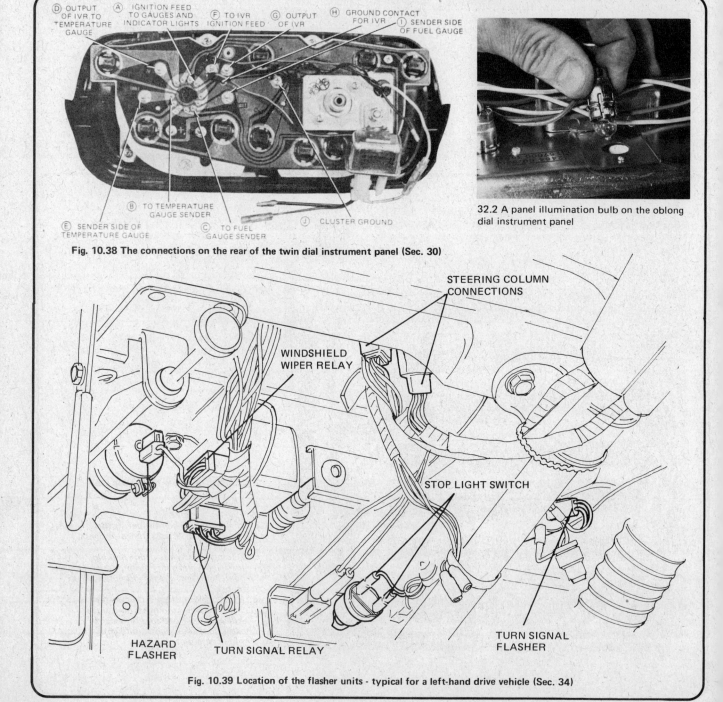

32.2 A panel illumination bulb on the oblong dial instrument panel

Fig. 10.38 The connections on the rear of the twin dial instrument panel (Sec. 30)

Ⓐ OUTPUT OF IVR TO TEMPERATURE GAUGE
Ⓐ IGNITION FEED TO GAUGES AND INDICATOR LIGHTS
Ⓕ TO IVR IGNITION FEED
Ⓖ OUTPUT OF IVR
Ⓗ GROUND CONTACT FOR IVR
Ⓘ SENDER SIDE OF FUEL GAUGE
Ⓑ TO TEMPERATURE GAUGE SENDER
Ⓔ SENDER SIDE OF TEMPERATURE GAUGE
Ⓒ TO FUEL GAUGE SENDER
Ⓙ CLUSTER GROUND

STEERING COLUMN CONNECTIONS
WINDSHIELD WIPER RELAY
STOP LIGHT SWITCH
HAZARD FLASHER
TURN SIGNAL RELAY
TURN SIGNAL FLASHER

Fig. 10.39 Location of the flasher units - typical for a left-hand drive vehicle (Sec. 34)

31 Speedometer drive cable - removal and installation

1   Disconnect the battery ground cable.
2   Unscrew the speedometer cable fitted at the left-hand side of the transmission.
3   For a person with small hands, it should be possible to unscrew the instrument panel end of the cable without removing the panel. Where this is not possible, withdraw the panel, as described previously, to enable this to be done.
4   Draw out the cable from inside the vehicle cab.
5   Installation is the reverse of the removal procedure. Make sure that the cable rubber boot and grommet are correctly installed on completion.

32 Instrument panel lamps - removal and installation

1   Instrument panel lamps are retained in bulb holders on the rear of the instrument panel.
2   To remove the bulbs, disconnect the battery ground lead, then reach up behind the panel and remove the appropriate bulb. For the bulbs at the top of the panel it may be necessary to remove the panel as previously described. The bulbs on the twin dial panels are retained by a bayonet-type fitting which requires pushing in and turning counter-clockwise; those in the oblong dial panel are in a push-in fitting which can be withdrawn for removal of the bulb (photo).
3   Installation is the reverse of the removal procedure. A trace of petroleum jelly on the bayonet fitting or bulb holder is beneficial when the bulbs are installed, to improve continuity of the bulb supply.

33 Switches (dash panel mounted) - removal and installation

1   To remove panel mounted switches, first disconnect the battery ground cable.
2   Loosen the grab screw which retains the switch knob, then remove the knob.
3   Remove the locknut on the front of the panel and push the switch out. Before disconnecting any leads, carefully identify them for correct installation.
4   Installation is the reverse of the removal procedure.

34 Flasher units

1   The hazard and turn signal flasher units are mounted to the left or right of the steering column beneath the instrument panel. Either can be removed after disconnecting the electrical connector and removing and retaining screw. Installation is the reverse of the removal procedure, but ensure that any replacements are of the same type as those removed.
2   The turn indicator relay is located adjacent to the hazard flasher unit. To remove it, disconnect the electrical connectors and remove the two retaining screws. Installation is the reverse of the removal procedure.

35 Fuses and fuse panel

1   A fuse panel containing four or six fuses is mounted on the rear

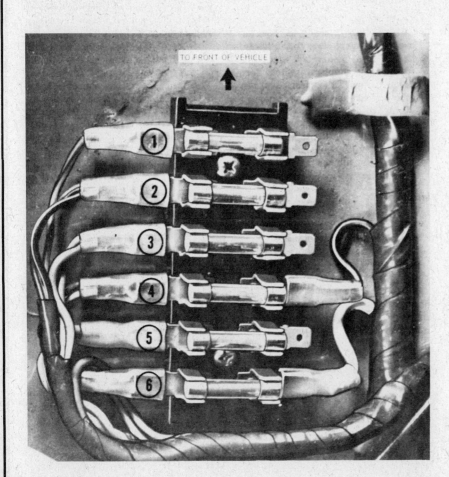

Fig. 10.40 The 6-fuse block (Sec. 35)

1   *10 amp (heater)*
2   *15 amp (engine)*
3   *15 amp (windshield wiper/washer)*
4   *15 amp (instruments indicator lights, and back-up lights)*
5   *20 amp (headlights, front parking, turn signal and side marker lights, domelight, and cluster illumination bulbs)*
6   *15 amp (horn, hazard flasher, turn signal flasher, stop lights turn signal indicator, rear parking, turn signal and side marker lights, tail lights and license plate lights)*

10

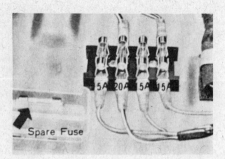

Fig. 10.41 The 4-fuse block (Sec. 35)

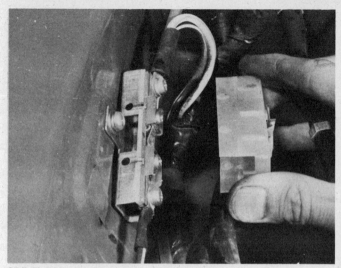

35.2 The 40 amp master fuse

corner of the engine compartment on the driver's side. These fuses are rated as shown in the appropriate illustration. Refer to the appropriate wiring diagram for the circuits which are protected.

2 The entire electrical system, except for the starter motor, is protected by a 40 amp fuse on the right-hand fender apron just to the rear of the battery (photo).

3 To replace a fuse, snap off the fuse cover and withdraw the appropriate fuse from the fuse panel. Replacements must be only of the correct type and current rating. Spare fuses are fitted inside the fuse covers.

36 Radio - removal and installation

Note: This Section covers the removal and installation of the standard fitment radio available for the vehicle in the USA. It is not envisaged that there should be any major deviation from the procedure given for other 'aftermarket' types of radio, but where a radio or similar equipment is being installed for the first time, refer to Section 37 and

38 which give general information and guidance.

Radio receiver

1 Remove the ashtray, ashtray retainer and rear retainer support, heater control knobs, bezel and right-hand defroster hose.

2 Remove the heater control (Chapter 12) and position it to the left (dash mounted control only).

3 Remove the radio receiver chassis rear support bracket. Bend the dash panel bracket downwards 90°.

4 Remove the radio receiver knobs, attaching nuts and bezel, then pull

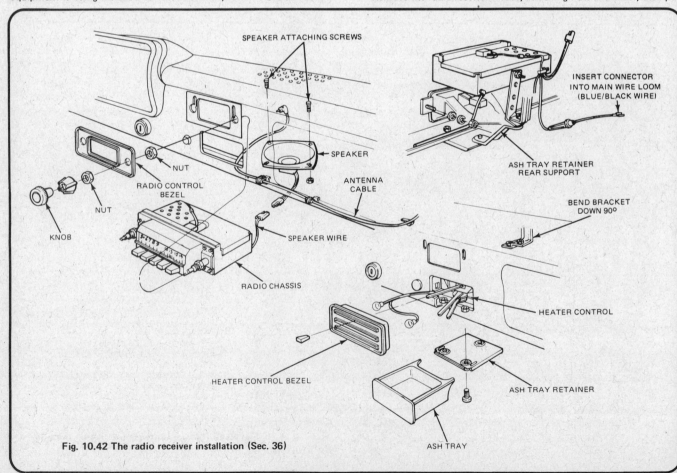

Fig. 10.42 The radio receiver installation (Sec. 36)

the chassis forwards until the control shafts clear the holes on the instrument panel. Rotate the chassis so that the control shafts are upwards, then lower the radio.

5 Disconnect the speaker wires, power lead and antenna (aerial) cable, then remove the radio chassis.

6 Installation is the reverse of the removal procedure.

Speaker

7 After removal of the radio receiver, the speaker assembly can be removed after taking out the retaining screws.

Antenna (aerial)

8 Disconnect the antenna lead from the radio receiver.

9 Remove the antenna lead from the clips beneath the instrument panel, then route the wire through the retainer wall.

10 Remove the antenna attaching nut, cap, gasket and ground strap attaching screw, and lower the antenna through the hole in the fender.

11 Installation is the reverse of the removal procedure but make sure that the ground strap screw is tight and free from rust or corrosion since this can lead to a sourse of reception interference. Ensure that any excess antenna cable is near the radio receiver rather than near the antenna itself.

---

37 Radios and tape players (aftermarket type) - installation (general)

A radio or tape player is an expensive item to buy, and will only give its best performance if installed properly. It is useless to expect concert hall performance from a unit that is suspended from the dashpanel on string with its speaker resting on the back seat or parcel shelf! If you do not wish to do the installation yourself there are many in-car entertainment specialists' who can do the job for you.

Make sure the unit purchased is of the same polarity as the vehicle. Ensure that units with adjustable polarity are correctly set before commencing installation.

It is difficult to give specific information with regard to installation,

as final positioning of the radio/tape player, speakers and antenna is entirely a matter of personal preference. However, the following paragraphs give guidelines to follow, which are relevant to all installations.

Radios

Most radios are a standardised size of around 7 inches wide, by 2 inches deep - this ensures that they will fit into the radio aperture provided in most cars. If your car does not have such an aperture, then the radio must be installed in a suitable position either in, or beneath, the dashpanel. Alternatively, a special console can be purchased which will fit between the dashpanel and the floor, or on the transmission tunnel. These consoles can also be used for additional switches and instrumentation if required. Where no radio aperture is provided, the following points should be borne in mind before deciding exactly where to install the unit.

   a) The unit must be within easy reach of the driver wearing a seat belt.
   b) The unit must not be mounted in close proximity to an electric tachometer, the ignition switch and its wiring, or the flasher unit and associated wiring.
   c) The unit must be mounted within reach of the antenna lead, and in such a place that the antenna lead will not have to be routed near the components detailed in the preceding paragraph 'b'.
   d) The unit should not be positioned in a place where it might cause injury to the car occupants in an accident; for instance, under the dashpanel above the driver's or passengers' legs.
   e) The unit must be installed really securely.

Some radios will have mounting brackets provided together with instructions; others will need to be installed using drilled and slotted metal strips, bent to form mounting brackets - these strips are available from most accessory stores. The unit must be properly grounded, by fitting a separate ground lead between the casing of the radio and the vehicle frame.

Use the radio manufacturer's instructions when wiring the radio into the vehicle's electrical system. If no instructions are available refer to

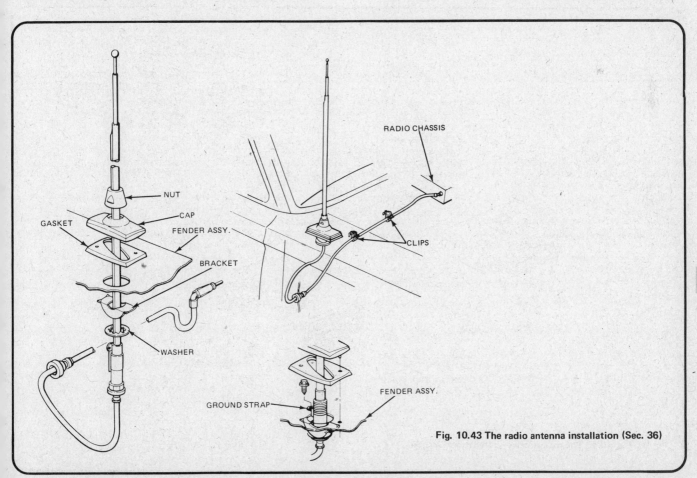

NUT
CAP
GASKET
FENDER ASSY.
BRACKET
WASHER
GROUND STRAP
RADIO CHASSIS
CLIPS
FENDER ASSY.

Fig. 10.43 The radio antenna installation (Sec. 36)

10

the relevant wiring diagram to find the location of the radio 'feed' connection in the vehicle's wiring circuit. A 1-2 amp 'in-line' fuse must be installed in the radio's 'feed' wire - a choke may also be necessary (see next Section).

The type of antenna used, and its installed position is a matter of personal preference. In general the taller the antenna the better the reception. It is best to install a fully retractable antenna - especially, if a mechanical car-wash is used or if you live in an area where cars tend to be vandalised. In this respect electric antennas which are raised and lowered automatically by switching the radio on or off are convenient, but are more likely to give trouble than the manual type.

When choosing a site for the antenna the following points should be considered:

a) *The antenna lead should be as short as possible - this means that the antenna should be mounted at the front of the vehicle.*

b) *The antenna must be mounted as far away from the distributor and HT leads as possible.*

c) *The part of the antenna which protrudes beneath the mounting point must not foul the roadwheels, or anything else.*

d) *If possible the antenna should be positioned so that the coaxial lead does not have to be routed through the engine compartment.*

e) *The plane of the panel on which the antenna is mounted should not be so steeply angled that the antenna cannot be mounted vertically (in relation to the 'end-on' aspect of the vehicle). Most antennae have a small amount of adjustment available.*

Having decided on a mounting position, a relatively large hole will have to be made in the panel. The exact size of the hole will depend upon the specific antenna being installed, although, generally, the hole required is of ¾ inch diameter. On metal bodied cars, a 'tank-cutter' of the relevant diameter is the best tool to use for making the hole. This tool needs a small diameter pilot hole drilled through the panel, through which, the tool clamping bolt is inserted. When the hole has been made the raw edges should be de-burred with a file and then painted, to prevent corrosion.

Fit the antenna according to the manufacturer's instructions. If the antenna is very tall, or if it protrudes beneath the mounting panel for a considerable distance it is a good idea to install a stay between the antenna and the vehicle frame. This stay can be manufactured from the slotted and drilled metal strips previously mentioned. The stay should be securely screwed or bolted in place. For best reception it is advisable to install a ground lead between the antenna body and the vehicle frame.

It will probably be necessary to drill one or two holes through bodywork panels in order to feed the antenna lead into the interior of the car. Where this is the case ensure that the holes are fitted with rubber grommets to protect the cable, and to stop possible entry of water.

Positioning and fitting of the speaker depends mainly on its type. Generally, the speaker is designed to fit directly into the aperture already provided in the car (usually in the shelf behind the rear seats, or in the top of the dashpanel). Where this is the case, installing the speaker is just a matter of removing the protective grille from the aperture and screwing or bolting the speaker in place. Take great care not to damage the speaker diaphragm whilst doing this. It is a good idea to position a 'gasket' between the speaker frame and the mounting panel in order to prevent vibration - some speakers will already have such a gasket fitted.

If a 'pod' type speaker was supplied with the radio, the best acoustic results will normally be obtained by mounting it on the shelf behind the rear seat. The pod can be secured to the mounting panel with self-tapping screws.

When connecting a rear mounted speaker to the radio, the wires should be routed through the vehicle beneath the carpets or floor mats - preferably through the middle, or along the side of the floorpan, where they will not be trodden on by passengers. Make the relevant connections as directed by the radio manufacturer.

By now you will have several yards of additional wiring in the car; use PVC tape to secure this wiring out of harm's way. Do not leave electrical leads dangling. Ensure that all new electrical connections are properly made (wires twisted together will not do), and completely secure.

The radio should now be working, but before you pack away your tools it will be necessary to 'trim' the radio to the antenna. Follow the radio manufacturer's instructions regarding this adjustment.

Tape players

Installation instructions for both cartridge and cassette stereo tape players are the same and in general the same rules apply as when fitting a radio. Tape players are not usually prone to electrical interference like radio - although it can occur - so positioning is not so critical. If possible the player should be mounted on an 'even-keel'. Also, it must be possible for a driver wearing a seat belt to reach the unit in order to change, or turn over, tapes.

For the best results from speakers designed to be recessed into a panel, mount them so that the back of the speaker protrudes into an enclosed chamber within the vehicle (eg; door interiors or the trunk cavity).

To install recessed type speakers in the front doors first check that there is sufficient room to mount the speaker in each door without it fouling the latch or window winding mechanism. Hold the speaker against the skin of the door, and draw a line, around the periphery of the speaker. With the speaker removed draw a second 'cutting' line, within the first, to allow enough room for the entry of the speaker back, but at the same time providing a broad seat for the speaker flange. When you are sure that the 'cutting-line' is correct, drill a series of holes around its periphery. Pass a hacksaw blade through one of the holes and then cut through the metal between the holes until the center section of the panel falls out.

De-burr the edges of the hole and then paint the raw metal to prevent corrosion. Cut a corresponding hole in the door trim panel - ensuring that it will be completely covered by the speaker grille. Now drill a hole in the door edge and a corresponding hole in the door surround. These holes are to feed the speaker leads through - so install grommets. Pass the speaker leads through the door trim, door skin and out through the holes in the side of the door and door surround. Re-install the door trim panel and then secure the speaker to the door using self-tapping screws. Note: if the speaker is supplied with a shield to prevent water dripping on it, ensure that this shield is at the top.

'Pod' type speakers can be fastened to the shelf behind the rear seat, or anywhere else offering a corresponding mounting point on each side of the car. If the 'pod' speakers are mounted on each side of the shelf behind the rear seat, it is a good idea to drill several large diameter holes through to the trunk cavity beneath each speaker - this will improve the sound reproduction. 'Pod' speakers sometimes offer a better reproduction quality if they face the rear window - which then acts as a reflector - so it is worthwhile experimenting before finally fixing the speakers.

38 Radios and tape players - suppression of interference (general)

To eliminate buzzes, and other unwanted noises, costs very little and is not as difficult as sometimes thought. With a modicum of common sense and patience and following the instructions in the following paragraphs, interference can be virtually eliminated.

The first cause for concern is the generator. The noise this makes over the radio is like an electric mixer and the noise speeds up when you rev up (if you wish to prove the point, you can remove the fanbelt and try it). The remedy for this is simple; connect a 1.0 mfd - 3.0 mfd capacitor between ground, probably the bolt that holds down the generator base, and the *large* terminal on the alternator (see Fig. 10.44).

A second common cause of electrical interference is the ignition system. Here a 1.0 mfd capacitor must be connected between ground and the SW or + terminal on the coil (see Fig. 10.45). This may stop the tick, tick, tick sound that comes over the speaker. Next comes the spark itself.

There are several ways of curing interference from the ignition HT system. One is to use carbon film HT leads but these are not recommended as they have a tendency to "snap" inside and you don't know then why you are firing on only half your cylinders. So the second, and more successful method is to use resistive spark plug caps (see Fig. 10.46) of about 10,000 ohm to 15,000 ohm resistance. If, due to lack of room, these cannot be used, an alternative is to use 'in-line' suppressors (Fig. 10.46) - if the interference is not too bad, you may get away with only one suppressor in the coil to distributor line. If the interference does continue (a "clacking" noise) then 'doctor' all HT leads.

At this stage it is advisable to check that the radio is well grounded, also the antenna and to see that the antenna plug is pushed well into the set and that the radio is properly trimmed (see preceding Section). In addition, check that the wire which supplies the power to the set is

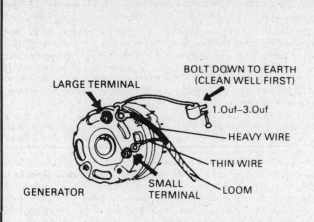

LARGE TERMINAL

BOLT DOWN TO EARTH
(CLEAN WELL FIRST)

1.0uf–3.0uf

HEAVY WIRE

THIN WIRE

SMALL TERMINAL

LOOM

GENERATOR

Fig. 10.44 The correct way to connect a capacitor to the alternator

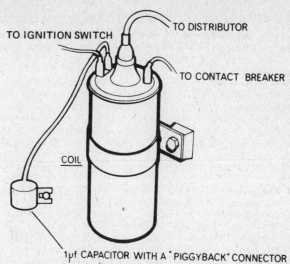

TO IGNITION SWITCH

TO DISTRIBUTOR

TO CONTACT BREAKER

COIL

1µf CAPACITOR WITH A "PIGGYBACK" CONNECTOR

Fig. 10.45 The capacitor must be connected to the ignition switch side of the coil (Sec. 38)

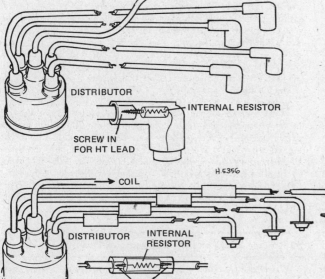

TO COIL

DISTRIBUTOR

INTERNAL RESISTOR

SCREW IN FOR HT LEAD

H.5356

Fig. 10.46 Ignition HT lead suppressors (Sec. 38)

Top: Resistive spark plug caps
Bottom: In-line suppressors

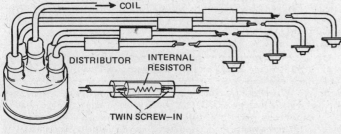

COIL

DISTRIBUTOR

INTERNAL RESISTOR

TWIN SCREW–IN

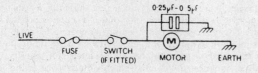

LIVE

FUSE

SWITCH
(IF FITTED)

0.25µF–0.5µf

M
MOTOR

EARTH

Fig. 10.47 Correct method of suppressing electric motors (Sec. 38)

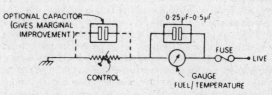

OPTIONAL CAPACITOR
(GIVES MARGINAL IMPROVEMENT)

0.25µF–0.5µf

FUSE

LIVE

CONTROL

GAUGE
FUEL/ TEMPERATURE

Fig. 10.48 Method of suppressing gauges and their control units (Sec. 38)

10

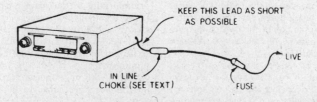

KEEP THIS LEAD AS SHORT AS POSSIBLE

LIVE

IN LINE CHOKE (SEE TEXT)

FUSE

Fig. 10.49 All 'in-line' chokes should be installed into the live supply lead as close to the unit as possible (Sec. 38)

as short as possible and does not wander all over the car. At this stage it is a good idea to check that the fuse is of the correct rating. For most sets this will be about 1 to 2 amps.

At this point the more usual causes of interference have been suppressed. If the problem still exists, a look at the causes of interference may help to pinpoint the component generating the stray electrical discharges.

The radio picks up electromagnetic waves in the air; now some are made by regular broadcasters, and some, which we do not want, are made by the car. The home made signals are produced by stray electrical discharges floating around the car. Common producers of these signals are electric motors, ie; the windshield wipers, electric screen washers, electric window winders, heater fan or an electric aerial if installed. Other sources of interference are electric fuel pumps, flashing turn signal and instruments. The remedy for these cases is shown in Fig. 10.47 for an electric motor whose interference is not too bad and Fig. 10.48 for instrument suppression. Turn signals are not normally suppressed. In recent years, radio manufacturers' have included in the line (live) of the radio, in addition to the fuse, an 'in-line' choke. If your pride and joy lacks one of these, put one in as shown in Fig. 10.49.

All the foregoing components are available from radio stores or accessory stores. If you have an electric clock installed this should be suppressed by connecting a 0.5 mfd capacitor directly across it as shown for a motor in Fig. 10.47.

If after all this, you are still experiencing radio interference, first assess how bad it is, for the human ear can filter out unobtrusive unwanted noises quite easily. But if you are still adamant about eradicating the noise, then continue.

As a first step, a few "experts" seem to favour a screen between thue radio and the engine. This is OK as far as it goes - literally! - for the whole set is screened anyway and if interference can get past that then a small piece of aluminium is not going to stop it.

A more sensible way of screening is to discover if interference is coming down the wires. First, take the live lead; interference can get between the set and the choke (hence the reason for keeping the wires short). One remedy here is to screen the wire and this is done by buying screened wire and using that. The loudspeaker lead could be screened also to prevent "pick-up" getting back to the radio - although this is unlikely.

Without doubt, the worst source of radio interference comes from the ignition HT leads, even if they have been suppressed. The ideal way of suppressing these is to slide screening tubes over the leads themselves. As this is impractical, we can place an aluminium shield over the majority of the lead areas, but for a straight engine the results are not particularly good.

Now for the really impossible cases, here are a few tips to try out. Where metal comes into contact with metal, an electrical disturbance is caused which is why good clean connections are essential. To remove interference due to overlapping or butting panels you must bridge the join with a wide braided ground strap (like that from the frame to the engine/transmission). The most common moving parts that could create noise and should be strapped are, in order of importance:

a) *Muffler to frame.*
b) *Exhaust pipe to engine block and frame.*
c) *Air cleaner to frame.*
d) *Front and rear bumpers to frame.*
e) *Steering column to frame.*
f) *Hood and trunk lids to frame.*
g) *Hood frame to frame on soft tops.*

These faults are most pronounced when (1) the engine is idling (2) labouring under load. Although the moving parts are already connected with nuts, bolts, etc, these do tend to rust and corrode, thus creating a high resistance interference source.

If you have a "ragged" sounding pulse when mobile, this could be wheel or tire static. This can be cured by buying some anti-static powder and sprinkling it liberally inside the tires.

If the interference takes the shape of a high pitched screeching noise that changes its note when the auto is in motion and only comes now and then, this could be related to the antenna especially if it is of the telescopic or whip type. This source can be cured quite simply by pushing a small rubber ball on top of the antenna (yes, really!) as this breaks the electric field before it can form; but it would be much better to buy yourself a new antenna of a reputable brand. If, on the other hand, you are getting a loud rushing sound every time you brake, then this is brake static. This effect is most prominent on hot dry days and is cured only by fitting a special kit, which is quite expensive.

In conclusion, it is pointed out that it is relatively easy, and therefore cheap, to eliminate 95 per cent of all noise, but to eliminate the final 5 per cent is time and money consuming. It is up to the individual to decide if it is worth it. Please remember also, that you cannot get an expensive radio's performance out of a cheap radio.

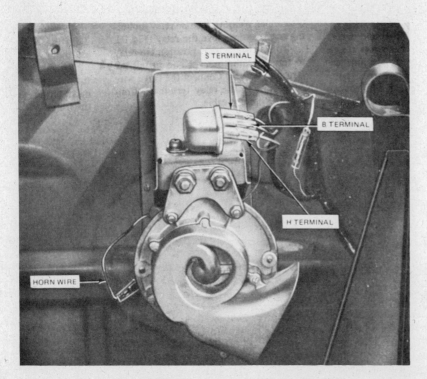

Fig. 10.50 The horn and relay installation (Sec. 39)

39.2 The horn relay

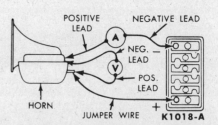

Fig. 10.51 The horn relay test set-up
(Sec. 39)

Finally, players and eight track players are not usually affected by car noise but in a very bad case, the best remedies are the first three suggestions plus using a 3 - 5 amp choke in the "live" line and in incurable cases screen the live and speaker wires.

Note: If your car is fitted with electronic ignition, then it is not recommended that either the spark plug resistors or the ignition coil capacitor be fitted as these may damage the system. Most electronic ignition units have built-in suppression and should, therefore, not cause interference.

39 Horn

1 A single horn is mounted under the hood on a bracket behind the left-hand headlight.
2 The horn switch on the steering wheel closes the circuit to the horn relay, which is mounted on the same bracket as the horn (photo).
3 The horn tone is adjustable by means of an adjusting screw on the horn casing.
4 To adjust the horn tone, connect an ammeter and voltmeter as shown in Fig. 10.52 and rotate the adjusting screw to obtain 4.0 ± 0.05 amps at a voltage of 12V dc.
5 In the event of the horn failing to operate, check that power is reaching the 'B' terminal of the relay by using a test lamp. If satisfactory, remove the relay 'S' terminal lead and use a jumper lead to ground the relay 'S' terminal. Connect a test light between the relay 'H' terminal and ground; if the bulb does not illuminate, the relay is defective. If the relay is to be renewed, note that the green/yellow wire connects to the 'H' terminal, the green/black wire connects to the 'B' terminal and the green wire connects to the 'S' terminal.

40 Windshield wiper arms and blades

1 To remove a windshield wiper blade, press down on the arm to unlatch the top stud. Depress the tab on the blade saddle and pull the blade from the arm. When installing, simply push the wiper arm into the blade until it latches (photo).
2 The rubber blade inserts can be removed by squeezing the latch lock release at the end of the blade, then pulling the insert out of the lever jaws. When installing, insert the new insert through each of the lever jaws.
3 To remove a wiper arm, either remove the arm retaining nut on the top surface of the arm or raise the arm from the windshield and loosen the retaining screw. Installation is the reverse of removal, but ensure that the arm is correctly positioned on the spindle with respect to the wiper mechanism park position. See Fig. 10.52 which shows the wiper blades in the 'Park' position for left-hand drive vehicles (photo).

41 Windshield wiper motor and linkage - removal and installation

1 Disconnect the battery ground cable then remove the wiper arms (see previous Section).
2 Remove the rubber cap, nut, tapered spacer and rubber grommet from each bracket pivot shaft.
3 Remove the two motor and bracket assembly mounting bolts and washers (photo).
4 Disconnect the motor leads at the connector and remove the assembly from the vehicle. Note the ground washer and rubber washer and the mounting.
5 Remove the plastic watershield.
6 Remove the linkage to motor output arm retaining clip, and move the link aside. Note the position of the washers before removing the bracket.
7 Remove the four motor to bracket retaining bolts, then remove the motor assembly.
8 Installation is the reverse of the removal procedure, but do not forget the washers between the wiper motor and the bracket, or the ground washer and rubber washer at the bracket mounting holes.

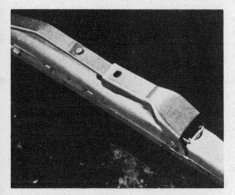

40.1 Removal of the windscreen wiper blades

40.3 The windshield wiper arm retaining screw

41.3 The windshield wiper motor (right-hand drive model illustrated)

10

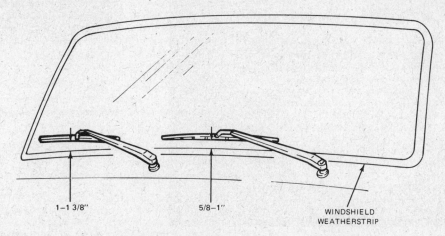

1 – 1 3/8"   5/8 – 1"   WINDSHIELD WEATHERSTRIP

Fig. 10.52 The wiper arm 'Park' position (Sec. 40)

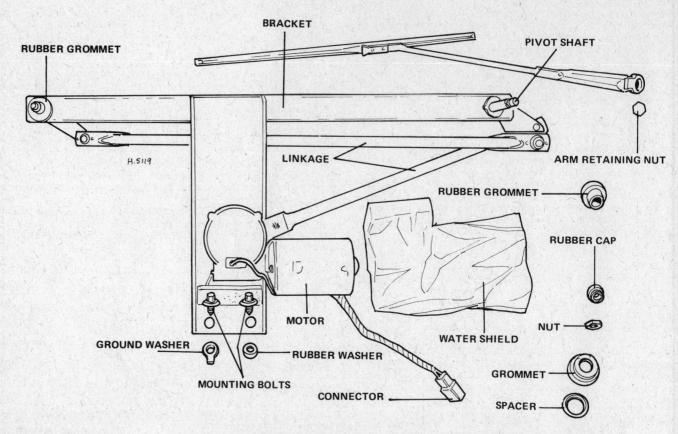

RUBBER GROMMET   BRACKET   PIVOT SHAFT

H.5119

LINKAGE

ARM RETAINING NUT

RUBBER GROMMET

RUBBER CAP

MOTOR

WATER SHIELD   NUT

GROUND WASHER   RUBBER WASHER

GROMMET

MOUNTING BOLTS

SPACER

CONNECTOR

Fig. 10.53 The windshield wiper motor, linkage and arms (Secs. 40 and 41)

(Left-hand drive vehicle illustrated)

42 Windshield wiper motor - dismantling and reassembly

1   Remove the wiper motor and bracket assembly, as described in the previous Section.
2   Remove the 'C' clip retaining the linkage to the output arm.
3   Remove the four bolts attaching the motor to the bracket assembly, and the four switch plate retaining screws.
4   Remove the two through-bolts and nuts, then slide the gear housing, brush plate and armature assembly out of the motor housing.
5   Pull out the armature from the gear housing.
6   Remove the three brush plate retaining screws; remove the brush plate and wire assembly.
7   Examine all the parts for wear and other damage. If the commutator shows signs of scoring or arcing, polishing with fine glass paper is permissible. However, in severe cases it will be necessary to purchase a replacement armature. If the motor is being dismantled for major servicing (eg; where it has failed to operate), it is recommended that new brushes are fitted, taking care to install one at a time so that the connections are not mixed up.
8   To commence assembly, position the brush plate assembly to the gear housing and install the screws.
9   Insert the worm gear end of the armature into the gear housing then pull back the three brushes to allow it to fully seat. The brushes should now be on the commutator.
10 Install the motor housing, checking that the grommet is properly seated. Install the through-bolts and nuts.
11 Install the switch plate and gasket.
12 Position the motor assembly to the bracket and linkage, and install the 'C' clip.
13 The assembly can now be installed in the vehicle.

43 Windshield washer system - removal and installation

Reservoir

1   Disconnect the hose and electrical connection from the pump, then slide the reservoir out of the mounting bracket. Installation is the reverse of this procedure.

Washer pump

2   Remove the reservoir, as described in paragraph 1.
3   Remove the two crosshead screws retaining the pump to the reservoir then remove the pump. Installation is the reverse of this procedure (photo).

Washer nozzle

4   Open the engine compartment hood (bonnet), reach under the cowl and pull the hose off the nozzle.
5   Remove the nozzle retaining clip to release the nozzle.
6   Installation is the reverse of the removal procedure; but adjust its position as necessary to obtain the correct spray pattern.

44 Windshield wiper motor - testing

1   If the wiper motor fails to operate, first check for obvious faults such as a blown fuse, faulty wiring or loose connector.
2   Next, check for 12 volts at the blue wire of the main harness connector when the ignition is on (not necessary if the washers are operating). If there is no supply, a blown fuse or open circuit connection is indicated.

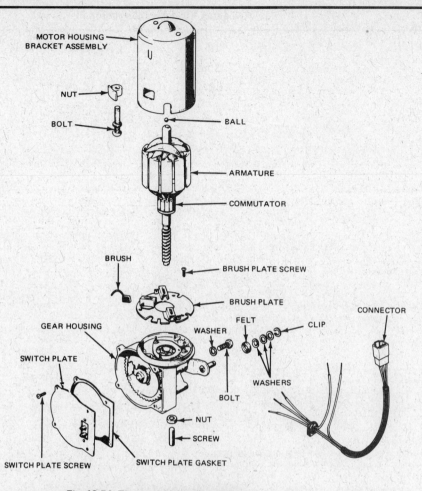

MOTOR HOUSING
BRACKET ASSEMBLY

NUT

BOLT

BALL

ARMATURE

COMMUTATOR

BRUSH PLATE SCREW

BRUSH

BRUSH PLATE

CONNECTOR

GEAR HOUSING

WASHER

FELT

CLIP

SWITCH PLATE

BOLT

WASHERS

SWITCH PLATE SCREW

SWITCH PLATE GASKET

NUT

SCREW

Fig. 10.54. The windshield wiper motor components

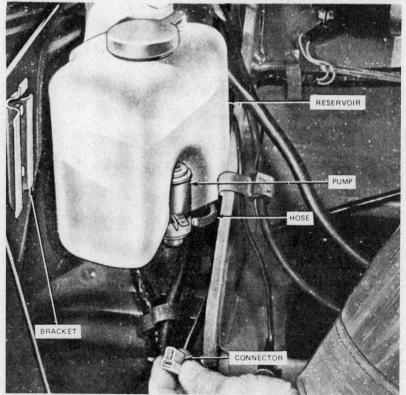

RESERVOIR

PUMP

HOSE

BRACKET

CONNECTOR

Fig. 10.55. The windshield washer reservoir and pump

43.3 The windshield washer pump

10

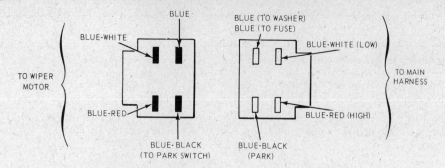

Fig. 10.56 The windshield wiper motor test set-up (Sec. 44)

3   Using a jumper wire, connect a +12 volt battery supply to the blue wire of the motor connector. Ground the blue/white wire and check that the wipers operate at low speed; ground the blue/red wire and check that the wipers operate at high speed. Stop the wipers in an 'up' position.

4   With the +12 volt battery lead connected as in paragraph 3, jumper the blue/black and blue/white wires. The wipers should now park.

5   If the motor does not operate, first check the ground before installing a replacement.

45 Windshield wiper relay - testing

1   Switch the ignition on and connect a jumper wire from the wiper relay blue/red wire to ground; the wipers should operate at high speed.

2   Connect a 12 volt testlamp between the blue wire and ground; the testlamp should glow.

3   Connect an ohmmeter or self-powered testlamp between the yellow/green wire and ground; there should be continuity with the wiper switch at high or low position.

4   Connect a jumper wire between the blue/white wire and ground; the wipers should operate at low speed.

5   Connect an ohmmeter or self-powered testlamp between the yellow/black wire and ground; there should be continuity when the wiper switch is in the high position.

6   Connect a jumper wire between the blue/black wire and the blue/white wire; the wipers should return to the high position.

7   If the above tests prove satisfactory, first check the relay case for ground before installing a replacement.

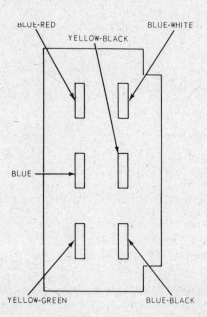

Fig. 10.57 The windshield wiper relay test set-up (Sec. 45)

46 Fault diagnosis - electrical system

Symptom	Reason/s
Starter motor fails to turn engine	Battery discharged.
	Battery defective internally
	Battery terminal leads loose or ground lead not securely attached to body.
	Loose or broken connections in starter motor circuit.
	Starter motor solenoid switch faulty.
	Starter brushes badly worn, sticking or brush wires loose.
	Commutator dirty, worn or burnt.
	Starter motor armature faulty.
	Field coils grounded.
Starter motor turns engine very slowly	Battery in discharged condition.
	Starter brushes badly worn, sticking or brush wires loose.
	Loose wires in starter motor circuit.
Starter motor operates without turning engine	Pinion or flywheel gear teeth broken or worn.
Starter motor noisy or engagement excessively rough	Pinion or flywheel teeth broken or worn.
	Starter motor retaining bolts loose.
Starter motor remains in operation after ignition key released	Faulty ignition switch.
	Faulty solenoid.

Symptom	Reason/s
Charging system indicator on with ignition switch off	Faulty alternator diode.
Charging system indicator light on - engine speed above idling	Loose or broken drivebelt. Shorted negative diode. No output from alternator.
Charge indicator light not on when ignition switched on but engine not running	Burnt out bulb. Field circuit open. Lamp circuit open.
Battery will not hold charge for more than a few days	Battery defective internally. Electrolyte level too weak or too low. Battery plates heavily sulphated.
Horn will not operate or operates intermittently	Loose connections. Defective switch. Defective relay. Defective horn.
Horns blow continually	Faulty relay. Relay wiring grounded. Horn button stuck (grounded).
Lights do not come on	If engine not running, battery discharged. Light bulb filament burnt out or bulbs broken. Wire connections loose, disconnected or broken. Light switch shorting or otherwise faulty.
Lights come on but fade out	If engine not running battery discharged. Light bulb filament burnt out, or bulbs or sealed beam units broken. Wire connections loose, disconnected or broken. Light switch shorting or otherwise faulty.
Lights give very poor illumination	Lamp glasses dirty. Lamps badly out of adjustment.
Lights work erratically - flashing on and off, especially over bumps	Battery terminals or ground connection loose. Lights not grounding properly. Contacts in light switch faulty.
Wiper motor fails to work	Blown fuse. Wire connections loose, disconnected, or broken. Brushes badly worn Armature worn or faulty. Field coils faulty.
Wiper motor works very slowly and takes excessive current	Commutator dirty, greasy or burnt. Armature bearings dirty or unaligned. Armature badly worn or faulty.
Wiper motor works slowly and takes little current	Brushes badly worn. Commutator dirty, greasy or burnt. Armature badly worn or faulty.
Wiper motor works but wiper blades remain static	Wiper motor gearbox parts badly worn or teeth stripped

10

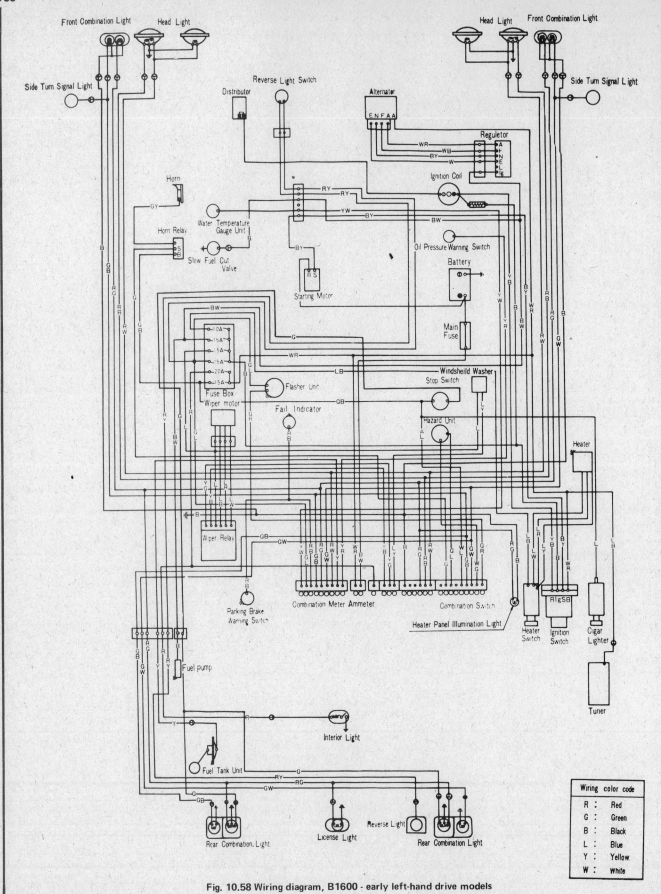

Fig. 10.58 Wiring diagram, B1600 - early left-hand drive models

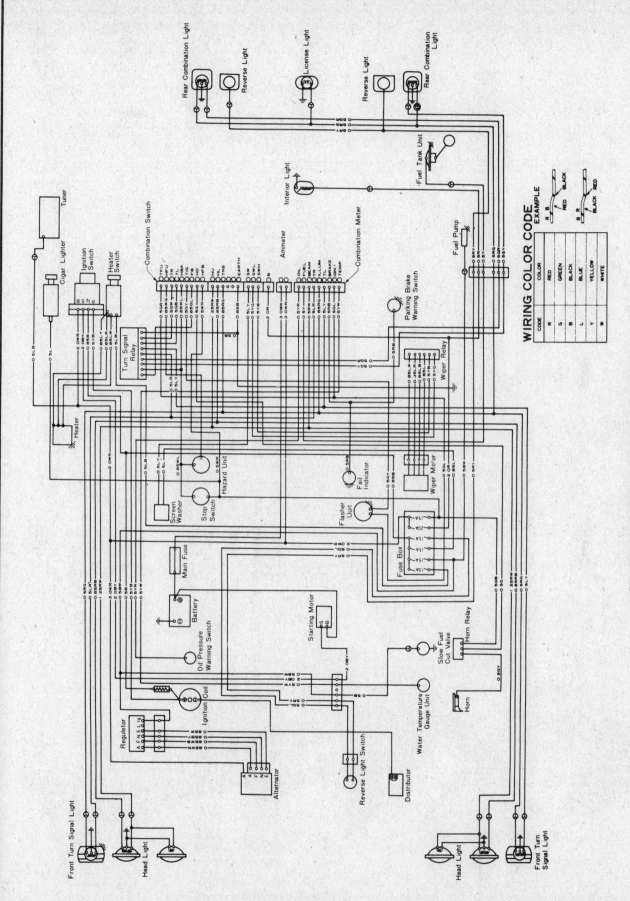

Fig. 10.59 Wiring diagram, B1600 - later left-hand drive models

10

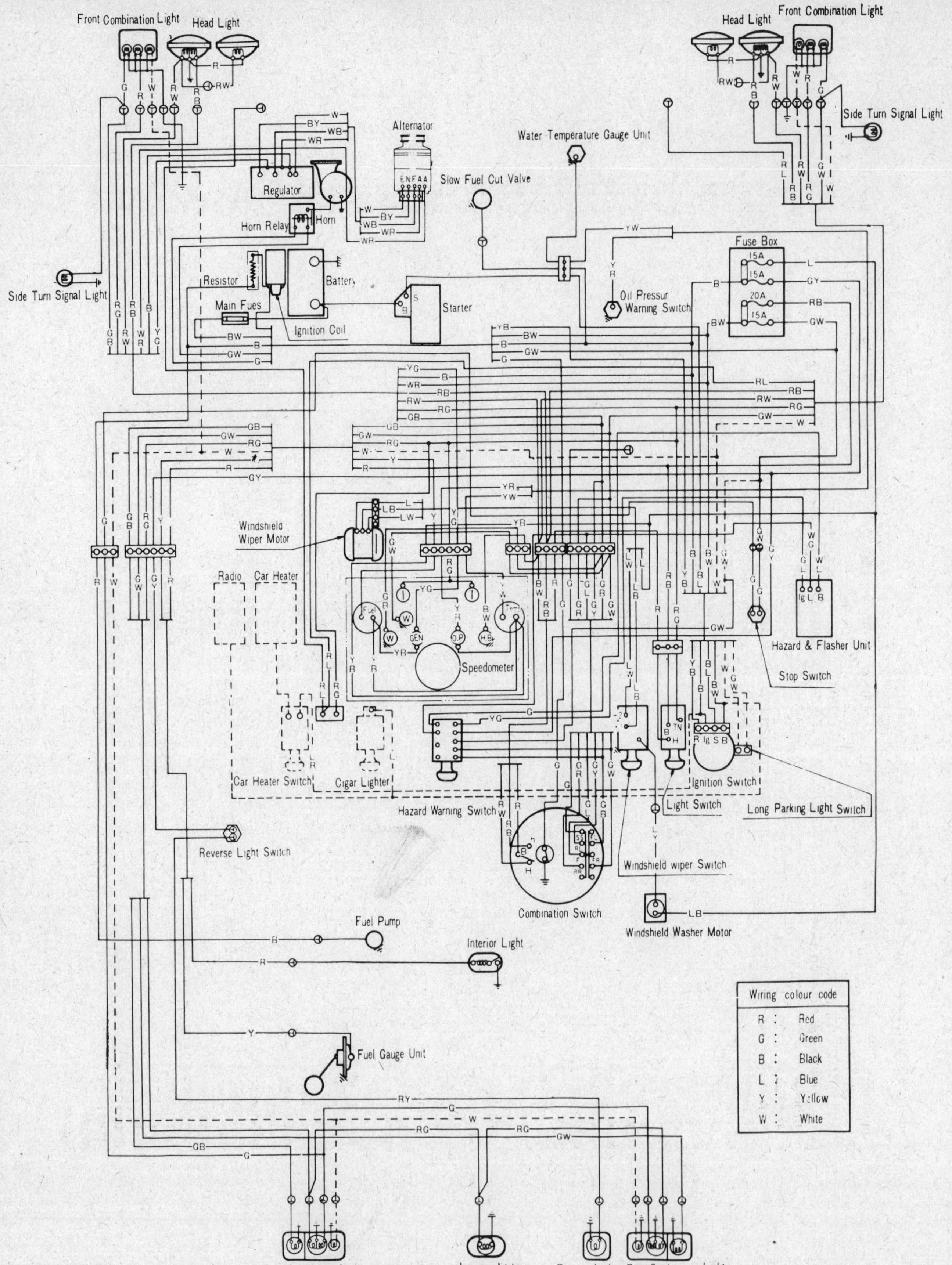

Fig. 10.60 Wiring diagram, B1600 - right-hand drive models

Code for Wiring diagrams, Courier, 1972 models (see pages 164 - 167)

Component	Location	Component	Location
Alternator	G-2	Pumps:	
Cigar lighter	B-23	Fuel	D-11
Coasting richer (deceleration valve)	F-12	Washer	D-15
Distributor	G-6	Regulator	J-6
Flashers:		Relays:	
Emergency warning	D-26	Horn	C-24
Turn signal	B-28	Speed switch (California only)	H-10
Horn	C-23	Turn signal	F-28
Lamps:		Wiper	E-14
Back-up	F-16	Sending units:	
Dome	B-19	Fuel	G-18
Headlamps:		Temperature	G-20
Left	F-21	Slow fuel cut valve (throttle solenoid)	F-12
Right	E-21	Switches:	
License plate	H-30	Accelerator	G-12
Parking lamps:		Back-up lamp	E-16
Left	J-25	Clutch (California only)	H-12
Right	H-25	Dimmer	C-22
Side marker lamps:		Dome light	B-19
Front:		Dual brake warning	G-16
Left	J-25	Emergency flasher	C-27
Right	G-25	Fan	C-10
Rear:		Horn	D-25
Left	J-30	Headlight	D-22
Right	F-20	Ignition	B-6
Tail lamps:		Oil pressure	F-18
Left	H-30	Parking brake	G-17
Right	G-30	Passing high beam	D-21
Ignition coil	C-7	Speed switch (California only)	H-10
Ignition resistor	B-9	Stoplight	C-26
Illumination:		Turn signal	C-28
Heater	D-23	Wiper/washer	G-14
Instrument cluster	E-24	Vacuum (49 states only)	G-11
Indicators:			
Ammeter	A-4	Wire colour code	
Brake warning	E-17	Black	BK
Fuel gauge	E-19	Green	DG
High beam	E-22	Blue	DB
Oil pressure	E-18	Red	R
Temperature gauge	E-20	White	W
Turn signal:		Yellow	Y
Left	G-28		
Right	G-26		
Motors:			
Blower	D-10		
Wiper	D-14		
Starter	D-2		

10

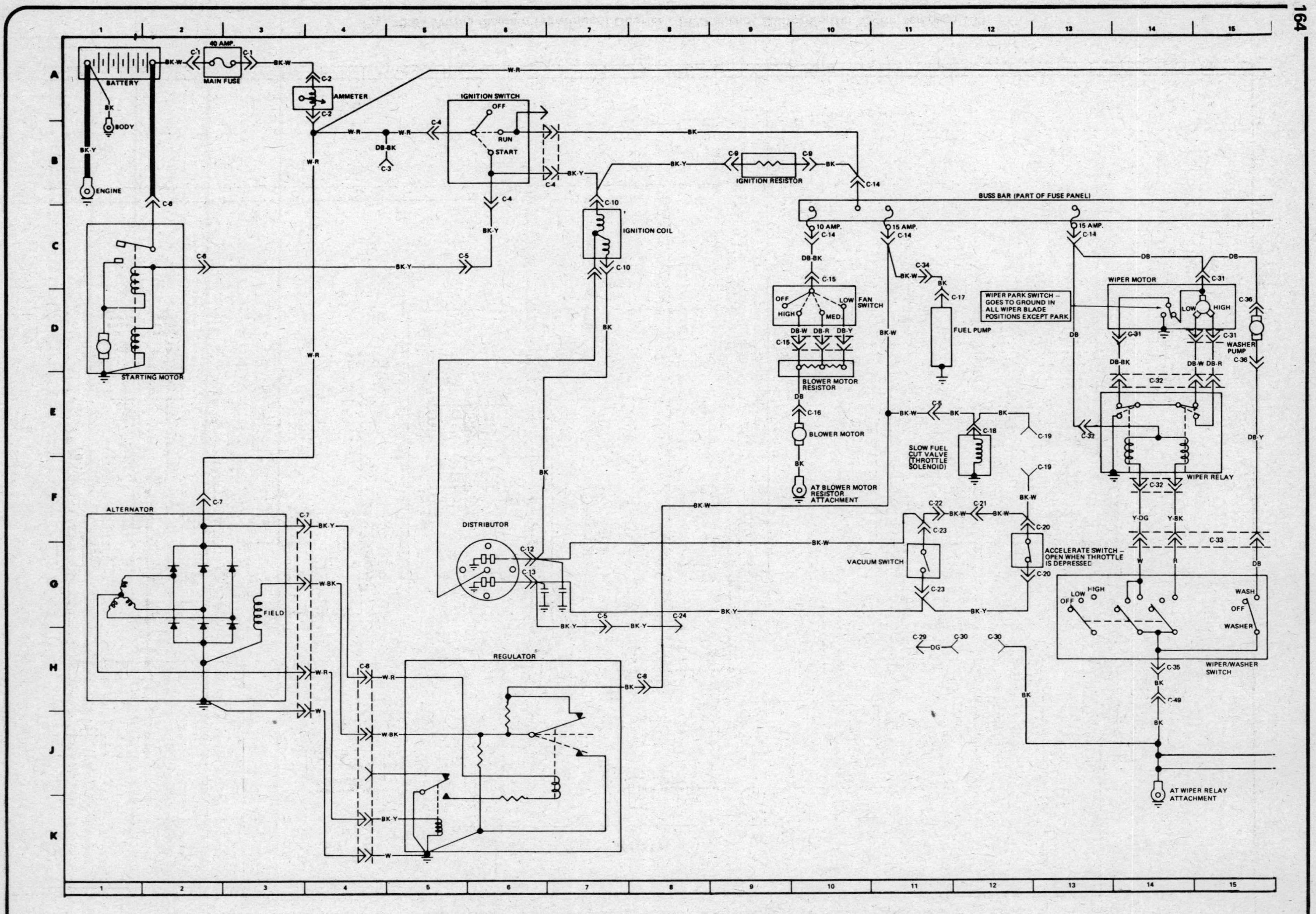

Fig. 10.61 Wiring diagram, Courier - 1972 except California (for 'Code' see page 163)

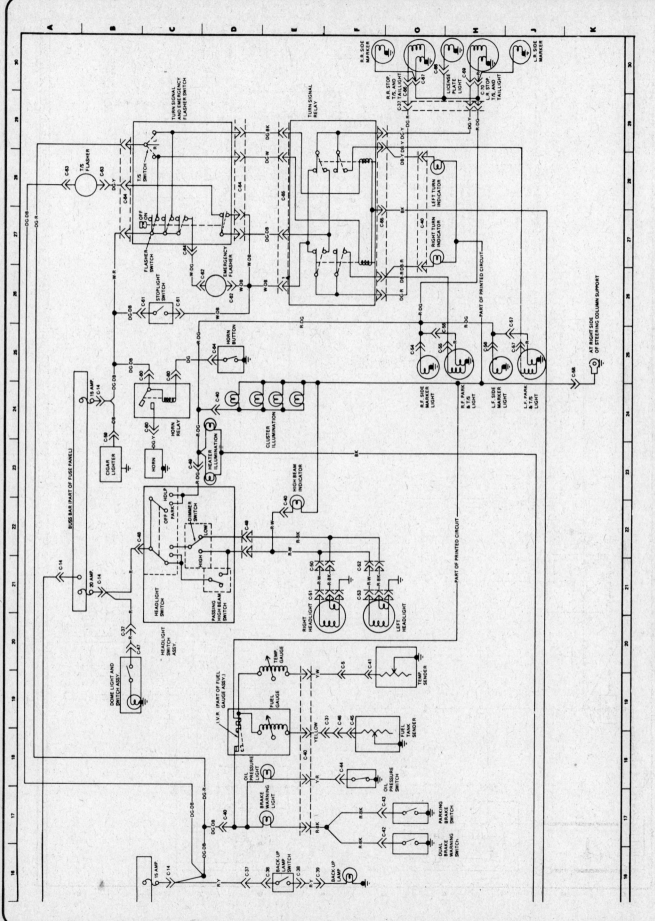

Fig. 10.61 Wiring diagram (continued) Courier - 1972 except California (for 'Code' see page 163)

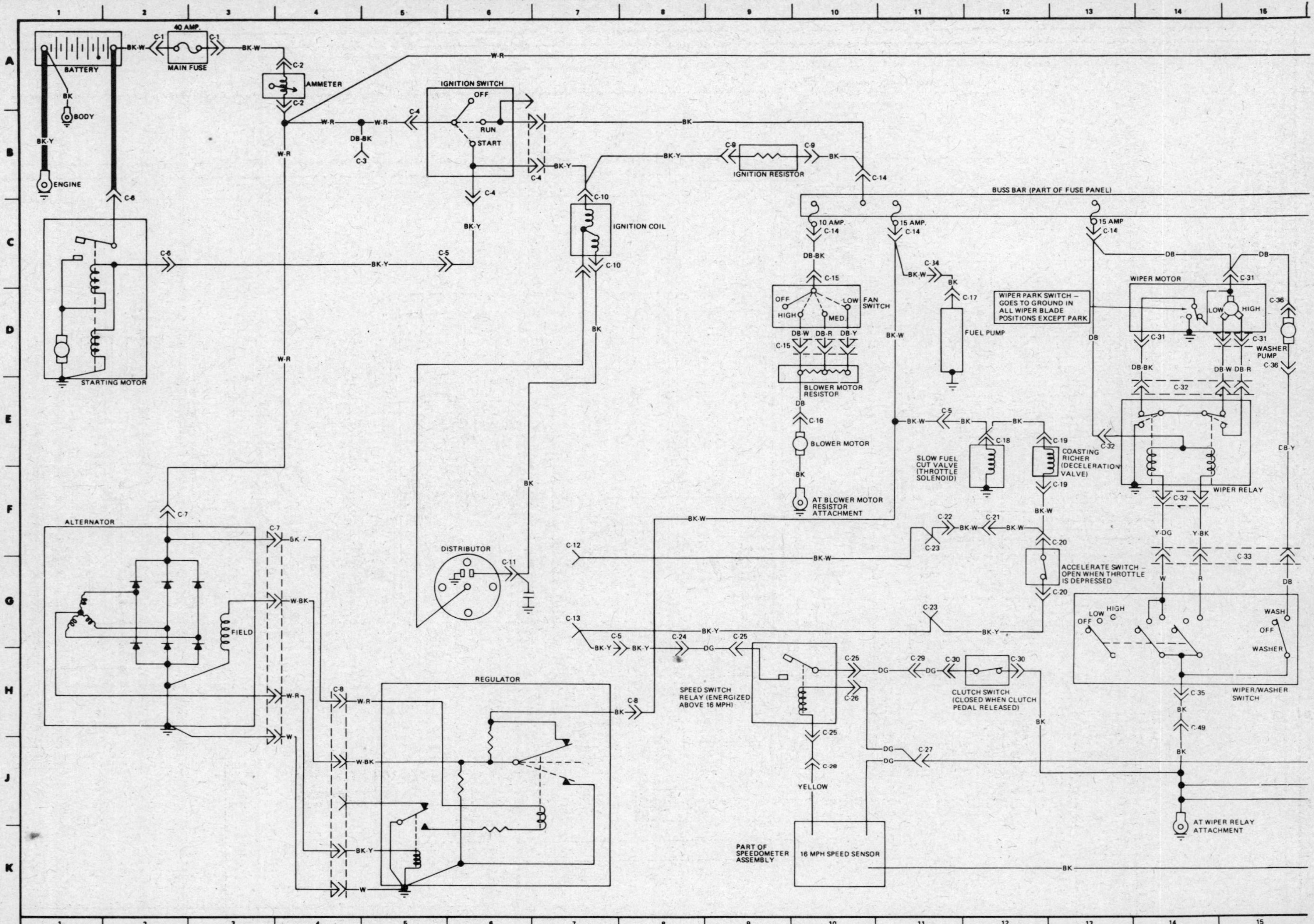

Fig. 10.62 Wiring diagram, Courier - 1972 California (for 'Code' see page 163)

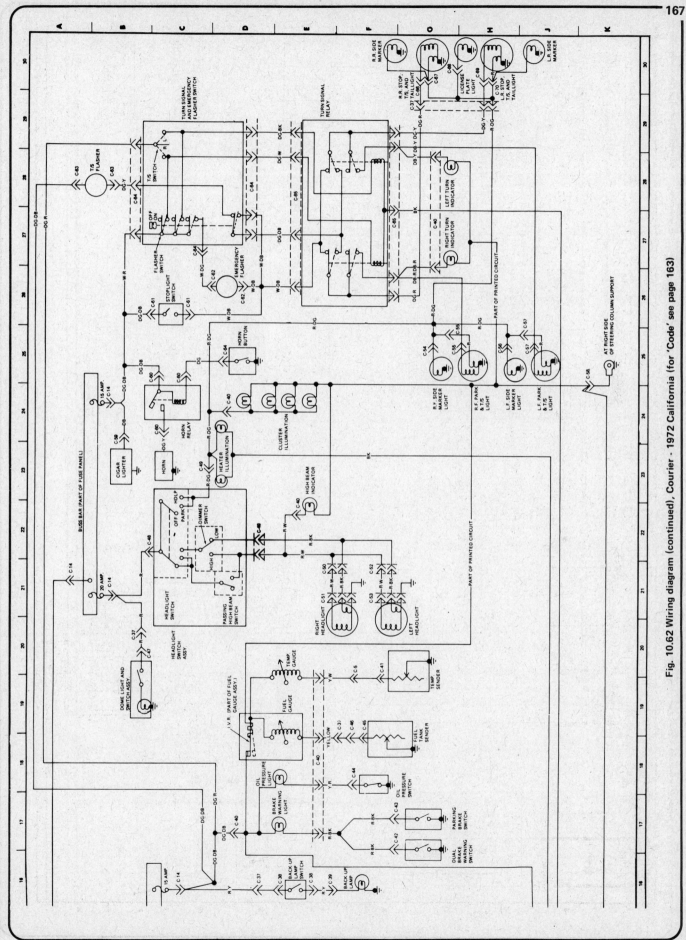

Fig. 10.62 Wiring diagram (continued), Courier - 1972 California (for 'Code' see page 163)

10

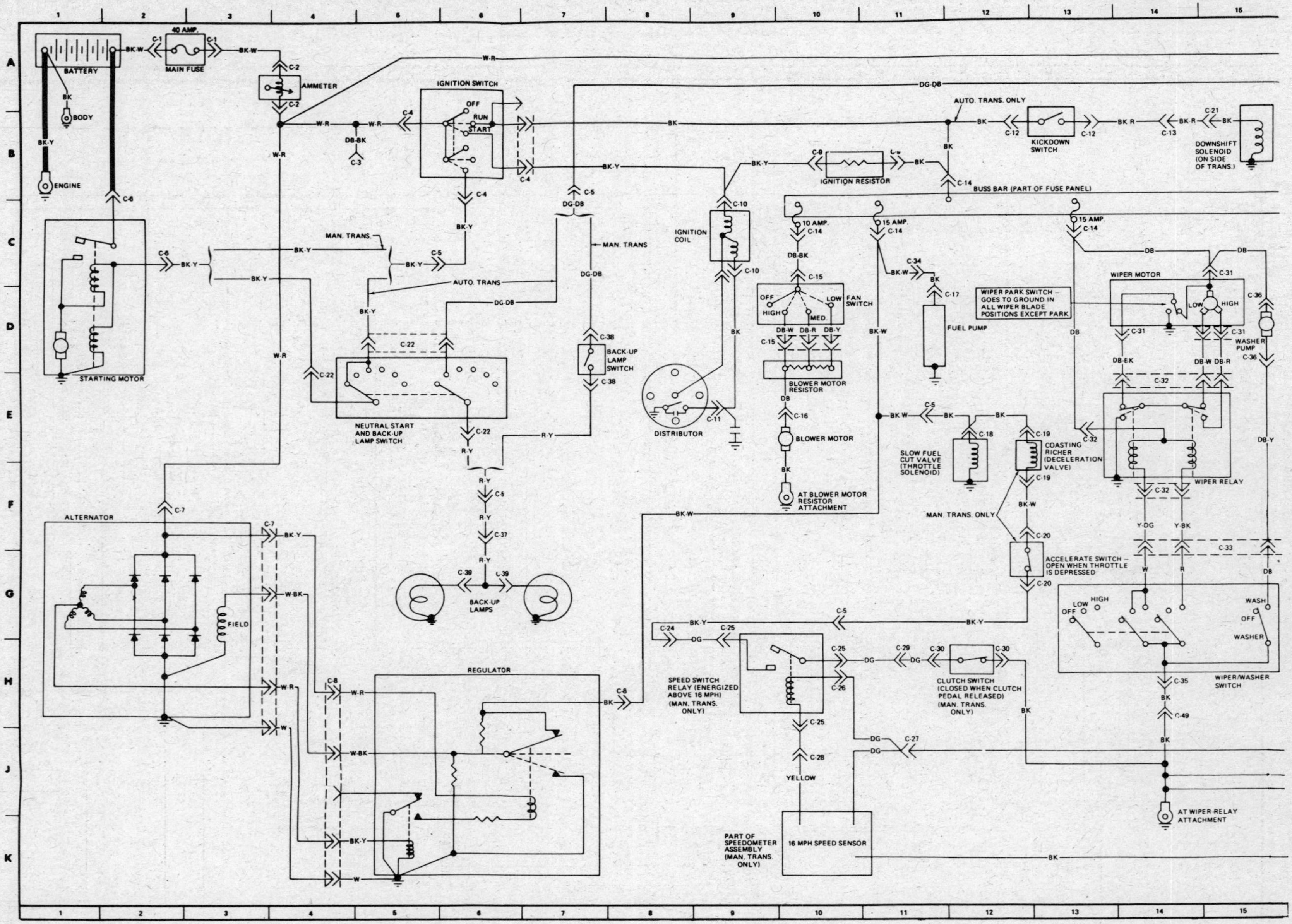

Fig. 10.63 Wiring diagram, Courier - 1973 (for 'Code' see page 172)

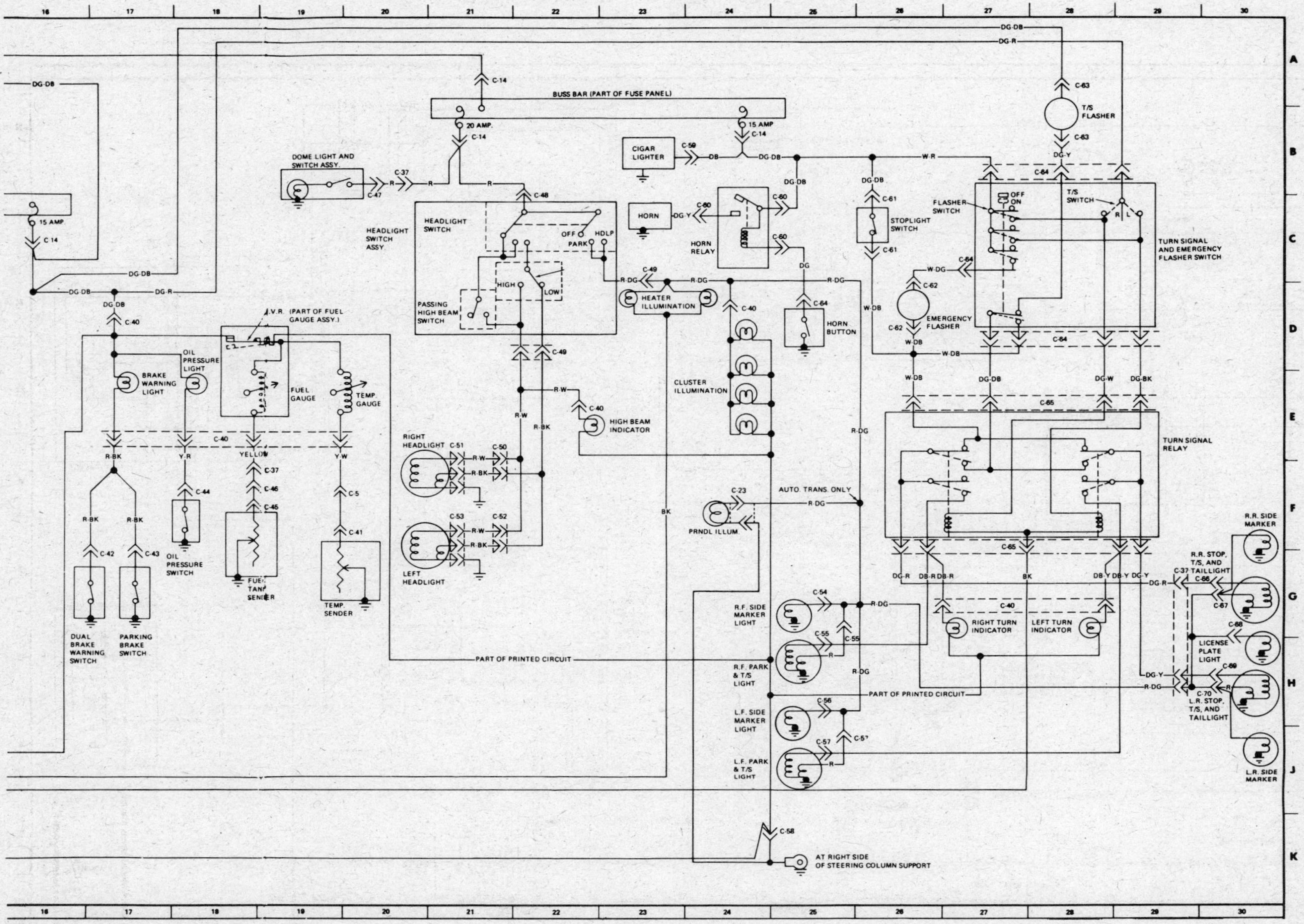

Fig. 10.63 Wiring diagram (continued), Courier - 1973 (for 'Code' see page 172)

10

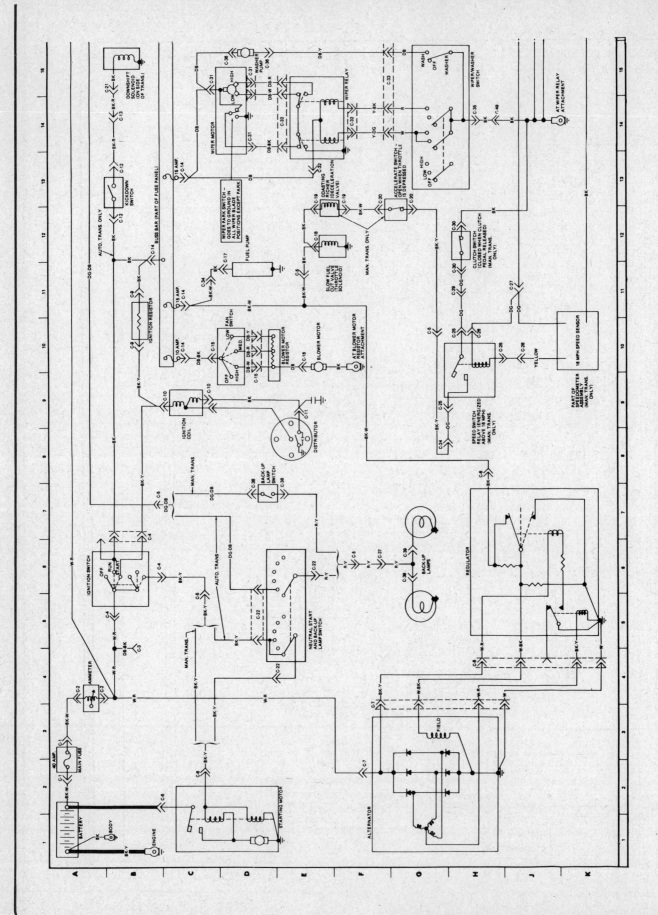

Fig. 10.64 Wiring diagram Courier - 1974 (for 'Code' see page 172)

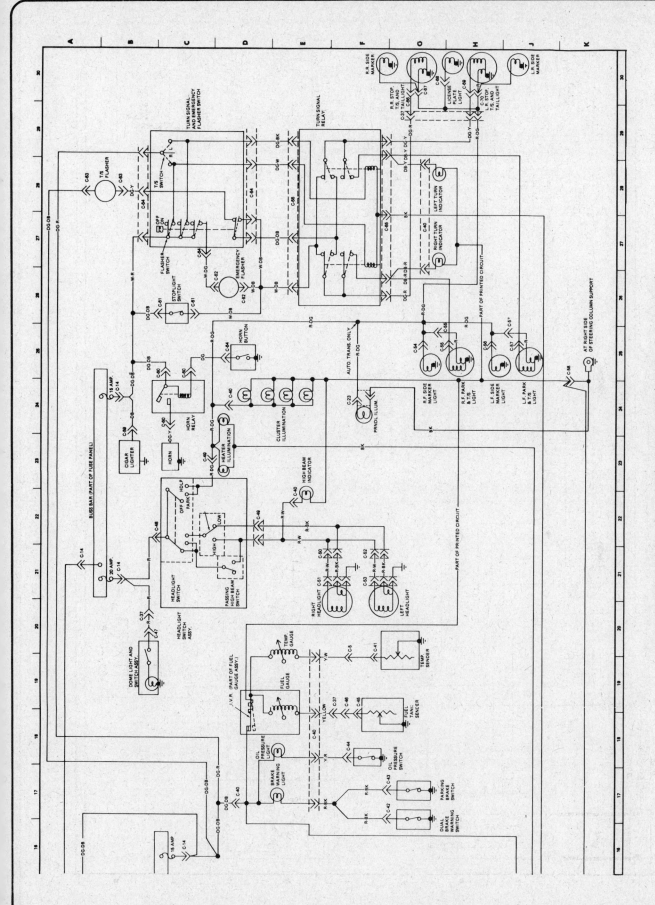

Fig. 10.63 Wiring diagram (continued), Courier - 1974 (for 'Code' see page 172)

(for 'Code' see page 172)

10

Code for Wiring diagrams, Courier, 1973 and 1974 models (see pages 168 - 171)

Component	Location
Alternator	G-2
Cigar lighter	B-23
Coasting richer (deceleration valve)	F-12
Distributor	D-8
Downshift solenoid	B-15
Flashers:	
Emergency warning	D-26
Turn signal	B-28
Horn	C-23
Lamps:	
Back up	G-6
Dome	B-19
Headlamps:	
Left	F-21
Right	E-21
License plate	H-30
Parking lamps:	
Left	J-25
Right	H-25
Side marker lamps:	
Front:	
Left	J-25
Right	G-25
Rear:	
Left	J-30
Right	F-30
Tail lamps:	
Left	H-30
Right	G-30
Ignition coil	C-9
Ignition resistor	B-10
Illumination:	
Heater	D-23
Instrument cluster	E-24
Prndl	F-24
Indicators:	
Ammeter	A-4
Brake warning	E-17
Fuel gauge	E-19
High beam	E-22
Oil pressure	E-18
Temperature gauge	E-20
Turn signal:	
Left	G-28
Right	G-26
Motors:	
Blower	D-10
Wiper	D-14
Starter	D-2

Component	Location
Pumps:	
Fuel	D-11
Washer	D-15
Regulator	J-6
Relays:	
Horn	C-24
Speed switch	H-10
Turn signal	F-28
Wiper	E-14
Sending units:	
Fuel	G-18
Temperature	G-20
Slow fuel cut valve (throttle solenoid)	F-12
Switches:	
Accelerator	G-12
Back up lamp	E-16
Clutch	H-12
Dimmer	C-22
Dome light	B-19
Dual brake warning	G-16
Emergency flasher	C-27
Fan	C-10
Horn	D-25
Headlight	D-22
Ignition	B-6
Kickdown	B-13
Neutral start and back up	E-5
Oil pressure	F-18
Parking brake	G-17
Passing high beam	D-21
Speed switch	H-10
Stoplight	C-26
Turn signal	C-28
Wiper/washer	G-14

Wiring color code	
Black	BK
Green	DG
Blue	DB
Red	R
White	W
Yellow	Y

Chapter 11 Suspension and steering

Refer to Chapter 13 for Specifications and information applicable to 1974 through 1982 models.

Contents

Fault diagnosis - suspension and steering 16	Steering gear - dismantling and reassembly 12
Front shock absorber - removal and installation 3	Steering gear - removal and installation 11
Front wheel bearings - adjustment 7	Steering geometry checks 8
Front wheel bearings - removal and installation 6	Steering linkage 14
General description 1	Suspension and steering - routine maintenance 2
Rear shock absorber - removal and installation 9	Suspension lower arm and spring - removal and installation ... 5
Rear spring - removal and installation 10	Suspension upper arm - removal and installation 4
Steering gear - adjustments 13	Wheels and tires 15

Specifications

Front suspension type	Coil spring and stabilizer bar, with double wishbones and hydraulic shock absorbers
Rear suspension type	Semi-elliptic leaf springs and hydraulic shock absorbers

Steering

Type	Recirculating ball nut
Reduction ratio	17.63 : 1
Free-play at steering wheel:	
Normal	0.8 to 1.2 in. (20 to 30 mm)
Limit	2 in. (50 mm)
Worm bearing preload (without sector shaft)	0.9 to 3.5 lb in. (1 to 4 kg cm)
Sector gear backlash	0 to 0.004 in. (0 to 0.1 mm)
Sector shaft/bush clearance:	
Normal	0.0003 to 0.0019 in. (0.007 to 0.049 mm)
Limit	0.008 in. (0.20 mm)
Sector shaft end-clearance	0 to 0.004 in. (0 to 0.1 mm)
Steering gearbox lubricant	SAE 90 EP gear oil

Steering geometry

King pin inclination	7° 37'
Camber	1° 23' ± 20'
Maximum camber difference, side-to-side	20'
Camber offset	1.57 in. (40 mm)
Caster angle	1° ± 20'
Maximum caster difference, side-to-side	20'
Caster trail	0.22 in. (5.6 mm)
Toe-in	0 to ¼ in. (0 to 6 mm)
Front wheel turning angle:	
Inside	34/38°
Outside	32/33°

Wheels

Type	Pressed steel
Size	4½J x 14WDC

Tires

Size:	
European market	6.70 - 14C, 8PR front and rear
USA market	6.00 - 14, 6PR front and rear
Other markets	6.00 - 14, 6PR front
	6.00 - 14, 8PR rear

Tire pressures:

European market:

Front	... ...	30 lbf/in^2 (2.1 kgf/cm^2) - light load
Rear	... ...	45 lbf/in^2 (3.2 kgf/cm^2) - light load
Front	... ...	30 lbf/in^2 (2.1 kgf/cm^2) - heavy load
Rear	... ...	65 lbf/in^2 (4.5 kgf/cm^2) - heavy load

USA market:

Front	... ...	25 lbf/in^2 (1.75 kgf/cm^2) - up to 60 mph
Rear	... ...	45 lbf/in^2 (3.2 kgf/cm^2) - up to 60 mph
Front	... ...	30 lbf/in^2 (2.1 kgf/cm^2) - over 60 mph
Rear	... ...	45 lbf/in^2 (3.2 kgf/cm^2) - over 60 mph

Other markets:

Front	... ...	25 lbf/in^2 (1.75 kgf/cm^2) - light load
Rear	... ...	45 lbf/in^2 (3.2 kgf/cm^2) - light load
Front	... ...	25 lbf/in^2 (1.75 kgf/cm^2) - heavy load
Rear	... ...	60 lbf/in^2 (4.25 kgf/cm^2) - heavy load

Note 1: In the above table, a heavy load is one in excess of 1100 lb (500 kg).
Note 2: Where a tire pressure decal is fitted, and the specified pressures do not conform to those given in this table, the decal information should be regarded as being correct.
Note 3: All tire pressures should be checked when the tires are cold.

Torque wrench settings

	lbf ft	kg fm
Front suspension		
Upper arm shaft to frame	62/76	8.6/10.5
Lower arm shaft to frame	54/69	7.4/9.5
Upper balljoint to upper arm	15/20	2.1/2.8
Lower balljoint to lower arm	60/70	8.3/9.7
Bumper to lower arm	60/70	8.3/9.7
Bumper to upper arm	15/20	2.1/2.8
Upper balljoint to steering knuckle	40/55	5.5/7.6
Lower balljoint to steering knuckle	58/73	8/10.1
Lower arm shaft to lower arm	43/80	5.9/11
Shock absorber mounting (upper)	18/26	2.5/3.6
Shock absorber mounting (lower)	12/17	1.7/2.3
Wheel bearing nut	6/8	0.83/1.1
Rear suspension		
Spring clip ('U' bolt) to plate	46/58	6.3/8
Spring pin to front hanger	62/76	8.6/10.5
Shackle plate to rear hanger	44/58	6.1/8
Shock absorber, upper and lower mounting	18/26	2.5/3.6
Spring pin to frame bracket	15/18	2.1/2.5
Steering		
Steering gear to frame	33/42	4.6/5.8
Side cover to gear	12/17	1.7/2.3
Steering wheel to shaft	22/29	3/4
Column bracket to instrument panel	12/17	1.7/2.3
Pitman arm to gear	109/130	15/18
Column jacket clamp to gear	7/9	1/1.2
Idler arm bracket to frame	33/42	4.6/5.8
Idler arm to shaft	43/50	5.9/6.9
Center link to Pitman arm	22/29	3/4
Center link to idler arm	33/47	4.6/6.5
Tie-rod to center link	18/25	2.5/3.5
Tie-rod to steering knuckle	22/29	3/4
Tie-rod clamps	13/18	1.8/2.5
Wheel nuts	58/65	8/9

Note: The wheel nuts are left-hand threaded on the left-hand side of the vehicle.

1 General description

1 The front suspension comprises double wishbones and a coil spring, with a double-acting, hydraulic shock absorber inside the spring, on each side of the vehicle (photo).
2 The front hub assemblies swivel on balljoints at the outer ends of the wishbones. They are adjustable for camber and castor angle by the use of shims behind the upper arm shaft (photo).
3 The rear suspension comprises semi-elliptic springs and double-acting, hydraulic shock absorbers. The spring rating is varied according to the particular application. The springs are mounted on a single pin at the forward end and on a shackle assembly at the rear end (photo).
4 Each spring is mounted to the axle tube using 'U' bolts (spring clips).
5 A recirculating ball nut type of steering is utilized which connects to the hub assemblies thru a center link, twin tie-rods and steering knuckles. All movement is transmitted thru balljoints, with an idler arm assembly mounted on the longitudinal chassis frame member opposite the steering gearbox.
6 Front wheel bearings are of the opposed, tapered roller type and are adjustable for hub endfloat. Rear wheel bearings form part of the axle halfshaft assembly and are dealt with in Chapter 8.

1.1 General view of the left side front suspension looking forwards.

1.2 Camber and caster are adjusted by shims behind the upper arm shaft

1.3 General view of the right side rear suspension looking rearwards

2 Suspension and steering - routine maintenance

1 At the intervals given in the 'Routine Maintenance' Section at the beginning of the manual, the following points require attention:

Steering wheel free-play
2 Examine for excessive play in the steering linkage and at the steering wheel rim — the maximum permissible play is given in the Specifications. Further information on suitable methods of checking, adjusting and renewing are given in Sections 13 and 14 of this Chapter.

Idler arm
3 When lubricating the idler arm, remove the grease plug and install a grease nipple. Remove the cotter pin (where applicable) and loosen the idler arm spindle nut, then apply grease from a grease gun fitted with a general purpose lithium base grease (eg; Castrol LM grease) until it is seen to exude from the dust seal. Tighten the nut on completion to the specified torque, install a new split pin (where applicable), remove the grease nipple and install the plug.

Front suspension balljoints
4 Remove the grease plug from each balljoint and install a grease nipple. Apply grease from a grease gun filled with a molybdenum disulphide lithium base grease until the joint rubber boot can be felt or seen to swell. Do not force the grease out of the boot or the seal will be destroyed. On completion remove the nipple and install the plug. Note: Where a vehicle has been stored at temperatures below 20°F (−6°C) it should be placed in a heated garage for about 30 minutes to permit the old lubricant in the joint to soften.

Steering balljoints and upper arm shaft
5 On some later models, grease nipples or plugs may be fitted to the steering balljoints and/or suspension upper arm shafts. Where applicable, apply two or three strokes from a grease gun filled with a molybdenum disulphide lithium base grease.

Wheel bearings
6 Clean and repack the wheel bearings. The full procedure is given in Section 6.

3 Front shock absorber - removal and installation

1 Apply the handbrake then raise the appropriate side of the vehicle and remove the roadwheel.
2 Remove the nuts securing the upper end of the shock absorber to the crossmember. Take off the rubber bushings and washers.
3 Remove the bolts securing the lower end of the shock absorber to the lower suspension arm, then withdraw it from below.
4 To test the shock absorber, hold it vertically and work it up and down three or four times throughout its full range of travel. If no resistance is felt, or if there is sudden free movement, the shock absorber should be discarded and a replacement fitted. Also, if there is evidence of oil leakage, the shock absorber should be replaced by a serviceable item.

5 When installing, always renew any worn or damaged bushings.
6 Position the shock absorber with its bushings and washers from below the lower arm, and install the bolts which attach it to the lower arm.
7 Fit the nuts at the upper end of the shock absorber and torque tighten them to the specified value.

4 Suspension upper arm - removal and installation

1 Apply the handbrake then raise the appropriate side of the vehicle, allowing the suspension to fall under its own weight.
2 Position suitable blocks beneath the lower arm and lower the vehicle until the upper arm is off the bump stop. Remove the roadwheel.
3 Remove the cotter pin and nut from the upper balljoint and separate the balljoint from the steering knuckle. This will ideally require the use of a balljoint separator or wedges, but a suitable tapered cold chisel driven between the joint and steering knuckle will usually suffice; it may even be possible to strike the steering knuckle eye sharply with a hammer to release the taper.
4 From beneath the bonnet, remove the two upper arm retaining bolts and nuts, then remove the arm from the vehicle. Do not lose the shim(s), if fitted.
5 If the balljoint is to be renewed, remove the three retaining nuts and bolts to permit the balljoint to be removed from the upper arm.
6 Whilst the arm is removed from the vehicle, check for any damage or cracks. If it was not intended to renew the balljoint, check the dust seal and renew it if it is damaged. If the balljoint endplay exceeds 0.031 in (0.79 mm) it must be renewed (see previous paragraph).
7 If the balljoint was removed, position the replacement assembly to the upper arm and fit the three bolts and nuts. Tighten to the specified torque.
8 Position the upper arm in the vehicle using the same shim(s) as originally fitted; fit the bolts and nuts, and tighten to the specified torque.
9 Fit the balljoint taper to the steering knuckle, torque-tighten the nut and fit a new cotter pin.
10 Fit the roadwheel and lower the vehicle to the ground.
11 If no new parts have been used, and front tire wear has always been satisfactory you may be lucky in not needing a steering geometry check. However, if new parts have been used, or front tire wear has not been satisfactory, or if you just wish to put your mind at ease, a steering geometry check should be carried out (refer to Section 8).

5 Suspension lower arm and spring - removal and installation

1 Raise the front of the vehicle and position suitable axle stands or blocks under each side of the frame just to the rear of the lower arms.
2 Remove the roadwheel.
3 Remove the two lower shock absorber mounting bolts and push the shock absorber up thru the spring.
4 Where applicable, remove the front stabilizer bar retaining bolt, nut and bushings and disconnect it from the lower arm.
5 Position a suitable jack under the lower arm and raise it sufficiently to relieve the spring pressure.

11

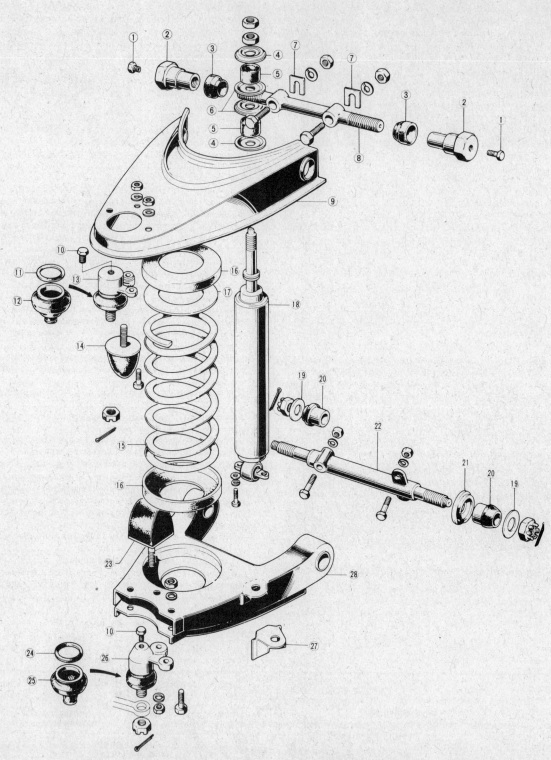

Fig. 11.1 The front suspension components (Secs. 3, 4 and 5)

1	Plug	8	Upper arm shaft	15	Coil spring	22	Lower arm shaft
2	Threaded bush	9	Upper arm	16	Seat	23	Bump stop
3	Dust seal	10	Plug	17	Adjusting plate	24	Set ring
4	Retainer	11	Set ring	18	Shock absorber	25	Dust seal
5	Bush	12	Dust seal	19	Washer	26	Balljoint
6	Retainer	13	Balljoint assembly	20	Bush	27	Bracket
7	Shim	14	Bump stop	21	Stopper	28	Lower arm

6 Remove the three lower arm to balljoint securing nuts and bolts, then pull the steering knuckle and balljoint away from the arm.

7 Lower the jack to permit the spring to be removed from the vehicle.

8 Remove the three bolts and nuts securing the lower arm shaft, then remove the arm from the vehicle.

9 Whilst the arm is removed from the vehicle, check for any damage or cracks. If it was not intended to renew the balljoint, check the dust seal and renew it if it is damaged. If the balljoint endplay exceeds 0.031 in (0.79 mm) it must be renewed (See paragraph 3 in the previous Section).

10 When installing, position the lower arm in the vehicle and fit the three lower arm retaining bolts and nuts finger-tight only.

11 Position the spring to the lower arm and in the retaining pocket at the upper end.

12 If a large 'G' clamp is available, position it thru the hole in the lower arm to clamp the lowest spring coil in position in its pocket. If no clamp is available, it will suffice to temporarily use iron wire or stout cord, but make sure that the spring is firmly held.

13 Raise the lower arm with the jack and position the balljoint and steering knuckle assembly to the lower arm.

14 Loosely fit the balljoint retaining nuts and bolts then remove the 'G' clamp (or retaining wire or cord). Tighten the nuts and bolts to the specifeid torque.

15 Tighten the three lower arm retaining nuts and bolts to the specified torque.

16 Pull down the shock absorber, fit the retaining nuts and bolts and tighten them to the specified torque.

17 Where applicable, position the stabilizer bar retaining bolt thru the bar with the bushings and washers, and install the retaining nut.

18 Fit the roadwheel, remove the axle stands or blocks and lower the vehicle to the ground.

Fig. 11.2 The mountings (arrowed) for the front stabilizer bar used on some models (Sec. 5)

19 If no new parts have been used, and front tire wear has always been satisfactory, you may be lucky in not needing a steering geometry check. However, if new parts have been used, or front tire wear has not been satisfactory, or if you just wish to put your mind at ease, a steering geometry check should be carried out (refer to Section 8).

6 Front wheel bearings - removal and installation

1 Apply the handbrake firmly, then raise the front of the vehicle and remove the roadwheel. Remove the brake drum, referring to Chapter 9, if necessary.

2 Carefully tap or prise out the hub grease cap then remove the cotter pin, castellated nut locking cap, nut and washer. Withdraw the outer bearing cone and roller assembly.

3 Pull off the hub assembly from the wheel spindle.

4 Remove and discard the old grease retainer then remove the inner bearing cone and roller assembly from the hub.

5 Clean all the old grease from the bearing caps using petrol (gasoline) and inspect each for scratches, pits, corrosion or other damage. If necessary they should be renewed, and can be removed from the hub by carefully driving them out or using a suitable extractor. If they are renewed it is essential that the cone and roller assemblies are renewed also.

6 Thoroughly clean the bearing cones and rollers to remove all old grease. This is essential since a sodium base grease is in general use during manufacture and is not compatible with the recommended lithium base replacement grease. Dry the cones and rollers using a lint-free cloth, but do not spin them with compressed air or damage may result. Inspect them for scratches, pits, corrosion and other damage, renewing as necessary. If they are to be renewed it is essential that the bearing cups are renewed also.

7 Thoroughly clean the spindle and the inside of the hub to remove all the old grease. Take care that loose dust and dirt does not remain on the spindle.

8 Pack the inside of the hub with a general purpose lithium base grease (eg; Castrol LM Grease), after ensuring that the bearing cups are fully seated (if renewed). The grease should be flush with the inside diameter of the bearing cups.

9 Pack the bearing cone and roller assemblies with the same type of grease working it in thoroughly with the fingers.

10 Place the inner bearing cone and roller assembly in the inner cup then apply a light film of grease to the grease retainer and carefully install it. If applicable, the sealing lips should be towards the hub.

11 Install the bearing spacer and hub on the wheel spindle, holding the hub centrally to prevent damage to the grease retainer and spindle threads.

12 Install the outer cone and roller assembly, flat washer and nut, but tighten the nut finger-tight only.

13 Install the brake drum and roadwheel.

14 Adjust the hub as detailed in the following Section, fit the hub cap and lower the vehicle to the ground. Pump the brake pedal several times to restore the normal brake travel.

11

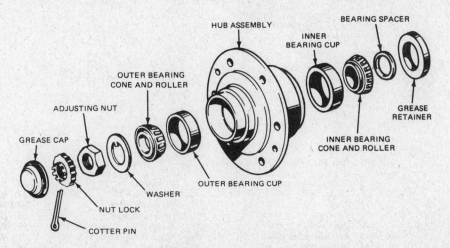

Fig. 11.3 The component parts of the front hub (Sec. 6)

7 Front wheel bearings - adjustment

1 Apply the handbrake firmly and raise the roadwheel clear of the ground.
2 Remove the hub cap and carefully tap or prise out the hub grease cap.
3 Remove any excess grease from the end of the wheel spindle then remove the cotter pin and castellated nut locking cap.
4 Turn back the adjusting nut about ¼ turn then tighten it to a torque of 17/25 lb f ft (2.35/3.45 kg f m) whilst rotating the roadwheel by hand.
5 Back off the adjusting nut ½ turn then retighten to the specified torque (see Specifications).
6 Position the castellated nut locking cap on the adjusting nut so that the castellations are aligned with the hole in the spindle. Fit a new cotter pin and bend over the ends (photo).
7 Check that the wheel rotates freely then install the grease cap and hub cap. **Note:** If the wheel does not rotate freely it indicates that the bearings require renewal (see previous Section).

8 Steering geometry checks

1 In order to obtain satisfactory tire wear and good steering stability, it is essential that the steering geometry is correctly set. This is not really a do-it-yourself job and it is always preferable to have the job done by your vehicle main dealer who will have the correct alignment gauges. However, if you feel competent to do the job yourself, the basic procedure is given below.

7.6 Install the cotter pin

8.6 The tie-rod clamp bolts (left side)

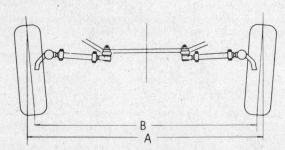
Fig. 11.4 Toe in: Dimension B should be less than A by the specified toe-in (Sec. 8)

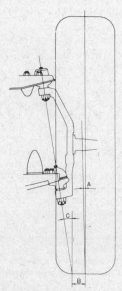
Fig. 11.5 Camber (Sec. 8)

A : Camber   B : Camber trail   C : Kingpin inclination

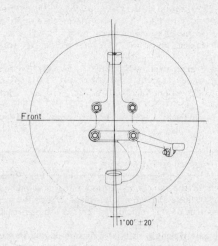
Fig. 11.6 Caster (Sec. 8)

2 Before commencing any checks, the vehicle must be standing on a level floor, the tires must be inflated to the correct pressures (cold), excessive mud must be removed from the vehicle underframe and the fuel tank, engine oil level and coolant level must be correct.

Toe-in

3 Raise the front end of the vehicle so that the wheels are clear of the ground.
4 Turn each wheel by hand and scribe a chalk line in the center of the tire tread around its circumference.
5 Measure between the chalk marks at the front and rear of the tire at equal heights from the ground. If the toe-in is correct, the distance between the chalk marks at the rear should be greater than the distance between them at the front by the amount given in the Specification.
6 If adjustment is required, loosen the tie-rod clamp bolts and rotate the tie-rod as necessary. Each tie-rod is threaded right-hand at one end and left-hand at the other end in order to retain the correct balance of the linkage; the two tie-rods must be the same length after any adjustment. On completion, ensure that clamps are positioned with the bolts horizontal and below the tie-rod in order to prevent contact with the center link (photo).

Camber

7 Camber angle is the angle by which the wheel tilts outwards when the weight is on the suspension. To obtain the specified camber, shims must be fitted between, or removed from, the upper suspension arm shaft and frame. Shims are available in thicknesses of 0.040, 0.064, 0.080 and 0.128 in (1.0, 1.6, 2.0 and 3.2 mm).

Caster

8 Caster angle is the forward or rearward tilt of the upper balljoint and is altered by the addition or removal of shims between the upper suspension arm shaft and the frame, or by turning the upper arm shaft as necessary until the correct angle is obtained.

Front wheel turning angle

9 Turning stop screws are fitted at each steering knuckle and should be adjusted as necessary to obtain the specified angle on each wheel.

9 Rear shock absorber - removal and installation

1 Raise the rear end of the vehicle as necessary, to obtain access to the shock absorber. Chock the front wheels to prevent movement of the vehicle, and preferably use axle stands or blocks to support the rear of the vehicle whilst the job is being carried out. Remove the rear roadwheel if considered necessary for better access to the lower end.
2 Remove the nuts, washers and rubber bushings at each end of the shock absorber.
3 Compress the shock absorber and remove it from the vehicle.
4 To test the shock absorber, hold it vertically and work it up and down three or four times throughout its full range of travel. If no resistance is felt, or if there is sudden free movement, the shock absorber should be discarded and a replacement fitted. Also, if there is evidence of oil leakage, the shock absorber should be replaced by a serviceable item.
5 When installing, always renew any worn or damaged bushings.
6 Compress the shock absorber and position it in the vehicle. Install the rubber bushings, washers and nuts at each end and tighten to the specified torque.
7 Install the roadwheel, if applicable, and lower the vehicle to the ground.

10 Rear spring - removal and installation

1 Raise the rear of the vehicle and support it on a suitable axle stand so that the spring relaxes under the axle weight. Chock the front wheels to prevent movement of the vehicle and remove the rear roadwheel for access.
2 Support the axle weight with a jack then undo the shock absorber lower mounting.
3 Remove the nuts, spacers and plate from the 'U' bolts (spring clips). Remove the 'U' bolts and bump stop from the axle.
4 Remove the spring pin nut and washers, and the two bolts and nuts attaching the spring pin to the frame bracket. Remove the pin and

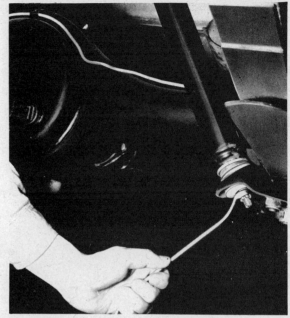

Fig. 11.7 Removing a rear shock absorber (Sec. 9)

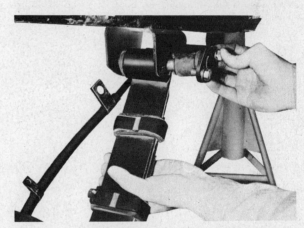

Fig. 11.8 Rear spring pin and bush removal (Sec. 10)

lower the front end of the spring.
5 Remove the shackle plate nuts and washers and the shackle plate and bar. Remove the spring from the vehicle.
6 Check the spring for damage, wear and excessive corrosion, and for looseness of the center bolt. If necessary, a new spring should be fitted. Also check the shackle pin and bushings, renewing as necessary.
7 When installing, fit the rubber bushings into the spring front eye and position the spring to the frame bracket. Align the holes in the bushings with the frame bracket hole.
8 Insert the spring pin from the outside, thru the rubber bushings and loosely fit the nut and washer.
9 Install the two bolts, nuts and washers retaining the spring pin, and tighten them to the specified torque.
10 Fit the rubber bushings into the rear spring eye and shackle plate. Install the spring and shackle plate to the frame bracket and loosely install the shackle bar, washers and nuts.
11 Lower the rear axle and place the center hole of the 'U' bolt plate over the head of the spring center bolt.
12 Place the spring plate under the spring, then fit the bumper, 'U' bolts, spacers, washers and nuts. Tighten the nuts to the specified torque.
13 Install the shock absorber at its lower mounting, then fit the roadwheel and lower the vehicle to the ground.
14 Bounce the vehicle several times to settle the spring, then tighten the nuts and bolts to the specified torque at each end of the spring.

11

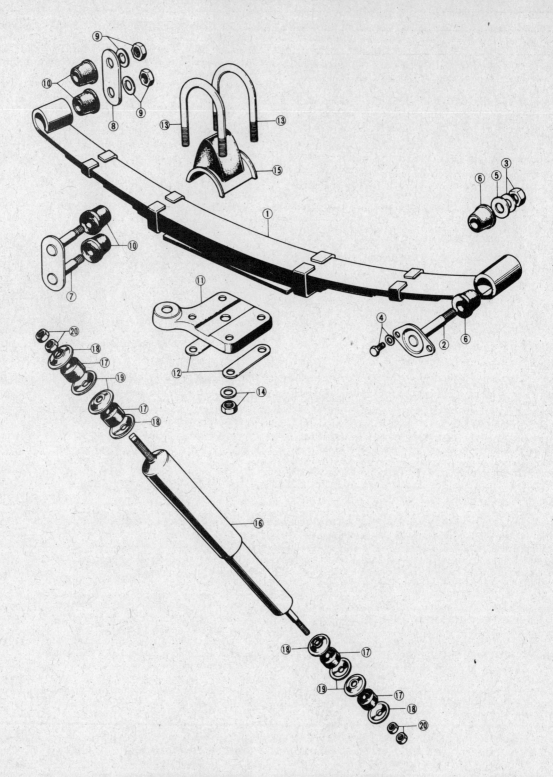

Fig. 11.9 The rear suspension components (Secs. 9 and 10)

1	Rear spring	6	Bushing	11	Spring clamp	16	Shock absorber
2	Spring pin assembly	7	Shackle plate assembly	12	Spacer	17	Bushing
3	Nut	8	Shackle plate	13	'U' bolt (spring clip)	18	Retainer
4	Bolt	9	Nut and washer	14	Nut and washer	19	Centering washer
5	Spacer	10	Bushing	15	Bump stop	20	Nut

11 Steering gear - removal and installation

1 Disconnect the battery ground lead then remove the horn button from the steering wheel by rotating it anticlockwise. Remove the horn contact spring.

2 Mark the relative installed positions of the steering wheel and column shaft then remove the wheel attaching nut and washer(s). Pull off the steering wheel.

B1600

3 Pull off the light switch knob.

4 Remove the column cover retaining screws and take off the cover. On column change models remove the shift linkage, as described in Chapter 6.

5 Remove the stop ring, cancel cam and spring from the end of the column shaft.

6 Disconnect the wiring in-line connectors from the combination switch assembly.

7 Remove the screws securing the combination switch assembly to the column jacket and remove the switch assembly.

Courier

8 Remove the cancelling cam snap-ring and cam from the top of the steering shaft.

9 Remove the dip-switch and direction indicator switch wires at the in-line connectors.

Both versions

10 Remove the steering column support bracket then loosen the nut securing the bottom of the column support bracket (see Fig. 11.10).

11 Remove the four screws and two bolts retaining the toe-plate and boot then withdraw the column jacket from the shaft.

12 According to the particular model and market, and the degree of access which you may feel is desirable, it may be considered necessary to remove the air cleaner, to remove the heater hoses from their clips and position them out of the way and to remove the brake and clutch master cylinders (refer to Chapters 9 and 5 for these last two items).

13 Raise the vehicle and remove the roadwheel on the steering gear side. On B1600 vehicles it may be necessary to temporarily remove the nuts and bolts retaining the upper arm shaft to the support bracket. If this is done, note the number and position of the adjusting shims to prevent alteration of the steering geometry when reassembled. Withdraw the upper arm.

14 The pitman arm can either be removed from the sector shaft using a suitable extractor after the nut and washer have been removed, or can be separated from the center link by the use of a suitable extractor. (See Section 14 and Fig. 11.12).

15 Remove the bolts and nuts securing the steering gear assembly to the frame. Collect any shims which may have been fitted for use when refitting.

16 Remove the steering gear, lowering the vehicle, if necessary, as it is being withdrawn.

17 Installation is essentially the reverse of the removal procedure, but

Fig. 11.10 The column support bracket nut (arrowed) (Sec. 11)

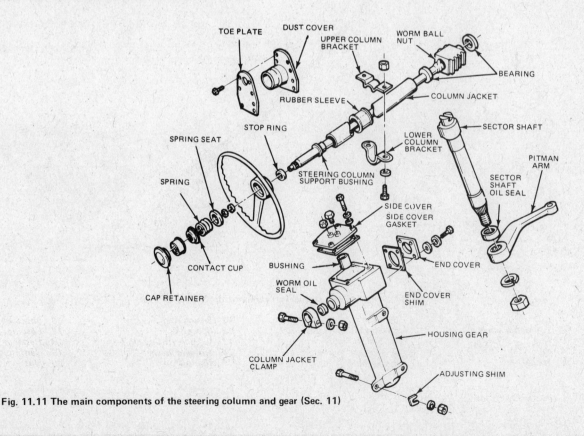

Fig. 11.11 The main components of the steering column and gear (Sec. 11)

the following points must be noted:

    a) *Do not torque tighten the steering gear attaching bolts until the steering column has been secured.*

    b) *Where it has been necessary to remove the clutch and brake master cylinders, the systems should be bled of air, as described in Chapters 5 and 9.*

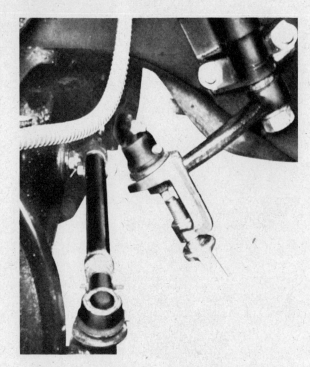

Fig. 11.12 Using a balljoint separator (Secs. 11 and 12)

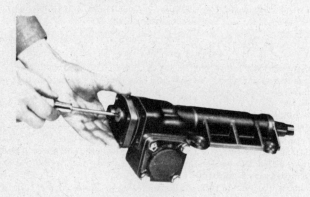

Fig. 11.13 Removing the side cover from the steering gear (Sec. 12)

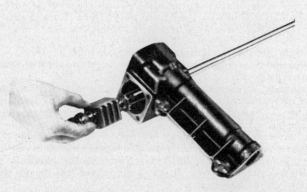

Fig. 11.15 Removing the worm and ball nut (Sec. 12)

12 Steering gear - dismantling and reassembly

1 Having removed the steering gear, as described in the previous Section, remove the filler plug and drain out the lubricant.

2 Support the gear in a vise. If not already removed, remove the nut and washer and draw off the pitman arm using a suitable extractor (see Section 14 and Fig. 11.12).

3 Remove the locknut from the sector shaft adjusting screw.

4 Remove the bolts from the side cover then turn the adjusting screw clockwise thru the cover so that the cover and gasket can be removed.

5 Removing the adjusting screw and shim from the end of the sector shaft.

6 Remove the sector shaft from the gear housing taking care not to damage the bushings and oil seal.

7 Remove the end cover bolts; take off the cover.

8 Remove the wormshaft and ball nut assembly thru the bottom of the gear housing.

9 Remove the oil seal from the gear housing if it is suspect.

10 Clean all the parts carefully using petrol (gasoline) and inspect for wear and damage. Check the operation of the ball nut assembly on the wormshaft; if it does not travel smoothly and freely the ballnut and worm shaft must be renewed as an assembly. Check for wear and damage in the bushings and bearings. Examine the oil seal for wear and damage; renew parts as necessary.

11 When reassembling, first install the housing oil seal if it was removed.

12 Insert the wormshaft and ball nut into the housing and adjust the worm bearing preload as described in the following Section.

13 Install the adjusting screw into the slot at the end of the shaft and check the end-clearance with a feeler gauge. By the use of shims, adjust this clearance to 0.001/0.003 in (0.02/0.08 mm); replacement shims are provided in the following sizes: 0.077 in (1.95 mm), 0.079 in (2.0 mm), 0.081 in (2.05 mm) and 0.083 in (2.10 mm).

14 Turn the wormshaft and place the rack in the center of the worm.

15 Insert the sector shaft and adjusting screw into the housing take care not to damage the oil seal. Ensure that the center of the sector gear aligns with the center of the rack.

16 Place the side cover and gasket on the adjusting screw, and turn the screw until the side cover seats.

17 Install the side cover bolts and adjust the backlash, as described in the following Section.

18 Tighten the adjusting screw locknut and, where applicable, fit the pitman arm, washer and nut.

Fig. 11.14 Withdrawing the sector shaft (Sec. 12)

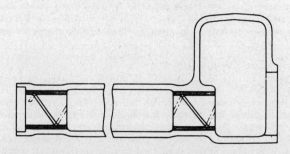

Fig. 11.16 Note that the oil ways in the steering gear bushes are not identical and must not be interchanged (Sec. 12)

Fig. 11.17 Installing the end cover and shims (Sec. 12)

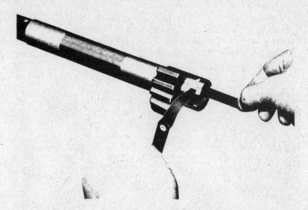
Fig. 11.18 Checking the adjusting screw and clearance (Sec. 12)

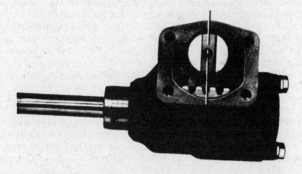
Fig. 11.19 Aligning the sector shaft and rack (Sec. 12)

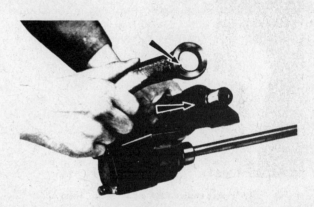
Fig. 11.20 Note the master spline (arrowed) on the pitman arm and sector shaft (Sec. 12)

Fig. 11.21 Backlash adjustment (Sec. 13)

13 Steering gear - adjustments

1 The steering system makes provision for adjustment to eliminate excessive play, and although this is not part of the routine maintenance procedure, it will need to be adjusted after a high mileage as wear occurs.

Steering wheel free-play check

2 If excessive play is suspected, set the front roadwheels to the 'straight-ahead' position and check that there is no play in the ball-joints, idler arm bushes and wheel bearings. This is best done by grasping the center link, tie-rods, idler arm and pitman arm and feeling for any movement. A large tire lever may help in detecting free-play but care should be taken not to lever against parts which might suffer damage. If any play exists in these parts, refer to Section 14; if they are satisfactory, first ensure that the steering gear is securely mounted then proceed to paragraphs 7 to 11. If this does not provide satisfactory

adjustment refer to paragraphs 3 to 6, then repeat paragraphs 7 to 11. If the adjustment cannot be carried out satisfactorily, the steering gear should be dismantled for overhaul (Section 12).

Worm bearing preload

3 Remove the pitman arm nut and washer, then withdraw the pitman arm using a suitable extractor (where applicable).
4 Drain the steering gear lubricant by removing the end cover (4 bolts and washers). Do not lose any shims which may be fitted. Refit the cover and shims afterwards.
5 Loosen the sector adjusting locknut on the side cover and turn the screw anticlockwise approximately 1 ½ turns.
6 Rotate the worm shaft using a suitable torque wrench and check for a preload reading as specified. If too low, reduce the shim thickness at the end cover; if too high, increase the shim thickness. Shims are available in the following sizes: 0.002 in (0.05 mm), 0.003 in (0.075 mm), 0.004 in (0.10 mm) and 0.008 in (0.20 mm).

Backlash (sector gear and ball nut meshload)

7 Remove the pitman arm nut and washer, then withdraw the pitman arm using a suitable extractor (where applicable).
8 Loosen the sector adjusting screw locknut on the side cover then turn the steering shaft slowly from stop-to-stop to avoid damage to the ball return guides. Count the number of turns of the shaft then set it in its mid-position of travel.
9 Turn the sector adjusting screw clockwise until a shaft torque of 5/7 lb f in (1.15 kg f cm) is obtained whilst rotating the worm past its center. This is equivalent to the backlash given in the Specifications.
10 Hold to adjusting screw against turning, tighten the locknut and recheck the backlash (photo).
11 Where applicable, top-up or refill the steering gear with the correct grade of lubricant, and reconnect the pitman arm.

11

13.10 Steering gear adjustment (column change gearshift)
The hexagon below the ring wrench is the steering gear filler plug.

14 Steering linkage

1   If excessive play occurs in the steering linkage (see previous Section, paragraph 2), it will be necessary to renew the appropriate ball joints and/or bushings. Before any attempt is made to remove the tie-rods, carefully measure and record the length from the steering knuckle ball-joint to the center link balljoint and ensure that after fitting new parts, this dimension is attained once more. Failure to do this will mean that the steering toe-in will need to be checked.

2   The center link can be removed from the tie-rods, pitman arm and idler arm by following the procedure given in paragraph 5.

3   The pitman arm can be disconnected from the sector shaft once the center link has been removed, by removing the nut and using a suitable extractor to pull it off. Note the master spline when installing.

4   The idler arm can be pulled off the shaft once the center link has been disconnected, by removing the split pin (where applicable) and nut. When installing, tighten the shaft nut and center link nut to the specified torques.

5   Removal of the tie-rod from the center link and steering knuckle is straightforward by reference to the following paragraph.

6   To remove a steering linkage balljoint, remove the appropriate cotter pin and nut and use a balljoint extractor to draw the balljoint taper out of the steering knuckle pitman arm or center link. If no extractor is available, suitable split wedges or even a tapered cold chisel will suffice. If these are not available it should be possible to free it by

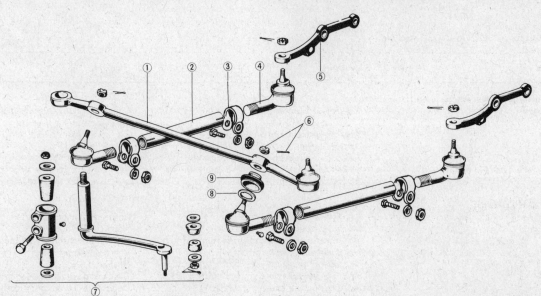

Fig. 11.22 The steering linkage (Sec. 14)

1 Centre link	4 Balljoint	6 Nut and split pin	8 Set ring
2 Tie rod	5 Steering knuckle	7 Idler arm assembly	9 Boot
3 Clamp, bolt and nut			

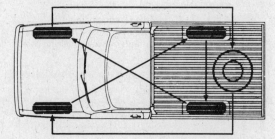

When the tire sizes are the same
on the front and the rear wheels

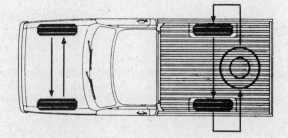

When the tire sizes differ between
the front and the rear wheels

Fig. 11.23 Suggested order for tire rotation (Sec. 15)

striking the steering knuckle or center link eye sharply whilst it is being supported. After releasing the taper unscrew the clamp bolts and screw the balljoint off the tie-rod. Installation is then straightforward, but use a new cotter pin on the balljoint studs. Ensure that the tie-rod clamps are positioned with the bolts horizontal and below the tie-rod in order to prevent contact with the center link.

15 Wheels and tires

1 Provided that they are not damaged during an accident or by striking the kerb, wheels can be expected to last the life of the vehicle with no maintenance other than cleaning and occasional painting.
2 The standard tires fitted to the B1600 and Courier models are crossply and the vehicle makers give no recommendations regarding the use of radial tires.
3 If radial tires are to be used, it is recommended that they are fitted in complete sets. It is permitted by law in the United Kingdom to use radials on the rear and crossplys on the front, but never the other way round. It may be found, though, that there is a slight tendency for the vehicle to wander if only the rear tires are radials and for this reason a full set is recommended if they are to be used.
4 Where tubeless tires are used, it is recommended that fitment is left to a dealer since it in all too easy to damage the seal by using tire levers.
5 It may be preferred by the owner to change the tires round at

Fig. 11.24 Wheel nut tightening sequence (Sec. 15)

intervals to equalize the tread wear. Where this is done, they should be rotated as shown in the illustrations, but it is advisable to take note of the wear pattern on each tire as this may give warning of the need for steering geometry adjustments or less severe driving habits (Fig. 11.23).
6 In order to obtain the best tire wear, and at the same time to reduce the out-of-balance loads on the steering and suspension, the wheel should be balanced dynamically. This not only balances the wheel and tire, but also compensates for the smaller out-of-balance forces in the hubs and brake drums. Therefore, if a balanced wheel is removed from a hub, it should always be refitted in the same hub-to-wheel relationship, and where it is refitted to another wheel it may well need re-balancing for optimum service.

16 Fault diagnosis - suspension and steering

Symptom	Reason/s	Remedy
Steering feels vague, car wanders, and floats at speed		
General wear or damage	Tire pressure uneven	Check pressures and adjust as necessary.
	Shock absorbers worn	Test, and replace if worn.
	Steering gear balljoints badly worn	Fit new balljoints.
	Suspension geometry incorrect	Check and rectify.
	Steering mechanism free play excessive	Adjust or overhaul steering mechanism.
	Front suspension and rear suspension pick-up points out of alignment	Normally caused by poor repair work after a serious accident. Extensive rebuilding necessary.
Stiff and heavy steering		
Lack of maintenance or accident damage	Tire pressure too low	Check pressures and inflate tires.
	No oil in steering gear	Top up steering gear.
	No grease in steering and suspension balljoints	Clean nipples and grease thoroughly.
	Front wheel toe-in incorrect	Check and reset toe-in.
	Suspension geometry incorrect after accident	Realign body.
	Steering gear incorrectly adjusted (too tight)	Check and adjust steering gear.
	Steering column badly misaligned	Determine cause and rectify (usually due to bad repair after severe accident damage, and is difficult to correct).
Wheel wobble and vibration		
General wear or damage	Wheel nuts loose	Check and tighten as necessary.
	Wheels and tires out of balance	Balance wheels and tires and add weights as necessary.
	Steering balljoints badly worn	Replace steering balljoints.
	Hub bearings badly worn	Remove and fit new hub bearings.
	Steering gear free play excessive	Adjust and overhaul steering gear.
Rattles		
General wear	Suspension bushes worn	Replace.
	Steering balljoints worn	Replace.
	Backlash in steering box	Adjust as necessary.

11

Chapter 12 Bodywork and fittings

Refer to Chapter 13 for Specifications and information applicable to 1974 through 1982 models

Contents

Blower motor and fan - removal and installation 27	Maintenance - bodywork and underframe 2
Bonnet (hood) release mechanism 14	Maintenance - locks and hinges 6
Bonnet (hood) - removal and installation 13	Maintenance - upholstery and carpets 3
Control assembly - removal and installation 25	Major bodywork damage - repair 5
Door glass and regulator - removal and installation 9	Minor bodywork damage - repair 4
Door latch and remote control - removal and installation ... 11	Radiator grille - removal and installation 19
Door outside handle - removal and installation 12	Seat and seat tracks - removal, adjustment and installation ... 18
Doors and hinges - removal and installation 8	Tailgate latches and hinges 15
Doors - rattles and their rectification 7	Ventilator and heater - adjustments 23
Front bumper - removal and installation 20	Ventilator and heater - general description 21
General description 1	Ventilator and heater - testing 22
Heater assembly - removal and installation 26	Weatherstrip and vent window assembly - removal and
Heater control cables - removal and installation 24	installation 10
Instrument panel pad - removal and installation 17	Windshield and rear window glass - removal and installation ... 16

Specifications

Basic capacities and dimensions

Overall length	172 in. (4370 mm)
Overall width	63 in. (1600 mm)
Overall height	62 in. (1565 mm)
Track, front and rear	51 in. (1300 mm)
Wheelbase	104 in. (2650 mm)
Road clearance	8 in. (200 mm)
Inside length, pick-up box	74 in. (1875 mm)
Inside width, pick-up box	57 in. (1460 mm)
Inside height, pick-up box	16 in. (410 mm)
Payload:	
B1600	2205 lb (1000 kg)
Courier	1400 lb (636 kg)
Curb weight:	
B1600	2325 lb (1055 kg)
Courier	2515 lb (1142 kg)

1 General description

1 An integral cab and pick-up body is bolted via rubber bushings to a box-section frame with tubular crossmembers. The engine compartment hood, the cab doors and rear tailgate are all fitted with removable hinges which incorporate provision for adjustment. The engine compartment hood release catch is operated from inside by a release lever beneath the dash panel. Both cab doors can be locked from the outside by a key or by pushing the inside handle forward and depressing the outside handle push button as the door is pushed shut. The tailgate is lowered by releasing 'over-center' type latches and is restrained in the horizontal position by plastic-sheathed chains.

2 Interior trim is fairly basic with a full three-seater bench seat which can be hinged forward for access to a tool compartment and some limited storage space (photo). A vinyl floor covering is standard equipment, although options for many markets include pile carpeting.

3 All models are equipped with a heater/ventilator system with a dash mounted control panel. For certain markets an air-conditioning pack is available but is not covered in this manual.

1.2 Storage space is provided behind the seat

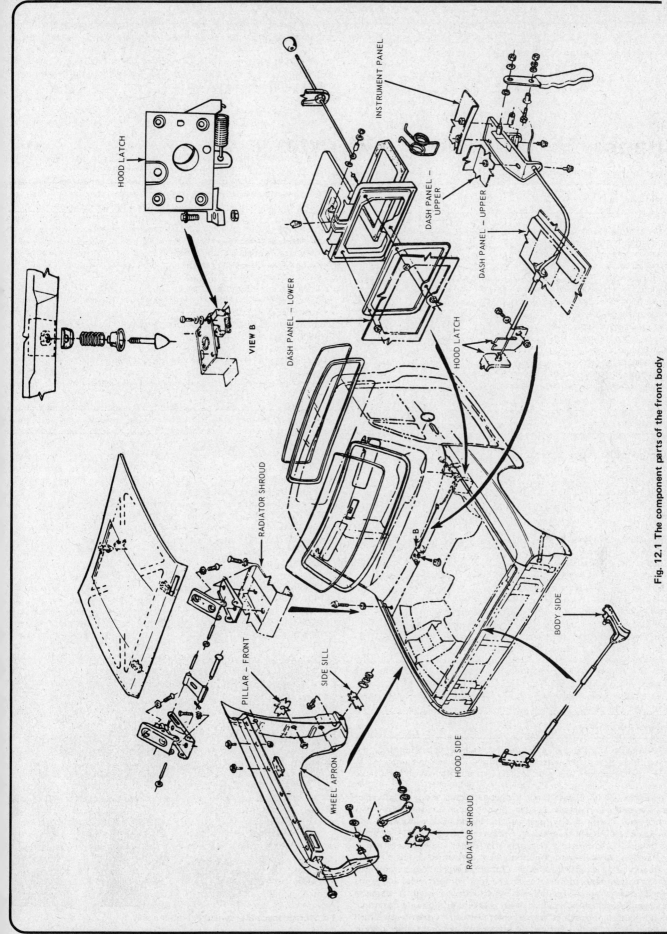

HOOD LATCH

VIEW B

DASH PANEL – LOWER

DASH PANEL – UPPER

DASH PANEL – UPPER

INSTRUMENT PANEL

HOOD LATCH

B

RADIATOR SHROUD

PILLAR – FRONT

SIDE SILL

WHEEL APRON

HOOD SIDE

RADIATOR SHROUD

BODY SIDE

Fig. 12.1 The component parts of the front body

12

2 Maintenance - bodywork and underframe

1   The general condition of a vehicle's bodywork is the one thing that significantly affects its value. Maintenance is easy but needs to be regular and particular. Neglect, particularly after minor damage, can lead quickly to further deterioration and costly repair bills. It is important also to keep watch on those parts of the vehicle not immediately visible, for instance the underside, inside all the wheel arches and the lower part of the engine compartment.

2   The basic maintenance routine for the bodywork is washing - preferably with a lot of water, from a hose. This will remove all the loose solids which may have stuck to the vehicle. It is important to flush these off in such a way as to prevent grit from scratching the finish.

The wheel arches and underbody need washing in the same way to remove any accumulated mud which will retain moisture and tend to encourage rust. Paradoxically enough, the best time to clean the underbody and wheel arches is in wet weather when the mud is thoroughly wet and soft. In very wet weather the underbody is usually cleaned of large accumulations automatically and this is a good time for inspection.

3   Periodically it is a good idea to have the whole of the underside of the vehicle steam cleaned, engine compartment included, so that a thorough inspection can be carried out to see what minor repairs and renovations are necessary. Steam cleaning is available at many garages and is necessary for removal of accumulation of oily grime which sometimes is allowed to cake thick in certain areas near the engine, gearbox and back axle. If steam facilities are not available, there are one or two excellent grease solvents available which can be brush applied. The dirt can then be simply hosed off.

4   After washing paintwork, wipe off with a chamois leather to give an unspotted clear finish. A coat of clear protective wax polish will give added protection against chemical pollutants in the air. If the paintwork sheen has dulled or oxidised, use a cleaner/polisher combination to restore the brilliance of the shine. This requires a little effort, but is usually caused because regular washing has been neglected. Always check that the door and ventilator opening drain holes and pipes are completely clear so that water can drain out. Bright work should be treated the same way as paintwork. Windscreen and windows can be kept clear of the smeary film which often appears if a little ammonia is added to the water. If they are scratched, a good rub with a proprietary metal polish will often clear them. Never use any form of wax or other body or chromium polish on glass.

3 Maintenance - upholstery and carpets

1   Mats and carpets should be brushed or vacuum cleaned regularly to keep them free of grit. If they are badly stained remove them from the vehicle for scrubbing or sponging and make quite sure they are dry before replacement. Seats and interior trim panels can be kept clean by a wipe over with a damp cloth. If they do become stained (which can be more apparent on light coloured upholstery) use a little liquid detergent and a soft nail brush to scour the grime out of the grain of the material. Do not forget to keep the head lining clean in the same way as the upholstery. When using liquid cleaners inside the car do not over-wet the surfaces being cleaned. Excessive damp could get into the seams and padded interior causing stains, offensive odours or even rot. If the inside of the vehicle gets wet accidentally it is worthwhile taking some trouble to dry it out properly particularly where carpets are involved. **Do not** leave oil or electric heaters inside the car for this purpose.

4 Minor bodywork damage - repair

See photo sequences on pages 190 and 191.

Repair of minor scratches in the vehicle's bodywork

If the scratch is very superficial, and does not penetrate the metal of the bodywork, repair is very simple. Lightly rub the area of the scratch with a paintwork renovator, or a very fine cutting paste, to remove loose paint from the scratch and to clear the surrounding bodywork of wax polish. Rinse the area with clean water.

Apply touch-up paint to the scratch using a thin paintbrush, continue to apply thin layers of paint until the surface of the paint in the scratch is level with the surrounding paintwork. Allow the new paint at least two weeks to harden; then, blend it into the surrounding paintwork by rubbing the paintwork, in the scratch area with a paintwork renovator, or a very fine cutting paste. Finally apply wax polish.

Where the scratch has penetrated right through to the metal of the bodywork, causing the metal to rust, a different repair technique is required. Remove any loose rust from the bottom of the scratch with a penknife, then apply rust inhibiting paint to prevent the formation of rust in the future. Using a rubber nylon applicator fill the scratch with bodystopper paste. If required, this paste can be mixed with cellulose thinners to provide a very thin paste which is ideal for filling narrow scratches. Before the stopper-paste in the scratch hardens, wrap a piece of smooth cotton rag around the top of a finger. Dip the finger in cellulose thinners and then quickly sweep it across the surface of the stopper-paste in the scratch; this will ensure that the surface of the stopper-paste is slightly hollowed. The scratch can now be painted over as described earlier in this Section.

Repair of dents in the vehicle's bodywork

When deep denting of the vehicle's bodywork has taken place, the first task is to pull the dent out, until the affected bodywork almost attains its original shape. There is little point in trying to restore the original shape completely, as the metal in the damaged area will have stretched on impact and cannot be reshaped fully to its original contour. It is better to bring the level of the dent up to a point which is about 1/8 inch (3 mm) below the level of the surrounding bodywork. In cases where the dent is very shallow anyway, it is not worth trying to pull it out at all.

If the underside of the dent is accessible, it can be hammered out gently from behind, using a mallet with a wooden or plastic head. Whilst doing this, hold a suitable block of wood firmly against the impact from the hammer blows and thus prevent a large area of bodywork from being 'belled-out'.

Should the dent be in a section of the bodywork which has a double skin or some other factor making it inaccessible from behind, a different technique is called for. Drill several small holes through the metal inside the dent area - particularly in the deeper sections. Then screw long self-tapping screws into the holes just sufficiently for them to gain a good purchase in the metal. Now the dent can be pulled out by pulling on the protruding heads of the screws with a pair of pliers.

The next stage of the repair is the removal of the paint from the damaged area, and from an inch or so of the surrounding 'sound' bodywork. This is accomplished most easily by using a wire brush or abrasive pad on a power drill, although it can be done just as effectively by hand using sheets of abrasive paper. To complete the preparations for filling, score the surface of the bare metal with a screwdriver or the tang of a file, or alternatively, drill small holes in the affected area. This will provide a really good 'key' for the filler paste.

To complete the repair see the Section on filling and respraying.

Repair of rust holes or gashes in the vehicle's bodywork

Remove all paint from the affected area and from an inch or so of the surrounding 'sound' bodywork, using an abrasive pad or a wire brush on a power drill. If these are not available a few sheets of abrasive paper will do the job just as effectively. With the paint removed you will be able to gauge the severity of the corrosion and therefore decide whether to replace the whole panel (if this is possible) or to repair the affected area. Replacement body panels are not as expensive as most people think and it is often quicker and more satisfactory to fit a new panel than to attempt to repair large areas of corrosion.

Remove all fittings from the affected area except those which will act as a guide to the original shape of the damaged bodywork (eg; headlamp shells etc.). Then, using tin snips or a hacksaw blade, remove all loose metal and any other metal badly affected by corrosion. Hammer the edges of the hole inwards in order to create a slight depression for the filler paste.

Wire brush the affected area to remove the powdery rust from the surface of the remaining metal. Paint the affected area with rust inhibiting paint; if the back of the rusted area is accessible treat this also.

Before filling can take place it will be necessary to block the hole in some way. This can be achieved by the use of one of the following materials: Zinc gauze, Aluminium tape or Polyurethane foam.

Zinc gauze is probably the best material to use for a large hole. Cut a piece to the approximate size and shape of the hole to be filled, then position it in the hole so that its edges are below the level of the surrounding bodywork. It can be retained in position by several blobs of filler paste around its periphery.

Aluminium tape should be used for small or very narrow holes. Pull a piece off the roll and trim it to the approximate size and shape required, then pull off the backing paper (if used) and stick the tape over the hole; it can be overlapped if the thickness of one piece is insufficient. Burnish down the edges of the tape with the handle of a screwdriver or similar, to ensure that the tape is securely attached to the metal underneath.

Polyurethane foam is best used where the hole is situated in a section of bodywork of complex shape, backed by a small box section (eg; where the sill panel meets the rear wheel arch - most vehicles). The unusual mixing procedure for this foam is as follows: Put equal amounts of fluid from each of the two cans provided in the kit, into one container. Stir until the mixture begins to thicken, then quickly pour this mixture into the hole, and hold a piece of cardboard over the larger apertures. Almost immediately the polyurethane will begin to expand, gushing frantically out of any small holes left unblocked. When the foam hardens it can be cut back to just below the level of the surrounding bodywork with a hacksaw blade.

Bodywork repairs - filling and re-spraying

Before using this Section, see the Sections on dent, deep scratch, rust hole, and gash repairs.

Many types of bodyfiller are available, but generally speaking those proprietary kits which contain a tin of filler paste and a tube of resin hardener are best for this type of repair. A wide, flexible plastic or nylon applicator will be found invaluable for imparting a smooth and well contoured finish to the surface of the filler.

Mix up a little filler on a clean piece of card or board - use the hardener sparingly (follow the maker's instructions on the packet) otherwise the filler will set very rapidly.

Using the applicator, apply the filler paste to the prepared area; draw the applicator across the surface of the filler to achieve the correct contour and to level the filler surface. As soon as a contour that approximates the correct one is achieved, stop working the paste - if you carry on too long the paste will become sticky and begin to 'pick-up' on the applicator. Continue to add thin layers of filler paste at twenty-minute intervals until the level of the filler is just 'proud' of the surrounding bodywork.

Once the filler has hardened, excess can be removed using a plane or Dreadnought file. From then on, progressively finer grades of abrasive paper should be used, starting with a 40 grade production paper and finishing with 400 grade 'wet-and-dry' paper. Always wrap the abrasive paper around a flat rubber, fork, or wooden block - otherwise the surface of the filler will not be completely flat. During the smoothing of the filler surface the 'wet-and-dry' paper should be periodically rinsed in water. This will ensure that a very smooth finish is imparted to the filler at the final stage.

At this stage the 'dent' should be surrounded by a ring of bare metal, which in turn should be encircled by the finely 'feathered' edge of the good paintwork. Rinse the repair area with clean water, until all of the dust produced by the rubbing-down operation is gone.

Spray the whole repair area with a light coat of grey primer - this will show up any imperfections in the surface of the filler. Repair these imperfections with fresh filler paste or bodystopper, and once more smooth the surface with abrasive paper. If bodystopper is used, it can be mixed with cellulose thinners to form a really thin paste which is ideal for filling small holes. Repeat this spray and repair procedure until you are satisfied that the surface of the filler, and the feathered edge of the paintwork are perfect. Clean the repair area with clean water and allow to dry fully.

The repair area is now ready for spraying. Paint spraying must be carried out in a warm, dry, windless and dust free atmosphere. This condition can be created artificially if you have access to a large indoor working area, but if you are forced to work in the open, you will have to pick your day very carefully. If you are working indoors, dousing the floor in the work area with water will 'lay' the dust which would otherwise be in the atmosphere. If the repair area is confined to one body panel, mask off the surrounding panels; this will help to minimise the effects of a slight mis-match in paint colours. Bodywork fittings (eg; chrome strips, door handles etc.), will also need to be masked off. Use genuine masking tape and several thicknesses of newspaper for the masking operation.

Before commencing to spray, agitate the aerosol can thoroughly, then spray a test area (an old tin, or similar) until the technique is mastered. Cover the repair area with a thick coat of primer; the thickness should be built up using several thin layers of paint rather than one thick one. Using 400 grade 'wet-and-dry' paper, rub down the surface of the primer until it is really smooth. While doing this, the work area should be thoroughly doused with water, and the 'wet-and-dry' paper periodically rinsed in water. Allow to dry before spraying on more paint.

Spray on the top coat, again building up the thickness by using several thin layers of paint. Start spraying in the center of the repair area and then, using a circular motion, work outwards until the whole repair area and about 2 inches of the surrounding original paintwork is covered. Remove all masking material 10 to 15 minutes after spraying on the final coat of paint.

Allow the new paint at least 2 weeks to harden fully; then, using a paintwork renovator or a very fine cutting paste, blend the edges of the new paint into the existing paintwork. Finally, apply wax polish.

5 Major body damage - repair

Where serious damage has occurred or large areas need renewal due to neglect, it means certainly that completely new sections or panels will need welding in and this is best left to professionals. If the damage is due to impact it will also be necessary to completely check the alignment of the bodyshell structure. Due to the principle of construction the strength and shape of the whole can be affected by damage to a part. In such instances the services of the official agent with specialist checking jigs are essential. If a body is left misaligned it is first of all dangerous as the car will not handle properly and secondly, uneven stresses will be imposed on the steering, engine and transmission, causing abnormal wear or complete failure. Tire wear may also be excessive.

6 Maintenance - hinges and locks

1 Periodically lubricate the hinges of the doors, bonnet (hood) and tailgate with a few drops of light oil.
2 Similarly lubricate the door catches, bonnet release mechanism and tailgate, and the release mechanism for the spare wheel.
3 Apply a smear of general purpose grease to lock strikers, striker plates and door pillar blocks.

7 Doors - rattles and their rectification

1 Check first that the door is not loose at the hinges and that the latch is holding the door firmly in position. Check also that the door lines up with the aperture in the body.
2 If the hinges are loose, or the door is out of alignment, it will be necessary to reset the hinge positions. This is a straightforward matter after slackening the hinge retaining screws slightly, following which the door can be repositioned in/out or up/down.
3 If the latch is holding the door properly it should hold the door tightly when fully latched and the door should line up with the body. If adjustment is required, slacken the striker plate screws slightly and reposition the plate in/out or up/down as necessary. Fore and aft adjustment of the striker plate is effected by the use of shims (photo).
4 Other rattles from the door could be caused by wear or looseness in the window winder, or the glass channels, seal strips and interior lock mechanism.

12

These photos illustrate a method of repairing simple dents. They are intended to supplement *Body repair - minor damage* in this Chapter and should not be used as the sole instructions for body repair on these vehicles.

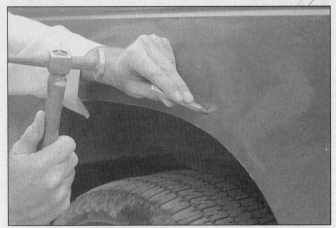

1   If you can't access the backside of the body panel to hammer out the dent, pull it out with a slide-hammer-type dent puller. In the deepest portion of the dent or along the crease line, drill or punch hole(s) at least one inch apart . . .

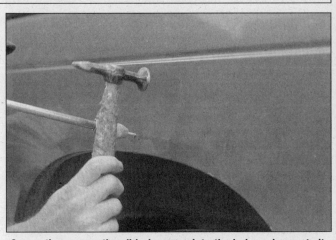

2   . . . then screw the slide-hammer into the hole and operate it. Tap with a hammer near the edge of the dent to help 'pop' the metal back to its original shape. When you're finished, the dent area should be close to its original contour and about 1/8-inch below the surface of the surrounding metal

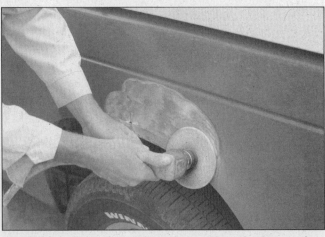

3   Using coarse-grit sandpaper, remove the paint down to the bare metal. Hand sanding works fine, but the disc sander shown here makes the job faster. Use finer (about 320-grit) sandpaper to feather-edge the paint at least one inch around the dent area

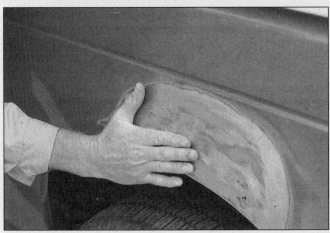

4   When the paint is removed, touch will probably be more helpful than sight for telling if the metal is straight. Hammer down the high spots or raise the low spots as necessary. Clean the repair area with wax/silicone remover

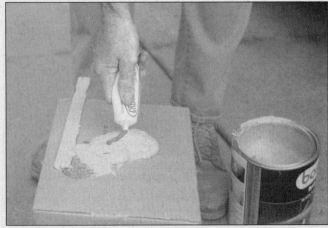

5   Following label instructions, mix up a batch of plastic filler and hardener. The ratio of filler to hardener is critical, and, if you mix it incorrectly, it will either not cure properly or cure too quickly (you won't have time to file and sand it into shape)

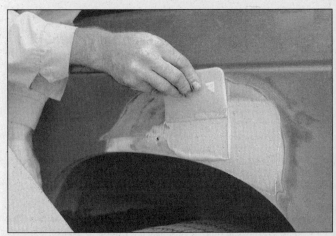

6   Working quickly so the filler doesn't harden, use a plastic applicator to press the body filler firmly into the metal, assuring it bonds completely. Work the filler until it matches the original contour and is slightly above the surrounding metal

7   Let the filler harden until you can just dent it with your fingernail. Use a body file or Surform tool (shown here) to rough-shape the filler

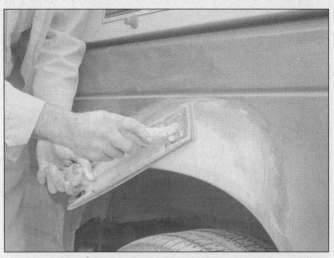

8   Use coarse-grit sandpaper and a sanding board or block to work the filler down until it's smooth and even. Work down to finer grits of sandpaper - always using a board or block - ending up with 360 or 400 grit

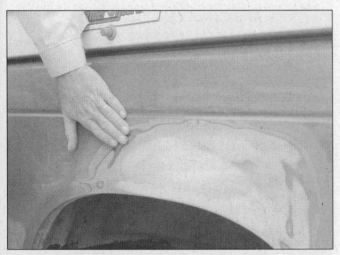

9   You shouldn't be able to feel any ridge at the transition from the filler to the bare metal or from the bare metal to the old paint. As soon as the repair is flat and uniform, remove the dust and mask off the adjacent panels or trim pieces

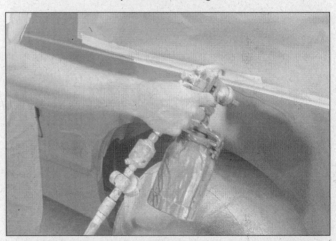

10   Apply several layers of primer to the area. Don't spray the primer on too heavy, so it sags or runs, and make sure each coat is dry before you spray on the next one. A professional-type spray gun is being used here, but aerosol spray primer is available inexpensively from auto parts stores

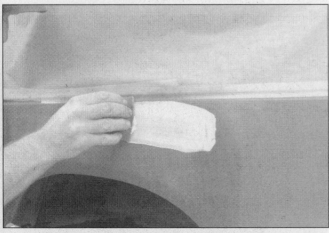

11   The primer will help reveal imperfections or scratches. Fill these with glazing compound. Follow the label instructions and sand it with 360 or 400-grit sandpaper until it's smooth. Repeat the glazing, sanding and respraying until the primer reveals a perfectly smooth surface

12   Finish sand the primer with very fine sandpaper (400 or 600-grit) to remove the primer overspray. Clean the area with water and allow it to dry. Use a tack rag to remove any dust, then apply the finish coat. Don't attempt to rub out or wax the repair area until the paint has dried completely (at least two weeks)

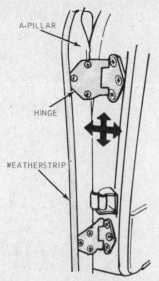

Fig. 12.2 Door hinge adjustment (Sec. 7)

8 Doors and hinges - removal and installation

1   Initially mark round the hinge with a ballpoint pen or a pencil as an aid to installation, then support the door whilst the hinge to body attaching screws are removed. Ideally, this requires help from an assistant as the door is an unwieldy object as well as being fairly heavy.
2   Remove the hinge from the door (if necessary) by removing the screws.
3   If a replacement door is to be fitted, remove the door latch and window regulator assemblies (Sections 9 and 11) and fit them to the replacement door.
4   Installation of the door is a straightforward reversal of the removal procedure, following which adjustment will be necessary as described in Section 7.

9 Door glass and regulator - removal and installation

1   Invert the door and regulator escutcheons and drive out the retaining pins using a suitable pin punch. Remove the handles, washers and escutcheons (photo).
2   Remove the pull handle and garnish plate (B1600) or plastic retainer and arm rest (Courier) (photo).
3   Carefully prise away the trim panel and clips from the door panel. If necessary remove the plastic weathersheets (photo).

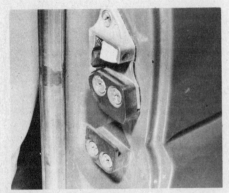

7.3 A door striker plate

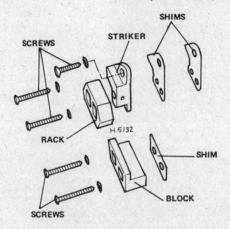

Fig. 12.3 Striker plate assembly - exploded view (Sec. 7)

Fig. 12.4 Removing the regulator retaining pins (Sec. 9)

9.1 Removing the window regulator handle

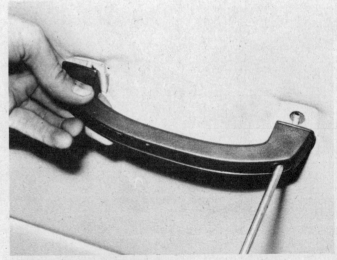

9.2 Removing the door pull handle

9.3 A door trim panel retaining clip

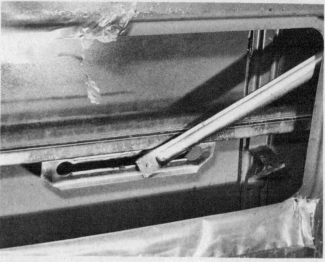

9.5 The regulator roller and arm

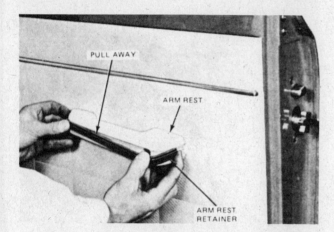

Fig. 12.5 Removing the plastic retainer and arm rest - Courier (Sec. 9)

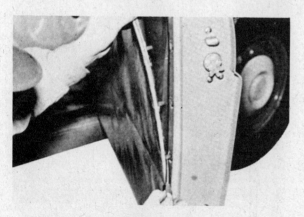

Fig. 12.6 Removing the trim panel (Sec. 9)

Door glass only
4   Remove the seven frame screws from the window frame assembly, then remove it and lower the door window glass.
5   Disengage the regulator roller and arm from the door glass channel, tilting the glass as necessary, then slide the window assembly up and out of the door (photo).
6   Remove the glass from the channel followed by the channel tape.

Regulator only
7   Remove the regulator retaining screws followed by the regulator and arm.

Door glass only
8   When installing, position 'Everseal' tape on the door glass, and fit the glass and tape into the channel.
9   Position the door glass assembly into the door cavity and engage the regulator roller into the glass channel.
10 Position the window frame assembly into the door, apply Loctite or a similar sealer to the frame screws, then fit and tighten them.
11 The remainder of the installation procedure is the reverse of removal.

Regulator only
12 When installing, fit the regulator into the door cavity, then fit the regulator roller and arm into the glass channel.
13 Apply Loctite or a similar sealer to the regulator retaining screws, then fit and tighten them.
14 The remainder of the installation procedure is the reverse of removal.

---

10 Weatherstrip and vent window assembly - removal and installation

1   Initially follow the procedure of Section 9, paragraphs 1, 2 and 3.
2   Remove the seven frame screws from the window frame assembly, then remove it from the door.
3   Remove the two vent frame screws.
4   Remove the two nuts, three washers and coil spring then remove the vent window assembly.
5   Pull out the weatherstrip from the vent window opening.
6   Installation is the reverse of the removal procedure, the spring tension of the vent window assembly being adjusted as necessary.

---

11 Door latch and remote control - removal and installation

1   Initially follow the procedure of Section 9, paragraphs 1, 2 and 3.
2   Using a screwdriver, prise up the lock cylinder retaining clip, noting the position of the lock cylinder as it is removed.
3   Remove the three door latch and two remote control assembly retaining screws. Remove the assembly from the door (photo).
4   When installing, position the assembly into the door and install the retaining screws. The remainder of the installation procedure is the reverse of removal.

12

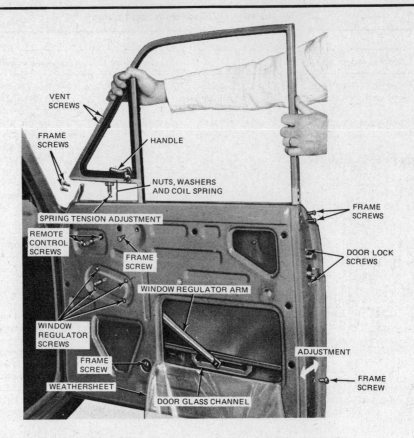

Fig. 12.7 Removing the window frame assembly (Sec. 9)

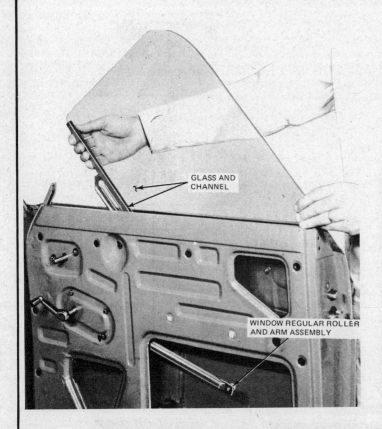

Fig. 12.8 Removing the door glass (Sec. 9)

Fig. 12.9 Removing the regulator assembly (Sec. 9)

12 Door outside handle - removal and installation

1   Initially follow the procedure of Section 9, paragraphs 1, 2 and 3.
2   Remove the screw and washer, and the nut and washer, and withdraw the handle.
3   Installation is the reverse of removal, making any necessary adjustment to the pushbutton as it is assembled to the door. Do not forget to fit the gaskets.

11.3 The door latch mechanism

13 Bonnet (hood) - removal and installation

1   Open the bonnet and mark the outline of the bonnet hinges with a pencil or ballpoint pen to aid installation.
2   With help from an assistant, remove the cotter key from the hinge stop retaining pin. Remove the pin and hood stop.
3   Tilt the bonnet forwards, position the torsion bar to one side then remove the hinge to body retaining screws.
4   Remove the bonnet then detach the hinges.
5   Installation is the reverse of the removal procedure. If adjustment is required, this can be done by repositioning the hinges or, if vertical adjustment is necessary, by shimming between the hinge and body at the front or by adjusting the bonnet bumpers at the rear.

14 Bonnet (hood) release mechanism

1   In the event of the release cable breaking, a screwdriver can be inserted through the access hole (after removing the rubber plug) directly behind the heater, and pushing the release lever to the left.
2   The bonnet latch dowel can be adjusted up or down using a screwdriver after slackening the locknut.
3   To renew the bonnet release cable, remove the nut from the bolt retaining the bonnet latch cable to the release lever.
4   Remove the windscreen wiper assembly as detailed in Chapter 10.
5   Remove the four hood latch retaining screws, loosen the nut and bolt retaining the cable, and remove the cable.
6   Feed the new cable through the dash panel, hook the cable end into the latch and tighten the retaining screw and nut.
7   Position the latch assembly to the latch retainer and install the four screws.
8   The remainder of the installation procedure is the reverse of removal.

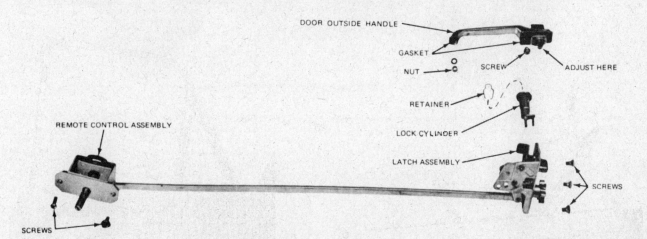

Fig. 12.10 Door latch, lock and handle (Secs. 11 and 12)

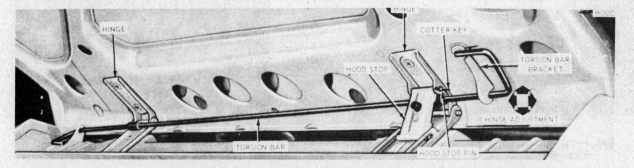

Fig. 12.11 The bonnet (hood) hinges and torsion bar (Sec. 13)

12

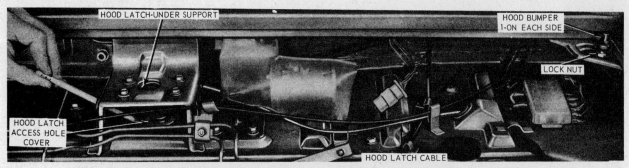

Fig. 12.12 Access to the bonnet (hood) release catch (Sec. 14)

Fig. 12.13 The tailgate latches and hinges (Sec. 15)

15 Tailgate latches and hinges

Latches

1 With the tailgate closed, loosen the chain retaining bracket and move it to one side, then remove the latch attaching screws.
2 Installation is the reverse of the removal procedure.

Hinges

3 Open the tailgate and support it in this position.
4 Remove the hinge pins, cotter keys and washers, then drive out the hinge pins.
5 Remove the hinge attaching screws and nuts if the hinges are to be renewed. If the tailgate is to be renewed, transfer the latches and chain brackets to the new tailgate.
6 Installation is the reverse of the removal procedure.

16 Windshield and rear window glass - removal and installation

1 In the event of windshield or rear window glass breaking, or the need to renew the sealing rubber, it must be appreciated that the procedure needs to be carried out very carefully to do the job properly. There is, of course, also the danger of breaking the new glass. For these reasons it is recommended that the job is entrusted to a properly equipped repair facility, and only in the event of this not being available, the following procedure should be followed:
2 Remove the windshield wiper arms and blades (refer to Chapter 10), if applicable.
3 Remove the rear view mirror, if applicable.

4 Using a wooden spatula, break the weatherstrip seal around the glass opening in the body.
5 With help from an assistant, push the glass out of the opening.
6 Where applicable remove the mouldings from the weatherstrip. Remove the weatherstrip from the glass.
7 Clean off all traces of old sealant from the glass and/or weatherstrip and/or body.
8 Apply a suitable sealer to the opening flange.
9 Position the weatherstrip on the glass and insert a draw cord in the pinch weld opening of the weatherstrip around its complete length. Overlap the cord at the lower center of the glass and tape the ends together as shown in the illustration (Fig. 12.15).
10 Coat the weatherstrip mounting surfaces with a suitable rubber lubricant. Where applicable insert the weatherstrip mouldings.
11 Position the glass and weatherstrip in the opening then, while an assistant applies hand pressure to the outside of the glass, pull the draw cord to pull the lip of the weatherstrip over the lower flange, along each side flange then over the upper flange.
12 Install the rear view mirror (if applicable), clean the glass and install the windshield wiper arms and blades (if applicable).

17 Instrument panel pad - removal and installation

1 Remove the windscreen, as described in Section 16, and the instrument panel cluster, as described in Chapter 10.
2 Remove the seven garnish moulding retaining screws; remove the mouldings (Fig. 12.16).
3 Remove the four instrument panel pad assembly retaining screws and remove the pad.
4 Installation is the reverse of the removal procedure.

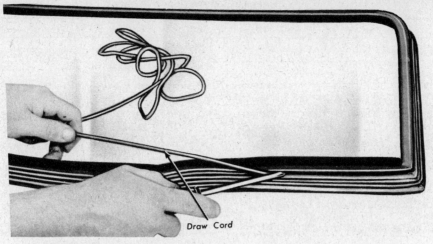

Fig. 12.14 Installing the draw cord prior to windscreen installation (Sec. 16)

Fig. 12.15 The draw cord in the installed state (Sec. 16)

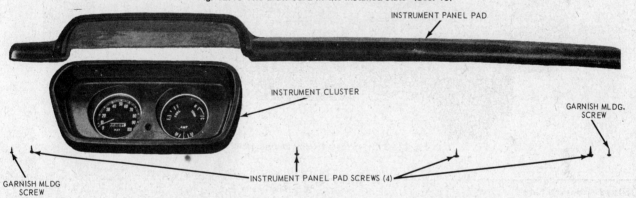

Fig. 12.16 Instrument panel pad removal - Courier illustrated (Sec. 17)

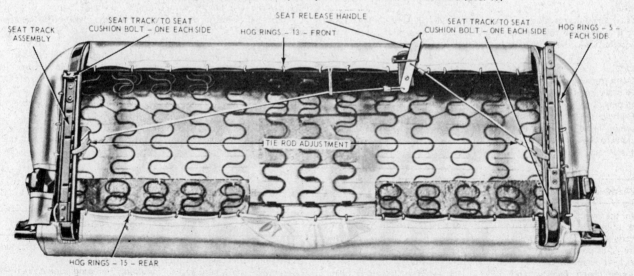

Fig. 12.17 The seat cushion and track assemblies (Sec. 18)

12

18 Seat and seat tracks - removal, adjustment and installation

1   To remove the seat tracks, disengage the seat back release lock on each side.

2   Remove the track to floor attaching nuts, bolts and washers then remove the seat back and cushion from the vehicle as an assembly.

3   Disengage the tie-rod adjustment wires from the seat track assemblies, and remove the track to cushion attaching bolts to permit removal of the tracks.

4   If adjustment of the tie-rod wire is necessary (eg; where the seat release handle is ineffective), straighten the tie-rod wire and either shorten or lengthen the bend in the wire, as appropriate.

5   To remove the seat back assembly, remove one bolt and two washers on each side, then disengage the seat back releases.

6   Installation is the reverse of the removal procedure.

19 Radiator grille and headlamp surround - removal and installation

Courier

1   Remove the six retaining screws and withdraw the grille assembly. Installation is the reverse of the removal procedure.

B1600

2   Remove the screws retaining the grille (or trim strips) and the headlamp surrounds. Installation is the reverse of the removal procedure (photos).

20 Front bumper - removal and installation

1   Disconnect the sidelight connectors.

Fig. 12.18 The seat back assembly
(Sec. 18)

19.2a Removal of the headlamp surround
UK B1600 models

19.2b Removal of the headlamp surround
UK B1600 models

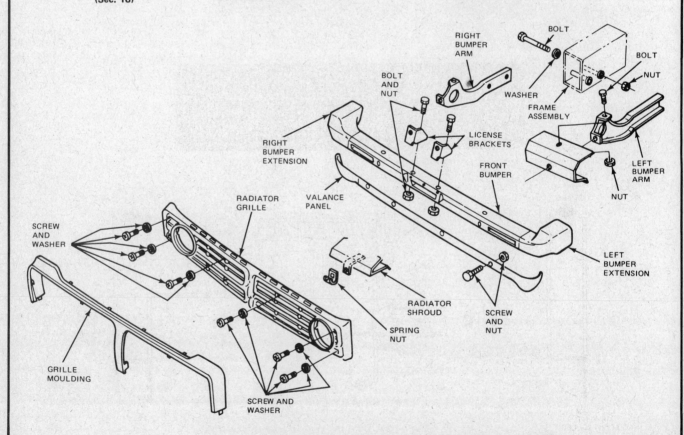

Fig. 12.19 The radiator grille and bumper - Courier illustrated (Secs. 19 and 20)

2 Remove the two bolts attaching each bumper arm to the frame and withdraw the bumper and arms as an assembly.

3 If the bumper side extensions or center strip are to be renewed, remove the parts as necessary and transfer them to the new assembly.

4 When installing, position the bumper and arms to the vehicle frame, lightly tighten the retaining nuts and re-make the sidelight connections.

5 Adjust the bumper as necessary and tighten the attaching bolts securely.

21 Ventilator and heater - general description

1 All models are fitted with a fresh-air type ventilating and heating system. Outside air enters by ram effect when the vehicle is in motion, being controlled by rod operated doors (see Fig. 12.21).

2 The heater blower (fan) draws either outside air or recirculating air into the heater housing and through the core to the discharge outlets. The position of the heater/defrost door determines the route through which the heated air passes.

3 The heater control assembly has two air control doors and a water valve controlled by levers and cables at the dash mounted control assembly. The upper lever also contains the blower control switch which is operated by pulling out the lever.

4 Fresh air ventilation can be obtained at low forward speeds by using the blower and shutting off the warm water supply to the heater core.

22 Ventilator and heater - testing

1 In the event of failure of the system to function properly, initially check for such things as blown fuses, loose or broken wires, collapsed hoses, loose ducts and correctly operating levers and controlling doors.

Motor test

2 Ensure that the motor is satisfactorily grounded (earthed) then disconnect the motor lead from the resistor and switch lead at the in-line connector. Connect the motor lead to the battery '+' terminal using a suitable length of wire. If the motor fails to run, it should be renewed; if the motor now operates check the blower switch and associated wiring.

Blower switch test

3 Remove the heater control (see Section 25). Set the switch to 'off' (lever pushed in) then use an ohmmeter or a lamp and battery to check for continuity between all of the terminals, two at a time. If there is continuity, the switch is faulty, which will mean renewal of the entire heater control assembly. If there is no continuity the switch is apparently serviceable.

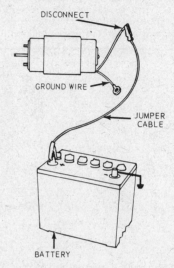

Fig. 12.20 Testing the blower motor (Sec. 21)

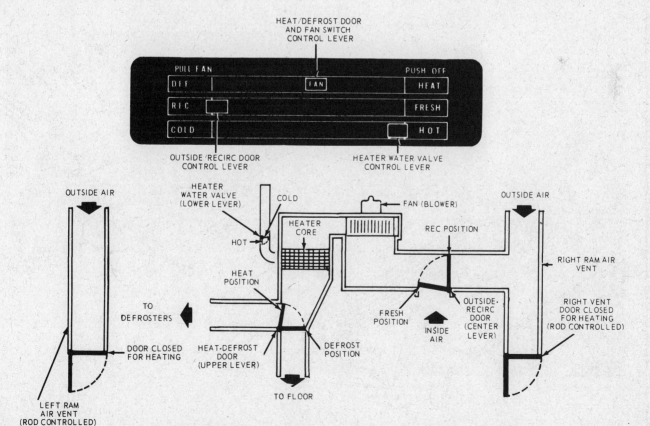

Fig. 12.21 Schematic diagram of the ventilating and heating system
(Sec. 21)

12

200

MOUNTING CLIP   HEAT DEFROST DOOR CRANK ARM   CABLE WIRE   CABLE HOUSING

VIEW A

CABLE HOUSING   MOUNTING CLIP   MOUNTING CLIP   OUTSIDE-RECIRC DOOR CRANK ARM

CABLE WIRE

CRANK ARM

ACTUATING LEVER

WATER VALVE   VIEW B

CABLE HOUSING   SET SCREW   CABLE WIRE

VIEW C

Fig. 12.22 Heater assembly control cable connections (Sec. 23)

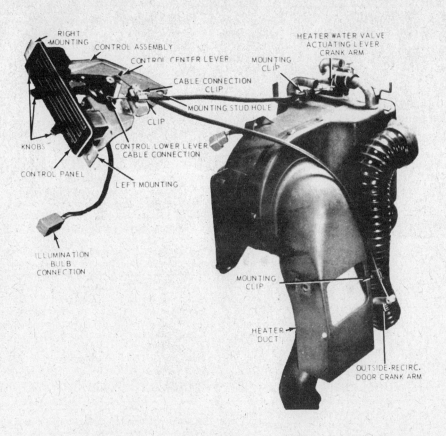

Fig. 12.23 Control cable connections to the control assembly - lower side (Sec. 24)

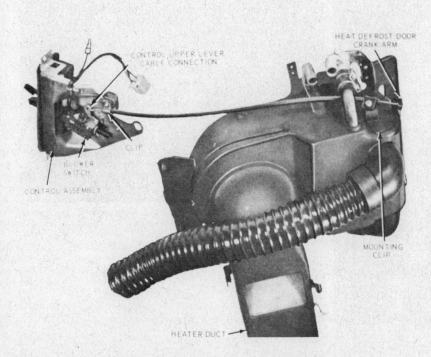

Fig. 12.24 Control cable connections to the control assembly - upper side (Sec. 24)

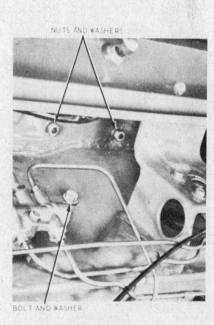

Fig. 12.25 The heater to dash panel mounting (Sec. 26)

12

Open circuit test

4   Where a wiring fault is indicated, this must be traced using a suitable lamp and battery or an ohmmeter, working from the wiring diagram given in Chapter 10. If an ohmmeter is used, the battery positive lead should be disconnected in order to prevent damage to the instrument.

Loose blower test

5   If only a hum is heard when the blower switch is 'on', a loose blower fan on the motor shaft is indicated.

Blocked heater core test

6   Start the engine then remove the hose from the water pump side of the heater core. Assuming that water is being delivered to the heater core, if there is little or no flow away from it, it must be assumed to be blocked.

Heater airlocks

7   If an airlock in the heater core is suspected, remove the hose which leads to the water pump and allow trapped air to flow out while the engine is running. Reconnect the hose when a continuous stream of coolant flows out.

23 Ventilator and heater - adjustments

Heat/defrost door cable (Fig. 12.22, View A)

1   Loosen the cable mounting clip screw and prise open the clip. Set the upper control lever at 'HEAT', turn the door crank arm towards the clip as far as possible then tighten the clip and screw.

Heater water valve cable (Fig. 12.22, View B)

2   Loosen the cable mounting clip screw and prise open the clip. Set the control lever to 'HOT' and pull the valve plunger and actuating lever fully outwards to move the lever crank arm as far as possible towards the cable mounting clip. Finally tighten the clip and screw.

Outside/recirculation door cable (Fig. 12.22, View C)

3   Loosen the cable mounting clip screw and prise open the clip. Set the control lever to 'REC', turn the door crank arm towards the clip as far as it will go, then tighten the clip and screw.

24 Heater control cables - removal and installation

Heater water valve cable

1   Remove the water valve shield from the lower left-hand side of the heater assembly (3 screws).
2   Disengage the cable assembly from the mounting clip, then disconnect the cable end from the heater water valve actuating lever.
3   Remove the ashtray and mounting bracket (3 bracket retaining screws).
4   Remove the cable housing to control assembly clip (1 screw) then disconnect the cable wire from the control lower lever and pull it out.
5   Installation is the reverse of the removal procedure. Adjust the heater water valve cable, as described in the previous Section.

Outside/recirculation door cable

6   Disengage the cable housing from the heater duct mounting clip.
7   Loosen the setscrew on the outside/recirculation door crank arm; pull the wire out of the crank arm.
8   Remove the ashtray and mounting bracket (3 bracket retaining screws).
9   Remove the cable housing to control assembly clip (1 screw), then disconnect the cable wire from the control lever and pull it out.
10 Installation is the reverse of the removal procedure. Adjust the outside/recirculation door cable, as described in the previous Section.

Heat/defrost cable

11 Disengage the cable from the mounting clip at the lower left-hand side of the heater assembly.
12 Remove the control assembly, as described in the following Section, but only remove the heat/defrost cable housing to control assembly clip. Disconnect the cable wire from the control upper lever and pull it out.

13 Installation is the reverse of the removal procedure. Adjust the heat/defrost cable as described in the previous Section.

25 Control assembly (dash mounted) - removal and installation

1   Disconnect the battery ground (earth) lead and remove the ashtray and mounting bracket (3 screws).
2   Pull off the heater control knobs then carefully prise out the control panel and remove the two illumination bulbs.
3   From beneath the instrument panel, remove the two control assembly retaining nuts.
4   Remove the nut retaining the forward end of the control assembly to the bracket on the upper section of the dashpanel.
5   Push the assembly forward and lower it from under the instrument panel. At each of the three cable connections, remove the retaining clip and disconnect the wire from the control lever.
6   When installing, connect the heat/defrost door cable wire to the upper control assembly lever, and the outside/recirculation door cable and the water valve cable wires to the center and lower levers respectively. Secure the housings in the clips.
7   Raise the control assembly up from beneath the instrument panel into the opening, ensuring that the mounting bracket stud on the upper section of the dash panel enters the stud hole in the forward end of the control assembly. Install the mounting nut.
8   Install the nuts (2) which secure the control assembly to the instrument panel and fit the two illumination bulbs.
9   Slide the control panel slots over the center levers and snap the panel into the control assembly.
10 Fit the three control knobs, install the ashtray mounting bracket and ashtray, and reconnect the battery ground lead.

26 Heater assembly - removal and installation

1   Disconnect the battery ground (earth) lead and drain the cooling system (refer to Chapter 2).
2   Remove the water valve shield (3 screws) at the left-hand side of the heater assembly, and loosen the hose clamp retaining screws. Remove the hoses.
3   Disengage the control cable housing from the heater at the heat/defrost door, water valve and the outside/recirculation door. Disconnect each cable wire at its crank arm.
4   Disconnect the fan motor leads.
5   Remove the glovebox (4 screws), and at the engine side of the dash panel, remove the retaining bolt and two retaining nuts.
6   Disconnect the two defrost ducts from the heater and remove the heater assembly from the vehicle.
7   If it is necessary to remove the heater core, remove the five screws and separate the two halves of the heater (Fig. 12.26, View A).
8   Loosen the hose clamps and slide the heater core from the case.
9   Install the replacement core into the case, connecting the core tube to the water valve tube with the short hose and clamps.
10 Assemble the two halves of the heater and fit the retaining screws, then install the heater core to the heater assembly.
11 Position the heater assembly to the dashpanel, ensuring that the heater duct aligns with the air intake duct and the two mounting studs enter the holes in the dash panel (Fig. 12.29).
12 From the engine side of the dash panel, install the nuts on the mounting studs. With an assistant lifting the heater up from inside, install the mounting bolt.
13 Connect the defrost ducts. Connect the heat/defrost door control cable wire to the door crank arm and adjust, as described in Section 23.
14 Connect the water valve control cable wire to the crank arm on the water valve actuating lever, and locate the housing in the mounting clip. Adjust as described in Section 23.
15 Insert the outside/recirculation door control cable wire into the door crank arm hole and tighten the setscrew. Adjust as described in Section 23.
16 Install the glovebox and secure with the four screws.
17 Reconnect the fan motor.
18 Reconnect the heater core hoses and tighten the clamp screws.
19 Install the water valve shield, fill the cooling system and connect the battery ground lead. Run the engine and bleed the cooling system, if necessary, referring to Chapter 2 and Section 22, of this Chapter.

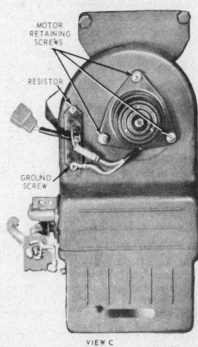

Fig. 12.26 The heater assembly (Secs. 26 and 27)

View A — side view
View B— front view (towards engine)
View C — rear view (towards driver's cab)

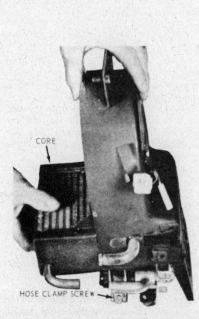

Fig. 12.27 Removing the heater core from the heater assembly (Sec. 26)

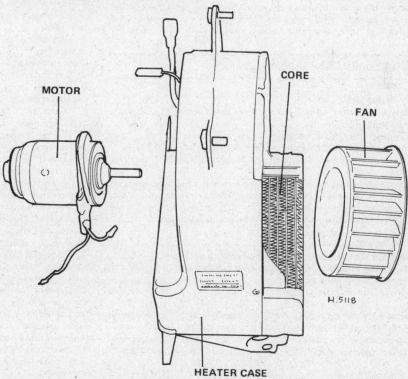

Fig. 12.28 The heater disassembled (Sec. 26)

12

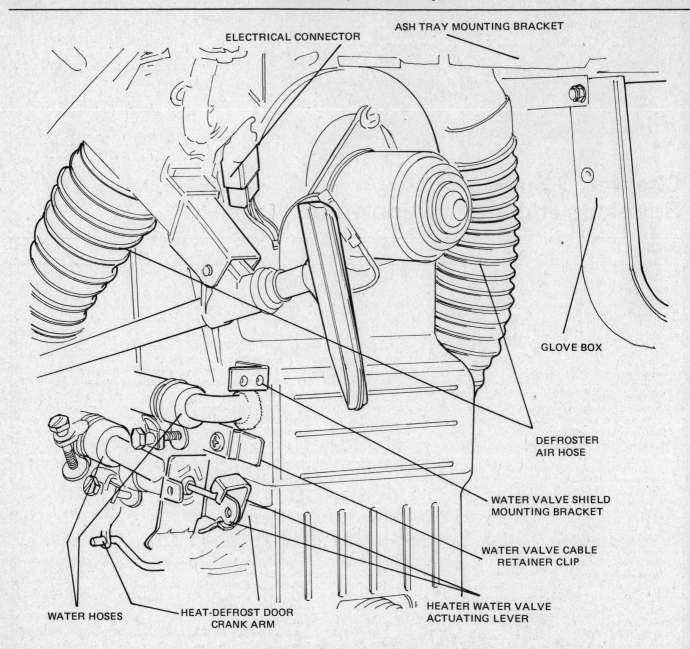

ELECTRICAL CONNECTOR

ASH TRAY MOUNTING BRACKET

GLOVE BOX

DEFROSTER
AIR HOSE

WATER VALVE SHIELD
MOUNTING BRACKET

WATER VALVE CABLE
RETAINER CLIP

WATER HOSES

HEAT-DEFROST DOOR
CRANK ARM

HEATER WATER VALVE
ACTUATING LEVER

Fig. 12.29 The heater installation (Sec. 26)

27 Blower motor and fan - removal and installation

1   Remove the heater assembly, as described in the previous Section.
2   Separate the two halves of the heater assembly (5 screws). Loosen the fan retaining nut then lightly tap the nut to loosen the fan so that it can be removed from the motor shaft (Fig. 12.26, View B).
3   Remove the three motor to case retaining screws (Fig. 12.26, View C); disconnect the in-line connector to the resistor and the ground screw.
4   Rotate the motor slightly to remove it from the case.
5   Installation of the motor and fan is a reversal of the removal procedure. Refer to Section 26 for installation of the heater assembly.

Chapter 13 Supplement:
Revisions and information on later models

Contents

Introduction 1
Specifications 2
Routine maintenance 3
Engine 4
Part A General information and removal procedures — 2.0 liter
    and 2.3 liter engines
    Major operations with engine in vehicle
    Major operations requiring engine removal
    Engine — removal
Part B Disassembly
    Disassembly — general
    Cylinder head removal — engine in place
    Auxiliary shaft — removal
    Flywheel and backplate — removal
    Oil pan and oil pump — removal
    Crankshaft sprocket, drivebelt inner cover and cylinder front cover —
        removal
    Pistons, connecting rods and big-end bearings — removal
    Crankshaft and main bearings — removal
    Camshaft drivebelt — removal (engine in place)
    Valves and lash adjusters — removal
    Camshaft — removal
    Thermostat and water pump — removal
    Piston pin — removal
    Piston rings — removal
Part C Lubrication and crankcase ventilation systems
    Oil pump — removal, inspection and replacement
    Oil filter — removal and installation
Part D Inspection
    General information
    Emission control components — checking
    Crankshaft, main bearings, cylinder bores and pistons/connecting
        rods
    Camshaft, camshaft bearings and camshaft followers
    Auxiliary shaft and bearings
    Valves and valve seats
    Hydraulic lash adjusters
    Timing gears and timing belt
    Flywheel
    Cylinder head, valve guides and oil pan
Part E Reassembly
    General information
    Crankshaft
    Pistons, piston rings and connecting rods
    Oil pump and strainer
    Auxiliary shaft and front covers
    Oil pan
    Engine backplate, flywheel and clutch
    Valves
    Camshaft
    Hydraulic lash adjusters and cam followers
    Cylinder head
    Water pump and thermostat
    Timing components and timing belt

Valve lash
Valve cover
Part F Installation
    Preparation
    Installation
    Initial start-up after overhaul or major repair
Part G Engine/transmission mount
    Front mounts — replacement with engine in vehicle
    Rear mounts — replacement with engine in vehicle
Fuel system 5
    Air cleaner — description
    Fuel cut valve — description, removal and checking
    Carburetor — general description
    Idle speed adjustment — all models
    Idle fuel mixture — 2.0 liter engine
    Idle fuel mixture — 2.3 liter engine
    High altitude adjustment
    Fast idle adjustment — 1976 through 1978
    Fast idle cam adjustment — 1979 through 1982
    Vacuum pulldown — adjustment — 1976 through 1978
    Float level — adjustment
    Choke — throttle valve opening angle
    Choke diaphragm — adjustment
    Exhaust system and catalytic converter — general information
    Catalytic converter
    Emission control systems — general
    Exhaust gas recirculation (EGR) system
    Spark timing control system
    EGR control valve test
    Spark delay valve test (manual transmissions)
Ignition system 6
    General description — 2.0 and 2.3 liter engines
    Distributor — removal and installation
    Ignition timing — breakerless distributors
Clutch 7
    Clutch adjustment
5-speed manual transmission 8
Part A Removal and installation
Part B Dismantling
    External components
    Shift rails, mainshaft, and countershaft bearings and gears
    Inspection
Part C Reassembly
    Mainshaft and countershaft assemblies
    Mainshaft and countershaft bearings
    Mainshaft and countershaft rear end components
    External components
Driveshaft 9
    Single section type — removal
    Universal joints
Brakes 10
Description
Brake shoes and pads — inspection

(continued on next page)

Contents (continued)

Brake pedal free travel — adjustment
Front disc pads — inspection and replacement
Front calipers — removal, overhaul and installation
Front brake disc — examination and replacement
Tandem master cylinder and dual hydraulic circuit
Brake booster — removal and installation
Brake booster — overhaul
Electrical system 11
Fuses
Fusible link
Alternator — removal, testing and installation — 1982
In vehicle tests — alternator
Bench tests — alternator
Lighting system — 1979 through 1982
Side marker lamps
Parking lights

License light bulb, lens and housing
Taillight/back-up light
Combination switch — 1982 only
Suspension and steering... 12
Front shock absorber — installation
Front wheel bearing — adjustment
Rear shock absorber — installation
Steering gear — removal and installation — 1977 through 1981
Steering linkage — 1977 through 1981
Front suspension — 1982
Steering linkage/steering column — 1982
Steering gear — removal and installation — 1982
Turning angle — adjustment
Wheel balancing
Wheels — removal and installation
Bodywork 13
Tailgate latches

1 Introduction

The purpose of this Chapter is to provide updated information on changes and additions made to the Ford Courier since 1974. The original material in the first 12 Chapters of the manual still applies unless amendments are given in this Chapter. Therefore, owners of Courier trucks manufactured from 1975 to 1982 should refer to this Chapter *before* using the information in the original Chapters of this manual.

Several major changes were made. In addition to the existing 109.6 cu in (1.8L) engine, two new four-cylinder engines were introduced: the 2.3 liter (2300 cc) in 1977 and a 2.0 liter (1969 cc) unit in 1979. A 5-speed manual transmission was also introduced in 1977 and was made available as an option on all Courier models. The automatic transmission was made available only on the largest (2.3L) engine.

2 Specifications

Note: *The information given in this Section is supplementary to the Specifications in the twelve main Chapters of the manual.*

1796 cc (109.6 cu in) engine

Valve lash (hot), intake and exhaust ... ...   0.012 in (0.30 mm)

Camshaft drive

Number of links in chain	106
Camshaft sprocket teeth	38
Crankshaft sprocket	19

Firing order 1-3-4-2

Cylinder location and distributor rotation

Valve timing

Intake opens	13° BTDC
Intake closes	57° ABDC
Exhaust opens	62° BBDC
Exhaust closes	8° ATDC

Pistons

Diameter ...	3.0691 to 3.0683 in (77.953 to 77.927 mm)
Piston ring groove width:	
Top compression	0.0600 to 0.0606 in (1.5240 to 1.6764 mm)
Second compression...	0.0598 to 0.0604 in (1.4986 to 1.6256 mm)
Oil control ...	0.1583 to 0.1587 in (4.0132 to 4.0386 mm)
Piston ring side clearance:	
Top compression	0.0014 to 0.0028 in (0.0254 to 0.0762 mm)

1969 cc (120.1 cu in) engine

General

Displacement ...	120.1 cu in (1969 cc)
Bore and stroke ...	3.15 x 3.86 in
Firing order ...	1,3,4,2
Oil pressure (hot @ 3000 rpm) ...	50 to 64 psi

Cylinder head

Valve guide bore diameter ...	0.3175 to 0.3183 in
Valve seat angle ...	45°
Valve stem-to-guide clearance:	
Intake ...	0.0007 to 0.0021 in
Exhaust ...	0.0021 to 0.0023 in

Valve head diameter:
   Intake ... ...   1.6497 to 1.6575 in
   Exhaust ... ...   1.2953 to 1.3031 in
Valve face run-out limit ... ...   0.0012 in
Valve face angle ... ...   45°
Valve stem diameter:
   Intake ... ...   0.3162 to 0.3168 in
   Exhaust ... ...   0.3160 to 0.3168 in
Valve springs:
   Free length ... ...   1.598 in
Rocker arm shaft:
   Diameter ... ...   0.7469 to 0.7477 in
   Bore diameter ... ...   0.7488 to 0.7501 in
   Clearance in bore ... ...   0.0011 to 0.0032 in

Camshaft

Camshaft endplay ... ...   0.001 to 0.007 in
   Wear limit ... ...   0.008 in
Camshaft journal diameter
   Front ... ...   I.7701 to I.7695 in
   Center ... ...   1.7691 to 1.7697 in
   Rear ... ...   1.7701 to 1.7695 in
Camshaft bearing running clearance ... ...   0.0007 to 0.0027 in
   Wear limit ... ...   0.002 in

Cylinder block

Cylinder bore ... ...   3.1497 to 3.1504 in
Maximum out-of-round ... ...   0.005 in
Maximum taper ... ...   0.010 in

Crankshaft and connecting rods

Main bearing journal diameter ... ...   2.4780 to 2.4786 in
Maximum out-of-round ... ...   0.0006 in
Maximum taper ... ...   0.0003 in (per inch of length)
Connecting rod journal:
   Diameter ... ...   2.0842 to 2.0848 in
   Maximum out-of-round ... ...   0.0006 in
   Maximum taper ... ...   0.0003 in (per inch of length)
Crankshaft endplay ... ...   0.003 to 0.009 in
Connecting rod bearing clearance ... ...   0.001 to 0.0026 in
   Wear limit ... ...   0.003 in
Main bearing running clearance ... ...   0.0005 to 0.0015 in
   Wear limit ... ...   0.0024 in
Piston pin bore diameter ... ...   0.7869 to 0.7873 in
Connecting rod length (between centers) ... ...   6.5335 to 6.5375 in
Connecting rod side clearance ... ...   0.004 to 0.008 in
   Wear limit ... ...   0.014 in

Pistons and piston rings

Diameter ... ...   3.1474 to 3.1482 in
   Oversizes available ... ...   0.010, 0.020, 0.030, 0.040 in
Piston-to-bore clearance ... ...   0.0014 to 0.0030 in
Ring groove width:
   Top compression ... ...   0.0480 to 0.0488 in
   Second compression ... ...   0.0598 to 0.0604 in
Oil control ... ...   0.1583 to 0.1587 in

Piston pin

Diameter
   Standard ... ...   0.7864 to 0.7866 in
Piston pin clearance ... ...   –0.0009 to –0.0003 in (interference fit)

Piston rings

Piston ring width:
   Top compression ... ...   0.0461 to 0.0469 in
   Second compression ... ...   0.0579 to 0.0587 in
Groove clearance:
   Top compression ... ...   0.0011 to 0.0027 in
   Second compression ... ...   0.0011 to 0.0025 in
Ring end gap:
   Compression ... ...   0.008 to 0.016 in
   Oil control ... ...   0.012 to 0.035 in

Lubrication system

Oil pump rotor end clearance ... ...   0.002 to 0.004 in
Outer rotor-to-body clearance ... ...   0.006 to 0.010 in
Oil capacity ... ...   4.1 US quarts (5.1 with filter change)

13

2300 cc (140.3 cu in) engine

Engine general

Displacement	2300 cc (140.3 cu in)
Bore and stroke	3.78 x 3.126 in (96.0 x 79.4 mm)
Firing order	1-3-4-2
Oil pressure (hot @ 2000 rpm)	40 to 60 psi

Cylinder head

Valve guide bore diameter	0.3433 to 0.3443 in (8.71 to 8.73 mm)
Valve seat width:	
Intake	0.060 to 0.080 in (1.5240 to 2.0320 mm)
Exhaust	0.070 to 0.090 in (1.7780 to 2.2860 mm)
Valve seat angle	45°
Valve sequence (front to rear)	1 Exhaust, 2 Intake, 3 Exhaust, 4 Intake, 5 Exhaust, 6 Intake, 7 Exhaust, 8 Intake
Valve lash adjuster bore	0.8430 to 0.8449 in (21.4122 to 21.4630 mm)
Valve stem-to-guide clearance:	
Intake	0.0010 to 0.0027 in (0.0254 to 0.0762 mm)
Exhaust	0.0015 to 0.0032 in (0.0508 to 0.0762 mm)
Valve head diameter:	
Intake	1.73 to 1.74 in (43.9420 to 44.1960 mm)
Exhaust	1.49 to 1.51 in (37.8460 to 38.3540 mm)
Valve face run-out limit	0.002 in (0.0508 mm) maximum
Valve face	44°
Valve stem diameter:	
Intake	0.3416 to 0.3423 in (8.6868 to 8.7122 mm)
Exhaust	0.3411 to 0.3418 in (8.6614 to 8.6868 mm)
Valve stem oversize availability	+0.003 in (0.0762 mm), +0.015 in (0.3810 mm), +0.030 in (0.762 mm)
Valve springs	
Free length:	
1982 only	1.89 in (48.00 mm)
All others	1.82 in (46.2 mm)
Fitted height	1-17/32 to 1-19/32 in (38.89 to 40.08 mm)
Rocker arm ratio	1.64 : 1
Valve tappet lifter:	
Diameter	0.8422 to 0.8427 in (21.3868 to 21.4122 mm)
Clearance in bore	0.0007 to 0.0027 in (0.1778 to 0.0762 mm)
Wear limit	0.005 in (0.1270 mm)

Camshaft

Lobe lift:	
Intake	0.2437 in (6.1976 mm)
Exhaust	0.2437 in (6.1976 mm)
Wear limit	0.005 in (0.1270 mm) maximum
Camshaft endplay	0.001 to 0.007 in (0.0254 to 0.1778 mm)
Wear limit	0.009 in (0.2286 mm)
Camshaft journal diameter	1.7713 to 1.7720 in (44.983 to 45.009 mm)
Camshaft bearing running clearance	0.001 to 0.003 in (0.0254 to 0.0762 mm)
Wear limit	0.006 in (0.1524 mm)

Cylinder block

Cylinder bore	3.7795 to 3.7831 in (95.98 to 96.01 mm)
Maximum out-of-round	0.005 in (0.1270 mm)
Maximum taper	0.010 in (0.2540 mm)

Crankshaft and connecting rods

Main bearing journal diameter	2.3982 to 2.3990 in (60.9092 to 60.9346 mm)
Maximum out-of-round	0.0006 in (0.0152 mm)
Maximum taper	0.0006 in (0.0152 mm) per inch of length
Length of thrust bearing:	
1982 only	1.199 to 1.201 (30.45 to 30.51 mm)
All others	2.3982 to 2.3990 in (60.9092 to 60.9346 mm)
Connecting rod journal:	
Diameter	2.0464 to 2.0472 in (51.9684 to 51.9938 mm)
Maximum out-of-round	0.0006 in (0.0152 mm)
Maximum taper	0.0006 in (0.0152 mm) per inch of length
Crankshaft endplay	0.004 to 0.008 in (0.1016 to 0.2032 mm)
Wear limit	0.012 in (0.3048 mm)
Auxiliary shaft endplay	0.001 to 0.007 in (0.0254 to 0.1778 mm)
Connecting rod bearing clearance	0.0008 to 0.0015 in (0.0203 to 0.0508 mm)
Wear limit	0.0008 to 0.0026 in (0.0203 to 0.0760 mm)
Main bearing running clearance	0.0008 to 0.0015 in (0.0203 to 0.0508 mm)
Wear limit	0.0008 to 0.0026 in (0.0203 to 0.0760 mm)

Auxiliary shaft running clearance ... ...   0.0006 to 0.0026 in (0.0152 to 0.0760 mm)
Piston pin bore diameter:
   1982 only ... ...   0.9096 to 0.9112 in (23.104 to 23.145 mm)
   All others ... ...   0.9104 to 0.9112 in (23.1140 to 23.1394 mm)
Connecting rod big-end bore ... ...   2.1720 to 2.1728 (55.1688 to 55.1942 mm)
Connecting rod length (between centers) ... ...   5.2031 to 5.2063 in (132.1562 to 132.2324 mm)
Connecting rod side clearance ... ...   0.0035 to 0.0105 in (0.1016 to 0.2540 mm)
   Wear limit:
      1982 only ... ...   0.014 in (0.356 mm)
      All others ... ...   0.0150 in (0.3810 mm)

Pistons and piston rings

Diameters:
   Red grade ... ...   3.7780 to 3.7786 in (95.9612 to 95.9866 mm)
   Blue grade ... ...   3.7792 to 3.7798 in (95.9866 to 96.0120 mm)
   Oversize (0.003 in) ... ...   3.7804 to 3.7810 in (96.0120 to 96.0374 mm)
Piston-to-bore clearance ... ...   0.0014 to 0.0022 in (0.0254 to 0.0508 mm)
Piston pin bore diameter in piston ... ...   0.9123 to 0.9126 in (23.1648 to 23.1902 mm)
Ring groove width:
   Top compression ... ...   0.080 to 0.081 in (2.0320 to 2.0574 mm)
   Second compression ... ...   0.080 to 0.081 in (2.0320 to 2.0574 mm)
Oil control ... ...   0.1880 to 0.1890 in (4.7752 to 4.8006 mm)

Piston pin

Length ... ...   3.010 to 3.040 in (76.454 to 77.2160 mm)
Diameter:
   Standard ... ...   0.9119 to 0.9124 in (23.1648 to 23.1902 mm)
   0.001 in oversize ... ...   0.9130 tp 0.9133 in (23.1902 to 23.1978 mm)
   0.002 in oversize ... ...   0.9140 to 0.9143 in (23.2156 to 23.2232 mm)
Piston pin clearance ... ...   0.0002 to 0.0004 in (0.0051 to 0.0102 mm)
Piston pin-to-rod clearance ... ...   Interference fit

Piston rings

Piston ring width:
   Top compression ... ...   0.077 to 0.078 in (1.9558 to 1.9812 mm)
   Second compression ... ...   0.077 to 0.078 in (1.9558 to 1.9812 mm)
Groove clearance:
   Top and second compression ... ...   0.002 to 0.004 in (0.0508 to 0.1016 mm)
   Wear limit ... ...   0.006 in (0.1524 mm)
Ring end gap:
   Top and second compression ... ...   0.010 to 0.020 in (0.2540 to 0.5080 mm)
   Oil control (steel rail) ... ...   0.015 to 0.055 in (0.3810 to 1.3970 mm)

Lubrication system

Oil pump driveshaft-to-housing bearing clearance ... ...   0.0015 to 0.0030 in (0.0381 to 0.0762 mm)
Relief valve-to-bore clearance ... ...   0.0015 to 0.0030 in (0.0381 to 0.0762 mm)
Oil pump rotor end clearance ... ...   0.004 in (0.1016 mm) maximum
Outer rotor-to-body clearance ... ...   0.001 to 0.013 in (0.0254 to 0.3302 mm)
Oil capacity:
   Without filter change ... ...   4 US qts (3.78 litres/3.34 Imp qt)
   With filter change ... ...   5 US qts (4.73 litres/4.17 Imp qt)

Torque wrench settings

1796 cc (109.6 cu in)

	lbf ft	kgf m
Cylinder head bolts:		
Cold	63 to 68	8.7 to 9.4
Hot	69 to 73	9.5 to 10.1
Oil pan bolts	5 to 9	0.7 to 1.2
Intake manifold bolts	14 to 19	1.9 to 2.6
Exhaust manifold bolts	16 to 21	2.2 to 2.9
Flywheel bolts	112 to 118	15.4 to 16.3
Main bearing cap bolts	61 to 65	8.4 to 9.0
Connecting rod bolts	30 to 33	4.1 to 4.6
Oil pump mounting bolts	13 to 20	1.8 to 2.8
Camshaft sprocket bolts	51 to 64	7.0 to 8.8
Rocker cover bolts	2	0.3
Oil pump sprocket bolts	22 to 26	3.0 to 3.6

1969cc (120.1 cu in)

	lbf ft	kgf m
Cylinder head bolts:		
Cold	65 to 69	8.97 to 9.52
Hot	69 to 72	9.52 to 9.94
Oil pan bolts	5 to 9	0.7 to 1.25
Intake manifold	14 to 20	1.93 to 2.76
Exhaust manifold	16 to 21	2.05 to 2.88

13

Torque wrench settings (continued)

Flywheel bolts	112 to 118	15.46 to 16.3
Distributor drive gear	51 to 58	7.04 to 8.0
Spark plug	11 to 15	1.52 to 2.07
Main bearing cap bolts	61 to 65	8.42 to 9.0
Connecting rod bolts	36 to 40	4.97 to 5.5
Oil pump bolts	13 to 19	1.8 to 2.62
Camshaft sprocket bolts	51 to 58	7.04 to 8.0
Rocker arm cover bolts	1.1 to 1.4	0.152 to 0.2
Oil pump sprocket	22 to 25	3.04 to 3.5

2300 cc (140.3 cu in)

Auxiliary shaft gear bolt	28 to 40	3.9 to 5.5
Auxiliary shaft thrust plate bolt	6 to 9	0.8 to 1.2
Timing belt tensioner pivot bolt	28 to 40	3.9 to 5.5
Timing belt tensioner adjusting bolt	14 to 21	1.9 to 2.9
Camshaft gear bolt		
1982 only	50 to 71	6.9 to 9.8
All others	80 to 90	11.1 to 12.9
Camshaft thrust plate bolt	6 to 9	0.8 to 1.2
Connecting rod nut	30 to 36	4.1 to 5.0
Crankshaft damper bolt	100 to 120	13.8 to 16.6
Cylinder head bolt		
Step 1	50 to 60	6.9 to 8.3
Step 2	80 to 90	11.1 to 12.5
Deceleration valve nut	10 to 15	1.4 to 2.1
Deceleration valve-to-intake manifold adaptor	23 to 28	3.2 to 3.9
Distributor clamp bolt	14 to 21	1.9 to 2.3
Exhaust manifold bolts and nuts	27 to 38	3.73 to 5.24
Flywheel bolts	54 to 64	7.5 to 8.8
Intake manifold bolts and nuts		
Step 1	5 to 7	0.7 to 0.97
Step 2	14 to 21	1.9 to 2.9
Main bearing cap bolt	80 to 90	11.1 to 12.5
Oil pump pick-up tube-to-pump	14 to 21	1.9 to 2.9
Oil pump-to-block	14 to 21	1.9 to 2.9
Oil drain plug	15 to 25	2.7 to 3.5
Oil pan bolts		
6 mm	6 to 8	0.7 to 1.1
8 mm	8 to 10	1.1 to 1.4
Spark plug	5 to 10	0.7 to 1.4
Auxiliary shaft cover bolts	6 to 9	0.7 to 1.2
Cylinder block front cover bolts	6 to 9	0.7 to 1.2
Timing belt inner cover stud	14 to 21	1.9 to 2.9
Timing belt outer cover bolt	6 to 9	0.8 to 1.2
Rocker arm cover shield bolt	28 to 40	3.9 to 5.5
Thermactor check valve-to-manifold	17 to 20	2.3 to 2.8
EGR tube-to-exhaust manifold	9 to 11	1.2 to 1.5

Cooling system

Thermostat

2000 cc engine	
Starts to open	180° F
Fully open	203° F
2300 cc engine	
Starts to open	188 to 195° F (86.6 to 90.6° C)
Fully open	212 to 215° F (100 to 101.6° C)

Coolant capacity

2000 cc engine	15.2 US pints (7.2 litres)
2300 cc engine	17.6 US pints (8.3 litres)

Fuel system

Carburetor calibration (2000 cc engine)

	Regular	High altitude (4000 + ft)
With manual transmission		
Primary main jet	1.06 mm	1.00 mm
Secondary main jet	1.45 mm	1.20 mm
With automatic transmission		
Primary main jet	1.06 mm	1.00 mm
Secondary main jet	1.45 mm	1.20 mm
Idle speed		
Manual transmission	650 rpm	
Automatic transmission	650 rpm	
CO level at idle speed	3.0 ± 0.5%	

Throttle valve opening (fast idle adjustment)
   California vehicles ... ...   1.4 ± 0.1 mm (0.055 ± 0.004 in)
   Other vehicles ... ...   1.4 ± 0.1 mm (0.055 ± 0.004 in)
Choke valve opening (choke/throttle adjustment)
   California vehicles ... ...   0.8 ± 0.2 mm (0.031 ± 0.008 in)
   Other vehicles ... ...   0.6 ± 0.2 mm (0.024 ± 0.008 in)
Choke valve opening (choke diaphragm adjustment)
   California vehicles ... ...   1.9 ± 0.25 mm (0.075 ± 0.010 in)
   Other vehicles ... ...   1.45 ± 0.25 mm 0.057 ± 0.010 in)
Choke valve opening (unloader adjustment)
   California vehicles ... ...   2.3 ± 0.4 mm (0.091 ± 0.016 in)
   Other vehicles ... ...   2.3 ± 0.4 mm (0.091 ± 0.016 in)
Float level adjustment ... ...   0.335 in

Carburetor calibration (2300 cc engine)

	Regular	High altitude (4000+ ft)
With manual transmission		
Primary main jet	No. 106	No. 100
Secondary main jet	No. 165	No. 140
With automatic transmission		
Primary main jet	No. 106	No. 98
Secondary main jet	No. 165	No. 140
Primary main air bleed	No. 110	No. 90

Vacuum pulldown adjustment ... ...   0.066 to 0.075 in (1.6764 to 1.9050 mm)
Vacuum pulldown adjustment (California only) ... ...   0.075 to 0.084 in (1.9050 to 2.1336 mm)
Idle speed
   Manual transmission ... ...   750 to 850 rpm (in Neutral)
   Automatic transmission ... ...   650 to 750 rpm (in Drive)
CO level at idle speed ... ...   4.0 ± 0.5%
Throttle valve opening (fast idle adjustment)
   California vehicles ... ...   1.67 ± 0.12 mm (0.066 ± 0.005 in)
   Other vehicles ... ...   1.57 ± 0.01 mm (0.062 ± 0.004 in)
Choke valve opening (choke/throttle adjustment)
   California vehicles ... ...   1.37 ± 0.32 mm (0.054 ± 0.013 in)
   Other vehicles ... ...   1.14 ± 0.15 mm (0.045 ± 0.006 in)
Choke valve opening (choke diaphragm adjustment)
   California vehicles ... ...   1.8 ± 0.2 mm (0.071 ± 0.008 in)
   Other vehicles ... ...   1.56 ± 0.25 mm (0.061 ± 0.010 in)
Choke valve opening (unloader adjustment)
   California vehicles ... ...   2.8 ± 0.4 mm (0.110 ± 0.016 in)
   Other vehicles ... ...   2.54 ± 0.25 mm (0.10 ± 0.010 in)
Float level adjustment ... ...   0.236 in

Fuel tank capacity (1977 through 1982)

   Standard ... ...   15.0 US gal (56.8 litres) 12.9 Imp gal
   Optional ... ...   17.5 US gal (66.2 litres) 15.0 Imp gal

Torque wrench settings

	lbf ft	kgf m
Carburetor-to-spacer stud ...	7.5 to 15	1.05 to 2.1
Carburetor spacer-to-manifold bolt ...	10 to 14	1.4 to 1.9

Ignition system

System type ... ...   Transistorized with breakerless distributor

Static timing
   2000 cc engine ... ...   8° BTDC
   2300 cc engine ... ...   6° BTDC

Armature-to-stator (pole) gap ... ...   0.008 to 0.024 in (0.2032 to 0.6096 mm)

Spark plug type ... ...   AGRF 52

Spark plug gap ... ...   0.029 to 0.033 in (0.7366 to 0.8382 mm)

Clutch
Pedal free movement ... ...   0.025 to 0.121 in (0.6350 to 3.0734 mm)

Manual transmission
Gear ratios (4-speed)
1st ... ...   4.359 : 1
2nd ... ...   2.519 : 1
3rd ... ...   1.507 : 1
4th ... ...   1.000 : 1
Reverse ... ...   4.024 : 1

13

Tolerances (4-speed)
Output shaft-to-gear bushing ... ...   0.008 to 0.0024 in (0.0203 to 0.0508 mm)
    Wear limit ... ...   0.006 in (0.1524 mm)
Reverse idler shaft-to-gear bushing ... ...   0.0012 to 0.0031 in (0.0254 to 0.0762 mm)
    Wear limit ... ...   0.006 in (0.1524 mm)

Gear ratios (5-speed)(1977 and 1978)
1st ... ...   4.030 : 1
2nd ... ...   2.370 : 1
3rd ... ...   1.514 : 1
4th ... ...   1.000 : 1
5th (overdrive) ... ...   0.862 : 1
Reverse ... ...   3.692 : 1

Gear ratios (5-speed) (1979 through 1982)
1st ... ...   4.317 : 1
2nd ... ...   2.455 : 1
3rd ... ...   1.514 : 1
4th ... ...   1.000 : 1
5th (overdrive) ... ...   0.862 : 1
Reverse ... ...   3.692 : 1

Tolerances (5-speed) (1977 through 1982)
Mainshaft run-out (maximum) ... ...   0.0012 in (0.03 mm)
Shift fork shaft-to-control lever (maximum) ... ...   0.031 in (0.8 mm)
Shift fork-to-clutch sleeve (maximum) ... ...   0.020 in (0.5 mm)
Synchro ring-to-conical face of gear ... ...   0.031 in (0.8 mm)
Mainshaft thrust play ... ...   0 to 0.0039 in (0 to 0.1 mm)
Countershaft thrust play ... ...   0 to 0.0039 in (0 to 0.1 mm)
3rd speed synchro key-to-synchro ring slot ... ...   0.026 to 0.079 in (0.66 to 2.0 mm)
5th gear thrust washer-to-snap-ring clearance ... ...   0.0039 to 0.018 in (0.1 to 0.3 mm)
Countershaft rear bearing (clearance between thrust washer and snap-ring)   0.0039 to 0.018 in (0.1 to 0.3 mm)
Mainshaft rear bearing (clearance between thrust washer and snap-ring) ...   0 to 0.0059 in (0 to 0.15 mm)

Lubricant capacity (5-speed)   ... ...   3.6 US pints (3.0 Imp pints) 3.4 litres

Lubricant type   ... ...   SAE EP 90

Torque wrench settings

	lbf ft	kgf m
Mainshaft lock nut (5-speed)	115 to 172	16 to 24

Automatic transmission
Stall speed   ... ...   1950 to 2200 rpm

Shift speeds

Throttle condition (manifold vacuum)	Range	Shift speed
Wide open	D1 to D2	31 to 43 mph (49 to 69 km/h)
	D2 to D3	55 to 71 mph (88 to 114 km/h)
	D3 to D2	50 to 64 mph (80 to 102 km/h)
	D2 to D1	22 to 32 mph (35 to 52 km/h)
Half throttle (7.87 in Hg)	D1 to D2	8 to 17 mph (13 to 27 km/h)
	D2 to D3	16 to 37 mph (26 to 60 km/h)
Throttle closed	D2 to D1	7 to 14 mph (11 to 23 km/h)

Braking system
Type (1977 through 1982) all models   ... ...   Disc front, drum rear, dual-circuit, booster-assisted

Brake pedal free travel   ... ...   0.33 to 0.39 in (8.5 to 10.0 mm)

Front disc brakes
Disc diameter ... ...   10.079 in (256.0 mm)
Disc thickness (new) ... ...   0.4724 in (11.988 mm)
Disc thickness (wear limit) ... ...   0.4331 in (10.9982 mm)
Maximum disc run-out ... ...   0.0039 in (0.1016 mm)
Pad friction material wear limit ... ...   0.079 in (2.0 mm)
Caliper piston bore ... ...   2.1248 in (53.9750 mm)

Electrical system
Lamp bulb specifications (1977 through 1981)

Bulb wattage	Trade No.	Lamp
50/40	6012	Headlamps
27/8	1157	Front turn and park
3.8	194	Front side marker

Bulb wattage	Trade No.	Lamp
27/8 x 2	1157	Rear tail, stop, turn
27	1156	Rear side marker, back-up
3.8	1895	Rear license plate
5	—	Interior lamp
5	—	Underhood
		Instrument panel
		Headlamp hi-beam indicator
		Oil pressure indicator
3.4	158	Brake warning
		Seat belt warning
		Turn signal warning
3	57	Radio bezel
1.7	53	Heater control

Lamp bulb specifications (1982)

60/50	6014	Headlamps

Suspension and steering
Steering angles, 1975 through 1976

Toe-in	0 to ¼ in (0 to 6.35 mm)
Camber	1 to 1¾°
Caster	¾ to 1¼°
Front wheel turning angle	
Inward	34 to 38°
Outward	32 to 33°

Steering angles 1977 through 1981

Toe-in	0 to ¼ in (0 to 6.35 mm)
Camber	½ to 1¼°
Caster	¾ to 1¼°
Front wheel turning angle	
Inward	32° 30'
Outward	30° 40'

Steering angles, 1982

Toe-in	0 to ¼ in (0 to 6.35 mm)
Camber	½ to 1¼°
Caster	¾ to 1¼°
Front wheel turning angle	
Inward	33° 53' with 195 SR 14 tire
	32° 34' with 600-14 tire
Outward	30° 38' with SR 14 tire
	30° 48' with 600-14 tire

Torque wrench setting

	lbf ft	kgf m
Tie-rod lock nut	80 to 87	11 to 12

Bodywork
Measurements and weights (1974 through 1982)

Overall length	
Standard	178 in (452.12 cm)
Optional	189 in (480.1 cm)
Overall width	63 in (160.02 cm)
Overall height	62 in (157.48 cm)
Pick-up box (inside length)	
Standard	76 in (193.04 cm)
Optional	87 in (220.98 cm)
Inside width	57 in (144.78 cm)
Inside height	16 in (40.64 cm)
Wheelbase	
Standard	107 in (271.78 cm)
Optional	113 in (287.02 cm)
GVW rating	4075 lb (1848 kg)
Maximum load rating	1400 lb (635 kg)
GAWR	
Front	1800 lb (816 kg)
Rear (standard)	2510 lb (1139 kg)
GVW (soft side option)	3575 lb (1622 kg)
Maximum load rating	900 lb (408 kg)
GAWR	
Front	1800 lb (816 kg)
Rear	2500 lb (1134 kg)

13

Lubricant general specifications

Component	Lubricant type
Engine oil ... ..., ...	SAE classification SE, SF, SF/CC
Manual transmission	SAE 90 EP
Automatic transmission	Type F fluid
Rear axle	Hypoid gear oil
Steering gear	SAE 90
Suspension points	Multipurpose grease
Steering idler	Multipurpose grease
Front wheel bearings	Multipurpose grease
Antifreeze	Ethylene glycol type
Hydraulic fluid	Extra heavy duty type
Body hinges, hood latch	Polyethylene grease
Lock cylinders	Graphite or lock lubricant

Note: *The above lubricants are general recommendations. Lubrication requirements may vary geographically and depend on vehicle usage. Consult the owners manual supplied with your vehicle.*

3 Routine maintenance

1975 through 1978 models

The recommended maintenance schedule for Courier trucks built from 1975 to 1978 is as follows. Follow the schedule in terms of months or miles, whichever comes first. Scheduled maintenance beyond 48 000 miles should be continued at the same intervals unless noted.

Every 250 miles (400 km) or weekly

Check the engine oil level and top-up if necessary.
Check the battery electrolyte level.
Check the windshield washer reservoir level.
Check the tire pressures (cold).
Check tires for wear and damage.
Check brake and clutch fluid reservoir levels.
Check radiator coolant level.
Check operation of all lights and switches.

At the first 2000 miles (3200 km) - new vehicles only

Engine
Check valve clearances (1796 cc engine only).
Check torque of cylinder head bolts (1796 cc engine only).
Check torque of intake and exhaust manifold bolts (1796 cc engine only).
Check drivebelt tension.

Fuel and emission control
Check carburetor adjustment.
Check carburetor dashpot setting (1796 cc engine).
Check servo diaphragm adjustment (1796 cc engine).
Check vacuum control valve adjustment (1796 cc engine).

Ignition system
Check timing.

Transmission
Check clutch adjustment.

Check automatic transmission fluid level.
Replace manual transmission oil.
Replace rear axle oil.

Chassis
Check torque of all bolts and nuts.

Every 6000 miles (9600 km), or at six month intervals

Engine
Replace engine oil.
Replace engine oil filter.
Clean and re-gap spark plugs.

Transmission
Check manual transmission oil level.
Check automatic transmission fluid level.
Check rear axle oil level.

Brakes
Check disc pad wear.
Adjust rear drum brakes.

Every 12 000 miles (19000 km) or at twelve month intervals

Engine
Check drivebelt tension.
Check cooling system hoses.
Adjust valve clearances (1796 cc engine).

Fuel and emission control systems
Check idle speed and mixture.
Check cold start enrichment (choke) system and fast idle.
Replace fuel filter.
Clean dust from air cleaner element by using compressed air and install in different position.
Check operation of automatic temperature-controlled type air cleaner.
Check fuel evaporative control system components and connections.
Check PCV hose connections.
Check carburetor dashpot setting (manual transmission).

Check operation and adjustment of servo diaphragm and vacuum control valve.

Ignition system
Check and adjust timing.
Replace spark plugs.

Steering gear
Check steering gear oil level.

Braking system
Adjust rear drum brakes.
Inspect brake lines for corrosion or damage.

Every 24 000 miles (38 000 km) or at two year intervals

Engine
Check torque of cylinder head bolts and manifold bolts.
Replace air cleaner element.
Replace engine coolant.

Emission control systems
Check carbon canister intake filter.
Replace PCV valve.

Transmission
Replace manual transmission oil.
Replace rear axle oil.

Braking system
Replace hydraulic fluid and all seals in hydraulic assemblies.

Suspension
Replace lubricant in front hub bearings and adjust.
Lubricate front suspension balljoints and upper arm shaft.

Every 48 000 miles (77 000 km) or at four year intervals

Braking system
Replace hydraulic flexible hoses.
Replace booster vacuum hose.

Routine maintenance

1979 through 1982 models

2 The following is the recommended maintenance schedule for models built from 1979 through 1982. Follow the schedule in terms of months or mileage, whichever comes first. Scheduled maintenance beyond 30 000 miles should be continued at the same intervals unless noted.

Every 250 miles (400 km) or weekly

Check the engine oil level and top-up if necessary.
Check the battery electrolyte level.
Check the windshield washer reservoir level.
Check the tire pressures (cold).
Check tires for wear and damage.
Check brake and clutch fluid reservoir levels.
Check radiator coolant level.
Check operation of all lights and switches.

At the first 2000 miles (3200 km) - new vehicles only

Engine
Check valve clearances
Check torque of cylinder head bolts.
Check torque of intake and exhaust manifold bolts.
Check drivebelt tension.

Fuel and emission control
Check carburetor adjustment.
Check carburetor dashpot setting.
Check servo diaphragm adjustment.
Check vacuum control valve adjustment.

Ignition system
Check timing.

Transmission
Check clutch adjustment.
Check automatic transmission fluid level.

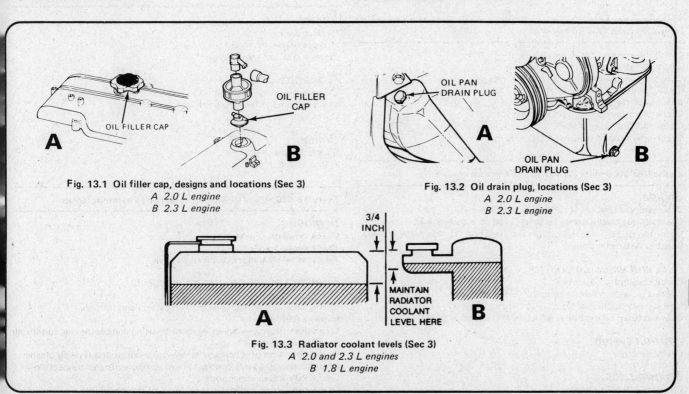

Fig. 13.1 Oil filler cap, designs and locations (Sec 3)
A 2.0 L engine
B 2.3 L engine

Fig. 13.2 Oil drain plug, locations (Sec 3)
A 2.0 L engine
B 2.3 L engine

Fig. 13.3 Radiator coolant levels (Sec 3)
A 2.0 and 2.3 L engines
B 1.8 L engine

13

Replace manual transmission oil.
Replace rear axle oil.

Chassis

Check torque of all bolts and nuts.

Every 7 500 miles (12 000 km) or at 7.5-month intervals

Change engine oil
Change engine oil filter.
Check battery electrolyte level and specific gravity.
Check automatic transmission fluid level.
Check fluid level.
Check brake fluid level.
Check clutch pedal free play.
Check disc brake pads.

Every 15 000 miles (24 000 km) or at 15-month intervals

Adjust valve clearance.
Check manual transmission oil.
Check rear axle oil.
Check steering gear oil.
Check steering wheel free play.
Check brake lines, hoses and connections.
Check rear brake unit and hoses.
Check drum brake linings.

Every 30 000 miles (48 000 km) or at 30-month intervals

Replace spark plugs.
Replace air cleaner element.
Check coolant system hoses and clamps.
Replace coolant.
Lubricate front wheel bearings.
Lubricate front suspension balljoints/upper arm shafts.
Check steering balljoints and idler arm.
Inspect and clean exhaust system heat shields.

4 Engine

Part A-general information and removal procedures

Description — 2.0 L (1969 cc) engine

The 2.0L engine is a four-cylinder, in-line, overhead camshaft engine. The cylinder head is cast aluminum alloy. The cylinder block is cast iron and supports the crankshaft in five main bearings. The oil pump is located at the front of the engine and is chain-driven. Lubrication is also provided by splash.

The distributor is mounted on the left side of the engine and is driven directly off the camshaft, which runs in four bearings.

A single two-barrel downdraft carburetor provides the fuel mixture. See Section 5 of this Chapter for further information on this carburetor. Depending on the year, the 2000 cc engine uses some or all of the emission control components found on the 2300 cc engine.

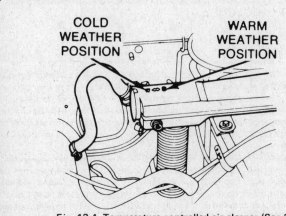

Fig. 13.4 Temperature-controlled air cleaner (Sec 3)

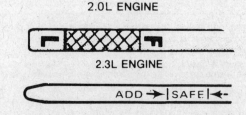

Fig. 13.5 Dipstick oil level marks (Sec 3)

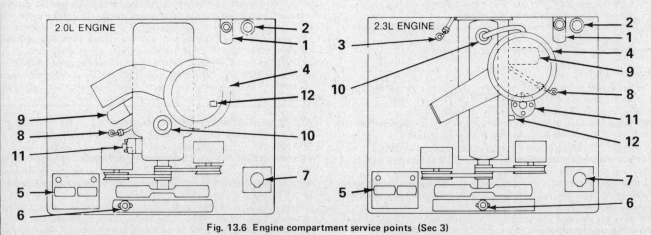

Fig. 13.6 Engine compartment service points (Sec 3)

1	Brake master cylinder reservoir	3	Automatic transmission dipstick and filler hose	6	Radiator filler cap
2	Clutch fluid reservoir (manual transmission)	4	Air filter	7	Windshield washer reservoir
		5	Battery	8	Engine oil dipstick

9	Engine oil filter
10	Engine oil filler cap
11	Distributor
12	PCV valve

The 2.0 liter engine is virtually identical in design to the 1.8 liter engine described in Chapter 1 or the text. For servicing and rebuilding the 2.0 liter engine, use the procedures in Chapter 1 as a guideline; however, do not use the specifications in that Chapter. Specifications for the 2.0 liter engine are found at the beginning of this Chapter.

Description — 2.3 L (2300 cc) engine

The 2300 cc (140.3 cu in) engine is a four-cylinder, in-line overhead camshaft unit. The crankcase, block and cylinder head are of lightweight steel construction.

The crankshaft turns in five main bearings, the camshaft runs in four. The main bearings, connecting rod big-end bearings, camshaft and auxiliary shaft bearings are all replaceable inserts.

The camshaft is driven from the crankshaft by a toothed belt which also operates the auxiliary shaft which drives the oil pump and distributor. Tension on the cam drivebelt is provided by a preloaded and locked idler pulley which applies pressure on the outside of the belt.

The water pump and the fan are driven separately from the crankshaft by a conventional V-belt which also drives the alternator.

Hydraulic valve lash adjusters are used in the valve train. These are placed at the fulcrum (or hinge) point of the cam followers (or rocker arms) and are similar to the hydraulic lifters used in pushrod engines. They are constructed and serviced in the same way. The cylinder head has drilled oil passages to provide engine oil pressure to the lash adjusters.

Some or all of the following emissions control systems have been used on the 2300 cc engine:
Air injection system
Oxidizing catalytic converter system
Exhaust Gas Recirculation system (EGR)
Deceleration control system
Positive Crankcase Ventilation system (PCV)
Evaporative emission control system
See the special Section for emissions systems in this supplement or Chapter 3 for further information.

Major operations with engine in vehicle

The following operations can be performed with the engine in place.
Removal and installation of the cylinder head.
Removal and installation of the camshaft drivebelt.
Removal and installation of the engine front mountings.
The camshaft can be removed after removal of the cylinder head.

Major operations requiring engine removal

The following major operations can be performed only with the engine out of the vehicle.
Removal and installation of the main bearings.
Removal and installation of the crankshaft.
Removal and installation of the flywheel.
Removal and installation of the crankshaft rear oil seal.
Removal and installation of the oil pan.
Removal and installation of the pistons, connecting rods and big-end bearings.
Removal and installation of the auxiliary shaft.

Engine — removal

1 We recommend that you remove the engine independently of the transmission, leaving the transmission in position in the truck.
2 Open the hood and cover the fenders to protect them.
3 Mark the position of the hood hinges with a crayon or permanent marker. With the help of an assistant, remove the hood.
4 Disconnect the positive and negative leads from the battery.
5 Drain the cooling system (Chapter 2).
6 Remove the air cleaner and heat stove assembly.
7 Disconnect all radiator hoses, being sure to check the condition of the clamps and the condition of the hoses at their point of connection for cracks and decomposition (Chapter 2).
8 Remove the radiator shroud bolts and push the shroud to the rear. Remove the radiator mounting bolts and lift out the radiator.
9 Remove the Thermactor hoses from the air pump (Chapter 3).
10 Disconnect the heater hose at the intake manifold and at the firewall.
11 Disconnect the vacuum hose from the brake booster and disconnect the vacuum lines from the vacuum amplifier.
12 Remove the choke cable and disconnect the accelerator linkage.

13 Disconnect the low tension wire from the distributor and the high tension lead from the ignition coil.
14 Remove the fan belt from the front of the engine by loosening the alternator mounting bolt.
15 Disconnect the fuel line from the carburetor. Plug it to prevent leakage.
16 Disconnect the battery ground wire from the side of the cylinder block.
17 Drain the engine oil and replace the plug and the oil pan.
18 Disconnect the exhaust pipe from the exhaust manifold and disconnect the exhaust pipe bracket (Chapter 1).
19 Attach the engine hoist and slings to the engine. Raise the engine slightly and remove the engine mount bolts and the right-hand mounting bracket.
20 Support the transmission on a small jack and remove the bolts securing the flywheel housing to the engine. The transmission must remain supported while the engine is out of place.
21 Unbolt the clutch operating cylinder and tie the operating rod up out of the way (Chapter 5).
22 Raise the engine slightly and pull it forward until it clears the clutch input shaft and then guide it up and out of the engine compartment being sure as you go that all disconnections have been made.
23 Clean the exterior surfaces of the engine using a water-soluable engine cleaner available at most automotive parts stores.
24 Remove the oil filter, spark plugs, fan, water pump, thermostat, oil pressure and temperature senders, emission control devices, etc. An instant photograph or rough sketch of these parts will aid you in reassembly. Refer to the appropriate Sections in Chapter 1 and other Sections of this Chapter for further information.
25 Remove the distributor, being sure to put an index mark on the distributor body and the engine block so you will know which way it fits during installation.

Part B — Disassembly

General disassembly

1 Disassemble the engine with it mounted on an engine stand if possible. If this is not possible, place the engine on a strong bench at a comfortable working height. During disassembly, inspection and reassembly, your working environment must be absolutely spotless. Do everything you can to keep the exposed parts, especially bearing surfaces, free from dirt and dust. Thoroughly clean the outside of the engine to remove all traces of oil and dirt. A good engine degreasing solvent is recommended.
2 When the engine has been cleaned completely, begin disassembly. As you proceed, clean each engine component in solvent. Do not use flammable products such as gasoline, kerosene or paint thinner.
3 Do not immerse parts with oilways drilled in them (such as the crankshaft and camshaft) in solvent. Clean these with a solvent-dampened rag and then blow out the holes with compressed air. Save your used gaskets for reference but under no circumstances re-use the gaskets. If you are rebuilding the engine, a complete gasket set can be bought from a dealer or auto parts supplier.
4 As you strip the engine from the top down, reinstall, wherever possible nuts, bolts and other fasteners from where they came. It is very important that the same bolts go back in the same place. If they cannot be reinstalled while disassembling the engine, clearly mark them or put them in a small container which is marked so that you will know where they go.

Cylinder head removal — engine removed

5 Remove the carburetor from the intake manifold (Chapter 3).
6 Remove the two gaskets and the EGR spacer (Chapter 3).
7 If there are any emission control hoses or fittings left on the intake manifold or block, carefully note their positions by labeling them with a piece of marked tape or take an instant photo to aid in reassembly. Remove these hoses now.
8 Noting that the intake manifold bolts are torqued to specific values, remove the bolts evenly in two stages and lift away the manifold.
9 Remove the four bolts from the timing belt outer cover and the two spacers near the bottom of the timing belt cover.
10 If you are going to completely disassemble the engine, remove the bolt and washer from the crankshaft pulley. The engine can be kept from turning by wedging a screwdriver into the flywheel teeth. It may be necessary to use a gear puller to remove the pulley. Remove the belt guide.

13

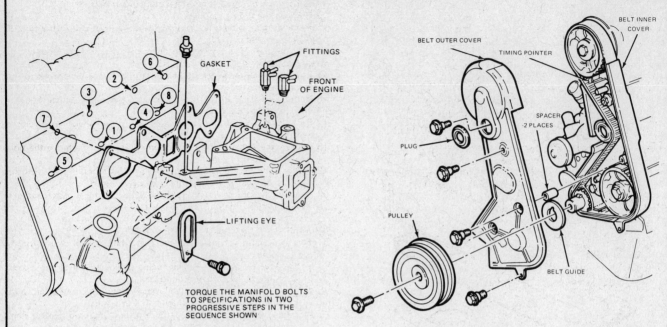

Fig. 13.7 Intake manifold details and torquing sequence (Sec 4)

GASKET

FITTINGS

FRONT OF ENGINE

LIFTING EYE

TORQUE THE MANIFOLD BOLTS TO SPECIFICATIONS IN TWO PROGRESSIVE STEPS IN THE SEQUENCE SHOWN

Fig. 13.8 Timing belt cover — exploded view (Sec 4)

BELT OUTER COVER

TIMING POINTER

BELT INNER COVER

PLUG

SPACER 2 PLACES

PULLEY

BELT GUIDE

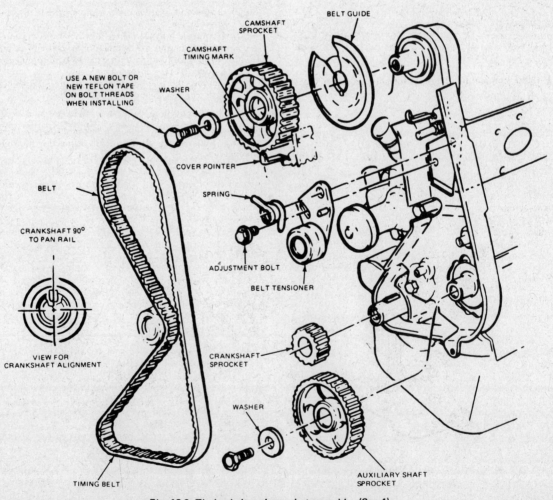

CAMSHAFT SPROCKET

BELT GUIDE

CAMSHAFT TIMING MARK

USE A NEW BOLT OR NEW TEFLON TAPE ON BOLT THREADS WHEN INSTALLING

WASHER

COVER POINTER

BELT

SPRING

CRANKSHAFT 90° TO PAN RAIL

ADJUSTMENT BOLT

BELT TENSIONER

VIEW FOR CRANKSHAFT ALIGNMENT

CRANKSHAFT SPROCKET

WASHER

TIMING BELT

AUXILIARY SHAFT SPROCKET

Fig. 13.9 Timing belt and sprocket assembly (Sec 4)

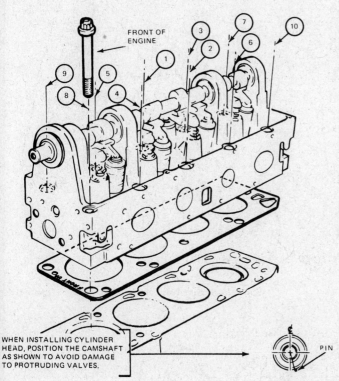

WHEN INSTALLING CYLINDER
HEAD, POSITION THE CAMSHAFT
AS SHOWN TO AVOID DAMAGE
TO PROTRUDING VALVES.

Fig 13.10 Cylinder head bolts — torquing sequence (Sec 4)

11 Loosen the timing belt tensioner adjustment bolts.

12 Remove the timing belt.

13 Remove the timing belt tensioner from the front end of the cylinder head. This is held on by two bolts.

14 Remove the eight screws from the rocker arm cover and remove the cover and the gasket.

15 Loosen the cylinder head bolts slightly in the reverse order to that shown in Fig. 13.10.

16 Remove all the bolts except bolts seven and eight, which should be fully loosened but not completely removed.

17 Break the cylinder head/gasket seal using the exhaust manifold for leverage.

18 Loosen the exhaust manifold retaining bolts and remove the bolts and manifold from the engine.

19 Remove the two remaining cylinder head bolts and lift off the head. Place it in a suitable work area (being sure it is clean).

20 Remove the old gasket from the block. Chemical gasket remover works well in this situation.

Cylinder head removal — engine in place

21 This procedure is similar to that described above except for the following points:

    a) Remove the hood from the engine compartment to gain access.

    b) Disconnect the battery ground lead.

    c) Drain the engine coolant and remove the hoses connected to the cylinder head. Refer to Chapter 1 if necessary.

    d) Remove the air cleaner, carburetor and emission control items attached to the carburetor and the intake and exhaust manifolds. It may help to make a quick sketch or take a photograph showing the various connections to avoid confusion when you are putting it back together.

    e) You won't need to remove the camshaft drivebelt or the crankshaft pulley.

    f) Remove the appropriate drivebelts from the engine-driven accessories to permit the drivebelt outer cover to be removed.

    g) If air conditioning lines need to be disconnected, this must be carried out by a specialist.

    h) Remove the spark plug leads and the oil pressure gauge connection from the cylinder head.

Auxiliary shaft — removal

22 Remove the sprocket retaining bolt and washer. It may be necessary to lock the auxiliary shaft sprocket in place with a metal bar or large screwdriver.

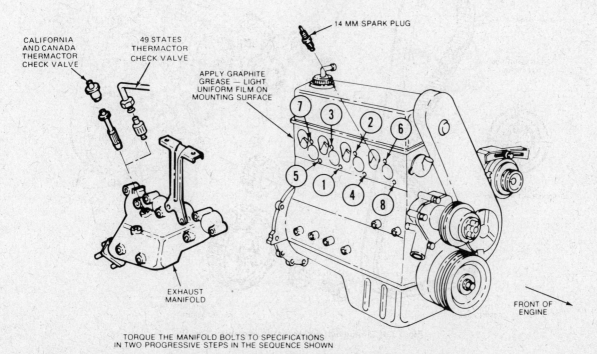

TORQUE THE MANIFOLD BOLTS TO SPECIFICATIONS
IN TWO PROGRESSIVE STEPS IN THE SEQUENCE SHOWN

Fig. 13.11 Exhaust manifold and torquing sequence (Sec 4)

13

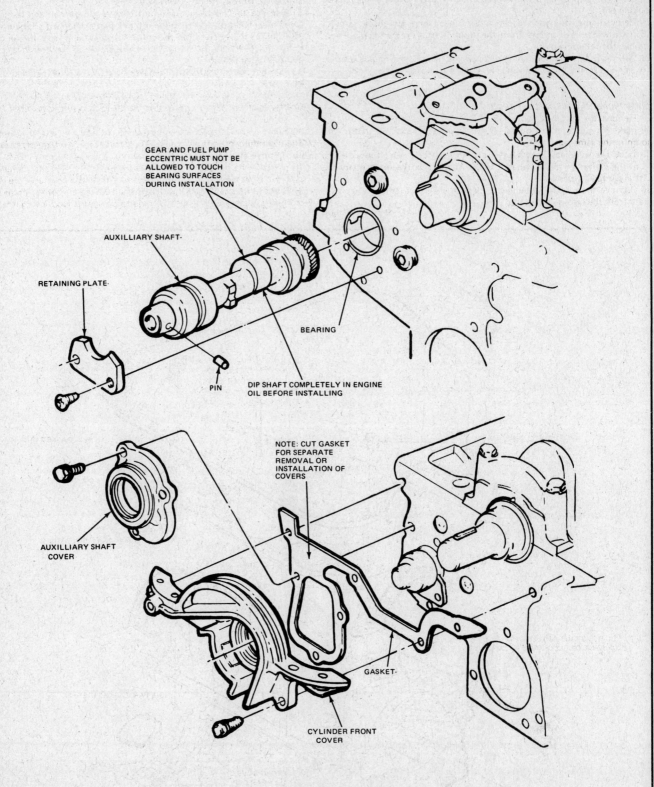

GEAR AND FUEL PUMP
ECCENTRIC MUST NOT BE
ALLOWED TO TOUCH
BEARING SURFACES
DURING INSTALLATION

AUXILLIARY SHAFT

RETAINING PLATE

BEARING

PIN

DIP SHAFT COMPLETELY IN ENGINE
OIL BEFORE INSTALLING

NOTE: CUT GASKET
FOR SEPARATE
REMOVAL OR
INSTALLATION OF
COVERS

AUXILLIARY SHAFT
COVER

GASKET

CYLINDER FRONT
COVER

Fig. 13.12 Auxiliary shaft and cylinder front cover (Sec 4)

23 Pull off the sprocket using a universal puller and remove the sprocket locking pin.

24 Remove the auxiliary shaft front cover and its three screws.

25 Remove the two screws from the auxiliary shaft retaining plate and remove the retaining plate.

26 Withdraw the auxiliary shaft through the front of the engine using a pry bar and spacer block for extra leverage if necessary.

Flywheel and backplate — removal

27 Remove the clutch (Chapter 5).

28 Make reference marks on the flywheel and crankshaft so that it will go on in the same position.

29 Lock the flywheel using a large screwdriver and remove the six bolts from the center of the flywheel using a progressive diagonal sequence. Lift away the flywheel.

30 Remove the remaining engine backplate bolts and remove the backplate from the two dowel pins.

Oil pan and oil pump — removal

31 Remove the oil pan bolts and lift away the oil pan and its gasket. Clean any gasket off of the cylinder block surface and off of the oil pan.

32 Remove the screws from the oil pick-up tube and from the oil pump body which attach the oil pump to the crankcase and remove the oil pump/strainer assembly.

33 Remove the oil pump driveshaft. Note how it is installed for re-assembly.

Crankshaft sprocket, drivebelt inner-cover and cylinder front cover - removal

34 Remove the crankshaft pulley if you have not already done so. Then, carefully pry off the crankshaft sprocket using a large screwdriver.

35 Remove the remaining bolt and pull off the engine front cover.

36 Remove the two bolts from the cylinder front cover and remove the cylinder front cover and gasket. Make sure the gasket surfaces are clean.

37 Remove the crankshaft key from its slot in the end of the crankshaft or hold it in place with a piece of tape to prevent it from being lost.

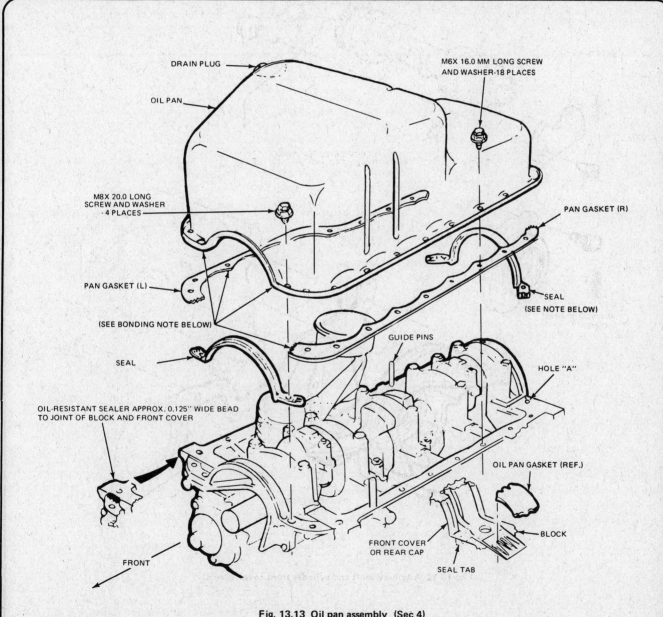

Fig. 13.13 Oil pan assembly (Sec 4)

13

Pistons, connecting rods and big-end bearings — removal

38 Note that the pistons are notched on their crowns showing the forward-facing side. Inspect the rod bearing caps and connecting rods to make sure there are visable identification marks. The rods and bearing caps must go on exactly the same way they came off. If there are no identification marks, punch marks into the metal as you pull each piston and rod out. Be sure to make the same number of punch marks on both the rod cap and the rod itself.

39 Remove the nuts from the connecting rod caps. Place them to one side in the order in which they were removed. Remove the big-end caps one at a time taking care to keep them in the order in which they were removed. Also, keep the bearing inserts in the correct connecting rods or caps unless the rods are to be replaced with new ones.

40 Tap the caps with a plastic or rubber hammer if they are difficult to remove. To remove the bearing inserts, press the bearing opposite the groove in both the connecting rod and its cap and the bearing will slide out easily.

41 Push small lengths of rubber hose over the threaded connecting rod studs to protect the cylinder walls as the piston/rod assemblies are removed. Remove the pistons and connecting rods by pushing them out through the top of the cylinders and make sure they are kept in the correct order for installation.

Crankshaft and main bearings — removal

42 The same policy on main bearing caps goes for the connecting rod caps — they must be installed in their original positions. Make the appropriate identification marks so you won't misplace them. Using proper reverse torqueing technique, loosen by one turn at a time, each of the bolts from the five main bearing caps. After all the bearing cap bolts have been loosened, continue to remove them and lift away each main bearing cap and the bottom half of each bearing insert. Be sure to keep the insert in the cap to which it belongs.

43 When removing the rear main bearing end cap, note that this also retains the crankshaft rear oil seal.

44 Note the thrust washers in the center main bearing. Both the center and rear bearing end caps are held in place by dowl pins. It may be necessary to tap the bearing caps gently to release them.

45 Remove the top halves of the bearing inserts and thrust washers by slowly rotating the crankshaft. Remove the bearing shells and thrust washers and place them with the correct bearing cap.

46 Lift away the crankshaft rear oil seal.

47 Remove the crankshaft by lifting it directly away from the crankcase.

Camshaft drivebelt — removal (engine in place)

48 The camshaft drivebelt can be removed with the engine in place.

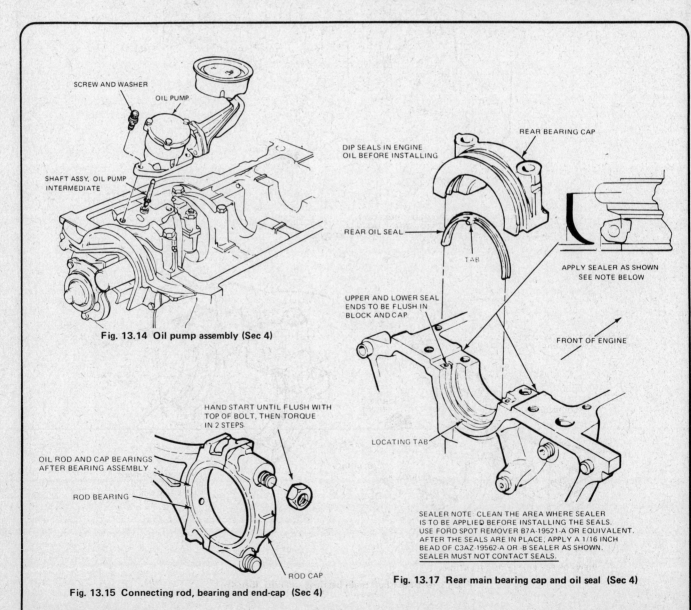

SCREW AND WASHER
OIL PUMP
SHAFT ASSY. OIL PUMP INTERMEDIATE

Fig. 13.14 Oil pump assembly (Sec 4)

HAND START UNTIL FLUSH WITH TOP OF BOLT, THEN TORQUE IN 2 STEPS.
OIL ROD AND CAP BEARINGS AFTER BEARING ASSEMBLY
ROD BEARING
ROD CAP

Fig. 13.15 Connecting rod, bearing and end-cap (Sec 4)

REAR BEARING CAP
DIP SEALS IN ENGINE OIL BEFORE INSTALLING
REAR OIL SEAL
TAB
APPLY SEALER AS SHOWN SEE NOTE BELOW
UPPER AND LOWER SEAL ENDS TO BE FLUSH IN BLOCK AND CAP
FRONT OF ENGINE
LOCATING TAB

SEALER NOTE: CLEAN THE AREA WHERE SEALER IS TO BE APPLIED BEFORE INSTALLING THE SEALS. USE FORD SPOT REMOVER B7A-19521-A OR EQUIVALENT. AFTER THE SEALS ARE IN PLACE, APPLY A 1/16 INCH BEAD OF C3AZ-19562-A OR -B SEALER AS SHOWN. SEALER MUST NOT CONTACT SEALS.

Fig. 13.17 Rear main bearing cap and oil seal (Sec 4)

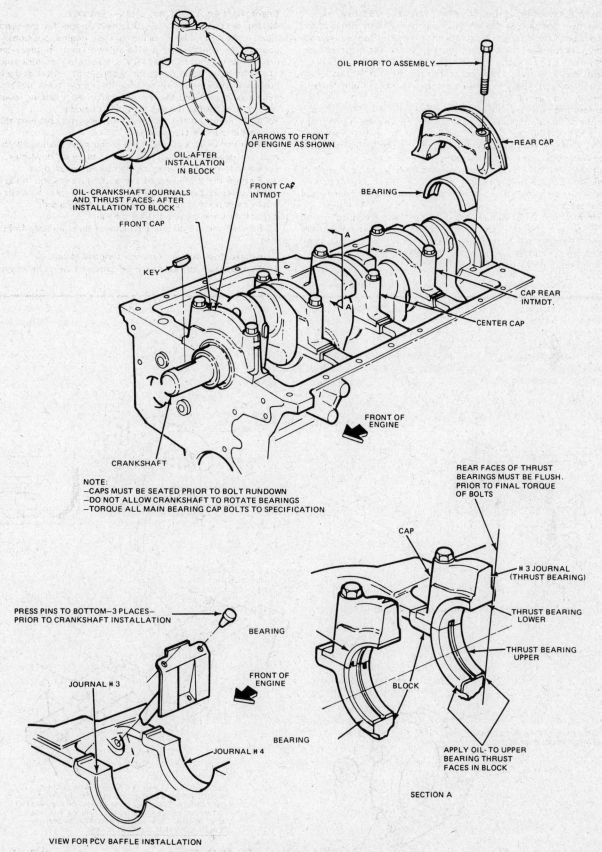

Fig. 13.16 Crankshaft main bearings and caps (Sec 4)

13

However, this type of belt is very durable and unlikely to break or stretch. If you are overhauling the engine, we recommend that you replace the belt anyway.

49 Drain the cooling system and remove the top hose.

50 Remove the fan belt by loosening the alternator mount bolts.

51 Remove the drivebelt guard from the front of the engine by removing the bolts that secure it.

52 Loosen the belt tensioner mounting plate securing bolt and release the tension on the belt. Place the car in gear and apply the brakes firmly or apply the parking brake. Remove the bolt and washer from the crankshaft pulley (on automatic transmission models the starter must be removed and the ring gear jammed to prevent the crankshaft from turning).

53 Use a gear puller or large screwdriver to carefully ease the pulley off the end of the crankshaft.

54 Remove the large belt guide washer and lift the drivebelt from the engine.

Valves and lash adjusters — removal

55 Remove the spring clip from the lash adjuster end of the cam followers (where applicable).

56 You will probably need the special Ford tool No. T74P-6565-A. Insert this beneath the camshaft and fully compress the lash adjuster to be removed making sure the cam peak is facing away from the follower. Be sure to keep the cam followers in order so that they can be installed in their original positions. **Note:** *It may be necessary to slightly compress the valve springs to remove the cam followers.*

57 Using a valve spring compressor, compress the valve springs and lift out the keys. Remove the spring retainer and valve spring and pry off the valve seal from the valve stem.

58 Push the valve out of the head and keep it with its cam follower. Repeat this procedure for the remaining valves. Lift out the hydraulic lash adjusters and place with the appropriate components.

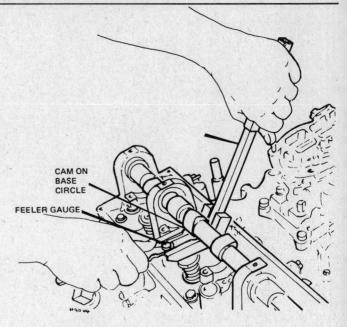

CAM ON BASE CIRCLE

FEELER GAUGE

Fig. 13.18 Using the valve lash adjuster compressor (Sec 4)

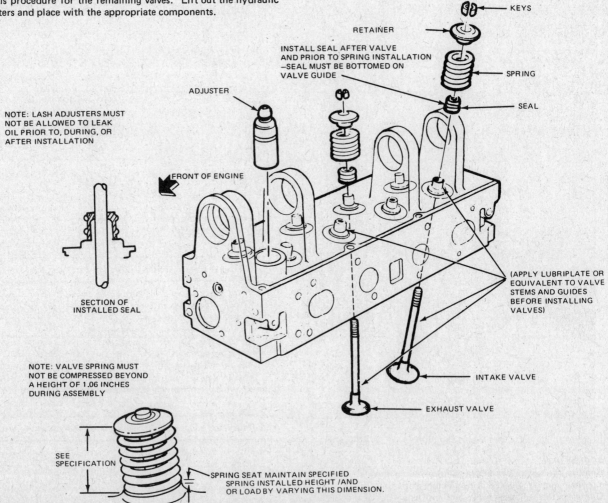

KEYS

RETAINER

INSTALL SEAL AFTER VALVE AND PRIOR TO SPRING INSTALLATION —SEAL MUST BE BOTTOMED ON VALVE GUIDE

SPRING

SEAL

ADJUSTER

NOTE: LASH ADJUSTERS MUST NOT BE ALLOWED TO LEAK OIL PRIOR TO, DURING, OR AFTER INSTALLATION

FRONT OF ENGINE

(APPLY LUBRIPLATE OR EQUIVALENT TO VALVE STEMS AND GUIDES BEFORE INSTALLING VALVES)

SECTION OF INSTALLED SEAL

INTAKE VALVE

EXHAUST VALVE

NOTE: VALVE SPRING MUST NOT BE COMPRESSED BEYOND A HEIGHT OF 1.06 INCHES DURING ASSEMBLY

SEE SPECIFICATION

SPRING SEAT MAINTAIN SPECIFIED SPRING INSTALLED HEIGHT /AND OR LOAD BY VARYING THIS DIMENSION.

Fig. 13.19 Valve train assembly (Sec 4)

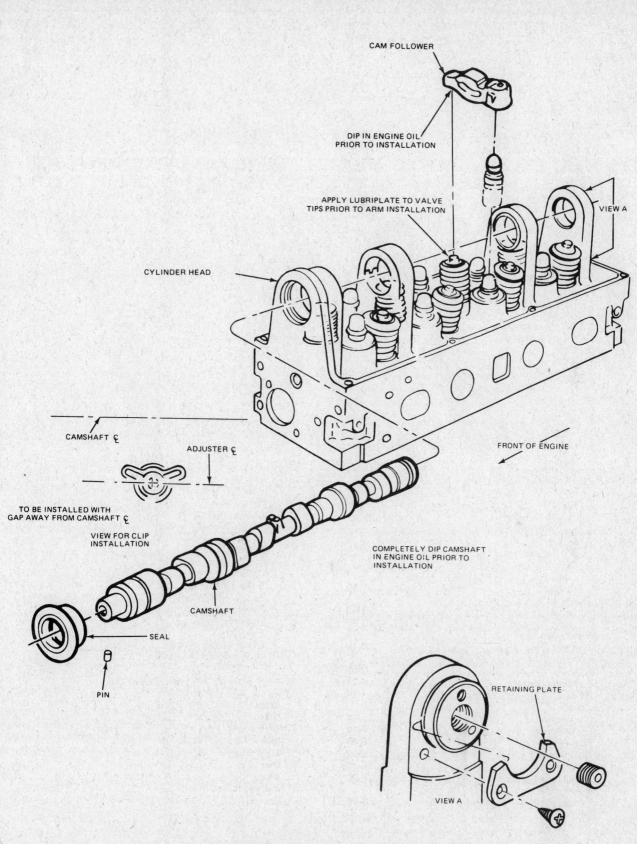

CAM FOLLOWER

DIP IN ENGINE OIL
PRIOR TO INSTALLATION

APPLY LUBRIPLATE TO VALVE
TIPS PRIOR TO ARM INSTALLATION

VIEW A

CYLINDER HEAD

FRONT OF ENGINE

CAMSHAFT ₵

ADJUSTER ₵

TO BE INSTALLED WITH
GAP AWAY FROM CAMSHAFT ₵

VIEW FOR CLIP
INSTALLATION

COMPLETELY DIP CAMSHAFT
IN ENGINE OIL PRIOR TO
INSTALLATION

CAMSHAFT

SEAL

PIN

RETAINING PLATE

VIEW A

13

Fig. 13.20 Camshaft assembly (Sec 4)

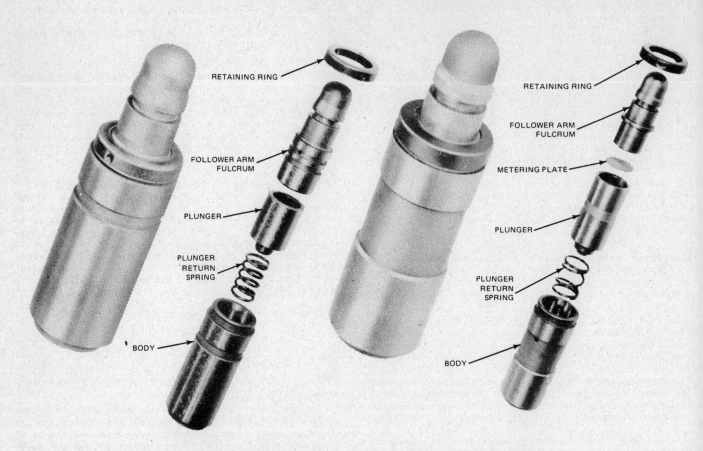

Fig. 13.21 Lash adjusters — Type I (left) and Type II (right) (Sec 4)

Camshaft — removal

59 The cam can be removed from the engine with the engine in the car.
60 Remove the cylinder head as described earlier in this Chapter and the cam followers as described in the preceding paragraphs.
61 Lock the camshaft drive sprocket with a metal bar or large screwdriver and remove the drive sprocket bolt and washer.
62 Remove the sprocket using a gear puller or carefully pry it off with a large screwdriver. Remove the belt guide.
63 Remove the sprocket indexing pin from the end of the camshaft.
64 Remove the camshaft retaining plate screws, followed by the plate itself.
65 Pull the camshaft out of position. Be very careful not to damage the camshaft bearings and journals as you remove the camshaft.

Thermostat and water pump — removal

66 Refer to Chapter 1 to remove the thermostat, thermostat housing and water pump if the cylinder head and block are being completely disassembled.

Piston pin — removal

67 Removal of the piston pin requires special equipment. Because of this, take the parts to your local Ford dealer service department or reputable garage to do this job.

Piston rings — removal

68 Remove the piston rings by sliding them carefully over the top of the piston. Do not scratch the piston. The rings are very brittle and break easily. Do this operation with extreme care.

Part C — Lubrication and crankcase ventilation systems
Oil pump — removal, inspection and installation

1 Remove the oil pump along with its intake pipe and screen by removing the two screws and spring washers. Pull the oil pump assembly directly off the block.
2 Remove the two bolts securing the oil pump tube and screen and separate these parts from the pump. Wash thoroughly in solvent. Note the condition of the oil pump shaft, looking for chipping, cracking or other signs of wear.
3 Check the oil pump clearances as described in Chapter 1, but use the specifications in this Chapter.
4 Replace the oil pump in the reverse of the removal procedure; however, prime the pump by filling the inlet port with oil. Then turn the pump shaft until oil flows out the outlet.

Oil filter — removal and installation

5 The oil filter is a disposable cartridge screwed into the left side of the cylinder block. Unscrew the old unit (it may be necessary to use a conventional oil filter strap wrench), clean the seating on the block and lubricate the filter gasket with fresh engine oil. Gently screw the new filter into position, being careful not to strip the threads. Follow the filter manufacturer's instructions for tightening, which is usually until the sealing ring touches the block face, then one-half turn more *by hand only*. Be sure to check for leaks after the engine has been run.

Part D — Inspection
General information

1 At this point the engine should be completely stripped and all parts properly cleaned in solvent. Decisions now have to be made as to what parts need to be replaced and the following text will help you make those determinations. If you are unsure of the condition of any part, have a professional mechanic check it out for you or replace it with a new one. It is always best to decide in favor of a new part. Even if a part may be servicicable its life will have been reduced by wear. Replacing it now may save you the trouble of pulling the whole engine apart for repairs later.

Note: *The following engine components can be inspected according to procedures in Chapter 1.*

    Head
    Crankshaft
    Block
    Cylinder bores
    Rods and rod bearings
    Rings
    Pistons
    Valves and valve seats
    Distributor drivegear
    Intake and exhaust manifolds
    Cam chain tensioner

Be sure to use the correct specifications for this engine.

Emissions control components — checking
2   See Chapter 3, Sections 19 through 24 and portions of this Chapter for descriptions, tests and adjustment of the emissions control components. The components described in that Chapter are essentially the same as on the 2300 cc engine.

Crankshaft, main bearings, cylinder bores and pistons/ connecting rods
3   See Chapter 1 and follow the procedures outlined there for the 1796 cc engine.

Camshaft, camshaft bearings and camshaft followers
4   Examine the camshaft bearing inserts for signs of scoring and pitting. Check the camshaft bearing bushes at the end of the camshaft. If these need to be replaced, they will require professional attention for installation.
5   Check the camshaft for signs of wear on the bearing journals and the cam lobes. Your decision will depend on the degree of wear. A camshaft is usually a fairly costly item. Any signs of scoring or damage to the bearing journals cannot be removed by grinding so you will have to replace the whole camshaft. If there is excessive cam lobe wear or cam follower wear, this might be due to a malfunction of the valve drive lubrication tube. If this is the case, replace the tube and the cam follower. If more than one cam follower is excessively worn, replace the camshaft, all the cam followers and the lubrication tube.
6   The cam lobes may show signs of ridging or pitting on the high points. If this happens, replace the cam.
7   Make sure the camshaft oilways are unobstructed by blowing them out with compressed air.
8   Check the faces of the cam followers for signs of pitting, chipping scoring or other forms of wear. They should fit snugly.
9   Inspect the cam follower faces. If they are pitted or indented replace the cam follower showing damage.
10 During any operation which requires removal of the valve rocker cover, ensure that oil squirts out of the lubrication holes by cranking the engine over with the starter motor. During routine maintenance operations this can be done after checking the valve clearance.

Auxiliary shaft and bearing
11 Check the auxiliary shaft bearings the same way you checked the camshaft bearings. Also check the bearing bushes in a similar way.
12 Examine the auxiliary shaft gear for wear and damaged teeth. If either is evident, replace the shaft.

Valves and valve seats
13 Check the valves and the valve seats according to the procedure described in Chapter 1, Section 34.

Hydraulic lash adjusters
14 Check each lash adjuster for wear and scoring on the outside. Light scoring and wear can be polished out with fine emery cloth, however, it is strongly recommended that the adjuster be replaced.
15 Pry off the retaining ring, remove the rocker arm and disassemble the adjuster. The component parts of the two different types of adjusters are shown in the accompanying Figure.
16 Check all the parts of the adjuster for damage, wear, corrosion and gum deposits or varnish. Obtain replacement parts for any which are unserviceable. Check one adjuster at a time to avoid mixing up the parts.
17 Reassemble the adjusters, lubricating the parts with fresh engine oil.

Do not attempt to fill them with oil — use just enough to make them slick.
18 If you doubt the condition of the lifters, take them to a machine shop or Ford dealer to have testing done.

Timing gears and timing belt
19 Probably the only wear which will occur with the timing assembly will be a stretched drivebelt. Always replace the cam drivebelt when you are overhauling the engine.
20 Since a belt is used it is unusual for the timing gears to wear at the teeth. Check the bolts and nuts on the gears, see if they have been loose and also check the keyway or hub bore for wear. If wear or damage is evident, replace the gear and/or the keyway.

Flywheel
21 Check the ring gear for missing teeth or severe wear. If you find these conditions, replace the ring gear. The old ring gear can be removed from the flywheel by cutting a notch between two teeth with a hack saw or file and splitting it with a cold chisel. A new ring gear can be installed by heating the ring to 400° F (204° C). This is most easily done by placing it in an oven or heating it evenly with a blow torch or butane torch. Be sure to prevent overheating. The gear has a beveled inner edge which should go against the shoulder of the flywheel. When hot enough, place the gear in position quickly, tap it around its perimeter with a plastic hammer and let it cool naturally.

Cylinder head, valve guides and oil pan
22 See Chapter 1, Sections 35 through 37 and follow the procedures given there.

Part E — Reassembly
Note: *Refer to Figures 13.7 - 13.23 for valuable reassembly information*

General information
1   Take this time to completely clean your shop working area. Clean all the engine components of oil, sludge, old gasket material and lay the components out in an exploded fashion on the floor or workbench. In addition to a good selection of metric socket wrenches and general tools, the following must be available before reassembly begins.
    Complete set of new gaskets
    A good supply of clean, lint-free cloths
    A clean oil can full of clean engine oil
    A torque wrench
    Any new spare parts which you have added to your shopping list
       during disassembly
    Multi-purpose grease
    One tube of anti-sieze-compound

Crankshaft
2   The crankcase should be absolutely clean and all oilways should be clear. A piece of broomstraw is useful to clean the oilways. Do not use a metallic instrument. If possible blow them out with compressed air and a blow gun.
3   Also clean the crankshaft thoroughly and the crankshaft oil holes. Squirt some engine oil into the oilways.
4   Install the crankshaft and main bearings by following this procedure:
5   Wipe the crankshaft journals. The bearing inserts and the bearing insert locations in the crankcase with a lint-free cloth.
6   If you are doing an overhaul, you should install new bearing inserts. Install the five upper halves of the inserts in their locations in the crankcase. Identify each main bearing cap and place them in order and ready to install. The numbers should be cast onto the cap. With intermediate caps, an arrow is also marked so that the cap is installed in the correct direction (arrow pointing to front). Wipe the end cap bearing shell location with a lint-free cloth. Install the other half of the bearing shell into each main bearing cap. Install the bearing half insert into each location in the crankcase and the rear half-seal in the crankcase groove. Note that the shells with the thrust washers are located at the center journal.
7   Lubricate all crankshaft journals with anti-sieze compound. Also lubricate the bearing shells with clean engine oil.
8   Carefully lower the crankshaft into its journals in the crankcase. Lubricate the crankshaft main bearing journals again and then install the number one bearing cap. Install the two bolts but do not tighten them. Apply a little non-setting gasket sealant to the crankshaft rear

13

main bearing end cap location. Insert the half-seal in the rear main cap. Install the cap but only screw in the bolts finger-tight at this stage.

9 Install the center main bearing cap and caps two and four. *Make sure that all the arrows point toward the front.*

10 Lightly tighten all main cap securing bolts, then fully tighten them in a progressive manner. This should be done in several steps, tightening it a little at a time until you reach the specified torque valve.

11 Ease the crankshaft fully toward the front of the engine (you may need to use a screwdriver for leverage) then check the clearance between the crankshaft journal side and the thrust washers with feeler gauges. The clearance must not exceed that given in the specifications for crankshaft endplay.

12 Rotate the crankshaft in its journals. If it is stiff or has high spots, check the crank journals with a micrometer. You may have oversize bearings.

Pistons, piston rings and connecting rods

13 There are at least two ways to assemble pistons. You can buy pistons as a unit with the rods connected or buy pistons and install then on your existing rods. If the later is the case, take the job to a Ford dealer or machine shop because the piston pin is an interference fit and requires special equipment for installation.

14 When installing the piston on the rod, the notch or arrow on the piston crown should face forward toward the front of the engine and the boss on the rod should be on the right.

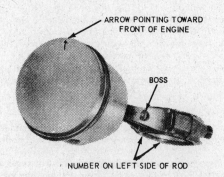

ARROW POINTING TOWARD FRONT OF ENGINE

BOSS

NUMBER ON LEFT SIDE OF ROD

Fig. 13.22 Piston and connecting-rod reference marks (Sec 4)

15 Wipe the rod and cap bearing seats with a soft cloth and install the new bearing inserts.

16 Install the new piston rings, oil ring (bottom) first then the second and the top compression rings. Be very careful not to break the rings as this is done.

17 Before installing the pistons in the cylinder bores, wipe the cylinder bores with a clean rag.

18 The pistons and connecting rods must be installed in the bores from the top of the block. As on removal, use small lengths of rubber hose over the threaded studs as the connecting rod/piston assemblies are installed.

19 Generously lubricate the piston and rings with engine oil. You will need a piston ring compressor. Fit the compressor over the piston to compress the rings and prepare to insert the first piston into the bore. Be sure it is the correct piston/connecting rod assembly for that particular bore, that the connecting rod is facing in the correct direction and that the front of the piston is toward the front of the bore.

20 Again, lubricate the skirt of the piston and insert the piston into the bore up to the bottom of the piston ring compressor.

21 Gently tap the piston through the piston ring compressor and into the cylinder bore with a wooden block and hammer or a plastic hammer or rubber-faced mallet.

22 Lubricate the crankshaft journals and turn the crankshaft so that the journal is in the best position for the connecting rod being inserted.

23 Lubricate the bearing shells and place the rod bearing caps onto the end of the connecting rods over the journals. Install the connecting rod nuts and tighten them finger-tight.

24 Tighten the bolts with a torque wrench to the specified torque.

25 When all the connecting rods have been installed, rotate the crankshaft to check that everything rotates freely and that there are no high spots.

Oil pump and strainer

26 The oil pump should have been cleaned completely in solvent and checked for play and clearances as described in Chapter 1. If there was too much play, you should purchase a new oil pump. Wipe the mating surfaces of the oil pump and underside of the cylinder block.

27 Insert the hexagon driveshaft into the end of the oil pump and install the oil pump onto the block. Install the two bolts. Prime the pump by referring to Step 4 of Part C.

28 Install the one bolt and spring washer that secures the oil pump pick-up pipe support bracket to the crankcase. Tighten all the oil pump bolts to specifications.

Auxiliary shaft and front covers

29 The auxiliary shaft bearing surfaces should be coated evenly with anti-sieze lubricant. Insert the shaft into the block and tap it gently with a soft-faced hammer until it is fully into place. Install the retaining plate and secure it with the two screws. **Note:** *If only one of the covers has been removed, the existing gasket may be cut away and a new gasket cut for it or it may be replaced with a factory gasket.*

30 Lubricate a new auxiliary shaft seal with clean engine oil and install it into the auxiliary shaft cover. The seal lip should be toward the cylinder block face.

31 Position a new gasket on the cylinder block end face, position the auxiliary shaft cover over the shaft and install the cover retaining bolts. Do not tighten them until the cylinder front cover has been fitted or the gasket may be distorted.

32 Install the cylinder front cover in a similar manner to that described above. Position the front cover over the crankshaft and loosely install the retaining bolts. Tighten the front cover bolts to the specified torque.

33 Tighten the auxiliary shaft cover bolts to the specified torque.

Oil Pan

34 The mating surfaces of the underside of the crankcase and of the oil pan should be absolutely clean. Smear some non-setting gasket sealant on the underside of the crankcase. Install the oil pan gasket and end seals making sure that the bolt holes line up. Smear some gasket sealant on the gasket surface of the oil pan and push the oil pan up onto the gasket, taking care not to dislodge it. Secure it in position with the oil pan bolts. Tighten the oil pan bolts finger-tight in a progressive manner and tighten them again to the final torque value found in the specifications.

Engine backplate, flywheel and clutch

35 Clean and wipe the faces of the backplate and cylinder block and carefully install the backplate on the two dowel pins. Wipe the mating faces of the flywheel and crankshaft and push the flywheel onto the crankshaft being sure to align the marks you made during disassembly.

36 Install the six flywheel bolts and tighten them lightly. Lock the flywheel using a screwdriver engaged in the starter ring gear and tighten the flywheel bolts in a diagonal and progressive sequence to the torque value in the Specifications.

37 Install the clutch disc and pressure-plate assembly (Chapter 5). Make sure the disc is facing in the correct direction. Secure the pressure plate assembly with the six retaining bolts and spring washers.

38 The clutch disc must be centered at this point. Special centering tools are commonly available or, an old input shaft or piece of wooden dowel will work. When the clutch disc is centered, fully tighten the retaining bolts.

Valves

39 The valves should have been fully serviced at this time and should be in the correct order. Start with number one cylinder and insert the valve into its guide. Lubricate the valve stem with anti-sieze compound and clean engine oil and slide on a new oil seal. The spring must be upper-most as shown. Install the valve spring and cap. Using a valve spring compressor, compress the valve spring until the split keys can be slid into position. Note the ridges in the keys which will engage in corresponding ridges in the valve stem. Release the valve spring compressor and tap the top of the valve several times lightly with a hammer to make sure that the keys are well seated.

40 Repeat this procedure with the remaining seven valves. Be sure that all valve keys are completely seated.

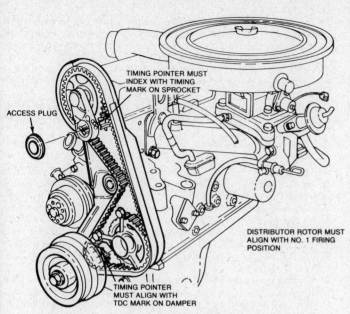

Fig. 13.23 Camshaft and drive train installation (Sec 4)

Camshaft

41 Lubricate the cam journals and bearings with anti-sieze lubricant. Carefully install the shaft in the cylinder head.

42 Install the retainer plate and screws at the rear end of the engine. Lubricate a new camshaft seal with clean engine oil. Carefully tap it into place at the front of the cylinder head. Install the belt guide and pin to the front end of the camshaft and carefully tap the sprocket onto the end of the cam. Be sure that the indexing key is in place.

43 Install a new sprocket bolt and tighten it to the specified torque.

Hydraulic lash adjusters and cam followers

44 Coat the hydraulic lash adjusters with assembly lube. Install each one into its respective bore. Smear the polished surfaces of the cam lobes and cam followers with assembly lube. Using the same technique you used to compress the lash adjusters during disassembly, compress them again and position each cam follower on its respective valve end and adjuster. Make sure the camshaft is rotated as necessary. Install the retaining spring clips (where applicable).

Note: *On some valves it may be necessary to compress the valve spring when installing the cam followers.*

Cylinder head

45 The cylinder head should be ready to install at this time. Wipe the mating surfaces of the cylinder head and cylinder block with a clean rag and carefully place the new head gasket on the cylinder block.

Note: *Do not re-use the old gasket. Make sure the gasket is facing up correctly* (each gasket is marked *front/up*).

46 When installing the head, rotate the camshaft so that the head will slide down completely onto the block. If the crankshaft needs to be rotated for any reason, make sure the pistons are approximately half way down the bores or they may contact the valves during head installation.

47 Install the cylinder head bolts and progressively tighten them using proper torque technique. Tighten them to the specified torque and in the order shown in Figure 13.10.

Water pump and thermostat

48 Install these according to the procedure described in Chapter 1 of this manual.

Timing components and timing belt

49 Install the engine front cover to the cylinder block with the two bolts. Ensure that the crankshaft sprocket key is in position and carefully tap on the crank sprocket. Ensure that the auxiliary shaft sprocket locking pin is in position, then carefully install this sprocket in the same way.

50 Install the auxiliary shaft washer and nut and tighten them to the specific torque.

51 Rotate the camshaft until the index mark on the sprocket aligns with the timing pointer on the belt inner cover. Rotate the crankshaft until the number one piston is at top-dead-center (TDC). Check this position either by rotating the crankshaft while inserting a screwdriver through the spark plug hole or by aligning the pulley O-mark with the timing pointer. The latter method is preferred.

52 Install the belt tensioner but do not tighten the bolt yet. *Be sure not to disturb the position of the crankshaft and camshaft during this procedure.* Install the timing belt over the crankshaft sprocket, then over the auxiliary shaft and the camshaft sprockets. If you pull the belt behind the cambelt wheel, it may be necessary to use leverage with a large screwdriver to pull the tensioner wheel away from the belt.

53 Rotate the crankshaft at least two full turns in a clockwise direction to remove all slack from the timing belt. Make sure the timing marks are correctly aligned then tighten the timing belt adjuster and bolts to the specified torques.

54 Position the belt guide on the end of the crankshaft and install the belt outer cover noting that spacers are used on two of the bolts. Install the crankshaft pulley, washer and retaining bolt. Tighten the bolt to the specified torque.

Valve lash

55 Rotate the crankshaft so that the point on the camshaft lobe of the first valve is facing away from the cam follower. Compress the valve lash adjuster fully and hold it in this position. Using a suitable feeler gauge, check that the gap is as given in the Specifications for valve lash. Insert the feeler blade between the cam and the follower. Proper adjustment is indicated when there is a slight drag on the feeler gauge blade. Repeat this procedure for the remaining valves.

56 If the measurement is outside the allowable limit, either the cam follower is worn or the lash adjuster is unserviceable and should be replaced.

Valve cover

57 The valve cover mating surfaces and the cylinder head mating surface should be absolutely clean. Apply a generous coat of non-setting gasket sealant to the gasket surfaces. Position the new valve cover gasket in the valve cover making sure that the locating tabs are correctly positioned in their slots. Install the rocker cover and tighten the eight screws around the base to the specified torque.

Part F — Installation
Preparation

1 Install all the sender units after smearing their threads with a non-setting sealant. Install the following components referring to the proper text and illustrations.

Install the intake manifold (Chapter 3)
Install the exhaust manifold (Chapter 3)
Install the spark plugs (Chapter 4)
Install the carburetor (Chapter 3 and 13)
Install the generator/alternator loosely on its mountings (Chapter 10)
Install the distributor (Chpater 4)
Install the emission control components (Chapters 3 and 13)
Install a new oil filter (Chapters 1 and 13)

Note: *Do not install the right engine mount at this time.*

Installation

2 Attach the lifting slings and hoist and raise the engine. Lift it over and into the engine compartment. Lower the engine and move it toward the rear of the car so that the splined clutch shaft slides into position in the clutch driven-plate. There should be no problem if the driven plate has been properly centered. If there is any difficulty aligning the splines, turn the crankshaft slightly using a wrench on the crank pulley bolt.

3 When the engine is snug against the clutch housing, insert and tighten the clutch housing bolts.

4 Install the right engine mount. Lower the engine onto its mounts and at the same time remove the transmission jack.

5 Install the engine-to-frame mount bolts.

6 Reconnect the clutch slave cylinder (Chapter 5).

7 Connect the accelerator linkage, the Thermactor hoses to the air pump, and the brake booster vacuum hose (Chapter 1).

8 Connect the heater hoses (Chapter 1).

13

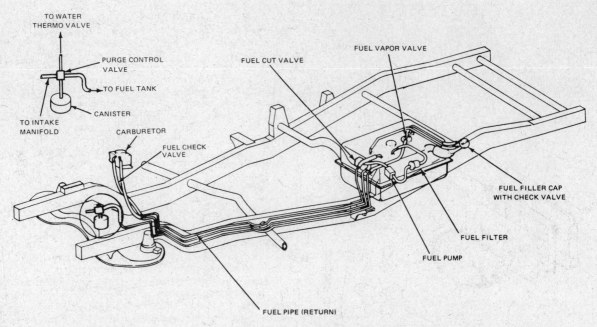

Fig. 13.24 Locations of fuel cut valve, fuel check valve and related fuel tank and fuel line components (Sec 5)

9 Connect the fuel lines to the carburetor.
10 Install and adjust the drivebelts.
11 Connect the distributor and coil leads.
12 Connect the battery ground lead to the cylinder block.
13 Position the fan shroud over the fan and push it toward the engine.
14 Install the radiator and shroud and connect the hoses.
15 Connect the exhaust pipe to the manifold and to the exhaust pipe support bracket.
16 Install the hood and the air cleaner. Connect the battery.
17 Fill the crankcase with engine oil and fill the cooling system with the proper ratio of water and anti-corrosive coolant.

Initial start-up after overhaul or major repair
18 Make sure the battery is fully charged and that all lubricants, coolant and fuel have been replaced. If the engine has been taken apart it may require several revolutions of the engine on the starter motor to start it. As soon as engine fires-up, keep it going at a fast idle only, no faster until it is brought up to normal operating temperature. During this time check for fluid leaks and sounds which would indicate an engine problem. If any such problems are indicated, shut off the engine and correct immediately. When the thermostat opens, the coolant level will fall and must be refilled again as necessary.
19 As the engine warms up there will be strange smells and some smoke from excess oil deposits. Also check the exhaust manifold connections (they will probably need tightening later).
20 When normal running temperature has been reached, adjust the idle speed as described later in this Chapter and in Chapter 3.
21 Stop the engine and wait a few minutes to see if any lubricant or coolant is dripping out.
22 After the engine has run for 20 minutes, remove the valve cover and re-check the tightness of the cylinder head bolts. Also check the tightness of the oil pan bolts. In both cases use a torque wrench.
23 Road test the vehicle to check that the timing is correct and that the engine is giving the necessary smoothness and power. Do not race the engine. If new bearings and/or pistons have been installed it should be treated as a new engine and run at a reduced speed for the first 500 miles.

Part G — Engine/transmission mounts
Front mounts — replacement with engine in vehicle
1 Remove the nuts from the rubber insulators. Raise the engine just high enough to permit the insulators to be removed by carefully jacking it beneath the mounting support brackets.
2 Installation is a direct reversal of the removal procedure.

Rear mounts — replacement with engine in vehicle
3 Support the transmission using a jack, then detach the right and left bracket from the side members.
4 Unscrew the center bolt and remove the bracket, then detach the rubber block and mounting plate from the bracket.
5 Installation is the reverse of the removal procedure. Do not fully tighten the bolts until the jack has been removed.

5 Fuel and emissions control systems

Air cleaner — description
1 The air cleaner comes in three different designs on each of the three engines. All three incorporate a winter/summer slide valve. All vehicles in the United States have an air cleaner with an automatic temperature control valve which regulates the ratio of warm air pulled past the exhaust manifold and outside air pulled through the air cleaner. Other models have manually controlled temperature valves.
2 Replace the disposable paper air cleaner element at the intervals specified in Routine Maintenance.

Fuel cut valve — description, removal and checking
3 Two valves are installed in the fuel lines on all later vehicles (except Canada). A fuel cut valve is installed in the fuel line between the fuel pump and carburetor. This valve is designed to cut the flow of fuel to the carburetor if the valve body is turned more than 60°. A fuel check valve is installed in the fuel return line between the carburetor and the fuel tank. It prevents fuel from the tank flowing through the return line and into the carburetor during an accident or overturning.
4 To remove the fuel cut valve, disconnect the hoses from it and unbolt the valve bracket. The valve can be checked by blowing air through the valve outlet port and then through the inlet port. Air should pass through in one direction only.
5 The fuel check valve can be removed and the hoses disconnected, but when installing, make sure that the arrow on the valve is pointing toward the carburetor.

Carburetor — general description
6 Since 1976 the carburetors used on Couriers are two-stage, two venturi downdraft units very similar to earlier carburetors. The carburetors on the 1796 cc engine and the 2300 cc engine are almost identical. However, the 2000 cc engine uses a carburetor with several minor modifications.

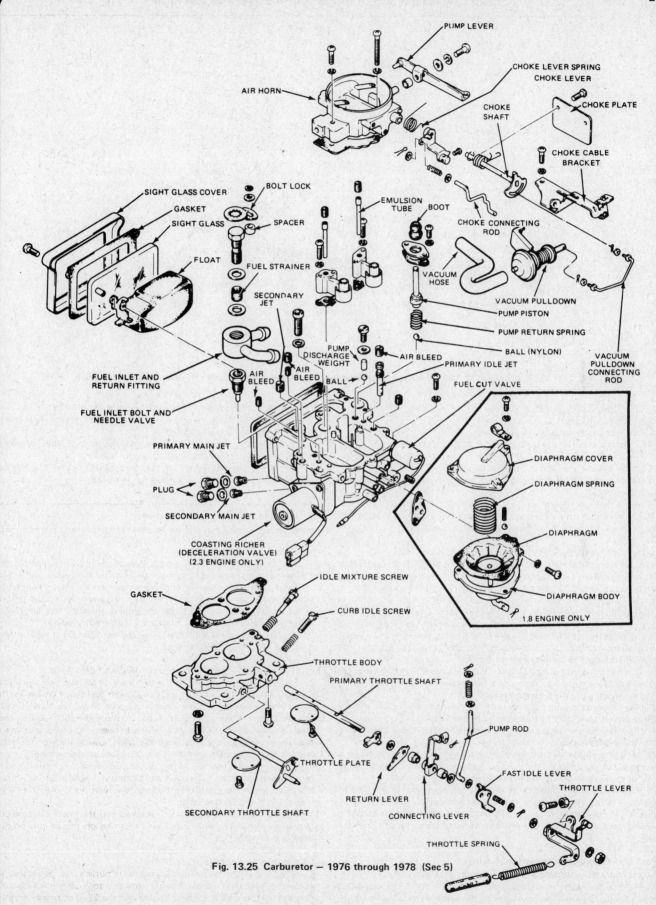

Fig. 13.25 Carburetor — 1976 through 1978 (Sec 5)

PUMP LEVER

AIR HORN

CHOKE LEVER SPRING
CHOKE LEVER

CHOKE SHAFT

CHOKE PLATE

CHOKE CABLE BRACKET

SIGHT GLASS COVER
BOLT LOCK

GASKET

SIGHT GLASS

SPACER

EMULSION TUBE
BOOT

CHOKE CONNECTING ROD

FLOAT

FUEL STRAINER

SECONDARY JET

VACUUM HOSE

VACUUM PULLDOWN

PUMP PISTON

PUMP RETURN SPRING

BALL (NYLON)

VACUUM PULLDOWN CONNECTING ROD

FUEL INLET AND RETURN FITTING

AIR BLEED

AIR BLEED

PUMP DISCHARGE WEIGHT

AIR BLEED

PRIMARY IDLE JET

FUEL INLET BOLT AND NEEDLE VALVE

BALL

FUEL CUT VALVE

PRIMARY MAIN JET

DIAPHRAGM COVER

DIAPHRAGM SPRING

PLUG

DIAPHRAGM

SECONDARY MAIN JET

DIAPHRAGM BODY

COASTING RICHER (DECELERATION VALVE) (2.3 ENGINE ONLY)

1.8 ENGINE ONLY

IDLE MIXTURE SCREW

GASKET

CURB IDLE SCREW

THROTTLE BODY

PRIMARY THROTTLE SHAFT

PUMP ROD

THROTTLE PLATE

FAST IDLE LEVER

THROTTLE LEVER

SECONDARY THROTTLE SHAFT

RETURN LEVER

CONNECTING LEVER

THROTTLE SPRING

13

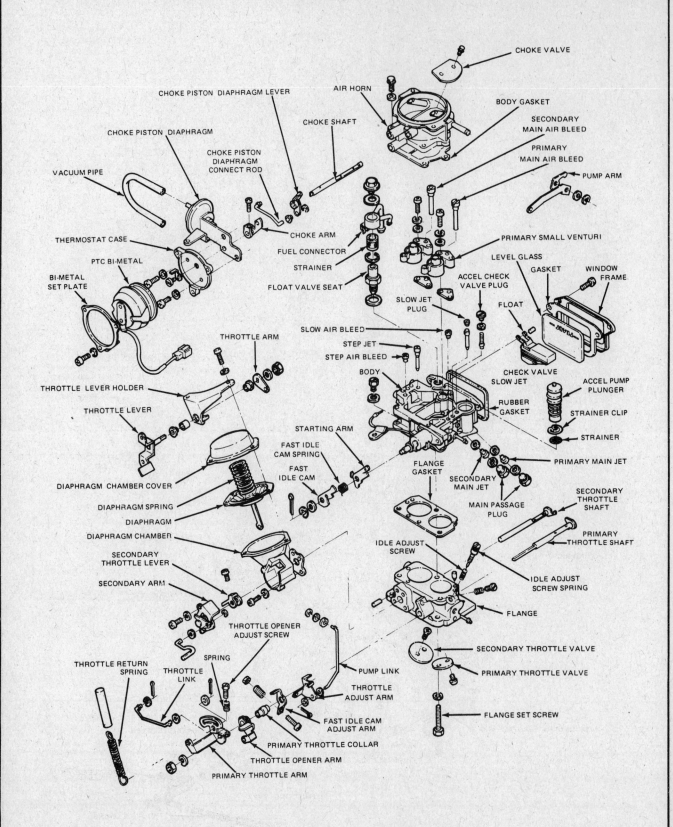

Fig. 13.26 Carburetor — 1979 through 1982 2000cc (Sec 5)

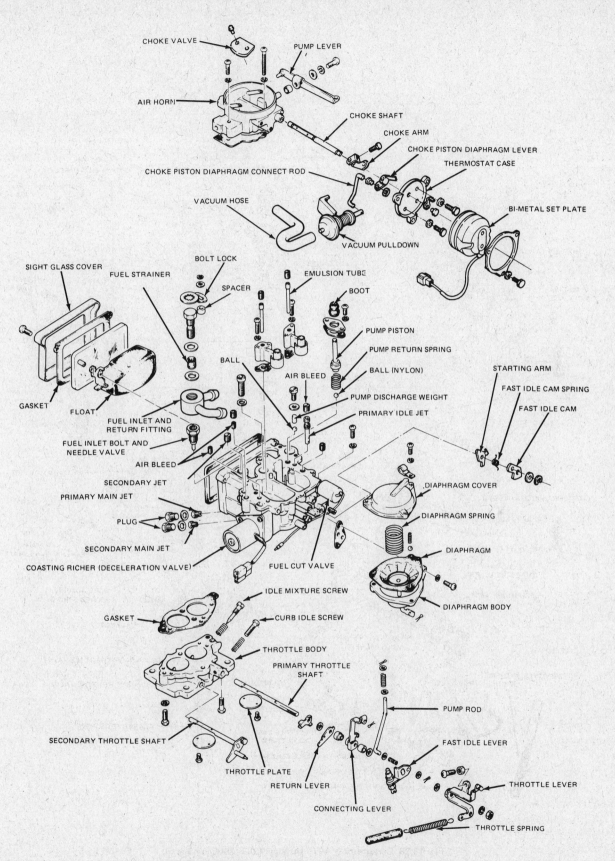

CHOKE VALVE

PUMP LEVER

AIR HORN

CHOKE SHAFT

CHOKE ARM

CHOKE PISTON DIAPHRAGM LEVER

THERMOSTAT CASE

CHOKE PISTON DIAPHRAGM CONNECT ROD

VACUUM HOSE

BI-METAL SET PLATE

VACUUM PULLDOWN

SIGHT GLASS COVER

FUEL STRAINER

BOLT LOCK

SPACER

EMULSION TUBE

BOOT

PUMP PISTON

PUMP RETURN SPRING

BALL

BALL (NYLON)

STARTING ARM

FAST IDLE CAM SPRING

FAST IDLE CAM

AIR BLEED

PUMP DISCHARGE WEIGHT

GASKET

FLOAT

FUEL INLET AND
RETURN FITTING

PRIMARY IDLE JET

FUEL INLET BOLT AND
NEEDLE VALVE

AIR BLEED

SECONDARY JET

PRIMARY MAIN JET

DIAPHRAGM COVER

DIAPHRAGM SPRING

PLUG

DIAPHRAGM

SECONDARY MAIN JET

COASTING RICHER (DECELERATION VALVE)

FUEL CUT VALVE

DIAPHRAGM BODY

IDLE MIXTURE SCREW

GASKET

CURB IDLE SCREW

THROTTLE BODY

PRIMARY THROTTLE
SHAFT

PUMP ROD

SECONDARY THROTTLE SHAFT

FAST IDLE LEVER

THROTTLE PLATE

THROTTLE LEVER

RETURN LEVER

CONNECTING LEVER

THROTTLE SPRING

Fig. 13.27 Carburetor — 1979 through 1982 2300cc (Sec 5)

13

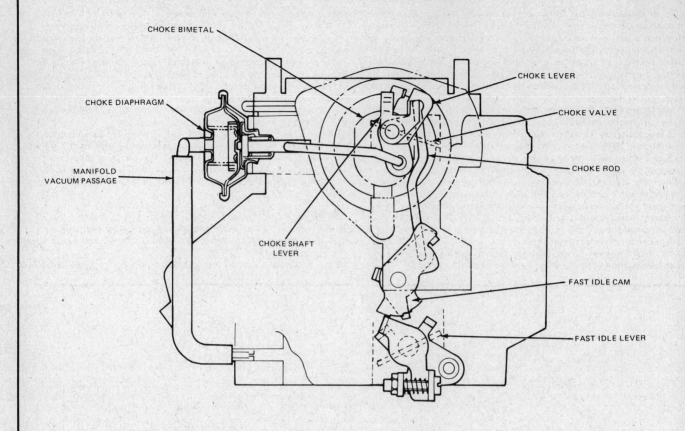

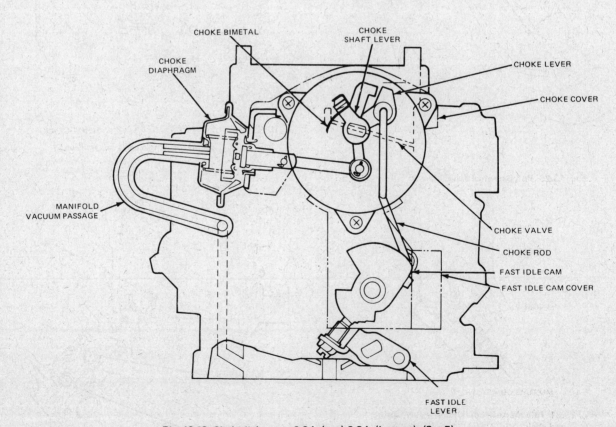

Fig. 13.28 Choke linkages — 2.0 L (top) 2.3 L (bottom) (Sec 5)

7 On all carburetors, the primary stage includes a curb idle system, an accelerator pump system, an idle transfer system, a main metering system and a power enrichment system. The secondary stage includes an idle transfer system and main metering system.

8 The electric heater warms a bi-metal valve interconnected to the choke and controls the position of the choke valve and the throttle valve in accordance with the warm-up condition of the engine and the outside temperature.

9 Models before 1979 incorporated a manual choke (cable operated) and an automatic choke release system which was operated by a solenoid actuated by a coolant temperature switch. On the automatic choke models (1979 through 1982), the automatic choke control serves to reduce exhaust gas emissions during warm-up by automatically selecting one of the two choke operation modes: fast acting or slow acting.

10 When the outside temperature is low, an electric current flows through the automatic choke relay to the heater and gradually warms the bi-metal strip. This causes the choke valve to open slowly. When the ambient temperature is high (64° F) a switch on the bi-metal strip closes which allows current to flow to an additional heater resulting in quicker opening of the choke valve.

11 The carburetors on all models may be removed, disassembled and reassembled according to the procedure described in Chapter 3.

Idle speed adjustment — all models
12 Before setting the idle speed check the ignition timing and the float level in the carburetor (Section 4, steps 39, 40). Make any necessary adjustments.

13 The transmission must be in Neutral. Start the engine and allow it to run until it reaches operating temperature. Check to see that the choke has fully opened.

14 Connect a tachometer to the engine, run the engine at 2000 rpm for three minutes. Disconnect the canister purge hose between the canister and air cleaner.

15 Set the curb idle speed to that specified at the beginning of this Chapter using the throttle adjustment screw. Refer to the Vehicle Emission Control Information label in the engine compartment for additional instructions or specifications specifically for your engine.

16 When the adjustments have been made reconnect the canister purge hose.

Idle fuel mixture — 2.0 L engine (low altitude only)
17 Remove the idle mixture adjustment screw and shell and install a new mixture adjustment screw and shell. Connect an exhaust gas analyzer to the vehicle.

18 On a California vehicle, disconnect the air hose between the air by-

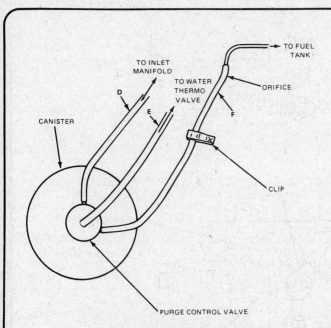

Fig. 13.29 Purge control valve (Sec 5)

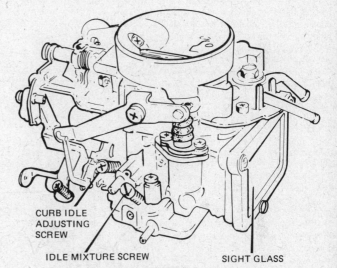

Fig. 13.30 Carburetor adjustment screws (Sec 5)

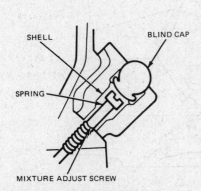

Fig. 13.31 Idle mixture adjustment screw, spring and shell — 2.0 L and 2.3 L (Sec 5)

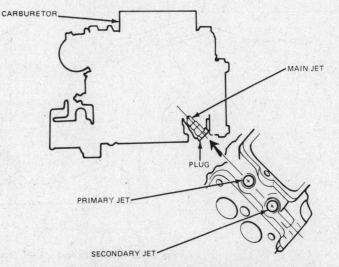

Fig. 13.32 Main jets — primary and secondary (Sec 5)

13

pass valve and the check valve and plug the port of the check valve. On non-California vehicles, disconnect the air hose between the air cleaner and the reed valve and plug the port of the reed valve.

19 Adjust the idle speed to specifications by turning the throttle adjustment screw.

20 Set the engine speed at the highest rpm by turning the mixture adjustment screw.

21 Now go back and reset the idle speed to specifications by turning the throttle adjustment screw. Now again, turn the mixture adjust screw clockwise until the specified idle speed is obtained.

22 Check the CO concentration. If it is less than one percent, turn the mixture adjustment screw counter-clockwise one quarter turn. Reconnect the disconnected air hose and check the idle speed again. If they are not at specifications turn the throttle adjust screw to meet them.

23 When the adjustments are complete, put a blind plug on the mixture adjustment screw shell.

Idle fuel mixture - 2.3 L engine

24 Follow the same procedure as for the 2.0L engine but use the idle speed specifications for the 2.3L engine at the beginning of this Chapter or on the Vehicle Emissions label. When finished, do not forget to install a blind plug on the mixture adjust screw shell.

High altitude adjustment

25 To adjust the carburetor from a low altitude calibration to a high altitude calibration, perform the following adjustments.

26 Remove the carburetor from the engine.

27 Remove the plugs, washers, main jets and washers from the carburetor. Install the high altitude jets shown in the Specifications and the plugs and washers.

28 Turn the mixture adjustment screw counter-clockwise and remove it, including the spring and shell.

29 Install a new mixture adjustment screw, spring and shell. Install the carburetor on the engine.

Fast idle adjustment - 1976 through 1978 carburetors

30 With the air cleaner removed, fully close the choke plate then measure the clearance between the edge of the primary throttle plate and the throttle bore. The clearance should be measured with a suitable gauge and for all vehicles except California it should be 0.071 in (1.803 mm). California vehicles should have measurements of 0.067 in (1.7018 mm). Bend the fast idle lever if necessary to adjust it.

Fast idle cam adjustment - 1979 through 1982 carburetors

31 Fully close the choke valve and place the fast idle cam on the first position.

32 Adjust the throttle valve opening clearance by turning the adjusting screw clockwise to increase or counter-clockwise to decrease the opening clearance. See Specifications for opening clearance measurements.

Vacuum pulldown adjustment - 1976 through 1978 vehicles

33 California vehicles have a vacuum pulldown adjustment. Disconnect the leads from the coolant thermo switch and bridge the leads. 34 Turn
34 Turn the ignition On.

35 Pull the choke control fully On to close the choke valve plate.

36 Disconnect the vacuum hose from the pulldown unit and connect a vacuum pump and gauge to the pulldown unit. Without this, the adjustment will have to be left to your dealer or professional mechanic.

37 The pulldown connecting rod should start to operate at a vacuum of 5.9 to 7.5 Hg.

38 Increase the vacuum to between 9.8 and 12.0 inches Hg. At this vacuum the clearance between the edge of the choke valve plate and the air horn wall should be according to specifications. Make this adjustment by bending the pulldown connecting rod.

Float level adjustment

39 With the engine operating, check the fuel level in the fuel bowl sight glass. If the fuel is not to the specified mark in the sight glass, remove the carburetor from the vehicle.

40 Remove the fuel bowl cover. Invert the carburetor on a stand and allow the float to lower by its own weight. Measure the clearance between the float and the edge of the bowl. If the clearance is not as specieied bend the float tang until the proper clearance is obtained.

Choke — throttle valve opening angle.

41 Adjust the fast idle cam as outlined in this Chapter.

42 Position the fast idle cam on the second position.

43 Adjust the choke valve opening clearance by bending the starting arm to obtain the specified clearance. If a large adjustment is required the choke rod can be bent.

Choke diaphragm — adjustment

44 Attach a vacuum pump to the choke diaphragm tube. Apply approximately 15.6 inches Hg.

45 Check to see that the fast idle cam is at the first position.

46 Press the choke valve slightly, then adjust the choke valve opening by bending the choke lever to obtain the specified clearance.

Exhaust system and catalytic converter — general information

47 The exhaust system must be free of leaks and excessive vibrations. These conditions are usually caused by loose, broken or misaligned clamps, brackets or pipes. Check the exhaust system components alignment. Adjust or replace as necessary.

48 If you find any brackets, clamps or insulators which are damaged, replace them with new ones. Do not attempt to repair these parts.

49 Inspect the inlet pipe, resonator assembly in the muffler and outlet pipe for cracked joints, broken welds and corrosion damage that will result in a leaking exhaust system. Look for badly corroded bolts or stripped bolt threads. When pipe clamps are loosened and/or removed to replace a pipe, muffler or resonater, replace the clamps with new ones if in doubt about their condition.

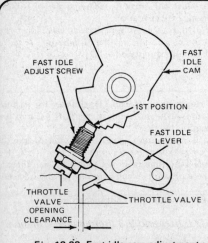

Fig. 13.33 Fast idle cam adjustment (Sec 5)

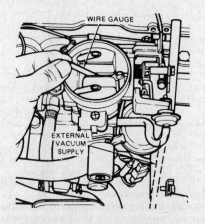

Fig. 13.34 Checking the choke valve clearance (vacuum pulldown) (Sec 5)

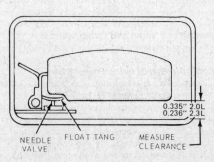

Fig. 13.35 Adjusting the float level clearance (Sec 5)

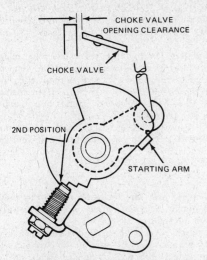

Fig. 13.36 Choke/throttle valve opening clearance measurement (Sec 5)

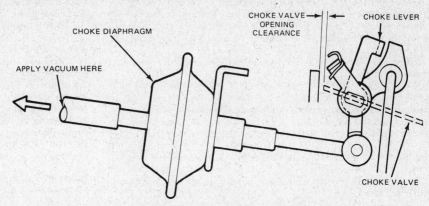

Fig. 13.37 Choke diaphragm adjustment (Sec 5)

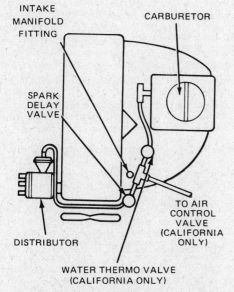

Fig. 13.38 Spark timing delay system (Sec 5)

Catalytic Converter

50 On all later models and all vehicles operating in California, the catalytic converter is used. This is an integral part of the exhaust system composed basically of a steel casing with a catalyst in it to help burn excess exhaust gases. As exhaust gases pass through the catalytic converter, the hydrocarbon and carbon monoxide content is burned and converted into water and carbon dioxide.

51 Never push-start a vehicle equipped with a catalytic converter.

Emission control systems — general

52 The systems used on later models in all 2.0 and 2.3 liter vehicles are very similar to those used earlier and described in Chapter 3.

53 The emission control system contains an air injector system, an oxidizing catalytic converter system, an Exhaust Gas Recirculation system (EGR), and a deceleration control system to reduce harmful composits in the exhaust gas. It also contains a PCV system which channels the blow-by gas from the crankcase into the combustion chamber to burn it and an evaporative emission control system which stores the fuel vapor from the fuel system and leads it to the combustion chamber.

54 A vehicle emission control information decal is located under the hood. This decal includes engine tune-up adjustment specifications. Always use the information on this decal in preference to other Specifications.

55 On California vehicles a vacuum hose routing diagram is included. The tune-up specifications on the decal include idle speed, ignition timing, fast idle speed, valve lash and dash pot setting, etc.

Exhaust gas circulation (EGR) system

56 The exhaust gas recirculation system on the 1.8, 2.0 and 2.3 liter engine is designed to reintroduce small amounts of exhaust gas into the combustion cycle which reduces combustion temperatures and the generation of nitrous oxides (NOX). The amount of exhaust gas re-introduced and the timing of the cycle are controlled by various factors such as engine vacuum temperature and speed. The EGR system is composed of three main components — the EGR control valve, the water thermo valve and the vacuum amplifier.

57 The EGR valve is a vacuum operated unit. When the valve is open, the exhaust gas goes into the intake manifold. When it is closed, the flow of exhaust gases is prevented.

58 The water thermo valve senses the coolant temperature and controls the vacuum control of the EGR control valve (except for 2.3 liter in California). When the coolant temperature is below approxiamtely 55° C (129° F) for the 2.0 liter engine and 60° C (140° F) for the 2.3 liter engine, the water thermo valve is closed which prevents the EGR valve from operating. When the coolant temperature is above these temperatures, the water thermo valve opens and vacuum is applied to the diaphragm of the EGR valve. The valve is located on the intake manifold.

59 The vacuum amplifier supplies various amounts of vacuum to the EGR valve diaphragm to open to close the valve during acceleration or at varying vehicle speeds.

Spark timing control system

60 The spark timing delay system is installed on all later models. It assists in reducing the exhaust emissions by delaying the distributor vacuum avance during periods of acceleration.

61 The main component of the system is a spark delay valve located in the vacuum line between the carburetor and the distributor. A faulty spark timing control valve should be replaced.

Testing
EGR control valve test

62 Start the engine and run it at idle speed. Disconnect the vacuum hose from the water thermo valve and connect the EGR vacuum line to the intake manifold vacuum.

63 When this connection is made, the engine should stall or idle unevenly. If the engine does not exhibit these symptoms, turn it off. Remove the EGR control valve and pipe from the engine. Clean the passages of the valve and pipe with a brush and wire. Install the valve and repeat the test.

64 Replace the EGR valve if the cleaning is not successful.

Spark delay valve test (2.0 liter and 2.3 liter engine — manual transmission vehicles)

65 Remove the air cleaner. Disconnect the vacuum line from the distributor. Remove the vacuum line from the side of the spark delay valve.

66 Start the engine, run it at idle speed and note the vacuum gauge

13

reading. Disconnect the vacuum line from the intake manifold and note the time it takes for the vacuum reading to decrease by 11.8 inches Hg. The vacuum should drop this amount within four to six seconds. Replace the spark delay valve if the vacuum does not drop within the specified time.

67 Return all vacuum lines to the original positions.

6 Ignition system

General description — 2.0 liter and 2.3 liter engines

1 A magnetic pulse distrubutor is used on the 2.0 liter and 2.3 liter engines. The distributor on the 2.0 liter engine is mounted on the right side of the engine. The distributor for the 2.3 liter engine is mounted on the left side of the engine.

2 Unlike a conventional distributor, this model contains no contact breaker points. The main components of the ignition system are an ignition amplifier, module, coil, distributor, battery and spark plugs.

3 For most purposes the ignition timing is carried out as for conventional ignition systems.

4 Troubleshooting a breakerless ignition system cannot be done without specialized equipment and should be left to an electrical professional or dealer service department. Many problems cannot be solved by substituting parts or cleaning/tightening connections.

Distributor — removal and installation (2.0 liter and 2.3 liter engines)

5 Remove the distributor cap and disconnect the vacuum hose from the distributor vacuum diaphragm.

6 Scribe a mark on the distributor to ease reassembly. Scribe another mark on the distributor body indicating the position of the rotor.
Note: *Do not crank the engine after the distributor has been removed*

from the cylinder head.

7 Disconnect the wire from the ignition module in the distributor.

8 Remove the distributor retaining nut, flat washer and lock washer.

9 Slide the distrubutor out of the cylinder head.

10 To reinstall the distributor, slide the distributor with a new rubber O-ring into the cylinder head making sure that all index marks previously made are in alignment.

11 Install, but do not tighten the flat washer, lock washer and attaching nut.

12 Install the distributor cap and connect the electrical wires to their respective terminals.

13 Start the engine and set the timing with a timing light then tighten the distributor lock nut.

14 Connect the vacuum line to the vacuum advance unit.

Ignition timing — breakerless distributor

15 No adjustments are to be made to the ignition system except armature gap, ignition timing and spark plug gap. The timing marks and their locations are illustrated in the accompanying Figure.

16 Clean and mark the timing marks on the crankshaft pulley. The static initial advance setting for the 2.0 liter engine is 8° BTDC. The advance setting for the 2.3 liter engine is 6° BTDC.

17 Disconnect the vacuum line from the distributor and temporarily plug the line.

18 Connect a timing light to the number one cylinder spark plug wire.

19 Connect a tachometer to the engine.

20 Start the engine and adjust the idle speed to 650 rpm (600 rpm for 2.0 liter engines). On 2.3 liter engines with a manual transmission the idle should be set at 850 rpm. 2.3 liter engines with an automatic transmission should be set at 700 rpm. Allow the engine to idle at the specified rpm and shine the timing light onto the pulley and note the position of the timing mark relative to the timing pointer. If the line and pointer do not coincide, loosen the distributor clamp bolt and twist

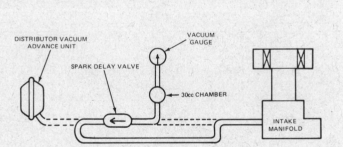

Fig. 13.39 Spark delay valve test (Sec 5)

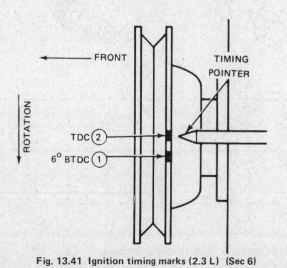

Fig. 13.41 Ignition timing marks (2.3 L) (Sec 6)

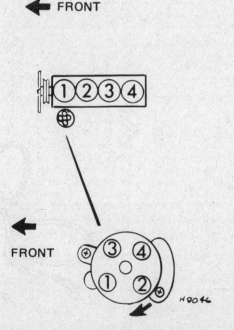

Fig. 13.42 Distributor positions and spark plug lead connections (2.3 L) (Sec 6)

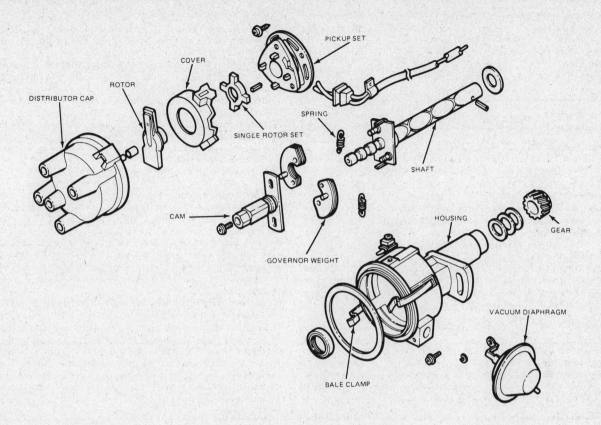

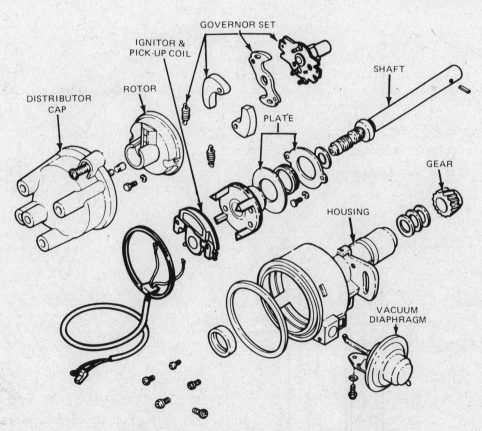

Fig. 13.40 Breakerless distributors — Pre 1980 (top), 1980-82 (bottom) (Sec 6)

13

the distributor until the timing marks do align.

21 You now have correct ignition timing. Stop the engine and tighten the distributor clamp bolt, then run the engine up to 2500 rpm and check that the timing advances. The indexing arrow should align with the BTDC mark. This will indicate that the centrifugal advance mechanism is operating properly.

22 Stop the engine. Unplug and reconnect the distributor vacuum line, then again run the engine up to 2500 rpm and check that the advance is greater than that obtained above. This will indicate that the vacuum advance is operating

23 If you are not achieving satisfactory results, take the distributor to an electrical specialist or Ford dealer. Overhaul kits are not available for this type of distributor and it usually must be replaced if the problems cannot be rectified.

7 Clutch

Clutch adjustment

1 On all vehicles between 1976 and 1982 the pedal free movement is adjusted by releasing the lock nut at the pedal pushrod and turning the pushrod.

2 No adjustment is carried out at the slave cylinder. When the free movement is as specified, tighten the lock nut. The return spring on these models is located at the clutch pedal arm, not on the release lever.

3 Service the slave cylinder as outlined in Chapter 5, Section 9.

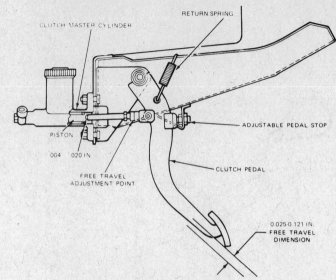

Fig. 13.43 Clutch pedal free-play adjustment (Sec 7)

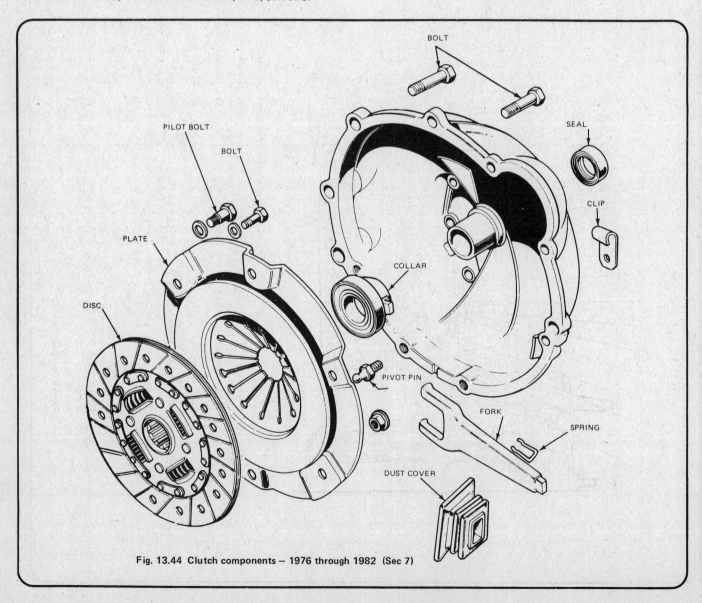

Fig. 13.44 Clutch components — 1976 through 1982 (Sec 7)

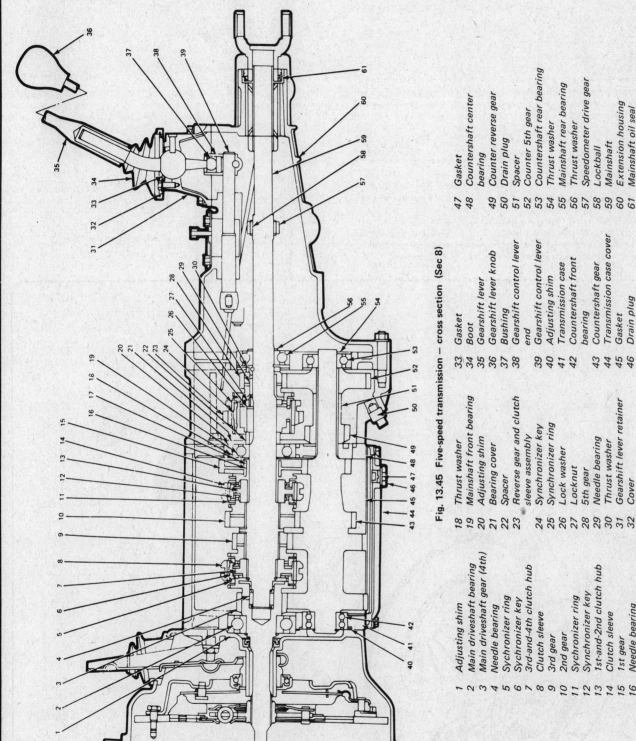

Fig. 13.45 Five-speed transmission – cross section (Sec 8)

1 Adjusting shim
2 Main driveshaft bearing
3 Main driveshaft gear (4th)
4 Needle bearing
5 Synchronizer ring
6 Sychronizer key
7 3rd-and-4th clutch hub
8 Clutch sleeve
9 3rd gear
10 2nd gear
11 Synchronizer ring
12 Synchronizer key
13 1st-and-2nd clutch hub
14 Clutch sleeve
15 1st gear
16 Needle bearing
17 Needle bearing inner race

18 Thrust washer
19 Mainshaft front bearing
20 Adjusting shim
21 Bearing cover
22 Spacer
23 Reverse gear and clutch sleeve assembly
24 Synchronizer key
25 Synchronizer ring
26 Lockwasher
27 Locknut
28 5th gear
29 Needle bearing
30 Thrust washer
31 Gearshift lever retainer
32 Cover

33 Gasket
34 Boot
35 Gearshift lever
36 Gearshift lever knob
37 Bushing
38 Gearshift control lever end
39 Gearshift control lever
40 Adjusting shim
41 Transmission case
42 Countershaft front bearing
43 Countershaft gear
44 Transmission case cover
45 Gasket
46 Drain plug

47 Gasket
48 Countershaft center bearing
49 Counter reverse gear
50 Drain plug
51 Spacer
52 Counter 5th gear
53 Countershaft rear bearing
54 Thrust washer
55 Mainshaft rear bearing
56 Thrust washer
57 Speedometer drive gear
58 Lockball
59 Mainshaft
60 Extension housing
61 Mainshaft oil seal

13

8   5-speed manual transmission

Part A — Removal and installation

The operations are almost identical with those described for the 4-speed unit in Chapter 6.

Part B — Dismantling

External components

1   With the transmission removed from the vehicle, unscrew the drain plug and allow the oil to drain.

2   Wipe any metallic debris from the drain plug magnet and screw it back into position.

3   Set the transmission in Neutral and then remove the four bolts which attach the gearshift lever retainer to the extension housing. Remove the retainer and gasket.

4   Remove the speedometer sleeve lockplate and driven gear assembly from the extension housing.

5   Unbolt the extension housing and lift the gearshift control lever to the left and slide it rearwards. At the same time, slide the extension housing from the main gearcase.

6   Remove the spring cap bolt, spring and friction piece from the extension housing.

7   Remove the bolt which holds the gearshift control lever end to the control lever, and remove the two components.

8   Unscrew the reverse light switch from the extension housing.

9   Remove the snap-ring and withdraw the speedometer drive gear from the mainshaft, retaining the locking ball. Extract the second snap-ring.

10 Unbolt and remove the bottom cover and gasket form the transmission case.

Shift rails, mainshaft, and countershaft bearings and gears

11 Scribe lines on the ends of the shifter rods as an aid to reassembly and then remove the bolts which hold the ends to the shift rods and remove the ends.

12 Pry the bearing housing away from the transmission case with a screwdriver and slide the housing from the mainshaft.

13 Remove the snap-ring and thrust washer from the face of the mainshaft rear bearing and then draw off the bearing with a suitable puller.

14 Now remove the countershaft rear bearing in a similar way after having first removed the snap-ring and washer.

15 Remove 5th gear and spacer from the rear end of the countershaft.

16 Unscrew the center housing attaching bolt and tap the housing off with a plastic-faced hammer.

17 Remove the three spring cap blots, detent springs and balls from

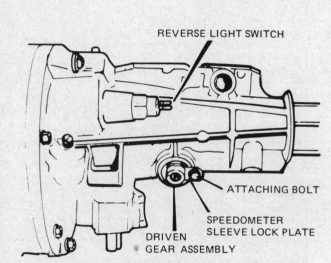

Fig. 13.46 Speedometer sleeve lockplate and driven-gear locations (Sec 8)

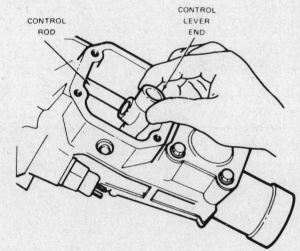

Fig. 13.47 Removing the gearshift control lever end (Sec 8)

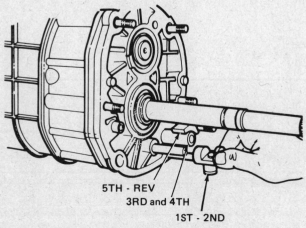

Fig. 13.48 Shift rod end-fitting removal (Sec 8)

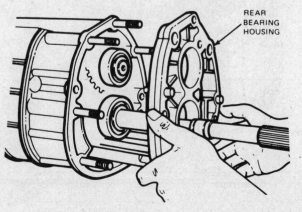

Fig. 13.49 Rear bearing housing removal (Sec 8)

the transmission case.
18 Remove the blind cover plates from the transmission case.
19 Unscrew the bolt from the 5th/Reverse shift fork and withdraw the shift rail.
20 Remove the bolt from the 3rd/4th shift fork (accessible through the front blind cover) and slide the shift rail out of the transmission.
21 Remove the bolt from the 1st/2nd shift fork and then slide the shift rail out of the transmission case.
22 Remove the snap-ring and remove the 5th gear from the mainshaft.
23 Remove the lock ball and needle bearing from the mainshaft.
24 Using a screwdriver, engage 2nd gear with the countershaft Reverse gear to lock up the mainshaft, and then bend back the lock washer tabs on the mainshaft bearing locknut. Unscrew the locknut.
25 Slide Reverse gear and synchro unit from the mainshaft.
26 Slide the spacer and countershaft Reverse gear from the rear of the countershaft.
27 Remove Reverse idler gear and shaft from the transmission case.
28 Remove the key spacer from the mainshaft.
29 Remove the snap-ring which secures the countershaft front bearing and then, using a suitable puller, remove the bearing.

30 Remove the adjusting shims from the countershaft bearing seat in the transmission case.
31 Remove the bolts which attach the bearing cover to the transmission case and remove the cover.
32 Again using a puller, draw off the countershaft center bearing.
33 Remove the snap-ring and shims which hold the mainshaft front bearing.
34 A sheet metal guard (tool No. T77J-7025E) should be used to prevent the synchro blocking ring from jamming onto the taper of the input shaft. Using a puller, draw off the mainshaft front bearing.
35 Remove the mainshaft center bearing, again using the puller.
36 Lift the countergear assembly from the transmission case.
37 If necessary, the countershaft center bearing inner race can be pressed off on a bench press.
38 Remove the input shaft from the transmission case.
39 Remove the synchro ring and needle bearing from the main drive gear.
40 Lift the mainshaft assembly from the transmission case.
41 Remove the shift forks and interlock pins from the transmission case.
42 Remove the snap-rings from the front of the mainshaft and then

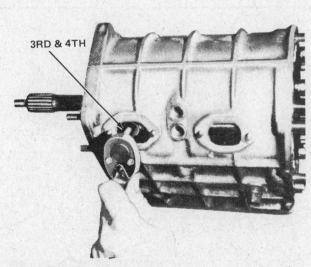

Fig. 13.50 Removing the 3rd/4th gear shift fork bolt (Sec 8)

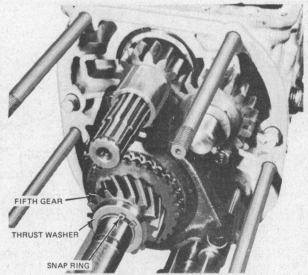

Fig. 13.51 Fifth gear — location (Sec 8)

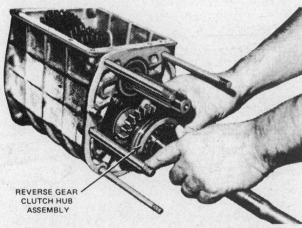

Fig. 13.52 Removing Reverse gear from the mainshaft (Sec 8)

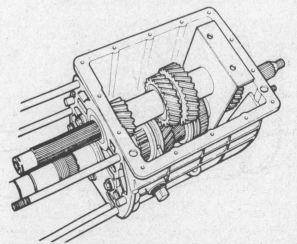

Fig. 13.53 Special tool to prevent synchro ring jamming (Sec 8)

13

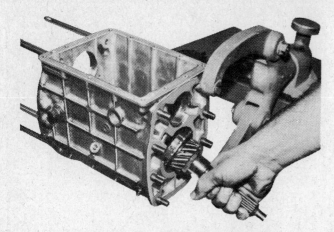

Fig. 13.54 Removing the input shaft (Sec 8)

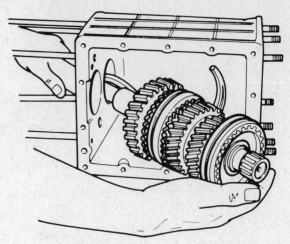

Fig. 13.55 Removing the mainshaft (Sec 8)

slide off 3rd/4th synchro assembly, 3rd speed synchro ring and 3rd gear. Do not mix up the synchronizer rings.

43 Slide the thrust washer, 1st gear and needle bearing from the rear end of the mainshaft.

44 Remove the needle bearing inner race and the 1st/2nd synchro unit from the mainshaft, and press off 2nd gear.

Inspection

45 Clean and inspect all components for wear, comparing clearances with those given in Specifications.

46 If the synchronizer assemblies are dismantled, reassemble them so that the key springs are installed in opposite (side-to-side) directional rotation as shown. If noisy gearshift has been evident previously, it is worthwhile buying new assemblies rather than individual components.

Part C - Reassembly

Mainshaft and countershaft assemblies

1 Place the synchronizer ring on 2nd gear and slide 2nd gear onto the mainshaft so that the synchro ring is toward the rear of the shaft.

2 Press in 1st gear needle bearing inner race, 1st/2nd synchro assembly to the mainshaft so that the oil grooves in the synchro clutch hub are toward the front of the mainshaft. Check that the three synchro keys engage with the notches in the 2nd speed synchro ring and that the hub direction is correct.

3 Place the synchro ring on the 3rd gear and slide the gear onto the front of the mainshaft so that the synchro ring is toward the front end of the mainshaft.

4 Slide 3rd/4th synchro clutch hub and sleeve onto the front of the mainshaft making sure that the three keys in the synchro unit engage with the notches in the synchro ring and that the hub direction is correct.

5 Install the snap-ring to the front of the mainshaft.

6 Slide the needle bearing for 1st gear onto the mainshaft.

7 Place the synchronizer ring onto 1st gear and slide the gear onto the mainshaft so that the ring is toward the front of the shaft. Rotate 1st gear to engage the three notches in the synchro ring with the synchro keys.

8 Install the original thrust washer to the mainshaft.

9 Install the mainshaft assembly into the transmission case.

10 Install the needle bearing to the front end of the mainshaft.

11 Place the synchronizer ring on 4th gear (input shaft) and install the input shaft onto the front end of the mainshaft. Make sure that the synchro keys and notches engage.

12 Place 1st/2nd shift fork and 3rd/4th shift fork in the groove of the synchro assembly.

13 Press the inner race of the countershaft center bearing onto the countershaft.

14 Install the countershaft gear assembly into the transmission case making sure that all the gear teeth mate with those on the mainshaft gears.

Mainshaft and countershaft bearings

15 At this time, check the mainshaft thrust play. To do this, measure the depth of the mainshaft front bearing bore (located in the clutch

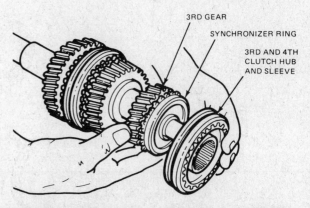

3RD GEAR

SYNCHRONIZER RING

3RD AND 4TH CLUTCH HUB AND SLEEVE

Fig. 13.56 Removing 3rd gear from the mainshaft (Sec 8)

housing). Now measure the height of the mainshaft front bearing. By subtracting the two measurements, the thickness of the packing shims will be indicated. Shims should be used from the two thicknesses available to ensure that the thrust play is within the tolerances specified.

16 Position the tool (referred to in paragraph 34 of Part B) between 4th synchro ring and the synchro gear on the input shaft.

17 Locate the input shaft and mainshaft front bearings into the bearing seats and then, using a suitable screw press with tubular distance pieces, press the bearings into position.

18 Install the input shaft bearing snap-ring.

19 Check the countershaft thrust play in the same way as described for the mainshaft in paragraph 15 and select suitable shims.

20 Install the countershaft front and center bearings in a similar way to that described for those on the input shaft in paragraphs 16 and 17, again using the special tool inserted between 4th synchro ring and gear on the input shaft.

21 Install the snap-ring to secure the countershaft front bearing.

22 Install the bearing cover to the transmission case and tighten the four securing bolts.

Mainshaft and countershaft rear end components

23 Install the Reverse idler gear and then slide the counter Reverse gear and spacer onto the countershaft.

24 Install the spacer and key to the mainshaft and then slide on the Reverse gear and synchro assembly. Install a new locknut hand-tight.

25 Using a screwdriver to move the synchro sleeves, engage 2nd and Reverse gears to lock up the mainshaft. Using a torque wrench, tighten the locknut to the setting given in Specifications. Stake the locknut on completion.

26 Locate 2nd/3rd synchro sleeve in 3rd gear and then check the clearance between the synchro key and the exposed edge of the synchro

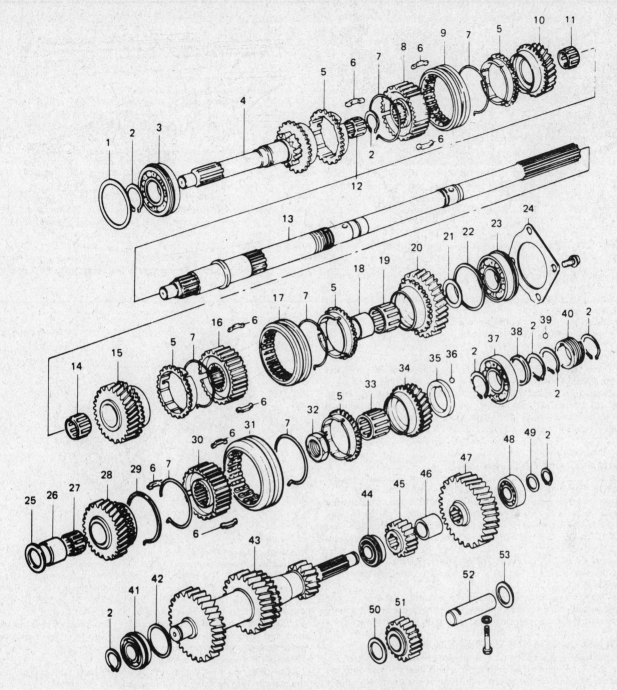

Fig. 13.57 5-speed transmission — gear train components (Sec 8)

1 Shim	15 2nd gear	29 Stop ring	42 Shim
2 Snap-ring	16 1st-and-2nd clutch hub	30 Rev-and-5th clutch hub	43 Countershaft
3 Main driveshaft bearing	17 Clutch sleeve	31 Clutch sleeve	44 Countershaft center
4 Main driveshaft gear	18 Bearing inner race	32 Mainshaft locknut	bearing
5 Synchronizer ring	19 Needle bearing	33 Needle bearing	45 Counter reverse gear
6 Synchronizer key	20 1st gear	34 5th gear	46 Spacer
7 Synchronizer key spring	21 Thrust washer	35 Thrust washer	47 Reverse gear
8 3rd-and-4th clutch hub	22 Shim	36 Lock-ball	48 Countershaft rear bearing
9 Clutch sleeve	23 Mainshaft front bearing	37 Mainshaft rear bearing	49 Thrust washer
10 3rd gear	24 Bearing cover	38 Thrust washer	50 Thrust washer
11 Needle bearing	25 Thrust washer	39 Lock-ball	51 Reverse idler gear
12 Needle bearing	26 Bearing inner race	40 Speedometer drive gear	52 Idler gear shaft
13 Mainshaft	27 Needle bearing	41 Countershaft front	53 Thrust washer
14 Needle bearing	28 Reverse gear	bearing	

13

ring using a feeler blade. If the measurement is greater than 0.079 in (2.0 mm) there is a danger of the synchro key popping out of engagement unless the thrust washer which is located between the mainshaft front bearing and 1st gear is changed. Thrust washers are available in the following thicknesses in order that the synchro key clearance can be brought within that specified.

    0.098 in (2.5 mm)
    0.118 in (3.0 mm)
    0.138 in (3.5 mm)

27 Install the needle bearing and lockball to the mainshaft.
28 Place 5th synchro ring onto 5th gear and slide 5th gear onto the mainshaft so that the synchro ring is towards the front of the shaft. Rotate the gear as necessary to engage the synchro keys and notches.
29 Install the thrust washer to the rear face of 5th gear and then install the snap-ring. Now check the clearance between the thrust washer and snap-ring with a feeler blade. If it is not as specified, change the thrust washer for one from the nine different thicknesses available.

Shifter and selector components
30 Working from the rear of the transmission case, slide the 1st/2nd shift shaft into the case. Secure the fork to the shaft with the lockbolt.
31 Insert the interlock pin into the hole just forward and below the oil filler plug on the side of the transmission casing.

32 From the rear of the transmission case, slide in 3rd/4th shift shaft and fit its shift fork.
33 From the rear of the transmission case, slide in reverse/5th shift shaft and install its shift fork.
34 Insert the three detent balls and springs into the transmission case followed by the spring cap bolts.
35 Install the two blind covers and gaskets.
36 Apply a film of gasket cement to the mating faces of the center housing and transmission case and install the center housing. Make sure that the Reverse idler gear shaft boss is aligned with the fixing bolt boss.
37 Slide the counter 5th gear onto the countershaft so that the F-mark on the gear is toward the front end of the shaft.
38 Press the countershaft rear bearing into position using a suitable hand press and tubular distance piece.
39 Fit the thrust washer and snap-ring to the rear of the countershaft rear bearing then check the clearance between the thrust washer and snap-ring with a feeler blade. Adjust the clearance if necessary to bring it within that specified by changing the thrust washer for one of four different thicknesses available.
40 Install the mainshaft rear bearing, the thrust washer and snap-ring. Again check the clearance and adjust if necessary as described in the preceding paragraph.

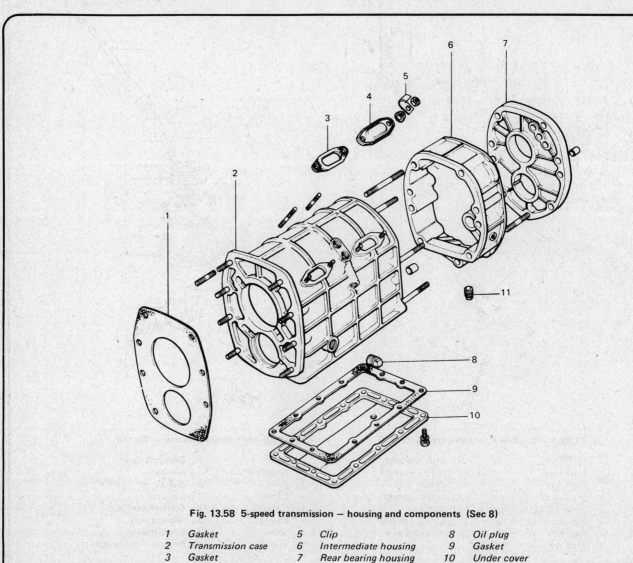

Fig. 13.58 5-speed transmission — housing and components (Sec 8)

1	Gasket	5	Clip	8	Oil plug
2	Transmission case	6	Intermediate housing	9	Gasket
3	Gasket	7	Rear bearing housing	10	Under cover
4	Blind cover			11	Oil plug

41 Apply a thin film of gasket cement to the mating faces of the bearing housing and center bearing. Locate the bearing housing on the center housing.

42 Install the shift shaft ends (dogs) to their respective shafts making reference to the scribe marks made before dismantling. Tighten the lockbolts.

43 Install the snap-ring, lock ball, speedometer drive gear and second snap-ring onto the mainshaft.

44 Insert the gearshift control lever through the holes, working from the front of the extension housing. Install the Woodruff key and slide the gearshift control lever end fitting onto the lever. Install the lockbolt.

45 Install the spring and friction piece into the extension housing and tighten the spring cap bolt.

46 Smear the mating surfaces of the extension housing and bearing housing with gasket cement, and then with the gearshift control lever

depressed to the left as far as it will go, bolt the extension housing to the bearing housing.

External components

47 Install the speedometer driven gear and lockplate.

48 Check the operation of the gearshift control.

49 Install the transmission case bottom cover using a new gasket.

50 Insert the select lock spindle and spring from the inside of the gearshift lever retainer. Set the lock ball and spring in alignment with the select lock spindle, and then tighten the spring cap bolt.

51 Bolt the gearshift lever retainer to the extension housing using a new gasket.

52 Measure the input shaft bearing thickness and the depth of the bearing recess in the clutch bellhousing. By subtraction, determine the thickness of the shim required to give the specified clearance.

53 Install the bellhousing, screw in and tighten the eight securing bolts.

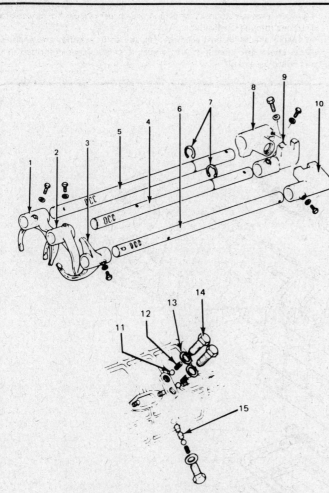

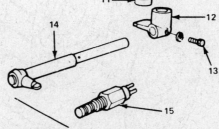

Fig. 13.59 Shift and selector components (Sec 8)

1	Shift fork	9	Shift rod end
2	Shift fork	10	Shift rod end
3	Shift fork	11	Detent ball
4	3rd-and-4th shift rod	12	Detent spring
5	1st-and-2nd shift rod	13	Washer
6	Rev-and-5th shift rod	14	Spring cap bolt
7	Stop ring	15	Interlock pin
8	Shift rod end		

Fig. 13.60 Shift lever components (Sec 8)

1	Knob	9	Gearshift lever
2	Gearshift lever		retainer
3	Boot	10	Gasket
4	Cover	11	Ball seat
5	Gasket	12	Control lever end
6	Spring	13	Reamer bolt
7	Shim	14	Control lever
8	Bush	15	Reverse lamp switch

13

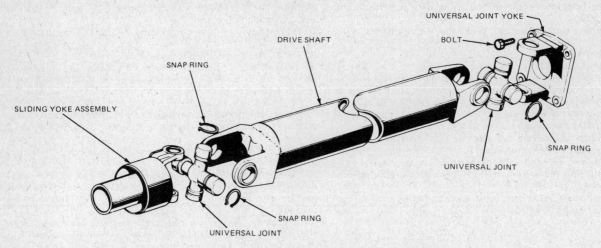

Fig. 13.61 One-piece driveshaft assembly (Sec 9)

9 Driveshaft

1   From 1977 to 1982, both two-section and single-section driveshafts are used depending upon the vehicle model and drive train with which it is equipped.

Single section type — removal

2   Unbolt the rear flange from the rear axle pinion flange and withdraw the shaft front sliding yoke from the transmission. Always mark the relative position of mating rear flanges before removal to ensure correct positioning on installation.

Universal joints

3   The overhaul of the universal joints on single-section driveshafts is carried out as described in Chapter 7.

4   It should be noted that the snap-rings which retain the bearing cups in position are located against the inner faces of the yokes. Make sure that the snap-rings used on each side of the same yoke are of identical thickness in order to maintain balance of the shaft. Snap-rings should be selected which will give a slight drag to the joint but which cannot be mistaken for binding.

10 Brakes

Description

1   Vehicles built from 1977 through 1982 are equipped with disc front brakes and a booster vacuum servo unit as standard equipment.

Brake shoes and pads — inspection (general note)

2   When examining the brake shoes and disc pads, take extreme care not to inhale any dust which may be brushed from them.

Brake pedal free travel — adjustment

3   A free movement of between 0.33 in (8.5 to 10.0 mm) should be maintained at the pedal pad on all vehicles equipped with a booster.

4   To adjust, release the locknut on the pushrod and turn the pushrod as necessary.

5   Tighten the locknut on completion to 20 ft-lbs torque.

Front disc pads — inspection and replacement

6   Raise the front of the vehicle, support securely and then remove the wheels.

7   Remove the four lock clips.

8   Tap out the two stopper plates using a thin drift.

9   Remove the caliper body and anti-rattle spring. Take care not to allow the caliper body to hang from the flexible hose. Instead wire it up to support its weight.

10 Inspect the thickness of the friction material of the pads. If it has worn down to 0.079 in (2.0 mm) or less, the pads must be replaced with new ones.

11 If the pads are in good condition, brush away any dust *avoiding*

inhaling it, and then reassemble the caliper by reversing the dismantling operations.

12 To replace the pads, remove them together with the shims and brush away any dust. *Avoid inhaling it.*

13 The caliper piston must now be depressed to accomodate the new thicker pads. This action will cause the fluid level in the master cylinder reservoir to rise and steps must therefore be taken to prevent overflowing. One of two methods may be used; either draw some fluid out of the reservoir using a poultry baster or old hydrometer, or release the bleed screw on the caliper at the precise moment that the piston is depressed and eject some of the hudraulic fluid into a container. Whichever method is used, discard the ejected fluid.

14 Install the new pads and shims, the anti-rattle spring and caliper body.

15 Apply a thin film of grease to the stopper plates and install them followed by the four locking clips.

16 Depress the brake pedal completely several times to bring the new pads into contact with the disc (rotor).

17 Always replace the front disc pads as an axle set, so the pads on the opposite wheel should now be replaced.

18 Install the wheels and lower the vehicle to the ground.

Front calipers — removal, overhaul and installation

19 Raise the front of the vehicle and support it securely on stands.

20 Remove the wheel.

21 Disconnect the hydraulic brake line at the front wheel apron. Cap the ends of the lines to prevent loss of fluid and entry of dirt.

22 Remove the clip which retains the flexible brake hose and release it from the front wheel apron.

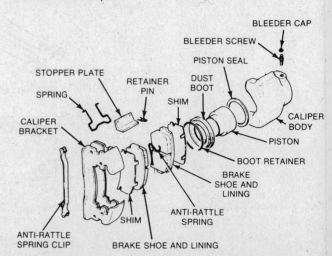

Fig. 13.62 Front disc brake caliper assembly (Sec 10)

23 Remove the bolts which hold the caliper bracket and remove the caliper and bracket.

24 The caliper is a single piston design and may be overhauled in the following way:

25 Clean away all external dirt.

26 Remove the retainer and flexible dust boot.

27 To remove the piston, apply air pressure to the brake line hole on the caliper body. Only low air pressure is needed to eject the piston such as can be generated by a hand pump. Take care not to trap the fingers as the piston comes out, and do not let the piston become damaged by striking the caliper body or by it dropping to the floor

28 Once the piston is removed, use a plastic tool or wood to pry out the seal from the caliper bore and discard it.

29 Examine the surfaces of the piston and caliper bore. If any scoring or 'bright' wear areas are evident, the caliper should be replaced as a complete assembly.

30 If these components are in good condition, obtain a repair kit which will contain the necessary seal and other items.

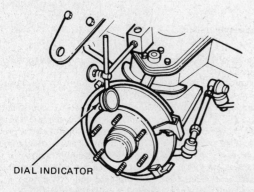

DIAL INDICATOR

Fig. 13.63 Checking brake disc runout (Sec 10)

31 Install the new seal into the cylinder bore using the fingers only to manipulate it into position.

32 Dip the piston in clean brake fluid and install it squarely into the cylinder.

33 Install the dust boot and its retainer.

34 Installation is a reversal of removal. On completion, bleed the front hydraulic circuit as described for tandem master cylinder (dual circuits) in Chapter 9, Section 4.

Front brake disc (rotor) — examination and replacement

35 Whenever the disc pads are being inspected, always check the discs themselves.

36 Light scoring is normal but any deep grooves or severe erosion due to rust must be removed.

37 The disc can be refaced, provided the final thickness of the disc will not be reduced below 0.433 in (11.0 mm) If this cannot be achieved, the disc must be replaced after dismantling the front hub as described previously.

38 Disc run-out (out-of-true) can give rise to faulty front brake operation and, if this is suspected, use a dial gauge to check that runout is within that specified. Before carrying out such a check, make sure that the hub bearings are correctly adjusted and unworn.

Tandem master cylinder and dual hydraulic circuit.

39 The master cylinder is mounted on the front face of the brake booster servo unit. The master cylinder can be unbolted from the servo unit once the rigid pressure lines and the reservoir connecting hoses have been disconnected from it.

40 The overhaul operations are similar to those described in Chapter 9, Section 11, but the slight variation in the design of the components will be observed from the accompanying illustration.

Brake booster — removal and installation

41 With the master cylinder mounted on the front face of the booster unit, removal may be done in one of three ways:

   a) *Remove the complete booster/master cylinder assembly.*

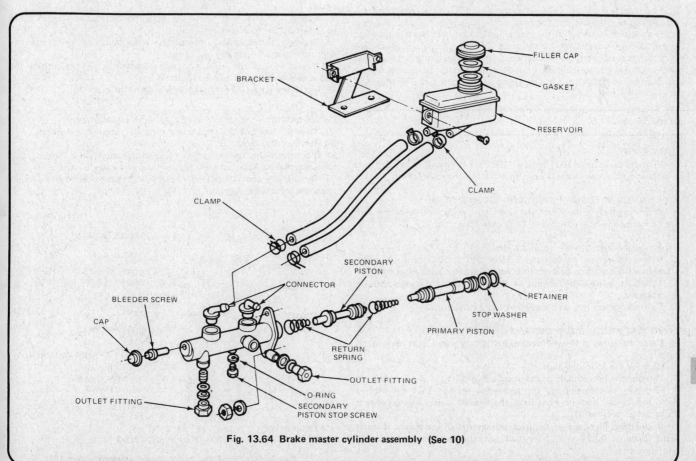

Fig. 13.64 Brake master cylinder assembly (Sec 10)

13

b) Remove the master cylinder first, separately.
c) Unbolt the master cylinder from the booster unit and without disconnecting the fluid lines, pull it just far enough forward to be able to unbolt and remove the booster. If this method is adopted, take care not to strain the pipelines.

42 Disconnect the booster pushrod from the brake pedal by removing the clevis and cotter pins.

43 Disconnect the vacuum hose.

44 Unscrew and remove the nuts from the booster mounting studs and remove the booster.

45 When installing a new booster, it is important that the specified clearance (0.004 to 0.020 in/0.1 to 0.5 mm) is maintained between the end of the master cylinder primary piston and the tip of the booster pushrod. This can only be measured satisfactorily using a narrow depth gauge. If adjustment is required, release the locknut on the booster pushrod, and screw the pushrod screw in or out. Retighten the locknut on completion.

Brake booster — overhaul

46 It is not recommended that the unit is dismantled. In the event of an overhaul being needed, exchange the complete assembly for a new or factory rebuilt one.

10 Electrical system

Fuses

1 1976 vehicles incorporate a seven-circuit fuseblock.
2 The fuse arrangement is as follows:

Fuse No.	Amp rating	Circuit protected
1	*15*	*Heated rear window*
2	*15*	*Horn, hazard warning lamps and flasher*
3	*15*	*Horn, hazard warning, turn signal, stop lamps*
4	*15*	*Engine, regulator, ignition coil, fuel pump, emission control*
5	*15*	*Instrument panel lamps, back-up lamps, turn signal flasher unit and lamps*
6	*15*	*Windshield wipers, washers, fuel gauge temperature gauge, brake warning lamp*
7	*15*	*Heater and radio*

3 The fuse block is located in the rear left-hand corner of the engine compartment.
4 1977 vehicles incorporate a nine-circuit fuse block.
5 The fuse arrangment is as follows:

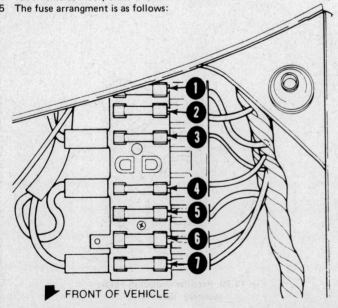

Fig. 13.65 Fuse block — 1976 vehicles (Sec 11)

Fuse No.	Amp rating	Circuit protected
1	*15*	*Horn, horn relay, stop lamps, hazard warning flasher, interior lamp, cigar lighter*
2	*15*	*Underhood lamp, glovebox lamp, heated rear window*
3	*15*	*Headlamps (high beam) and indicator lamp*
4	*15*	*Headlamps (low beam)*
5	*10*	*Taillights, rear license plate, front parking, front side marker instrument panel, ashtray and auto-transmission indicator lamps*
6	*10*	*Windshield wipers and washers*
7	*15*	*Heater blower motor, radio, defroster switch and relay*
8	*10*	*Front and rear turn signal lamps, turn signal relay and indicator lamps, turn signal flasher, seat belt warning lamp and buzzer, oil pressure and brake warning lamps, fuel and temperature gauges, alternator warning, back-up lamps*
9	*15*	*Regulator, fuel pump, choke solenoid, EGR 3-way solenoid, kickdown solenoid, coasting richer solenoid.*

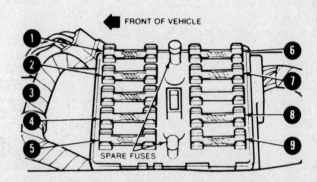

Fig. 13.66 Fuse block — 1977 vehicles (1978 -1982 similar) (Sec 11)

Fusible link

6 On 1977 through 1982 vehicles, the previously-used master fuse has been replaced with a fusible link still located on the right fender apron.
7 Never replace a master fuse or fusible link until the source of trouble has been traced and the fault rectified.
8 1978 and 1979 vehicles have the same fusible link as 1977 models, but use a ten fuse block in the following configuration:

Fuse No.	Amp rating	Circuit protected
1	*15*	*Horn, stop system, hazard warning flasher, interior light, lighter*
2	*15*	*Hood light, glove box light, rear window defroster*
3	*---*	*Blank*
4	*15*	*Headlights (high beam)*
5	*15*	*Headlights (low beam)*
6	*10*	*Taillights, license plate light, front parking lights and side markers, instrument panel lights*
7	*10*	*Windshield wipers and washers*
8	*15*	*Heater blower motor, radio*
9	*10*	*Turn signal lights, oil pressure and brake system warning lights, fuel gauge, engine temperature gauge, back-up lights*
10	*15*	*Engine electrics*

9 1980 through 1982 models use the same fusible link as previous models and a ten fuse block in the following configuration:

Fuse No.	Amp rating	Circuit protected
1	15	Engine electrics
2	10	Turn signal lights, oil pressure light, brake warning light, fuel gauge, engine temperature gauge, back-up lights
3	---	Blank
4	15	Heater blower motor, radio
5	10	Windshield wipers and washers
6	10	Taillights, license plate light, front parking lights and side markers, instrument panel lights
7	15	Headlights (low beam)
8	15	Headlights (high beam)
9	15	Hood light, glove box lights, rear window defroster
10	15	Horn, stop system, hazard warning light, interior light, lighter

Alternator — Removal, testing and installation — 1982 model

10 The alternator charging system consists of a 35 amp (490 watt) alternator, with built-in regulator, an ammeter, battery, fuse and associated wiring. It is mounted differently than previous units and requires a different in-vehicle testing procedure.

11 To remove the alternator, open the hood and disconnect the battery ground cable.

12 Disconnect the wire at the alternator single-wire terminal and pull the block connector from the rear of the alternator.

13 Remove the single strap bolt, rock the alternator toward the engine block and pull the drive belt off the alternator pulley.

14 Remove the pivot bolt from the bracket at the bottom of the alternator.

Alternator — In-vehicle tests

15 Before performing any tests, check all electrical connections for corrosion and looseness. Check the drivebelt tension and battery terminals.

16 With the ignition switch Off, use a voltmeter to check the voltage at the 'B' terminal on the alternator and on the battery. Both voltages should be the same.

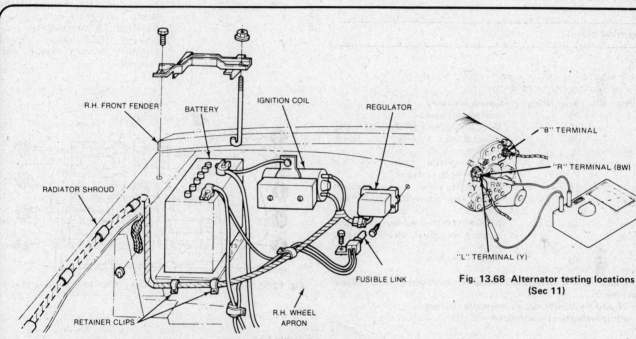

Fig. 13.67 Location of fusible link — 1977 through 1982 (Sec 11)

Fig. 13.68 Alternator testing locations (Sec 11)

Fig 13.69 Location of 'F' terminal (Sec 11)

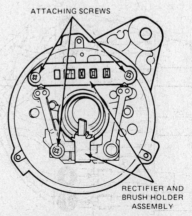

Fig. 13.70 Rectifier and brush-holder assembly (Sec 11)

13

17 Check the 'R' terminal (BW) voltage and the 'L' terminal (Y) voltage at the alternator. If either voltage reads other than zero, the alternator, not the regulator, is causing the problem and should be removed, disassembled and tested.

18 Turn the ignition switch to the On position and check the 'L' terminal (Y) voltage. This should be about two volts. If the reading is zero, the alternator and regulator are causing the problem.

19 If the voltage reading in the above test is approximately that of the battery voltage, short-circuit the 'F' terminal to the rear alternator bracket. Read the 'L' terminal voltage again. If the voltage is lower than the battery voltage, the regulator is at fault. If the voltage is still close to that of the battery, the alternator is at fault.

Alternator — Bench tests

20 The alternator must first be disassembled.

21 Remove the through-bolts and separate the front housing assembly with a large screwdriver.

22 Unsolder the stator leads from the rectifier. This should be done in less than 20 seconds to avoid damage to the rectifier.

23 Remove the stator, then remove the three screws attaching the rectifier/brush holder and remove these units.

24 Remove the pulley, fan, spacer and front washer.

25 Remove the front housing and rear washer.

26 If bearing replacement is necessary, remove the rear bearing from the rotor shaft using a suitable puller.

27 To replace the front bearing, remove the bearing retainer and press the bearing out from the front housing. The bearings are pre-lubricated and do not require additional lubrication.

28 Brushes should be replaced when they are worn to the wear limit line on the side of each brush. Brush spring tension should be 11 to 15 ounces. Replace weak or corroded springs.

29 Turn to Chapter 10, Section 9 and perform the two stator tests, the open rotor test, the grounded rotor test, and the diode (rectifier) test. Replace any defective components.

30 Reassemble the alternator in the reverse of disassembly, noting the following points.

31 When installing the rotor assembly to the rear housing and stator assembly, hold the brushes in position by inserting a piece of stiff wire into the brush hole, through the rear housing.

32 Soldering the rectifier leads should be done quickly (20 seconds or less) to avoid rectifier damage.

33 Adjust the drivebelt tension according to the procedure in Chapter 10.

Lighting system — 1979 through 1982

34 Later model vehicles have different side marker light assemblies, taillight assemblies, parking light assemblies and license plate light assemblies. All bulbs are of the same voltage except for the 1982 headlight. See the Specifications for the proper lights for these units.

Side marker lamps

35 The side marker lamps can be serviced similarly to the procedure described in Chapter 10, Section 18. Note the additional gasket behind the light body and the fact that there is no nut on the screw.

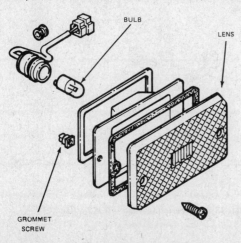

Fig. 13.71 Side-marker light assembly (Sec 11)

Parking lights

36 To remove the parking light body, disconnect the parking light wires at the connectors. Remove the retaining screws and pull the parking light body from the bumper and remove the light. To replace the parking light bulb, remove the bulb from the light body by rotating it and pulling the socket from the body. Remove the bulb by pushing it into the socket and twisting it counterclockwise.

37 To install the bulb push it into the socket and rotate it clockwise.

38 Check the operation of the parking light and turn signal.

39 Replace the parking light body into the bumper in the reverse of removal procedure.

License light bulb, lens and housing

40 To remove the license light, disconnect the wire at the connector and working behind the license support bracket, remove the two screws attaching the light assembly to the vehicle. Remove the light assembly.

41 Remove the two cover attaching screws and remove the cover from the light body. To remove the bulb, depress the bulb in the socket and rotate it counterclockwise.

42 Reassemble the license light bulb and housing in the reverse of the disassembly procedure.

Taillight/backup light

43 Later model trucks have a combination taillight assembly. Remove the six lens attaching screws and remove the lens. To remove the bulb, press the bulb in the socket and rotate it counterclockwise. To install the bulb, position it in the socket, press it inward and rotate it clockwise. Position the lens to the light body and install the six attaching screws.

44 The taillight assembly can be removed by disconnecting the wires at the connectors and unhooking the wires from the wire clip. Then remove the four bolts retaining the taillight assembly to the box in the rear fender. Remove the taillight. Replace the taillight assembly in the reverse order of disassembly.

Combination switch — 1982 only

45 The combination switch is mounted to the steering column and will have to be replaced as a complete assembly if there are any defects.

46 To remove the combination switch assembly disconnect the battery ground cable and remove the steering wheel (Chapter 11). Remove the steering column shroud and disconnect the multiple connectors at the combination switch.

47 Remove the switch retaining snap-ring and pull the turn indicator cancelling cam off the shaft.

48 Remove the one retaining bolt near the bottom of the switch and pull the complete switch from the column.

49 To install the combination switch, position the switch on the steering column and install the one retaining bolt.

50 Position the turn indicator cancelling cam and install the snap-ring.

51 Connect the block connectors at the combination switch assembly and install the steering column shroud.

52 Install the steering wheel and reconnect the battery ground cable.

53 Check the operation of the switch.

---

12 Suspension and steering

Front shock absorber — installation

1 When attaching the upper mounting, tighten the nut until the length of the exposed thread above the nut conforms to that shown.

Front wheel bearing — adjustment

2 The following revised adjustment procedure is now recommended for the front wheel bearings.

3 Raise the wheel off the ground.

4 Pry off the hub cap and remove the grease cap.

5 Wipe away excess grease so that the cotter pin and nut lock can be removed.

6 Rotate the wheel, at the same time tightening the hub nut to a torque of between 17 and 25 lbf ft (2.3 and 3.5 kgf m).

7 Back off the nut ¼ turn.

8 Install the nut lock so that the two notches are aligned with the cotter pin hole, then insert a new pin and bend the ends well over.

9 Install the grease cap and hub cap. **Note:** *On later vehicles equipped*

with disc front brakes, should any confusion arise when carrying out the adjustment operation because of the rubbing of the brake pads on the disc, the pads should be removed before adjustment begins.

Rear shock absorber — installation
10 When connecting the upper and lower mountings, tighten the nuts until the lengths of the exposed threads conform to the dimensions shown.

Steering gear — removal and installation (1977 through 1981)
11 Disconnect the battery negative lead.
12 Remove the steering wheel.
13 Remove the shrouds from the upper steering column.
14 Remove the snap-ring from the top of the steering shaft.
15 Remove the combination switch from the upper end of the steering shaft.
16 Unbolt the steering column upper clamp.
17 Pull the carpet away from the bottom of the steering column and unbolt the toe-plate and boot from the dash panel.
18 Unscrew the jacket lower bolt and withdraw the jacket from the steering shaft.
19 Remove the air cleaner.

20 Disconnect the heater hose clips and move the hoses out of the way of the steering shaft.
21 Disconnect the hydraulic lines from the brake and clutch master cylinders. Plug or cap the openings.
22 Unbolt and remove the brake booster/master cylinder, and the clutch master cylinder.
23 Working under the vehicle, disconnect the Pitman arm from the steering shaft using a heavy duty extractor.
24 Unbolt and remove the steering gear from the frame but check for alignment shims located between the gear and frame, marking their exact position.
25 Withdraw the gear from the vehicle.
26 Installation is a reversal of removal but on completion, bleed the brake and clutch hydraulic systems.

Steering linkage (1977 through 1981)
27 The difference in components of the steering linkage will be observed from the accompanying illustration. Note particularly that the tie-rod ends are retained by locknuts, and not clamps as on earlier models.
28 Disassembly and reassembly is as described in Chapter 11, Section 14, but after reassembly always check and adjust the front wheel alignment (toe-in).

Fig. 13.72 Shock absorber upper mounts (Sec 12)

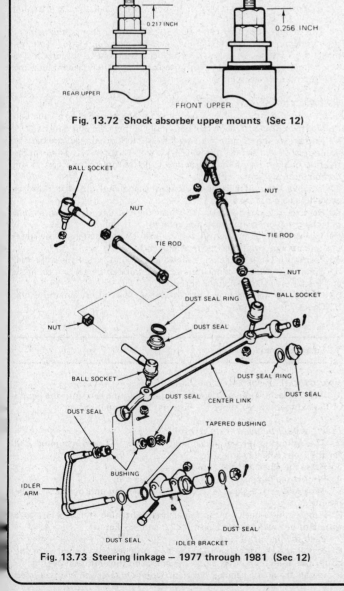

Fig. 13.73 Steering linkage — 1977 through 1981 (Sec 12)

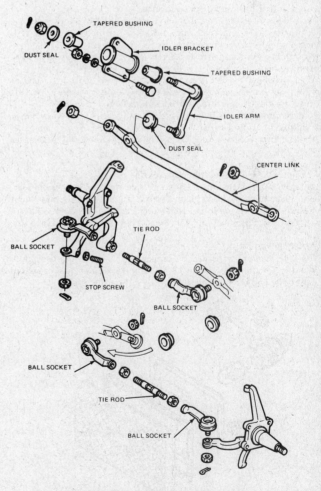

Fig. 13.74 Steering linkage — 1982 (Sec 12)

13

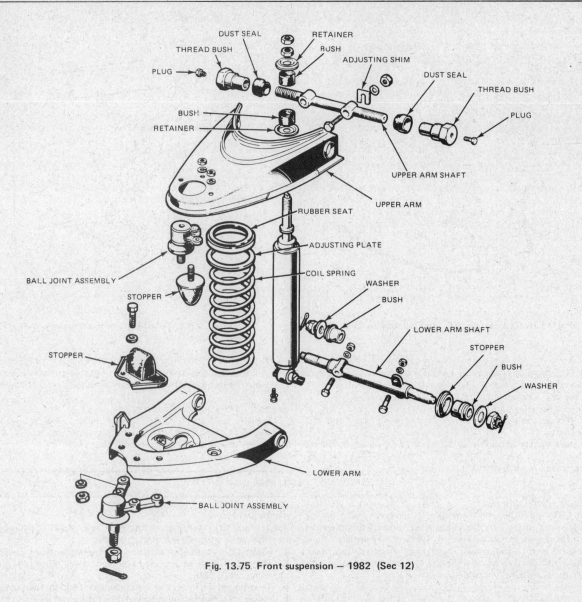

Fig. 13.75 Front suspension — 1982 (Sec 12)

29 The camber and caster adjusting shims are located between the upper arm shaft and the frame. Adding or removing shims equally will alter the camber. The upper arm pivot shaft has mounting bosses of unequal length and the shaft can be unbolted and turned through 180° to achieve greater adjustment. The caster angle can be altered by moving shims between the front and rear mounting bosses.

Front suspension — 1982
30 The front suspension was changed in 1982 in the following minor ways:
31 The balljoint assembly is now a sealed unit attached to the lower arm by four bolts rather than two. The dust seal has been eliminated.
32 The lower rubber stopper is now mounted to a plate and attached by four bolts instead of one.

Steering linkage/steering column (1982)
1 The steering linkage and steering column assembly was completely changed in 1982. These changes require a different procedure for removing the steering gear. Once removed, follow the procedures in Chapter 11 for steering gear disassembly, checking and reassembly.

Steering gear — removal and installation (1982)
Removal
2 Disconnect the negative battery cable at the battery.
3 Remove the horn cap from the center of the steering wheel and scribe an indexing mark on the steering wheel and the column shaft.

Remove the steering wheel by removing its retaining nut and washer.
4 Remove the steering column cover by removing the retaining screws.
5 Remove the stop-ring, cancel cam and spring from the end of the steering column shaft. Disconnect the combination switch assembly wiring connectors.
6 Remove the combination switch assembly by removing the single screw attaching the assembly to the column jacket.
7 Remove the steering column mounting bracket bolts from the dash panel. Pull the column jacket off of the steering shaft.
8 Clear the carpet and pad away from the bottom of the steering column and remove the bolts attaching the set plate to the dash panel.
9 Pull the steering shaft toward the rear of the vehicle and remove the bolts attaching the yoke joint to the worm shaft. Remove the steering shaft.
10 Disconnect the hoses from the air cleaner assembly. Remove the air cleaner assembly.
11 Remove the hydraulic lines from the brake master cylinder outlet and plug the lines and outlet to prevent fluid leakage.
12 Remove the master cylinder by removing its attaching nuts.
13 Raise the front end of the truck, support it with jackstands and remove the left front wheel.
14 Disconnect the center link from the idler arm. Remove the retaining nut from the idler arm and remove the idler arm.
15 Remove the bolts and nuts holding the steering gear assembly to the frame and remove the steering gear from the vehicle.

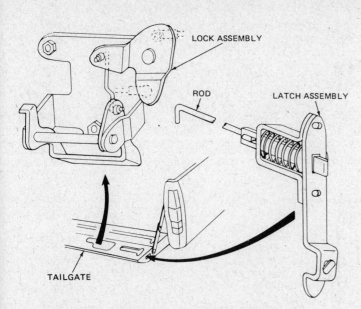

Fig. 13.76 Tailgate lock and latch assemblies (Sec 13)

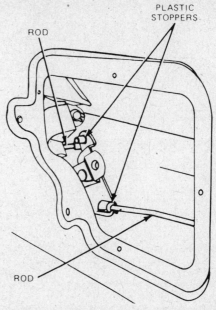

Fig. 13.77 Tailgate latch rod arrangement (Sec 13)

Installation

16 Install the steering gear assembly by reversing the removal procedure. Note the following:

17 Tighten the gear housing nuts to 33 to 41 ft-lbs.

18 Tighten the yoke joint bolt to 13 to 20 ft-lbs.

19 Be sure to align the indexing mark on the steering wheel with the mark on the shaft.

20 Fill the steering gear housing with 90 weight gear oil up to the oil level hole.

21 Bleed the brake lines (Chapter 11).

Turning angle — adjustment

22 Although this should be set on suitable equipment at your service station, the location of the lock stop bolts is just below the suspension lower balljoint on the steering knuckle at each side of the vehicle.

23 If you are carrying out adjustment as an emergency measure, make sure that under full steering lock conditions, the front tires do not rub against the frame or suspension components.

Wheel balancing

24 The wheels should be balanced statically and dynamically. If all the tires are of the same size it is an advantage to have them balanced off the vehicle as all four wheels can then be interchanged periodically to even-out tread wear.

25 If the tires are balanced on the vehicle, do not interchange the wheels, also, before removing a wheel, always mark the relationship of one of the mounting studs to the wheel so that the wheel can be re-installed in its original position in relation to the hub.

Wheels — removal and installation

26 Vehicles built from 1977 on no longer have wheel securing nuts on the left-hand side of the vehicle with left-hand threads. All wheel nuts now have conventional, right-hand threads.

12 Bodywork

Tailgate latches

1 As from 1977, vehicles are equipped with modified tailgate latches installed flush into the ends of the tailgate.

2 Support arms are substituted for the chains previously used.

3 The tailgate can be removed complete if the hinge pins are driven out using a thin drift.

4 To remove a latch, first remove the control handle (two screws).

5 Extract the five retaining screws from the cover-plate on the inside of the tailgate and remove the plate.

6 Pull off the plastic stoppers from the latch rods, and disconnect the rods from the latch.

7 Remove the lock assembly.

8 Remove the latch assembly (two screws).

9 Installation is a reversal of removal.

13

Code for wiring diagrams

Component	Location
Alternator...	G-2
Air control valve solenoid	G-12
Catalytic converter thermo-sensor	C-8
Choke control	J-19
Cigar lighter	B-23
Coasting richer valve	F-12
Control unit	G-8
Distributor	D-8
Downshift solenoid	B-15
EGR meter reset switch	F-4
EGR mileage warning light	G-19
EGR solenoid	K-13
Electric rear window defroster	D-19
Electric rear window defroster relay	B-20
Electric rear window defroster switch	B-18
Emission control box	F-8
Flashers:	
Emergency warning	D-26
Turn signal	B-28
Horn	C-23
Lamps:	
Back-up	G-6
Dome	B-19
Headlamps:	
Left	F-21
Right	E-21
License plate	H-30
Parking lamps:	
Left	J-25
Right	H-25
Side marker lamps	
Front:	
Left	J-25
Right	G-25
Rear:	
Left	J-30
Right	F-30
Tail lamps:	
Left	H-30
Right	G-30
Ignition coil	C-9
Ignition resistor	B-10
Illumination:	
Heater	D-23
Instrument cluster	E-24
PRNDL	F-24
Indicators:	
Ammeter	A-4
Brake warning	E-17
Fuel gauge	E-19
High beam	E-22
Oil pressure	E-18
Temperature gauge	E-20
Turn signal:	
Left	G-28
Right	G-26
Motors:	
Blower	D-10
Wiper	D-14
Starter	D-2
Pumps:	
Fuel	D-11
Washer	D-15
Regulator	J-6
Relays:	
Horn	C-24
Speed switch	H-10
Turn signal	F-28
Wiper	E-14
Seat belt seat switch	K-21
Seat belt timer	J-21
Seat belt warning buzzer	K-30
Seat belt warning light	G-22
Sender units:	
Fuel	G-18
Temperature	G-20
Slow fuel cut valve	F-12
Switches:	
Accelerator	G-12
Back-up lamp	E-16
Dimmer	H-17
Dome light	B-19
Dual brake warning	G-16
Emergency flasher	C-27
Fan	C-10
Horn	D-25
Headlight	D-22
Ignition	B-6
Instrument panel light:	
Resistor switch	H-18
Kickdown	B-13
Neutral start and back-up	E-5
Oil pressure	F-18
Parking brake	G-17
Passing high beam	D-21
Speed switch	H-10
Stoplight	C-26
Turn signal	C-28
Water thermo switch	H-18
Wiper/washer	G-14

Wiring color key

Black	BK
Green	DG
Grey	GY
Blue	DB
Light Blue	LB
Red	R
White	W
Yellow	Y
Brown	BR

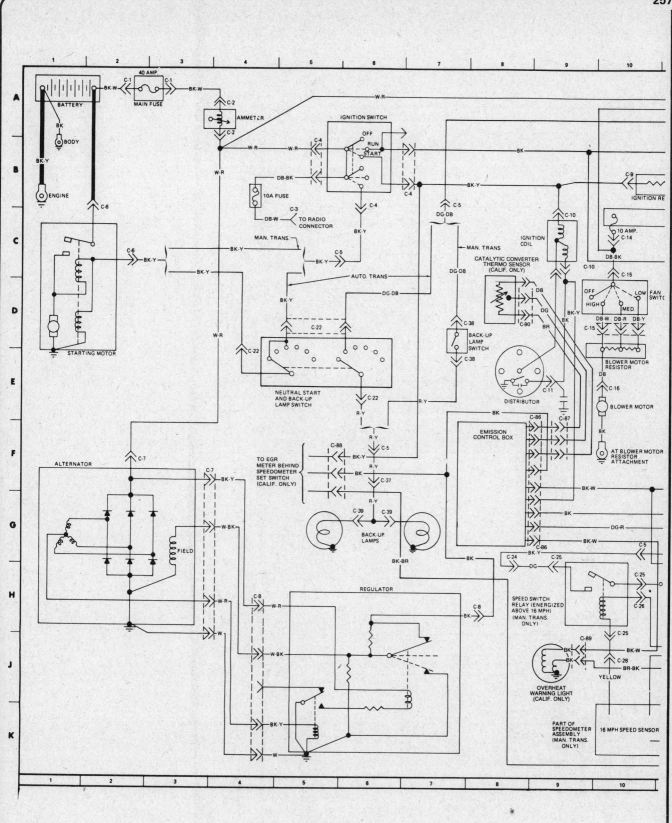

Wiring diagram for 1976 Ford Courier

11 12 13 14 15 16 18 19 20

DG-DB

AUTO. TRANS. ONLY

DG-DB

BK C-12 KICKDOWN SWITCH C-12 BK-R C-13 BK-R C-21 BK DOWNSHIFT SOLENOID (ON SIDE OF TRANS.)

C-9 BK C-81 Y-W Y-W

BK-W C-82 DB ELECTRIC REAR WINDOW DEFROSTER RELAY

LB

BK DOME LIGHT AND SWITCH ASSY.

SISTOR BK BK C-14 BUSS BAR (PART OF FUSE PANEL)

C-83 ELECTRIC REAR WINDOW DEFROSTER SWITCH

C-82 C-37 R

C-47 R

15 AMP. C-14 15 AMP. C-14 C-14 15 AMP. C-14

LB-BK

HEADLIGHT SWITCH ASSY.

HEADLI SWITCH

C-34 BK-W BK DB DB

C-17 WIPER MOTOR C-31 LOW HIGH

C-84 DG-DB DG-DB ELECTRIC REAR WINDOW DEFROSTER

PASSING HIGH BEA SWITCH

BK-W FUEL PUMP

WIPER PARK SWITCH — GOES TO GROUND IN ALL WIPER BLADE POSITIONS EXCEPT PARK

DB C-31 C-36 WASHER PUMP C-36

DG-DB DG-R

C-40 DG-DB I.V.R. (PART OF FUEL GAUGE ASSY.)

BRAKE WARNING LIGHT OIL PRESSURE LIGHT FUEL GAUGE TEMP. GAUGE

C-5 BK-W BK BK-W

C-18 SLOW FUEL CUT VALVE (THROTTLE SOLENOID) C-19 COASTING RICHER (DECELERATION VALVE)

DB-BK DB-W DB-R C-32

BK C-32 G

WIPER RELAY

C-40 R-BK Y-R YELLOW Y-W

C-37 C-46 C-5

C-44 C-45 C-41

RIGHT HEADLIGHT

MAN. TRANS. ONLY

BK-W C-72 BK AIR CONTROL VALVE SOLENOID C-20 ACCELERATE SWITCH — OPEN WHEN THROTTLE IS DEPRESSED C-20

C-32 Y-DG Y-BK C-33

BK R-BK R-BK

C-42 C-43

OIL PRESSURE SWITCH

LEFT HEADLIGHT

BK W R DB DB-Y

BK-Y

LOW HIGH OFF ON WASH OFF WASHER

FUEL TANK SENDER

C-85 BK-BR BK BK EGR MILEAGE WARNING LIGHT (CALIF. ONLY)

TEMP. SENDER

C-29 BK

DUAL BRAKE WARNING SWITCH PARKING BRAKE SWITCH

BR-R

C-35 BK WIPER/WASHER SWITCH

C-49 BK

C-73 WATER THERMO SWITCH C-74 BK-W

SEAT BELT TIMER

DG C-27 DG

BK C-75 INSTRUMENT PANEL LIGHT RESISTOR SWITCH

BK-W

CHOKE CONTROL C-73

BK BK BK BK-W

C-76 EGR SOLENOID (CALIF. ONLY) C-76 AT WIPER RELAY ATTACHMENT

BK-W BK-BR

SEAT BELT SEAT SWITCH

BK-W

BK

BK-BR

11 12 13 14 15 16 17 18 19 20

Wiring diagram for 1976 Ford Courier (contd.)

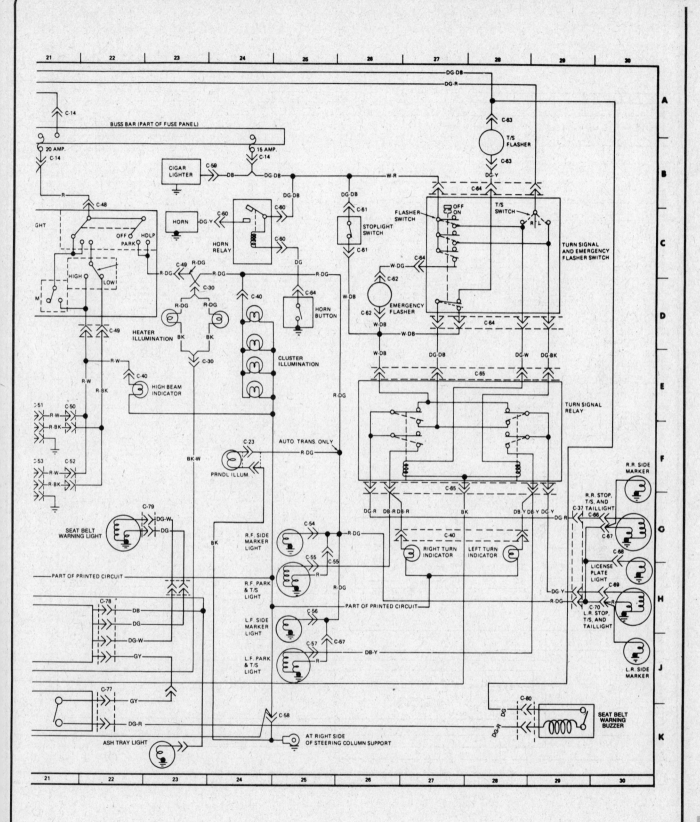

Wiring diagram for 1976 Ford Courier (contd.)

260

Wiring diagram for 1977 Ford Courier

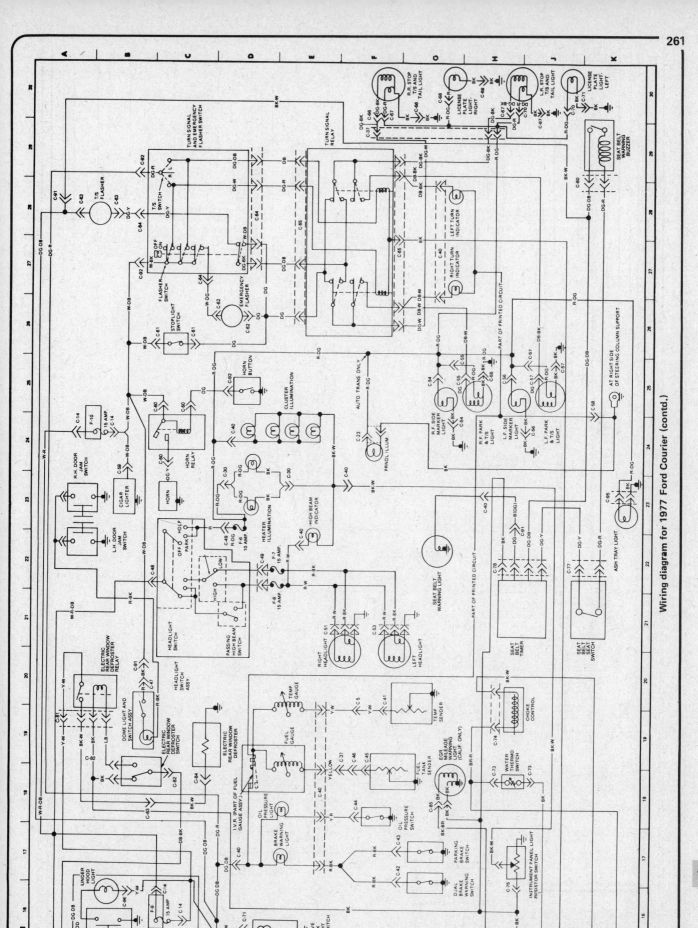

Wiring diagram for 1977 Ford Courier (contd.)

13

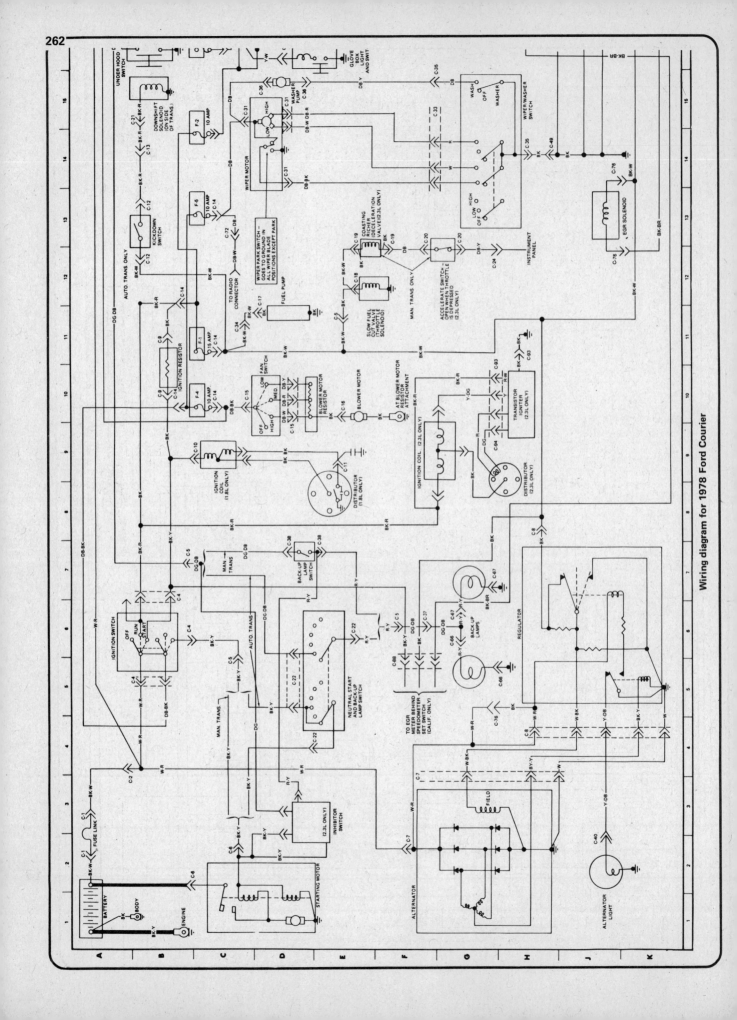

Wiring diagram for 1978 Ford Courier

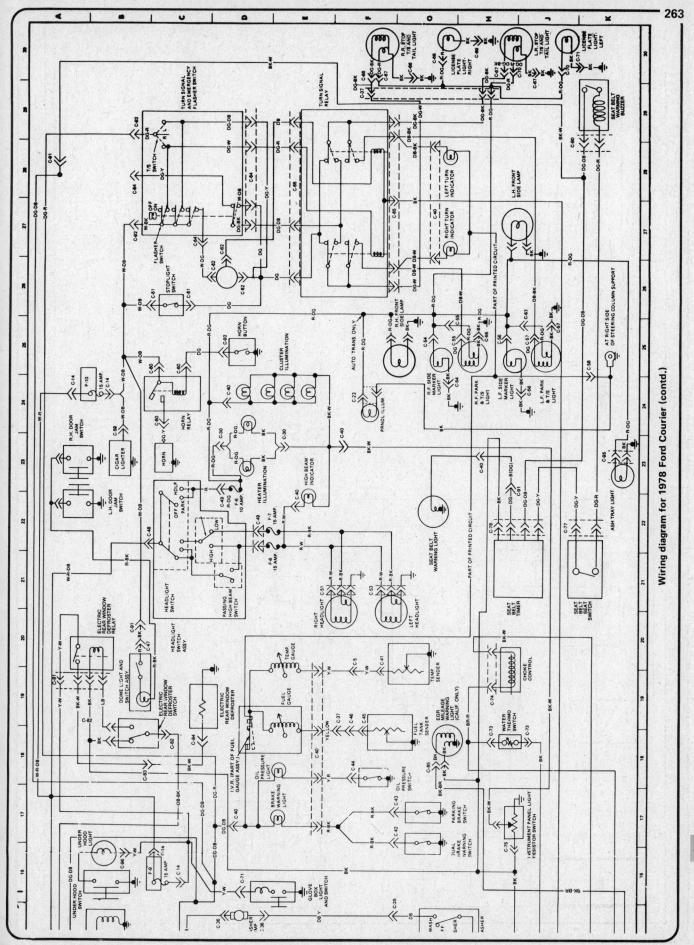

Wiring diagram for 1978 Ford Courier (contd.)

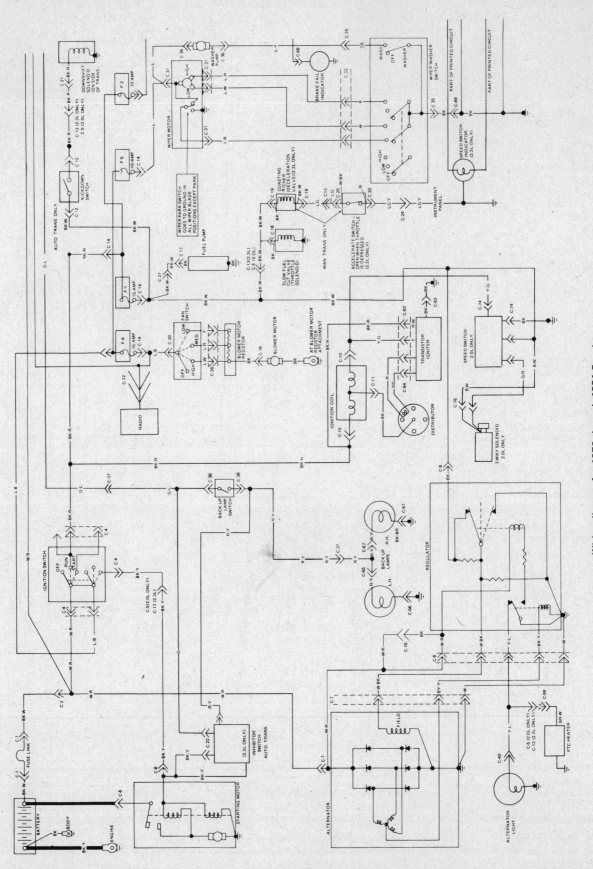

Wiring diagram for 1979 through 1981 Courier

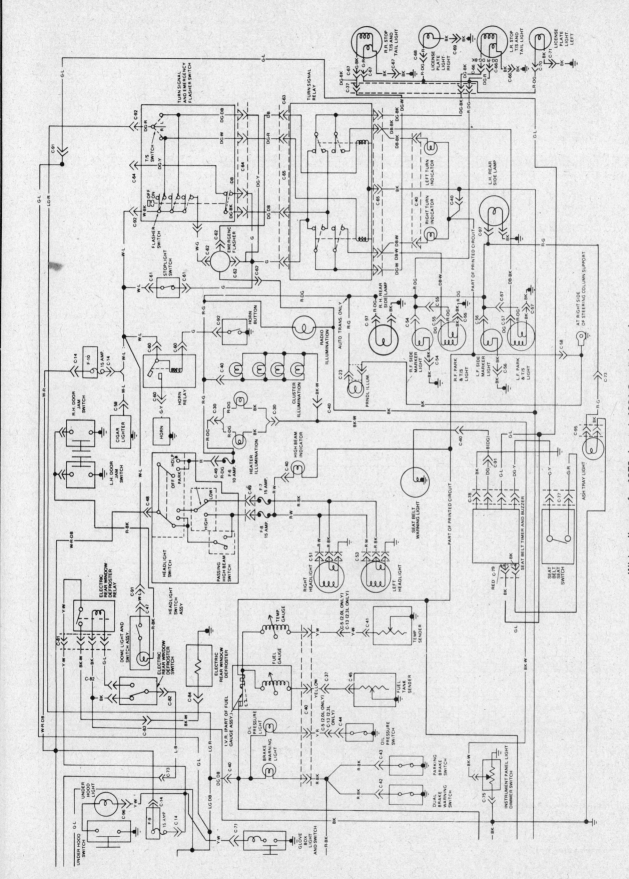

Wiring diagram for 1979 through 1981 Courier (cont)

13

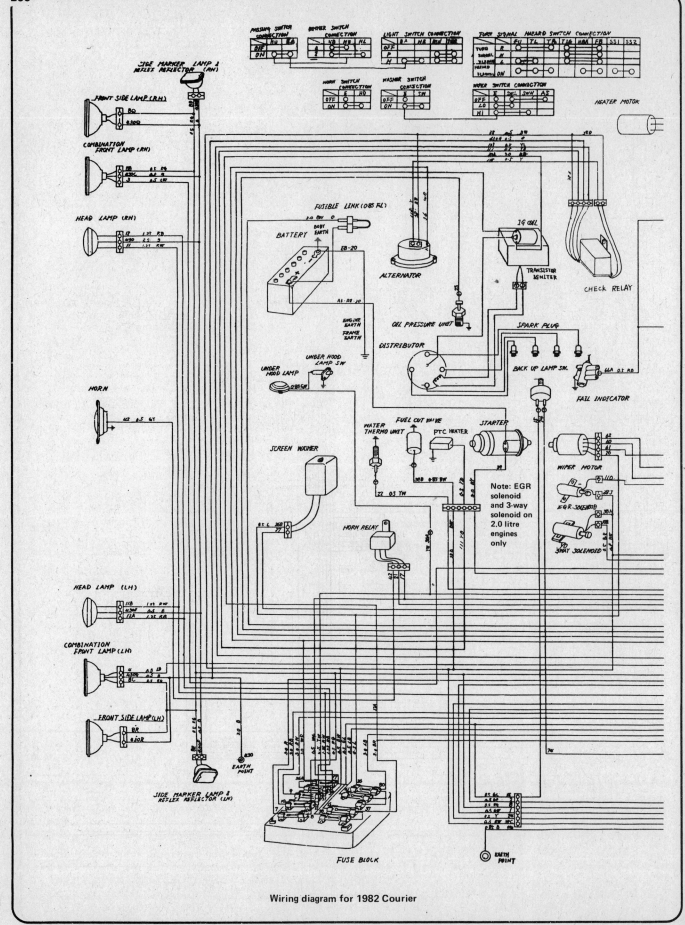

Wiring diagram for 1982 Courier

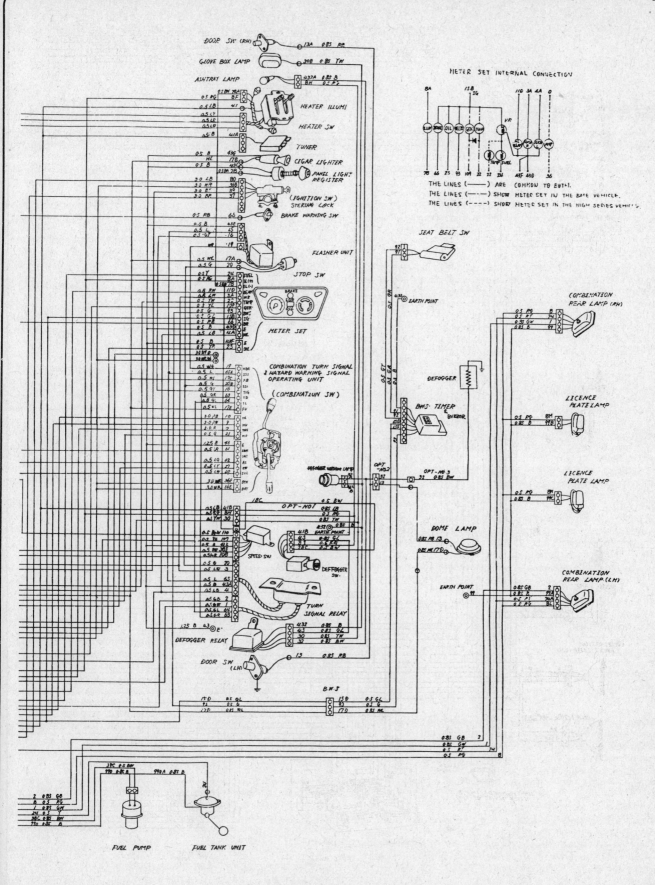

Wiring diagram for 1982 Courier (cont)

Safety first!

Regardless of how enthusiastic you may be about getting on with the job at hand, take the time to ensure that your safety is not jeopardized. A moment's lack of attention can result in an accident, as can failure to observe certain simple safety precautions. The possibility of an accident will always exist, and the following points should not be considered a comprehensive list of all dangers. Rather, they are intended to make you aware of the risks and to encourage a safety conscious approach to all work you carry out on your vehicle.

Essential DOs and DON'Ts

DON'T rely on a jack when working under the vehicle. Always use approved jackstands to support the weight of the vehicle and place them under the recommended lift or support points.

DON'T attempt to loosen extremely tight fasteners (i.e. wheel lug nuts) while the vehicle is on a jack — it may fall.

DON'T start the engine without first making sure that the transmission is in Neutral (or Park where applicable) and the parking brake is set.

DON'T remove the radiator cap from a hot cooling system — let it cool or cover it with a cloth and release the pressure gradually.

DON'T attempt to drain the engine oil until you are sure it has cooled to the point that it will not burn you.

DON'T touch any part of the engine or exhaust system until it has cooled sufficiently to avoid burns.

DON'T siphon toxic liquids such as gasoline, antifreeze and brake fluid by mouth, or allow them to remain on your skin.

DON'T inhale brake lining dust — it is potentially hazardous (see *Asbestos* below)

DON'T allow spilled oil or grease to remain on the floor — wipe it up before someone slips on it.

DON'T use loose fitting wrenches or other tools which may slip and cause injury.

DON'T push on wrenches when loosening or tightening nuts or bolts. Always try to pull the wrench toward you. If the situation calls for pushing the wrench away, push with an open hand to avoid scraped knuckles if the wrench should slip.

DON'T attempt to lift a heavy component alone — get someone to help you.

DON'T rush or take unsafe shortcuts to finish a job.

DON'T allow children or animals in or around the vehicle while you are working on it.

DO wear eye protection when using power tools such as a drill, sander, bench grinder, etc. and when working under a vehicle.

DO keep loose clothing and long hair well out of the way of moving parts.

DO make sure that any hoist used has a safe working load rating adequate for the job.

DO get someone to check on you periodically when working alone on a vehicle.

DO carry out work in a logical sequence and make sure that everything is correctly assembled and tightened.

DO keep chemicals and fluids tightly capped and out of the reach of children and pets.

DO remember that your vehicle's safety affects that of yourself and others. If in doubt on any point, get professional advice.

Asbestos

Certain friction, insulating, sealing, and other products — such as brake linings, brake bands, clutch linings, torque converters, gaskets, etc. — contain asbestos. *Extreme care must be taken to avoid inhalation of dust from such products since it is hazardous to health.* If in doubt, assume that they *do* contain asbestos.

Fire

Remember at all times that gasoline is highly flammable. Never smoke or have any kind of open flame around when working on a vehicle. But the risk does not end there. A spark caused by an electrical short circuit, by two metal surfaces contacting each other, or even by static electricity built up in your body under certain conditions, can ignite gasoline vapors, which in a confined space are highly explosive. Do not, under any circumstances, use gasoline for cleaning parts. Use an approved safety solvent.

Always disconnect the battery ground (–) cable *at the battery* before working on any part of the fuel system or electrical system. Never risk spilling fuel on a hot engine or exhaust component.

It is strongly recommended that a fire extinguisher suitable for use on fuel and electrical fires be kept handy in the garage or workshop at all times. Never try to extinguish a fuel or electrical fire with water.

Torch (flashlight in the US)

Any reference to a "torch" appearing in this manual should always be taken to mean a hand-held, battery-operated electric light or flashlight. It DOES NOT mean a welding or propane torch or blowtorch.

Fumes

Certain fumes are highly toxic and can quickly cause unconsciousness and even death if inhaled to any extent. Gasoline vapor falls into this category, as do the vapors from some cleaning solvents. Any draining or pouring of such volatile fluids should be done in a well ventilated area.

When using cleaning fluids and solvents, read the instructions on the container carefully. Never use materials from unmarked containers.

Never run the engine in an enclosed space, such as a garage. Exhaust fumes contain carbon monoxide, which is extremely poisonous. If you need to run the engine, always do so in the open air, or at least have the rear of the vehicle outside the work area.

If you are fortunate enough to have the use of an inspection pit, never drain or pour gasoline and never run the engine while the vehicle is over the pit. The fumes, being heavier than air, will concentrate in the pit with possibly lethal results.

The battery

Never create a spark or allow a bare light bulb near a battery. They normally give off a certain amount of hydrogen gas, which is highly explosive.

Always disconnect the battery ground (–) cable *at the battery* before working on the fuel or electrical systems.

If possible, loosen the filler caps or cover when charging the battery from an external source (this does not apply to sealed or maintenance-free batteries). Do not charge at an excessive rate or the battery may burst.

Take care when adding water to a non maintenance-free battery and when carrying a battery. The electrolyte, even when diluted, is very corrosive and should not be allowed to contact clothing or skin.

Always wear eye protection when cleaning the battery to prevent the caustic deposits from entering your eyes.

Mains electricity (household current in the US)

When using an electric power tool, inspection light, etc., which operates on household current, always make sure that the tool is correctly connected to its plug and that, where necessary, it is properly grounded. Do not use such items in damp conditions and, again, do not create a spark or apply excessive heat in the vicinity of fuel or fuel vapor.

Secondary ignition system voltage

A severe electric shock can result from touching certain parts of the ignition system (such as the spark plug wires) when the engine is running or being cranked, particularly if components are damp or the insulation is defective. In the case of an electronic ignition system, the secondary system voltage is much higher and could prove fatal.

Conversion factors

Length (distance)

Inches (in)	X	25.4	=	Millimetres (mm)	X	0.0394	= Inches (in)
Feet (ft)	X	0.305	=	Metres (m)	X	3.281	= Feet (ft)
Miles	X	1.609	=	Kilometres (km)	X	0.621	= Miles

Volume (capacity)

Cubic inches (cu in; in³)	X	16.387	=	Cubic centimetres (cc; cm³)	X	0.061	= Cubic inches (cu in; in³)
Imperial pints (Imp pt)	X	0.568	=	Litres (l)	X	1.76	= Imperial pints (Imp pt)
Imperial quarts (Imp qt)	X	1.137	=	Litres (l)	X	0.88	= Imperial quarts (Imp qt)
Imperial quarts (Imp qt)	X	1.201	=	US quarts (US qt)	X	0.833	= Imperial quarts (Imp qt)
US quarts (US qt)	X	0.946	=	Litres (l)	X	1.057	= US quarts (US qt)
Imperial gallons (Imp gal)	X	4.546	=	Litres (l)	X	0.22	= Imperial gallons (Imp gal)
Imperial gallons (Imp gal)	X	1.201	=	US gallons (US gal)	X	0.833	= Imperial gallons (Imp gal)
US gallons (US gal)	X	3.785	=	Litres (l)	X	0.264	= US gallons (US gal)

Mass (weight)

Ounces (oz)	X	28.35	=	Grams (g)	X	0.035	= Ounces (oz)
Pounds (lb)	X	0.454	=	Kilograms (kg)	X	2.205	= Pounds (lb)

Force

Ounces-force (ozf; oz)	X	0.278	=	Newtons (N)	X	3.6	= Ounces-force (ozf; oz)
Pounds-force (lbf; lb)	X	4.448	=	Newtons (N)	X	0.225	= Pounds-force (lbf; lb)
Newtons (N)	X	0.1	=	Kilograms-force (kgf; kg)	X	9.81	= Newtons (N)

Pressure

Pounds-force per square inch (psi; lbf/in²; lb/in²)	X	0.070	=	Kilograms-force per square centimetre (kgf/cm²; kg/cm²)	X	14.223	= Pounds-force per square inch (psi; lbf/in²; lb/in²)
Pounds-force per square inch (psi; lbf/in²; lb/in²)	X	0.068	=	Atmospheres (atm)	X	14.696	= Pounds-force per square inch (psi; lbf/in²; lb/in²)
Pounds-force per square inch (psi; lbf/in²; lb/in²)	X	0.069	=	Bars	X	14	= Pounds-force per square inch (psi; lbf/in²; lb/in²)
Pounds-force per square inch (psi; lbf/in²; lb/in²)	X	6.895	=	Kilopascals (kPa)	X	0.145	= Pounds-force per square inch (psi; lbf/in²; lb/in²)
Kilopascals (kPa)	X	0.01	=	Kilograms-force per square centimetre (kgf/cm²; kg/cm²)	X		= Kilopascals (kPa)
Millibar (mbar)	X	100	=	Pascals (Pa)	X	0.01	= Millibar (mbar)
Millibar (mbar)	X	0.0145	=	Pounds-force per square inch (psi; lbf/in²; lb/in²)	X	0.947	= Millibar (mbar)
Millibar (mbar)	X	0.75	=	Millimetres of mercury (mmHg)	X	1.333	= Millibar (mbar)
Millibar (mbar)	X	0.401	=	Inches of water (inH₂O)	X	2.491	= Millibar (mbar)
Millimetres of mercury (mmHg)	X	0.535	=	Inches of water (inH₂O)	X	1.868	= Millimetres of mercury (mmHg)
Inches of water (inH₂O)	X	0.036	=	Pounds-force per square inch (psi; lbf/in²; lb/in²)	X	27.68	= Inches of water (inH₂O)

Torque (moment of force)

Pounds-force inches (lbf in; lb in)	X	1.152	=	Kilograms-force centimetre (kgf cm; kg cm)	X	0.868	= Pounds-force inches (lbf in; lb in)
Pounds-force inches (lbf in; lb in)	X	0.113	=	Newton metres (Nm)	X	8.85	= Pounds-force inches (lbf in; lb in)
Pounds-force inches (lbf in; lb in)	X	0.083	=	Pounds-force feet (lbf ft; lb ft)	X	12	= Pounds-force inches (lbf in; lb in)
Pounds-force feet (lbf ft; lb ft)	X	0.138	=	Kilograms-force metres (kgf m; kg m)	X	7.233	= Pounds-force feet (lbf ft; lb ft)
Pounds-force feet (lbf ft; lb ft)	X	1.356	=	Newton metres (Nm)	X	0.738	= Pounds-force feet (lbf ft; lb ft)
Newton metres (Nm)	X	0.102	=	Kilograms-force metres (kgf m; kg m)	X	9.804	= Newton metres (Nm)

Power

Horsepower (hp)	X	745.7	=	Watts (W)	X	0.0013	= Horsepower (hp)

Velocity (speed)

Miles per hour (miles/hr; mph)	X	1.609	=	Kilometres per hour (km/hr; kph)	X	0.621	= Miles per hour (miles/hr; mph)

Fuel consumption*

Miles per gallon, Imperial (mpg)	X	0.354	=	Kilometres per litre (km/l)	X	2.825	= Miles per gallon, Imperial (mpg)
Miles per gallon, US (mpg)	X	0.425	=	Kilometres per litre (km/l)	X	2.352	= Miles per gallon, US (mpg)

Temperature

Degrees Fahrenheit = ($°C$ x 1.8) + 32   Degrees Celsius (Degrees Centigrade; °C) = (°F - 32) x 0.56

*It is common practice to convert from miles per gallon (mpg) to litres/100 kilometres (l/100km), where mpg (Imperial) x l/100 km = 282 and mpg (US) x l/100 km = 235

Index

A

Air cleaner — 51, 230
Alternator
  precautions — 136
  removal and installation — 136, 251
  testing and servicing — 137, 252
  testing in the vehicle — 136, 251
Antifreeze — 44
Automatic transmission
  brake band adjustment — 109
  description — 107
  fluid level checking — 109
  inhibitor switch — 111
  kick-down switch — 110
  removal and installation — 109
  selector lever — 110
  specifications — 107, 212
  torque wrench settings — 107
  vacuum diaphragm — 110
Auxiliary shaft — 219, 227, 228

B

Battery
  charging — 136
  electrolyte replenishment — 136
  maintenance — 135
  removal and installation — 135
Big-end bearings — see Connecting rod bearings
Bodywork
  capacities and dimensions — 186
  description — 186
  front bumper — 198
  instrument panel pad — 196
  maintenance — 188, 189
  radiator grille — 198
  rear window glass — 196
  repair, major damage — 189
  repair, minor damage — 188
  repair, minor damage (color) — 190, 191
  seat — 198
  specifications — 186, 213
  tailgate latches and hinges — 196, 255
  vent window — 193
Bonnet — 195
Braking system
  bleeding — 120
  brake adjustment — 119
  brake booster — 249, 250
  brake lines and hoses — 124
  brake pedal adjustment — 120, 248
  description — 119, 248
  fault diagnosis — 133
  front brake disc — 249
  front brake shoes — 120, 248
  front brake wheel cylinder — 122
  front calipers — 248
  master cylinder
    removal and installation — 128
  master cylinder (single)
    servicing — 129
  master cylinder (tandem)
    servicing — 128, 249
  parking brake — 130
  parking brake warning light switch — 132
  pressure differential valve — 130
  rear brake shoes — 123, 248
  rear brake wheel cylinder — 124
  specifications — 118, 212
  tandem master cylinder — 249
  torque wrench settings — 118

C

Camshaft
  drivebelt — 222, 227, 229
  installation — 38, 229
  removal — 28, 29, 226
  renovation — 32, 227
Carburation
  specifications — 48, 49, 210
Carburetor
  accelerator pump lever adjustment — 59
  description — 230
  fast idle adjustment — 60, 236
  float level adjustment — 59, 236
  high altitude adjustment — 236
  idle speed and mixture adjustments — 60, 235
  removal and installation — 55
  secondary throttle valve adjustment — 60
  servicing — 57
  vacuum pull-down — 236
Catalytic converter — 236, 237
Choke controls — 53, 236
Clutch
  adjustment — 240
  bleeding — 85
  description — 85
  fault diagnosis — 91
  linkage adjustment — 88
  master cylinder
    dismantling and reassembly — 90
    removal and installation — 88
  pilot bushing
    removal and installation — 20
  release cylinder — 90
  release lever and bearing — 87
  removal and installation — 86, 228
  specifications — 85, 211
  torque wrench settings — 85
Condenser — 78
Connecting rods
  bearings, removal and installation — 25, 222
  bearings, renovation — 31
  dismantling and reassembly — 25
  examination — 32
  removal and installation — 25, 222
Cooling system
  description — 43
  draining — 44
  fault diagnosis — 47
  filling — 44
  flushing — 44
  routine maintenance — 43
  specifications — 43, 210
Crankcase Ventilation System — 237
Crankshaft
  pulley renovation — 34
  rear oil seal
    removal and installation — 20
  removal — 215, 222
  renovation — 31
  sprocket removal — 221
Cylinder block
  core plugs renovation — 34
  dismantling — 31
  reassembly — 34
Cylinder bores
  renovation — 32
Cylinder head
  decarbonisation — 33
  dismantling and reassembly — 30
  installation — 38, 229
  removal — 28, 29, 217, 219

D

Decarbonisation — 33
Distributor
contact points — 77
drive gear
renovation — 34
dwell angle — 80
removal and installation — 78, 238
servicing — 78
Doors
glass and regulator — 193
latch and remote control — 193
outside handle — 195
rattles — 189
removal and installation — 192
vent window — 193
Driveshaft
balance and run-out checks — 114
description — 112
dismantling and reassembly — 113
removal and installation — 112, 248
single selector type — 251
specifications — 112
torque wrench settings — 112
universal joints — 248

E

Electrical system
description — 135
fault diagnosis — 158
flasher units — 149
instrument panel — 147, 149
instrument, testing — 148
sender units — 147
specifications — 134, 212
voltage regulator — 139
wiring diagrams — 160—172, 257—267
Emission control system
components
removal and installation — 73
description — 66, 237
tests and adjustments — 69, 237
Engine
ancillary components
removal — 27
description — 16, 216
dismantling — 27, 217
examination and renovation — 226
fault diagnosis — 41
front cover oil seal
renewal — 21
front cover
removal and installation — 21
installation — 39, 229
operations requiring engine removal — 16, 217
operations possible with engine installed — 16, 217
reassembly — 34, 227
removal methods — 16, 217
removal without transmission — 17
removal with transmission — 17
renovation — 31
specifications — 12, 206
start-up after overhaul — 40, 230
support (mounts) — 19, 230
torque wrench settings — 16, 209
Exhaust Gas Recirculation System — 237
Exhaust system — 60, 236

F

Fan/alternator drivebelt — 45
Fan drive clutch — 46

Fault diagnosis
braking system — 133
clutch — 91
cooling system — 47
electrical system — 158
engine — 41
fuel system — 74
gearbox (manual) — 106
ignition system — 82
rear axle — 117
steering — 185
suspension — 185
Flywheel
removal and installation — 20, 221, 228
Fuel cut valve — 230
Fuel pump
removal, installation and testing — 51
servicing — 52
Fuel system
description — 49, 228
fault diagnosis — 74
routine maintenance — 49
specifications — 48, 49, 210
torque wrench settings — 49
Fuel tank — 53
Fuses and fuse panel — 149, 250

G

Gearbox (manual)
clutch housing — 101
countershaft (layshaft) — 98, 242
description — 93
dismantling — 242
extension housing — 101
extension housing rear bushing — 106
extension housing rear seal — 105
fault diagnosis — 106
input shaft — 97
output shaft — 97
reassembly — 244
removal and installation — 242
shift rails — 98, 242
shift tower and lever — 101
specifications — 92, 211
torque wrench settings — 92, 212
transmission
cleaning and inspection — 102
dismantling — 95
reassembly — 104
removal and installation — 93

H

Headlights
aim adjustment — 145
removal and installation — 143
Heater — 199, 202, 204
Hood — 195
Horn — 155

I

Ignition system
description — 76, 238
fault diagnosis — 82
routine maintenance — 76
specifications — 75, 211
timing — 81, 238
Instrument panel — 147, 149

L

Lights — 145, 149, 252
Lubrication — 11, 214

M

Main bearings
removal and installation — 24, 222
renovation — 31
Maintenance
routine — 7, 214
Manifolds
exhaust — 61
intake — 61

O

Oil filter
removal and installation — 27, 226
Oil pan
removal and installation — 23, 221,228
renovation — 34, 227
Oil pump
chain removal and installation — 21
dismantling and reassembly — 26
inspection — 226
removal and installation — 23, 221, 226, 228

P

Piston pin — 226
Piston rings
renovation — 32
removal — 226
Pistons
dismantling and reassembly — 25, 228
removal and installation — 25, 222
renovation — 32

R

Radiator — 45
Radio (aftermarket type)
installation — 151
removal and installation — 150
suppression of interference — 152
Rear axle
axle housing — 116
axleshaft assembly — 116
description — 115
differential carrier assembly — 116
fault diagnosis — 117
rear wheel bearing and seals — 116
specifications — 115
torque wrench settings — 115
Rocker arm assembly
dismantling and reassembly — 29
renovation — 33
Routine maintenance — 7, 214

S

Safety first! — 268
Spare parts
buying — 6
Spark plugs — 82
Spark plugs color chart — 83
Spark Timing Control System — 237

Speedometer drive cable — 149
Starter motor — 141
Steering
description — 174
fault diagnosis — 185
gear adjustments — 183
gear dismantling and reassembly — 182
gear removal and installation — 181, 253, 254
geometry checks — 178
linkage — 184, 253, 254
routine maintenance — 175
specifications — 173, 212
torque wrench settings — 174
turning angle — 255
Sump — see 'Oil pan'
Suspension
description — 174
fault diagnosis — 185
front shock absorber — 175, 252
lower arm and spring — 175
rear shock absorber — 179, 253
rear spring — 179
routine maintenance — 175
specifications — 173, 213
torque wrench settings — 174
upper arm — 175

T

Tape players — 151, 152
Thermostat — 45, 226, 229
Throttle controls — 53
Timing chain
removal and installation — 21
renovation — 34
tensioner
adjustment, removal and installation — 22
Tires
general — 185
pressures — 174
size — 173

U

Universal joints
inspection — 112

V

Valve lash (clearance)
adjustment — 39, 229
Valves
renovation — 33, 227
removal — 224
Vehicle identification numbers — 6
Ventilator and heater — 199, 202

W

Water pump — 46, 226, 229
Wheel balancing — 255
Wheel bearings
front — 177, 252
Wheels — 173, 185, 255
Windshield glass — 196
Windshield washer — 156
Windshield wiper
arms and blades — 155
motor and linkage — 155, 156
relay testing — 158
Wiring diagrams — 160-172, 257-267